on the Market!

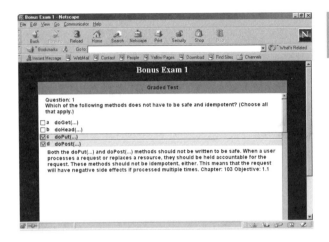

Get the explanations you need when you need them!

■ Review the explanations for our hundreds of test questions without having to flip through the book.

■ The correct answer will appear in green along with a handy explanation.

Search through the complete book in PDF!

■ Access the entire *Java 2 Web Developer Certification Study Guide,* complete with figures and tables, in electronic format.

■ Search all of the Study Guide's chapters to find information on any topic in seconds.

■ Use Adobe Acrobat Reader (included on the CD-ROM) to view the electronic book.

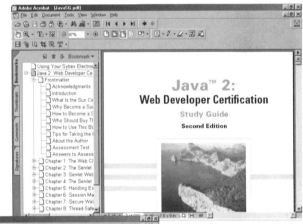

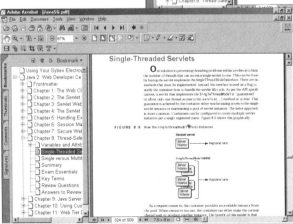

SYBEX

Java™ 2 Web Developer Certification Study Guide

Sun Certified Web Component Developer for J2EE™ Platform (310-080)

SYBEX

SYBEX

Java™ 2:
Web Developer Certification
Study Guide
Second Edition

Natalie Levi

San Francisco • London

Associate Publisher: Richard Mills, Neil Edde
Acquisitions Editor: Denise Santoro Lincoln
Developmental Editor: Elizabeth Hurley
Editor: Sharon Wilkey, Suzanne Goraj
Production Editors: Leslie H. Light, Erica Yee, Elizabeth Campbell
Reviser: Kathryn Collina
Technical Editor: Steven Potts
Reprint Coordinator: Neachan Harvey
Book Designer: Bill Gibson
Graphic Illustrator: Tony Jonick
Electronic Publishing Specialists: Interactive Composition Corporation
Proofreaders: Amey Garber, Dave Nash, Laurie O'Connell, Yariv Rabinovitch, Nancy Riddiough
Indexers: Lynnzee Elze, Rebecca Plunkett
CD Coordinator: Dan Mummert
CD Technician: Kevin Ly
Cover Designer: Archer Design
Cover Illustrator/Photographer: Natural Selection

Library of Congress Card Number: 2002114266

ISBN: 0-7821-4202-8

SYBEX

To our valued readers,

The success of Sun's Java certification program has surpassed all expectations; it is now widely recognized as the hottest programmer certification. Java is now a first-class citizen in the world of programming languages and increasing use of the Java 2 Platform for enterprise-class applications has fueled demand for the related certifications.

The Sun Certified Web Component Developer for Java 2 Platform exam is relatively new but is aimed at the part of the Java market that is growing the fastest. Java 2 Enterprise Edition technologies, such as JSP and Servlets, are used in corporate web applications of all kinds. Sybex is proud to have helped thousands of candidates already prepare for the Programmer and Developer certifications with the best-selling *Complete Java Certification Study Guide*. These exams are a prerequisite for the Web Component Developer exam, and in the new Study Guide, author Natalie Levi gives candidates exactly what they need to pass the first time.

The authors and editors have worked hard to ensure that the book you hold in your hands is comprehensive, in-depth, and pedagogically sound. We're confident that *Java 2 Web Developer Certification Study Guide* will exceed the demanding standards of the certification marketplace and help you succeed in your endeavors.

As always, your feedback is important to us. Please send comments, questions, or suggestions to support@sybex.com. At Sybex we're continually striving to meet the needs of individuals preparing for IT certification exams.

Good luck in pursuit of your Java certification!

Richard Mills
Associate Publisher—Programming
Sybex Inc.

Software License Agreement: Terms and Conditions

For my Dad, Mom, and brother. Thank you for always being there for me and teaching me the importance of family.

—Natalie

Acknowledgments

There are a group of people who are very dear to me, who seem to believe in every endeavor I tackle. Thank you Yoav, Ariela, Delon, Sara, Osher, Scott Learned, Noelle Aardema and family, Steve Stelting, Chris Cook (Cookie-Monster), Johnnie Antinone, Eleni and Bill Miller, Tressa (Stressa) Cavigliano, Jonathan Newbrough, Phillip Heller, Simon Roberts, Justin Schwab, Mike, Victor Peters, other friends, and the SuperC group for inspiration and support.

—Natalie

Contents at a Glance

Contents

Introduction

If you are preparing to take the Sun Certified Web Component Developer for J2EE Platform exam, you will undoubtedly want to find as much information as you can concerning servlets and Java Server Pages (JSPs). The more information you have at your disposal and the more hands-on experience you gain, the better off you will be when attempting to pass the exam. This study guide was written with that in mind. We have utilized a variety of valid resources to explicitly define all characteristics associated with the exam objectives. We attempted to dispense as much information as we could about servlet and JSP web components so that you will be prepared for the test—but not so much that you will be over-loaded. This book is arranged in a format that follows the Sun-specified exam objectives. If you need to concentrate on a particular objective, you will find everything you need within the chapter on which the objective is based.

This book presents the technical material at an intermediate level. You should be experienced with the Java language and have passed the Sun Certified Programmer for the Java 2 Platform exam. You should also have some experience with servlets or Java Server Pages. If you do not, it is still possible to acquire the knowledge necessary to pass the exam by using this book. You will, however, need to study each chapter carefully and write practice code to ensure you thoroughly understand each concept.

Each chapter provides review questions to help you test your comprehension of the material. If you can answer 80 percent or more of the review questions correctly for a given chapter, you can probably feel safe moving on to the next chapter. If you're unable to answer that many correctly, reread the chapter and try the questions again. Your score should improve.

Don't just study the questions and answers—the questions on the actual exam will be different from the practice ones included in this book and on the CD. The exam is designed to test your knowledge of a concept or objective, so use this book to learn the objective *behind* the question.

What Is the Sun Certified Web Component Developer for J2EE Certification?

Businesses are often intrigued and interested in incorporating new technologies to improve their existing systems. However, because the technologies are fairly new, it is difficult for developers to prove their level of competence in the desired area. A thorough understanding of the rules associated with web component development can assure an employer that you can begin developing these components to provide a successful web solution for their applications. Those programmers who successfully complete the exam can be assured that their certification is respected in the computer industry, as it tests your knowledge on the basic fundamentals and the ability to utilize these web components in an advanced fashion.

Now that J2EE technologies are accepted in the computer industry as providing an enterprise-level solution to robust systems, it is critical that Java programmers understand the key components that drive this architecture to the web user. With each layer managing distinct tasks, the design offers expandability, maintainability, and flexibility; and servlets and JSPs are the foundation components used to communicate with the front end of the application. Becoming a Sun certified web component developer proves to companies that you not only know of the technologies and their techniques, but that you are proficient in understanding when and how to use servlets and JSPs within a J2EE architecture.

Why Become a Sun Certified Programmer?

There are a number of reasons for becoming a Sun certified web component developer:

- It demonstrates proof of professional achievement.

- It increases your marketability.

- It provides greater opportunity for advancement in your field.

- It is increasingly found as a requirement for some types of advanced training.

- It raises customer confidence in you and your company's services.

Let's explore each reason in detail.

Provides Proof of Professional Achievement

Specialized certifications are the best way to stand out from the crowd. In this age of technology certifications, you will find thousands of programmers who have successfully completed the Sun Certified Programmer for the Java 2 Platform exam. This level of certification proves that you understand the fundamentals. To set yourself apart from the crowd, you need a little bit more. With Java finally making an impact on the web user, a developer must prove that their skill set expands beyond the fundamentals and encompasses web development.

The Sun Certified Web Component Developer for J2EE Platform exam is either the second or third level of Java certification. After you pass the Sun Certified Programmer for Java 2 Platform, you are eligible to either take the Sun Certified Developer for Java 2 Platform exam or the Sun Certified Web Component Developer for the J2EE Platform exam. The standard developer exam consists of a programming assignment, along with an essay. The web component exam is a multiple choice test to determine your understanding of servlets and JSPs within a J2EE architecture. Each level of certification further solidifies your credibility and knowledge in this competitive programming market. J2EE certification will give you the recognition you deserve.

Increases Your Marketability

Almost anyone can bluff their way through an interview. After you have been certified on a product such as the Sun Certified Web Component Developer for the J2EE Platform, you will have the credentials to prove your competency. And certifications are not something that can be taken from you when you change jobs. Once certified, you can take that certification with you to any of the positions you accept.

Provides Opportunity for Advancement

Those individuals who prove themselves as competent and dedicated are the ones who will most likely be promoted. Becoming certified is a great way to prove your skill level and shows your employers that you are committed to improving your skill set. Look around you at those who are certified. They are probably the ones who receive good pay raises and promotions when they come up.

Fulfills Training Requirements

Many companies have set training requirements for their staff so that they stay up-to-date on the latest technologies. Having a certification program for the Java family of products provides developers another certification path to follow when they have exhausted some of the other industry-standard certifications.

Raises Customer Confidence

As companies discover the J2EE architectural advantage, they will undoubtedly require qualified staff to implement this technology. Many companies outsource the work to consulting firms with experience working with J2EE web components. Those firms that have certified staff have a definite advantage over other firms that do not.

How to Become a Sun Certified Programmer

Exams must be taken at an authorized Prometric testing center. To register for the Sun Certified Web Component Developer exam, you must first purchase an exam voucher by calling 1-800-422-8020 or visiting the Sun Educational Services website at `http://suned.sun.com/US/certification/register/index.html`. Payment of $150 will be requested at the time you register, giving you one year in which to take the exam. Exams can be scheduled up to six weeks out or as early as the next day.

When you schedule the exam, you will receive instructions regarding appointment and cancellation procedures, ID requirements, and information about the testing center location. In addition, you will receive a registration and payment confirmation letter from Prometric.

The exam consists of 60 questions, and you will be given 90 minutes to complete it. Make sure you use your time wisely. Follow the guidelines later in this introduction on how to take the exam.

In addition to reading the book, you might consider downloading and reading the white papers that Sun has provided on their website.

Who Should Buy This Book?

If you want to acquire a solid foundation in Java web component development, and your goal is to prepare for the exam by learning how to use and manage servlets and JSPs, this book is for you. You'll find clear explanations of the concepts you need to grasp, and plenty of help to achieve the high level of professional competency you need in order to succeed in your chosen field.

If you want to become certified as a Java web component developer, this book is definitely for you. However, if you just want to attempt to pass the exam without really understanding web components, this study guide is not for you. It is written for people who want to acquire hands-on skills and in-depth knowledge of Java web components.

How to Use This Book and the CD

We've included several testing features both in the book and on the CD-ROM bound at the front of the book. These tools will help you retain vital exam content as well as prepare you to sit for the actual exam. Using our custom test engine, you can identify weak areas up front and then develop a solid studying strategy using each of these robust testing features. Our thorough readme file will walk you through the quick and easy installation process.

Before You Begin   At the beginning of the book (right after this introduction, in fact) is an Assessment Test that you can use to check your readiness for the actual exam. Take this test before you start reading the book. It will help you determine the areas you may need to brush up on. The answers appear in a separate section after the last question of the test. Each answer also includes an explanation and a note telling you in which chapter this material appears.

Chapter Review Questions   To test your knowledge as you progress through the book, there are review questions at the end of each chapter. As you finish each chapter, answer the review questions and then check to see if your answers are right—the correct answers appear on the pages following the last review question. You can go back to reread the section that covers each question you got wrong to ensure that you get the correct answer the next time you are tested on the material.

Test Engine   In addition to the Assessment Test and the chapter review tests, you'll find three Bonus exams. Take these Bonus exams just as if you were taking the actual exam (i.e., without any reference material). When you have finished the first exam, move onto the next one to solidify your test-taking skills. If you get more than 90 percent of the answers correct, you're ready to go ahead and take the certification exam.

Full Text of the Book in PDF   Also, if you have to travel but still need to study for the Java web developer exam and you have a laptop with a CD-ROM drive, you can carry this entire book with you just by taking along the CD-ROM. The CD-ROM contains this book in PDF (Adobe Acrobat) format so it can be easily read on any computer.

Tips for Taking the Exam

Here are some general tips for taking your exam successfully:

- Bring two forms of ID with you. One must be a photo ID, such as a driver's license. The other can be a major credit card or a passport. Both forms must contain a signature.

- Arrive early at the exam center so you can relax and review your study materials, particularly tables and lists of exam-related information.

- Read the questions carefully. Don't be tempted to jump to an early conclusion. Make sure you know exactly what the question is asking.

- Don't leave any unanswered questions. Unanswered questions are scored against you.

- There will be questions with multiple correct responses. When there is more than one correct answer, a message at the bottom of the screen will prompt you to "Choose all that apply." Be sure to read the messages displayed.

- When answering multiple-choice questions you're not sure about, use a process of elimination to get rid of the obviously incorrect answers first. This will improve your odds if you need to make an educated guess.

- On form-based tests, because the hard questions will eat up the most time, save them for last. You can move forward and backward through the exam. (When the exam becomes adaptive, this tip will not work.)

- For the latest pricing on the exams and updates to the registration procedures, call Sun Microsystems at (800) 422-8020. If you have further questions about the scope of the exams or related Sun certifications, refer to the Sun website, `http://suned.sun.com/US/certification/register/index.html`.

About the Author

Natalie Levi is a Sun Certified Java instructor, programmer, distributed developer, and web component developer. As owner of Educational Edge, Inc., she and her group consult for various companies, such as Sun Microsystems, to provide educational solutions to current Java technologies. Besides running a business, teaching and developing, Natalie performed the technical edit to the Java 2 Certification Study Guide, as well as coauthored the Sybex practice exam software package to supplement the guide. You can e-mail her at `nlevi@educationaledge.net`.

Assessment Test

1. Hidden values are retrieved by using which of the following mechanisms?

   A. The URI

   B. The ServletRequest object

   C. The HttpServletRequest object

   D. The HttpSession object

2. Which of the following methods is used to extract a session ID from a manually rewritten URL?

   A. getParameter(*String name*)

   B. getSessionID()

   C. getPathInfo()

   D. getID()

3. In which of the following scenarios will a session always be invalidated? (Choose all that apply.)

   A. A site using hidden values displays a static e-mail page.

   B. A client disconnects.

   C. close() is called on the session object.

   D. The session times out.

4. Which object type is used to invoke the method encodeURL (*String url*)?

   A. HttpServletRequest

   B. HttpServletResponse

   C. HttpSession

   D. ServletRequest

5. What approach should be used to rewrite the URL if a servlet needs to send the current request to another servlet?

   A. encodeRedirectURL(*String url*)

   B. encodeURL(*String url*)

   C. All URLs must have the session ID concatenated to the value.

   D. It is done automatically.

6. Which of the following names must be used to identify a session ID when rewriting the URL?

   A. JSESSIONID

   B. sessionID

   C. ID

   D. jsessionid

7. Which of the following statements is false?

   A. Cookies can be stored to the browser, request object, or other resource.

   B. An HttpSession object can store cookie or URL rewritten data.

   C. URL rewriting stores data in a session object or other resource.

   D. Hidden values store data to the request object.

   E. None of the above.

8. Which of the following methods is invoked when remove-Attribute(*String name*) is called on a session object?

   A. valueRemoved(*HttpSessionBindingEvent event*)

   B. attributeRemoved(*HttpSessionBindingEvent event*)

   C. valueUnbound(*HttpSessionBindingEvent event*)

   D. attributeUnbound(*HttpSessionBindingEvent event*)

9. Which of the following methods is called when a session object is destroyed?

    A. class: `HttpSessionListener`, method: `sessionDestroyed(HttpSessionEvent event)`

    B. class: `HttpSessionBindingListener`, method: `sessionDestroyed(HttpSessionBindingEvent event)`

    C. class `HttpSessionListener`, method: `sessionInvalidated(HttpSessionEvent event)`

    D. class `HttpSessionBindingListener`, method: `sessionInvalidated(HttpSessionEvent event)`

10. Which of the following options causes the server to invalidate a session after 15 seconds?

    A.
    ```
    <session-config>
        <session-timeout>
            15
        </session-timeout>
    </session-config>
    ```

    B.
    ```
    <session-config>
        <session-timeout>
            <timeout-value-seconds>
                    15
            </timeout-value-seconds>
        </session-timeout>
    </session-config>
    ```

    C. class: `SerlvetContext`, method: `setMaxInactiveTime(15)`

    D. class: `HttpSession`, method: `setMaxInactiveInterval(15)`

11. Which of the following variable types are intrinsically thread-safe? (Choose all that apply.)

    A. Local

    B. Class

    C. Instance

    D. Method parameters

12. Synchronizing code can cause which of the following effects?

    A. Increased resource utilization

    B. Reduction in performance

    C. Deadlock

    D. All of the above

13. Which of the following statements is false?

    A. Class variables are shared among all instances of a servlet.

    B. A server can create a new instance of the same servlet for each registered name defined.

    C. Class variables are not thread-safe.

    D. Class variables are treated the same as instance variables.

14. Which of the following attributes are rarely thread-safe?

    A. Request attributes

    B. Session attributes

    C. Context attributes

    D. None of the above

15. Given a class implements the `SingleThreadModel` interface, which of the following statements is false?

    A. The container could create multiple instances of the servlet and store them within a pool.

    B. Only one thread can access the `service(...)` method at a time.

    C. Class variables are protected.

    D. Instance variables are protected.

16. When a servlet implements the `SingleThreadModel` interface, which of the following value types are thread-safe? (Choose all that apply.)

    A. Instance variables

    B. Class variables

    C. Request attributes

    D. Session attributes

17. Synchronizing which of the following can ensure thread-safety?

    A. Local variables

    B. Session attributes

    C. Context attributes

    D. All of the above

18. Which of the following methods returns the outer tag's handle from within an inner tag? (Choose all that apply.)

    A. `getOuterTag()`

    B. `getTag()`

    C. `getParent()`

    D. `findAncestorWithClass(Tag from, Class type)`

19. Which of the following tags is used within a tag library descriptor to define the type of data that the tag accepts?

    A. `body`

    B. `body-content`

    C. `bodyData`

    D. `bodycontent`

20. Which of the following statements is true?

    A. The JSP page must include a `taglib` element to identify which tag libraries to load into memory.

    B. The `web.xml` document must use a `taglib` element to identify the location of the TLD file.

    C. The TLD file must use the `taglib` element to identify each custom tag and its attributes.

    D. All of the above.

21. Given the following tag description, which tag element is invalid?

```
<tag>
    <name>goodbye</name>
    <tag-class>tagext.GoodByeTag</tag-class>
    <body-content>JSP</body-content>
    <info>Second example</info>
    <attribute>
        <name>age</name>
        <isRequired>true</isRequired>[
        <rtexprvalue>true</rtexprvalue>
        <type>java.lang.Integer</type>
    </attribute>
</tag>
```

A. name

B. isRequired

C. rtexprvalue

D. body-content

22. Which of the following tag elements within the TLD is used to define the tag suffix within the JSP?

A. name

B. tag-name

C. tag-class

D. tag

23. Which of the following options enables a custom tag access to a JSP page's implicit variables?

A. If the custom tag implements the Tag interface, the pageContext handle is automatically provided.

B. If the custom tag implements the BodyTag interface, a local instance of the pageContext must be saved using the setPage-Context(*PageContext pageContext*) method.

C. If the custom tag extends the BodySupportTag, the pageContext is automatically provided.

D. None of the above.

24. What is the default return value for the doAfterBody() method when a custom tag extends the BodySupportTag class?

    A. EVAL_BODY_BUFFERED

    B. EVAL_BODY_INCLUDE

    C. EVAL_BODY_AGAIN

    D. SKIP_BODY

25. Which of the following options is not a valid return type for the doStartTag() method, if the custom tag implements the IterationTag interface? (Choose all that apply.)

    A. EVAL_BODY_INCLUDE

    B. SKIP_BODY

    C. EVAL_BODY_BUFFERED

    D. EVAL_PAGE

26. If a SKIP_PAGE is returned, which of the following statements is correct?

    A. If the request was created from a forward or include, both the original and new request are complete.

    B. The rest of the page should not be evaluated.

    C. The body should be reevaluated.

    D. The doAfterPage() method is evaluated next.

27. Your current application performs slowly due to the number of times the database must be accessed to retrieve a record. What design pattern should be incorporated to reduce the number of calls necessary to complete a single transaction?

    A. Value Objects

    B. MVC

    C. Data Access Object

    D. Business Delegate

28. Which of the following patterns helps separate work tasks, improve maintainability, and enable extensibility?

   A. Value Objects

   B. MVC

   C. Data Access Object

   D. Business Delegate

29. If the server's root directory is called /root and your application context is /test, which of the following options describes the default location for the application's WAR file called app.war?

   A. web-server/root/test/app.war

   B. web-server/test/app.war

   C. web-server/test/WEB-INF/app.war

   D. web-server/root/WEB-INF/applwar

30. Assuming the application's context directory is defined as /context, which of the following files are visible to the client? (Choose all that apply.)

   A. /context/index.html

   B. /context/WEB-INF/image.gif

   C. /context/welcome.jsp

   D. /context/WEB-INF/lib/audio.au

31. In which directory are JAR files placed?

   A. Directly in the application's context directory

   B. Directly within the /WEB-INF directory

   C. Directly within the /WEB-INF/classes directory

   D. Directly within the /WEB-INF/lib directory

32. In which directory should you find the web.xml file?

   A. The context directory

   B. The /WEB-INF directory

   C. The /WEB-INF/classes directory

   D. The /WEB-INF/lib directory

33. Which option best describes how to define a servlet's name and class type within the deployment descriptor?

   A.
```
<servlet>
    <name>Search</name>
    <class>SearchServlet</class>
</servlet>
```

   B.
```
<servlet>
    <servletName>Search</servletName>
    <servletClass>SearchServlet</servletClass>
</servlet>
```

   C.
```
<servlet>
    <servlet-name>Search</servlet-name>
    <servlet-class>SearchServlet</servlet-class>
</servlet>
```

   D. `<servlet name="Search" class="SearchServlet" />`

34. Which of the following tags represents a servlet instance?

   A. servlet-name

   B. servlet-instance

   C. servlet

   D. instance

35. If MyServlet needs to have a variable initialized to a value of 5, which of the following tag groups enables the servlet to extract the appropriate information using its request object?

A.
```
<context path="/features" docbase="
    c:/projects/features" reloadable="true">
    <context-param>
        <name>SEARCH_PATH</name>
        <value>/features/utilities</value>
    </context-param>
</context>
```

B.
```
<context path="/features" docbase="
    c:/projects/features" reloadable="true">
    <context-param>
        <param-name>SEARCH_PATH</param-name>
        <param-value>/features/utilities</param-value>
    </context-param>
</context>
```

C.
```
<servlet>
    <servlet-name>MyServlet</servlet-name>
    <servlet-class>MyServlet</servlet-class>
    <param>
        <param-name>defaultType</param-name>
        <param-value>5</param-value>
    </param>
</servlet>
```

D.
```
<servlet>
    <servlet-name>MyServlet</servlet-name>
    <servlet-class>MyServlet</servlet-class>
    <init-param>
        <param-name>defaultType</param-name>
        <param-value>5</param-value>
    </init-param>
</servlet>
```

36. Which tags will you use to enable the server to locate a servlet if it is located in a directory other than the standard /WEB-INF/classes? (Choose all that apply.)

A. url

B. url-pattern

C. url-mapping

D. servlet-mapping

37. If you are monitoring your system by checking logs and ensuring certain groups are accessing only their designated areas, which option best describes your actions?

　　A. Authorizing

　　B. Authenticating

　　C. Auditing

　　D. Assuring integrity

38. Which deployment descriptor element is used to define the type of authentication?

　　A. `authentication`

　　B. `auth`

　　C. `auth-role`

　　D. `auth-method`

39. What is the immediate parent element to the `form-login-page` or `form-error-page` tag?

　　A. `form-login-config`

　　B. `form-login`

　　C. `form`

　　D. `config`

40. Which of the following tags is used to define an application's resource areas and the different roles and request types that have access to those areas?

　　A. `security`

　　B. `security-config`

　　C. `security-constraint`

　　D. `security-role`

41. In which of the following classes will you find the `sendError()` method?

    A. HttpServletRequest

    B. HttpServletResponse

    C. ServletContext

    D. ServletResponse

42. Which of the following is a legal exception-type 42. description?

    A. javax.servlet.ServletException

    B. ServletException

    C. javax.servlet.http.UnavailableException

    D. UnavailableException

43. Which of the following methods is invoked when an HTTP PUT request is made?

    A. doGet(...)

    B. doPost(...)

    C. doPut(...)

    D. doAll(...)

44. Which of the following objects would you use to set an attribute if your goal is to have that value shared among all application servlets for the life of the application?

    A. HttpSession

    B. ServletContext

    C. ServletConfig

    D. GenericServlet

45. Which listener is notified when a context is destroyed?

    A. ServletContextListener

    B. ContextListener

    C. ServletContextAttributeListener

    D. ServletListener

46. Which deployment descriptor tag is used to declare a session attribute listener?

   A. `distributable`

   B. `distributable-listener`

   C. `listener`

   D. `listener-name`

47. Which option provides the best location to store data in a distributable environment?

   A. Static variable

   B. Instance variable

   C. `ServletContext`

   D. `HttpSession`

48. Which directive is used to import a Java class into a JSP page?

   A. `<%= page import="java.io.*, java.util.*" %>`

   B. `<%@ page import="java.io.*" />`

   C. `<%@ page import="java.io.*, java.util.*" %>`

   D. None of the above

49. Which option provides the correct XML translation for the following scriptlet?

   `<%@ taglib uri="URIForLibrary" prefix="tagPrefix" %>`

   A. `<jsp:taglib taglibDirective />`

   B. `<jsp:directive.taglib taglibDirective />`

   C. `<jsp:directive.taglib taglibDirective >`

   D. None

50. Which statement best describes the purpose of the following syntax?

`<% ... %>`

A. Declares Java variables and methods

B. Is a valid statement of logic

C. Provides global information to the page

D. Provides code fragments

51. What is the expected outcome of the following code snippet?

```
<% for(int i=0; i<1; i++)  %>
do something!
<%    System.out.println("i is equal to: " + i ); %>
```

A. The loop displays "do something! i is equal to: 0."

B. The loop displays "do something!" on the first line and "i is equal to: 0" on the next.

C. The loop displays "do something!"

D. The code does not compile.

52. Which of the following listeners is called when a session is created?

A. `HttpSessionBindingListener`

B. `HttpSessionListener`

C. `HttpSessionChangedListener`

D. `SessionListener`

53. Which of the following deployment descriptor tags identifies the HTML page used to validate a user with FORM authentication?

A. `<form-login></form-login>`

B. `<form-login-page> </form-login-page>`

C. `<form-access-page></form-access-page>`

D. `<form-authentication></form-authentication>`

54. Which of the following elements is used to list all security roles?

   A. security-constraint

   B. web-resource-collection

   C. auth-constraint

   D. role-constraint

55. Where must modifications be made to limit security access within a method for a particular user?

   A. Within the deployment descriptor

   B. Within the servlet program

   C. Within the index.html file

   D. Within the web server's configuration file

56. In what order must the following security elements be listed in the deployment descriptor?

   A. security-constraint, login-config, security-role.

   B. login-config, security-role, security-constraint.

   C. security-constraint, security-role, login-config.

   D. Order does not matter.

57. What is the expected output of the following code snippet?

```
<% if(true)  %>
    To be
<% else { %>
    or not to be
<% } %>
```

   A. To be

   B. or not to be

   C. To be, or not to be

   D. The code will not compile.

58. Which of the following is not a valid implicit object?

  A. pageContext

  B. config

  C. out

  D. page

  E. None of the above

59. Which of the following attributes is set for a RequestDispatcher using the getRequestDispatcher(...) method? (Choose all that apply.)

  A. context_path

  B. path_info

  C. query_string

  D. None of the above

60. Which of the following implicit objects has a page scope? (Choose all that apply.)

  A. exception

  B. request

  C. config

  D. pageContext

61. Which of the following options is not a valid attribute for the jsp: setProperty action?

  A. name

  B. scope

  C. param

  D. value

62. If you would like to include an applet in your JSP page, which of the following directives or tags would you use?

A. `<%@ page name="applet" value="MyApplet.class" />`

B. `<%@ include file="home/MyApplet.class" %>`

C. `<jsp:plugin type="applet" code="MyApplet.class" />`

D. `<jsp:include page="home/MyApplet.class" />`

63. When a JSP page is translated, in which method are scriptlets placed?

A. `jspInit()`

B. `_jspInit()`

C. `_jspService()`

D. `service()`

64. Assuming a JavaBean instance `accountData`, the JSP line `<jsp:set-Property name="accountData" property="*" />` will do what?

A. Set all the fields of `accountData` that have a corresponding `HttpServletRequest` property

B. Instantiate another identical instance of `accountData`

C. Call the constructor of the `accountData` bean

D. Allow any property on `accountData` to be accessed via a corresponding "get" method

65. Identify the deployment descriptor tags used to define a filter:

A. `<filter><filter-name></filter-name><filter-url></filter-url></filter>`

B. `<filter><filter-name></filter-name><filter-class></filter-class></filter>`

C. `<filter-mapping><filter-name></filter-name><filter-url></filter-url></filter-mapping>`

D. `<filter-mapping><filter-name></filter-name><url-pattern></url-pattern></filter-mapping>`

Answers to Assessment Test

1. B.   When a request object is triggered within a form, its hidden values are stored within the actual request object. Using the `Servlet-Request`'s method `getParameter(String name)`, you can extract the hidden value by passing its name to the method. For more information, see Chapter 2.

2. C.   The `HttpServletRequest` class contains the path information containing the session ID. The method `getPathInfo()` returns the path information listed after the servlet path and before the query string. For more information, see Chapter 6.

3. D.   A session can exist beyond the client. To manually discard a session, you must call `invalidate()`—not `close()`. Hidden values are useful only if you can propagate the values through dynamic pages. After a static page is used, hyperlinks or browser triggers are the only way to navigate. Those options do not allow for the inclusion of hidden values. However, if the site is configured to use cookies for session management, the session may continue, and using hidden values will not result in the removal of the session. Finally, a session can time out, resulting in the removal of the session object. For more information, see Chapter 6.

4. B.   To *extract* a rewritten URL, the `HttpServletRequest` class is used. To *rewrite* the URL by using provided methods, you must use the `HttpServletResponse` class. For more information, see Chapter 6.

5. A.   When redirecting a response, the `encodeRedirectURL(...)` method should be used to encode the current session ID in the URL. Because a redirect URL is stored differently than a normal URL, you must use a different method to generate the appropriate URL output. For more information, see Chapter 6.

6. D.   The specification states that the name associated to the session value must be `jsessionid`. For cookies, the session name is written with all capitals; however, for URL rewriting, the specification SRV.7.1.3 states that the name must be written with lowercase letters. For more information, see Chapter 6.

7. E.   Cookies are data objects written to the response object and stored on the browser. They can be retrieved by using the request object. Cookies can also be added as an attribute to the session object or written to a database. A session object acts like a storage unit. It can contain data from cookies or URL rewriting. URL rewriting is a way to store the session ID. The ID can then be linked to any resource that allows data to be stored. Finally, hidden values can be accessed via the request object. For more information, see Chapter 6.

8. C.   When an attribute is unbound from a session, an `HttpSessionBindingEvent` is generated and sent to all registered `HttpSessionBindingListeners` via the `valueUnbound(...)` method. For more information, see Chapter 6.

9. A.   A class that implements the interface `HttpSessionListener` must define the method `sessionDestroyed(HttpSessionEvent event)`. This method is then called when a session is invalidated. For more information, see Chapter 6.

10. D.   When the session-time value is set within the deployment descriptor, it is defined using minutes. There is no tag available to change that time measurement to any other value. For granular control using seconds, you can set the maximum inactive period by using the session object. For more information, see Chapter 6.

11. A, D.   Local variables and method parameters are stored on the stack. Because each thread is provided its own stack, there are no threading issues to be concerned with, in regard to these variables. For more information, see Chapter 8.

12. D.   Synchronized code blocks are usually encouraged to ensure the integrity of instance variables. Their use, however, can cause an increase of resources, because the system needs to transfer the lock between threads. In addition, locking code causes a reduction in performance as other threads must wait for the lock. Finally, deadlock can result from locking too much information. For more information, see Chapter 8.

13. D.   Class variables are shared among all instances of a servlet. Because the server can create a new servlet instance for each registered name, the instance variable is handled differently than the class variable. The instance variable is accessed each time a particular instance is used, whereas the class variable is accessed each time any instance of that servlet is used. Because more than one thread can access a class variable at a time, it too is not thread-safe. For more information, see Chapter 8.

14. D.   Request attributes are tied to the request object and managed by the RequestDispatcher to ensure that each request is assigned to a separate thread. Session attributes act in a similar way. They are assigned to each client through the request object, and threading is handled internally. Consequently, there is no need to worry about threading issues. Finally, context attributes are safe assuming the setAttribute(...) method is synchronized. Usually it is, so context attributes are almost always thread-safe. For more information, see Chapter 8.

15. C.   Because a container can pool many instances of the same servlet, each thread can access a different instance and utilize any service(...) method simultaneously with another thread. Consequently, if one thread changes the value of a class variable, and another does the same, the first might expect a certain result after the change, but might experience the effects of another servlet's alteration instead. For more information, see Chapter 8.

16. A, C, D.   Instance variables are protected because the SingleThread-Model interface ensures that only one thread will access an instance's service(...) method at a time. Class variables are not so fortunate. Because request and session attributes are inherently thread-safe, implementing the interface has no effect. For more information, see Chapter 8.

17. D.   Synchronizing changes to any attribute or value will ensure that only one thread can access that variable in that block at a time. For more information, see Chapter 8.

18. C, D.   The getParent() method returns the immediate outer tag handle, whereas the findAncestorWithTag(...) method can return any outer tag surrounding the current tag. For more information, see Chapter 10.

19. B.   The body-content tag is used to define how the tag should handle content existing between the opening and closing tags. The three options are empty, JSP, or tagdependent. For more information, see Chapter 10.

20. D.   The `taglib` element serves a different purpose within each document. For more information, see Chapter 10.

21. B.   The element `name` is used to identify the name used to access the tag, whereas `rtexprvalue` is used to define wither the attribute value can be dynamically specified. Finally, `bodycontent` is used to identify how to handle the content between the tags. `isRequired` is incorrect. The correct element is `required`. It is used to define whether a tag attribute is required. For more information, see Chapter 10.

22. A.   The value assigned to the `name` element is used to define the custom tag suffix within the JSP page. For more information, see Chapter 10.

23. C.   A custom tag that implements any interface must define the method `setPageContext(PageContext pageContext)` and save a local instance to have access to all other implicit variables. Support classes define this method and enable the `pageContext` handle to be accessed by subclasses. For more information, see Chapter 10.

24. D.   By default, the `doAfterBody()` and `doStartTag()` methods return the constant SKIP_BODY. For more information, see Chapter 10.

25. C, D.   The EVAL_BODY_BUFFERED constant is a valid return type only if the tag utilizes the body content. This feature is available only when the tag uses a class or interface that implements the `BodyTag` interface. The EVAL_PAGE constant is a valid return only for the `doEndTag()` method. For more information, see Chapter 10.

26. B.   The first option is not true because only the current request is complete, not the originating page. After SKIP_PAGE is returned, the body is complete, as is the rest of the page. For more information, see Chapter 10.

27. A.   By creating a value object for each record, you need to make only a single request instead of multiple calls for each element of a record. For more information, see Chapter 11.

28. B.   The Model View Controller design pattern separates controller code from graphical or view code. Pulling the model out of the Presentation layer enables the application to grow without affecting existing pieces. It also provides easier maintainability because each piece is designated to accomplish a specific task. For more information, see Chapter 11.

29. A. The WAR file should be placed in the web server's application root directory (the directory preceding the context). For more information, see Chapter 3.

30. A, C. All files located in the /context directory, *and any subdirectory other than* WEB-INF, are visible to the client. For more information, see Chapter 3.

31. D. All JAR files should be placed in the /WEB-INF/lib directory for a particular application. For more information, see Chapter 3.

32. B. The deployment descriptor should be placed directly in the /WEB-INF directory. For more information, see Chapter 3.

33. C. When defining a servlet, the name is specified by using the tag servlet-name, whereas the class name uses the tag servlet-class. For more information, see Chapter 3.

34. A. The servlet-class tag can be used several times within a servlet tag. What distinguishes one instance from another is the servlet-name. Most containers will create an instance for each registered name. For more information, see Chapter 3.

35. D. A servlet can have its own set of initialization parameters by using the tag init-param. Parameters that apply to the entire application context are placed within the context-param tags. For more information, see Chapter 3.

36. B, D. The servlet-mapping outer tag specifies the servlet-name and url-pattern, defining where the server can locate the specified servlet. For more information, see Chapter 3.

37. C. Auditing is the act of monitoring a system to ensure that all users are accessing files within their defined security realm. For more information, see Chapter 7.

38. D. The auth-method tag defines one of four authentication types: BASIC, FORM, DIGEST, and CLIENT-CERT. For more information, see Chapter 7.

39. A. The form-login-config tag is used to define any custom or error pages. It is used only with the FORM authentication method. For more information, see Chapter 7.

40. C. The security-constraint tag is used to define all web-resource-collection elements, which include the name, URL, accessible method, and all auth-constraint roles that can access those areas. For more information, see Chapter 7.

41. B. The HttpServletResponse class provides the sendError() method to provide the client with an HTML-formatted error page created by the server. For more information, see Chapter 5.

42. A. The exception-type tag requires the fully qualifying exception name that includes the package name. The third option fails because the UnavailableException is part of the javax.servlet package, not the javax.servlet.http package. For more information, see Chapter 5.

43. C. A PUT request is sent to a servlet's doPut(…) method to enable the client to place a resource on the server. For more information, see Chapters 1 and 2.

44. B. An HttpSession provides access for the life of the session of a single client rather than for the life of the application. The Servlet-Config object is incorrect because it is used to get initialization parameters rather than set attributes. Finally, GenericServlet applies only to the servlet at hand. For more information, see Chapter 4.

45. A. The ServletContextListener's method contextDestroyed-(ServletContextEvent e) is called when a context is removed. For more information, see Chapter 4.

46. C. The distributable tag marks whether an application is likely to run on multiple systems. The listener tag, however, identifies any listener-class names that must be registered with the container. For more information, see Chapter 4.

47. D. Static variables are shared only within the same JVM. In a distributed environment, a new static variable is initialized when a servlet is accessed in a different system. The same is true with instance variables, except they have an even smaller scope. The ServletContext applies to the entire application; however, in a distributable environment, a new ServletContext is created when an application is moved. A session object is the ideal location, because all serializable data is transferred in a distributed environment. For more information, see Chapter 4.

48. C. A page directive uses the <%@ %> syntax. It can import more than one class group by using commas to separate each package type. For more information, see Chapter 9.

49. D. There is no XML translation for the taglib directive. You must use the scriptlet syntax. For more information, see Chapter 9.

50. D. The syntax <% %> identifies a scriptlet. Its code is translated into the JSP's service method as code fragments. For more information, see Chapter 9.

51. D. If a for loop does not have an opening and closing brace, the loop applies only to the first line after the block declaration. As a result, the variable i is out of scope, because it is referenced on the second line after the block declaration. For more information, see Chapter 9.

52. B. The HttpSessionListener is called when a session is created and destroyed. For more information, see Chapter 6.

53. B. The <form-login-page> tag identifies the form used when protected code is requested in an application that uses form-based authentication. For more information, see Chapter 7.

54. C. The auth-constraint element contains a role-name tag used to define each role with access to the specified file. For more information, see Chapter 7.

55. B. Modifications to the deployment descriptor enable an application to control file access for roles. User security must be handled from within the servlet itself. For more information, see Chapter 7.

56. A. The security-constraint tag must be used first to list the resources and roles that require security. The login-config is defined next to specify the type of container authentication. Finally, the security-role tag is listed to identify the roles with access. For more information, see Chapter 7.

57. A. When a scriptlet is translated within the servlet, tags are removed and text outside the scriptlet code is written to the output stream buffer. The code snippet translates to the following:

```
if(true)
  out.println("To be");
else {
  out.println("or not to be");
}
```

Consequently, the if block is entered and "To be" is printed. For more information, see Chapter 9.

58. E.   The first four options are all valid implicit objects; config, out, and page are bound to the pageContext object. For more information, see Chapter 9.

59. A, B, C.   When accessing a RequestDispatcher through the method getRequestDispatcher(...), all defined attributes are set; if, however, the dispatcher was accessed by using the getNameDispatcher(...) method, these values would not be defined. For more information, see Chapter 2.

60. A, C, D.   Six implicit objects have a page scope. They are config, response, pageContext, out, page, and exception. After these variables exit the current page, a new instance is used. For more information, see Chapter 9.

61. B.   The scope attribute is actually used with the jsp:useBean action to define the bean's availability. For more information, see Chapter 9.

62. C.   The first option fails because the page directive is used to define attributes for the entire JSP page, rather than to include a component in the page. The second option is invalid because the include directive is used for static files. Finally, the last option fails because you cannot include an applet as a page. An applet requires the interpreter to run, rather than the container to read a static or dynamic file—instead the jsp:plugin action should be used. For more information, see Chapter 9.

63. C.   A JSP page is translated to a servlet that includes the method _jspService(). All scriptlet code is placed inside this method. For more information, see Chapter 9.

64. A.   By using a setProperty tag and identifying the property value as an asterisk, all instance variables that map to the request parameters will be defined. For more information, see Chapter 9.

65. B.   A Filter is defined using the outer tag filter, and the inner tags filter-name, which defines the name of the filter, and filter-class, which defines the actual class name. The last option is incorrect because since the filter-mapping tag is used to identify which files or objects the filter will be performed on. For more information, see Chapter 4.

The Web Client Model

THE FOLLOWING SUN CERTIFIED WEB COMPONENT DEVELOPER FOR J2EE PLATFORM EXAM OBJECTIVES ARE COVERED IN THIS CHAPTER:

- ✓ 1.1 For each of the HTTP methods, GET, POST, and PUT, identify the corresponding method in the HttpServlet class.

- ✓ 1.2 For each of the HTTP methods, GET, POST, and HEAD, identify triggers that might cause a browser to use the method, and identify benefits or functionality of the method.

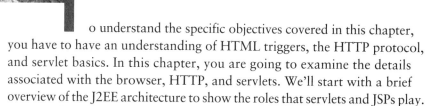

To understand the specific objectives covered in this chapter, you have to have an understanding of HTML triggers, the HTTP protocol, and servlet basics. In this chapter, you are going to examine the details associated with the browser, HTTP, and servlets. We'll start with a brief overview of the J2EE architecture to show the roles that servlets and JSPs play.

We will do the following:

- Introduce the Java Enterprise (J2EE) model

- Present the Hypertext Markup Language (HTML) tags

- Present the Hypertext Transmission Protocol (HTTP)

- Define an HTTP client request, server response, and HTTP request methods

After discussing the J2EE model, we will zero in on its Presentation tier (or the Web Client model). Beginning with HTML, each tag will be covered to identify its functionality and associated trigger. Because the browser uses the HTTP protocol to transfer client-entered data to its intended destination, the protocol will be discussed next. The information is transferred in the form of a request, which contains one of several HTTP request methods. We will thoroughly cover each possible method and the characteristics of the respective response. Our goal is to ensure that you have a detailed understanding of each method and its associated components.

Introduction to the J2EE Model

"Write once, *run* anywhere" was the first phrase Java developers grew accustomed to hearing. As the language developed and matured, it began to have an impact on the entire network and took on an additional phrase, "Write once, *implement* anywhere." This phrase is the foundation behind the Java 2 Enterprise Edition (J2EE) architecture. Although complex architectures existed before Java, they were limited in flexibility because their applications were forced to be vendor dependent. Prior to J2EE, the code for each component was directly linked to a particular manufacturer. Consequently, changes could not be made in one area without hugely affecting another. Java took vendor dependence out of the equation. The J2EE model enables you to develop components independent of the operating system or server vendor. These components are re-usable and fully capable of communicating between the specific tier layers. To ensure success and consistent behavior of the J2EE model, vendors must provide servers that comply with the associated J2EE Java Application Programming Interface (API) specification, and developers must write components that utilize these same interfaces. Compliance results in components that are both swappable and reusable among different J2EE servers.

Figure 1.1 displays the various components that make up the architecture. The acronym *EJB* stands for *Enterprise Java Bean*. This is a server-side component that manages business objects, their logic, and interaction with all storage mechanisms, referred to as *EIS*, or *Enterprise Information Systems*. The other acronym is JSP, which stands for Java Server Page. Both JSPs and servlets manage the Presentation layer by interacting with server-side business logic.

This book focuses on two important object types in this enterprise model: servlets and Java Server Pages. The first half of the book is based on servlets, and the second on Java Server Pages (JSPs).

Servlets are platform-independent *web components*—elements that bridge the gap between the Presentation tier and the Business Logic, or EIS Integration tier. In simple terms, they are Java classes that implement specific interfaces allowing the container to manage their life cycle and communicate their data to a browser. A *web server* is an application written by a vendor that meets the J2EE specification. Within the server exists a *container*. This component within the server manages the life cycle and communicates the data of a servlet or JSP to the browser. Servlets are saved to a container and loaded dynamically on an as-needed basis to process business logic and generate a graphical layout for the client. Specifically, servlets are designed to optimize business logic executed on the server side.

FIGURE 1.1   The J2EE model

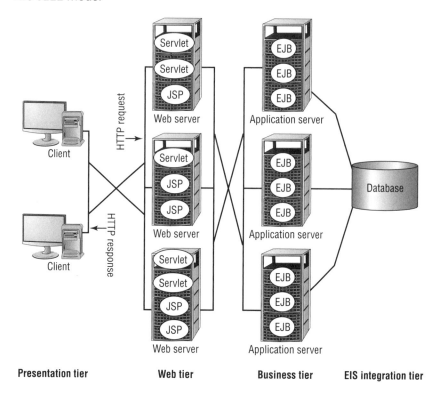

Java Server Pages are also Java objects used to communicate between the client and server. They, too, execute business logic; however, processing Java code is not their specialty. Unlike servlets, JSPs are optimized for the layout. Their elegance lies within their ability to generate easy-to-read graphical interface code—while servlets provide the opposite. The servlet priority is to primarily process a request and then create a response. Figure 1.2 defines the architecture for the Servlet model.

The Servlet model, in its simplest form, defines a transaction in four steps. The user begins by making a request, an object containing client intent and data. The request is first sent to the web sever. The server then invokes the appropriate servlet in step 2. After the servlet receives and processes the request, it then generates a response, an object containing the information requested by the client. This response is sent back to the web server in step 3. As the intermediary, the web server completes the final step by sending the response back to the client for an update to the interface.

FIGURE 1.2 The Servlet model

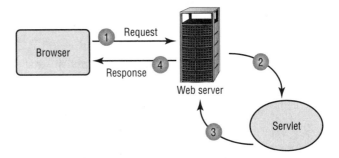

This book provides a detailed look at each topic to help you understand the rules and information necessary to pass the Sun Certified Web Component Developer for J2EE Platform certification exam. In the following "HTML" section, our focus begins by looking at the technologies necessary to enable the client to communicate with the web server, or more specifically, the servlet. The process starts with the client accessing the server via their web browser, which reads HTML.

HTML

The *Hypertext Markup Language (HTML)* is the intermediary language between the browser/client and all other technologies, such as Java or networking protocols. Before learning how the information is transferred and what the servlet or JSP does with this information (and how it does it), you need to understand all the rules associated with web interface.

A large portion of client and server interaction is done by using HTML forms. A form usually contains one or more HTML tag components. These components enable a user to select or enter an item for a particular request. For example, you might encounter an online order form to access market information. Each field might represent a filter or characteristic used to locate the stocks you are looking to learn more about. These specifics within an HTML form notify the server of your needs. Once triggered, a request is sent with your criteria. Although the purpose of the book is not to teach you HTML, it is important you understand forms and their associated tags. This next section covers the various HTML tags and their triggers; later we will show you how these forms actually trigger a request to the server.

Real World Scenario

When to Use HTML

Your company is developing a website that surveys the public's purchasing preferences. In designing the project, a decision must be made on how to develop the most effective front end. Because the application will be accessed through browsers, your choices consist of HTML or Java.

Java applets are useful when your site is looking to utilize complex graphical user interface (GUI) functionality or render multidimensional images. They are also used to stream data, such as music or videos, and to display dynamic data without having to refresh the entire page.

HTML, on the other hand, is best suited for displaying static data, often seen in news pages or forms. Unlike updating an applet, updating a client HTML display requires the server to reload the entire page.

When comparing capabilities, Java seems to offer more advantages. For this site, however, HTML is all that is needed. The site needs to contain fields of information and choices for the user to select. After the user enters the necessary data, the site then needs to send all the information to the server and reload a new or the same page. By using HTML and HTTP, the site can be developed to be both functional and efficient.

HTML Tags

A variety of HTML tags are used to create custom web pages. Some tags define components used to display data and/or accept input. Other tags are used for formatting purposes. In this section, we will present the common tags used to communicate with servlets and JSPs. Their purpose and associated triggers will be covered as well.

FORM Tag

A form is a section of an HTML page that can contain a variety of controls. It has two main attribute tags: ACTION, which defines location of the request target, and METHOD, which defines the type of request. Contained within the form are controls. Programmatically they are often referred to as a(n) INPUT, SELECT, or TEXTAREA. Conceptually, *controls* are GUI components that enable the user to interact with the interface. Some examples are radio buttons, text fields, buttons, and menus. A user modifies these controls by entering data or selecting available options. In certain cases, a user's action can trigger a request to the server. Before you move on to that stage, take a closer look at the FORM tag and its controls:

```
<HTML>
  <BODY>
   <FORM ACTION='/servlet/example/NameForm' METHOD='POST'>
    <P>First name:
    <INPUT TYPE='text' SIZE='20' NAME='first'></P>
    <P>Last name:
    <INPUT TYPE='text' SIZE='20' NAME='last'></P>
    <INPUT TYPE='submit' VALUE='Send'>
   </FORM>
  </BODY>
</HTML>
```

The following is the resulting image.

A form can contain several control types. Some enable a client to communicate with the server, while others do not. Only components used to acquire or transfer client information are covered. Labels and images are strictly visual and will not be addressed. The three main control tags are INPUT, SELECT, and TEXTAREA.

> **TIP** If you do not specify a method type for the FORM tag, the browser will assume the appropriate method type for you and generate a GET request when triggered.

INPUT Tag

The INPUT tag identifies a control and its attributes, both of which should be included in the form. The most significant attribute is TYPE. It identifies which control should be used. Following is a list of the possible attributes used in an input tag:

TYPE   specifies the type of control to create. Your choices are the following:

```
text|password|hidden|submit|reset|button|checkbox
radio|file|image
```

NAME   is often the human-language name assigned to the control. It is also used to identify the element in the servlet.

VALUE   specifies the initial value of the control. It is not a required attribute for any control.

SIZE   identifies the initial width of the control. In general, the width is measured in pixels. For text or password controls, size is measured by characters.

MAXLENGTH   is used for text and password to specify the maximum number of characters the user is allowed to enter.

CHECKED   is an attribute used for radio or checkbox controls. It's a Boolean value that identifies whether the control should be selected.

SRC   specifies the location of the image control type.

A closer look at each control will reveal how each attribute affects the INPUT tag.

INPUT TYPE='text'

In an HTML form, the type text creates a text field GUI component that enables the user to enter a single line of text. Here is an example of the code and resulting image:

```
<INPUT TYPE='text' NAME='firstName'
  VALUE='Enter your name here' SIZE='20' MAXLENGTH='30'>
```

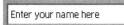

The NAME is simply a way to identify the data accessed from this control, while its VALUE pre-fills the text field. If the VALUE attribute is excluded, the text field would be empty. The visual width or SIZE of this text field is 20 characters wide, yet the user's name cannot be greater than 30 characters, given the MAXLENGTH specification.

INPUT TYPE='password'

In an HTML form, the type password creates a password GUI component that alters the entered characters to hide their true value. Here is an example of the code and resulting image:

```
<INPUT TYPE='password' NAME='loginPassword'
  VALUE='P433w0rd' SIZE='20' MAXLENGTH='20'>
```

You can define all the same attributes as you can for the text field. The difference between the two is how the characters appear. Although a password component conceals the true value from the user's view, the characters are not encrypted. When a password is sent to the server, the original characters are transmitted.

INPUT TYPE='hidden'

In an HTML form, the type hidden creates a control that is not rendered, but whose values can be transmitted back to the server. Here is an example:

```
<INPUT TYPE='hidden' NAME='taxRate' VALUE='.0725' >
```

In general, the NAME is a string whose VALUE remains the same regardless of user interaction.

The user cannot directly modify the VALUE of the control. However, the HTML designer can set up a trigger (JavaScript) to update the control if some predefined action occurs, such as the user selecting a different state.

In our example, this control would be useful on a form that took information for an order. After the order was placed, the taxRate value would be sent to the server. Although this value might not remain constant for an infinite period, it can be changed by the developer or updated dynamically without performing any compilations.

INPUT TYPE='submit'

In an HTML form, the type submit creates a submit button GUI component that triggers an HTTP request to submit a form to the server. There are three ways to create a submit button. Each procedure has a different effect.

Example 1:

```
<INPUT TYPE='submit'>
```

The first example creates a default button. Because we do not provide a VALUE attribute, the label is set to a default string determined by the browser—for example, "Submit Query" or "Submit."

Example 2:

```
<INPUT TYPE='submit' VALUE='Place Order'>
```

By including the VALUE attribute, we can now customize the label on our submit button, as shown here.

Example 3:

```
<INPUT TYPE='submit' NAME='btnOrder' VALUE='Order'>
```

The NAME attribute serves two purposes. It gives us a handle to the component, and it captures the name/value pair btnOrder=Order to include in the data being sent to the server via a request object. (We'll talk more about the details in the upcoming "HTTP" section.) The following is the resulting image.

While other input controls take in data, the submit button actually triggers a request to be sent. As a side note: if you have a form that contains multiple submit buttons, each button will capture all the data from the controls defined within the same <FORM></FORM> body tags.

INPUT TYPE='reset'

In an HTML form, the type reset creates a reset button GUI component. Here is an example of the code and resulting image:

```
<INPUT TYPE='reset' VALUE='RESET'>
```

The reset button component is designed to set all control types back to their original values. It does not provide any form data for a request.

INPUT TYPE='button'

In an HTML form, the type button creates a basic button GUI component. Here is an example of the code and resulting image:

```
<INPUT TYPE='button' NAME='btnOK' VALUE='OK'>
```

The button component receives events but does not directly trigger a request. Instead, it is used to extend the HTML functionality. By using a client-side scripting language, such as JavaScript, you can cause this component to trigger other processes to take place.

INPUT TYPE='checkbox'

In an HTML form, the type checkbox creates a check box GUI component. Here is an example of the code and resulting image:

```
<INPUT TYPE='checkbox' NAME='state' VALUE='CA'
 CHECKED> California <BR>
<INPUT TYPE='checkbox' NAME='state' VALUE='TX'> Texas <BR>
<INPUT TYPE='checkbox' NAME='state' VALUE='AZ'
 CHECKED> Arizona <BR>
```

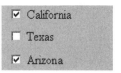

 Placing quotes around the attribute definitions is not mandatory, but it is considered good programming practice.

The check box component enables the user to select or deselect multiple items. These components are independent from one another, so selecting one will not affect another. When the information is ready to be sent to the server, all selected items will be paired by using their assigned name and value, and then sent with the request. For example, if a request were triggered and both California and Arizona were selected, the request data would include state=CA and state=AZ. Notice that we assign the VALUE attribute, not the label. If none were selected, then the request would not include data from these controls.

INPUT TYPE = 'radio'

In an HTML form, the type radio creates a radio button GUI component. Here is an example of the code and resulting image:

Example 1:

```
<INPUT TYPE='radio' NAME='question' VALUE='Yes'
 CHECKED> Loves me<BR>
<INPUT TYPE='radio' NAME='question' VALUE='No'>
 Loves me not<BR>
<INPUT TYPE='radio' NAME='question' VALUE='Confused'>
 Not sure <BR>
```

The radio button component links multiple buttons, but only one can be selected at a time. All three buttons in the example are joined because they share the same NAME attribute of question. This named group represents a mutually exclusive set of options. If you attempted to make the third option checked as well, only the last checked control in the group would be selected. See the following code example and resulting image:

Example 2:

```
<INPUT TYPE='radio' NAME='question' VALUE='Yes'
 CHECKED> Loves me<BR>
<INPUT TYPE='radio' NAME='question' VALUE='No'>
 Loves me not<BR>
<INPUT TYPE='radio' NAME='question' VALUE='Confused'
 CHECKED> Not sure <BR>
```

As you can see, the first checked item is ignored and only the last one selected is marked. Again, if a request were created, this last example would create a name/value data pair of question=Confused to send to the server.

SELECT Tag

Now that you've gone through all the desired INPUT type tags, you are ready to understand the SELECT tag. It is designed to create a component that enables the user to select options. You can set it up to allow either single or multiple selections. Syntactically, SELECT has an open and close tag. Within its body, you identify the available choices by using the OPTION attribute. We'll first show you the code for a single selection control and its resulting image.

Example 1 (single selection):

```
<SELECT NAME='Food Preference'>
    <OPTION VALUE='Vegetarian'> Vegetarian
    <OPTION VALUE='Kosher' SELECTED> Kosher
    <OPTION VALUE='None'> None
</SELECT>
```

By default, the SELECT tag allows only single selection. Marking an option SELECTED causes that choice to appear highlighted when the image is first rendered or reset. The NAME attribute is used to create the data name/value pair to send with a request. In the preceding example, a triggered request would include Food Preference=Kosher. Next we will show you how to create a multiple selection control.

Example 2 (multiple selection):

```
<SELECT NAME='Meat' MULTIPLE>
    <OPTION VALUE='Beef'> Beef
    <OPTION VALUE='Chicken' SELECTED> Chicken
    <OPTION VALUE='Pork'> Pork
    <OPTION VALUE='Fish' SELECTED> Fish
</SELECT>
```

Adding the MULTIPLE attribute enables you to select more than one option. In fact, the control takes on a list-like appearance. Again, a request would produce name/value pairs for Meat=Chicken and Meat=Fish in this example.

TEXTAREA Tag

A TEXTAREA tag creates a text area GUI component, which enables the user to enter multiple rows of data. Here is an example of the code and resulting image:

```
<TEXTAREA NAME='message' ROWS='5' COLS='30'>
You can pass the exam if you know all the rules!
Let us help you get there.
</TEXTAREA>
```

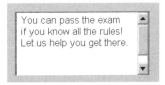

The text area component is created with a ROWS attribute to identify the number of visible lines. Without this attribute, the number of rows is set to a default value determined by the browser.

The COLS attribute identifies the visible number of characters per line without the use of a scrollbar. Because the letter *l* has a smaller width than *w*, the average width is used to measure a character. If the attribute value is excluded, the browser will apply a reasonable default column width.

The HTML spec encourages browsers to provide automatic word wrap for this component. Because word wrap is not mandatory, you can programmatically enforce this behavior by including the following attribute: WRAP='VIRTUAL'.

The controls within a form are used to help the developer gather user data and send client information to the web server. Next, we'll discuss how the information is formatted into a query string in preparation for transportation.

Query String

With a better understanding of HTML tags, you can start examining elements more closely associated with the browser. A *query string* is a URL-encoded string that contains data stored in name/value pairs.

Say you had an HTML form with the following controls:

```
<INPUT TYPE='text' NAME='firstName' VALUE='Name:'
     SIZE='20'>
<INPUT TYPE='password' NAME='passwd' VALUE='Password:'
     SIZE='20'>
<INPUT TYPE='submit' NAME='bttn' VALUE='Send Now'>
```

Clicking the submit button triggers a request that generates the following query string:

```
firstName=Name%3A&passwd=Password%3A&bttn=Send+Now
```

Here are a few important query string rules to remember:

- Data is transferred in name/value pairs.

- Names and values are URL encoded (hexadecimal ASCII), including white space, question marks, and most non-alphanumeric values. For example, a percent sign (%) would be denoted with the Unicode value 0025 and displayed as %25.

- Name and value pairs are separated by an ampersand (&).

- Spaces in the name are encoded as a plus sign or a hexadecimal code by the browser, because URLs cannot contain spaces.

- URL

A *Uniform Resource Locator (URL)* defines the information the client needs to make a connection to the server. For example:

```
http://book.com/
```

or

```
http://book.com:8080/servlet/Registration?
name=Ariela&address=1234+Happy+Street
```

The full signature consists of the following:

```
<protocol>://<servername>[:port]/<url-path>
[?query-string]
```

The following list is a more detailed breakdown of the various elements found in a URL and their functions:

Protocol   The set of rules used to transmit information. For simple website access, you will most often see HTTP used. However, depending on what information you are trying to access and how, you might see other types of protocols such as HTTPS, FTP, or NNTP.

Servername Defines the domain name used for the web server. It usually ends with a `.com`, `.net`, `.org`, `.gov`, `.edu`, `.biz`, `.info`, `.tv`, `.ws`, `.to`, `.co`, `.uk`, or something similar.

Port Required only if the default port 80 is not being used. It is a numeric value (from 0 to 65,535) designated by the web server for that particular service.

URL path Defines additional directories to locate the resource.

Query string A URL-encoded string that represents data being sent in an HTTP request.

URI

The *Uniform Resource Identifier (URI)* is the part of the URL excluding the domain name and the query string—in other words, all information after the domain name and before the query string. It specifies the resource.

Given the following address, you can see both the URL and URI:
Request address:

```
http://java.sun.com/products/servlet/index.html?id='09'
```

URL:

```
http://java.sun.com/products/servlet/index.html?id='09'
```

URI:

```
/products/servlet/index.html
```

HTTP

The success behind client-server architecture is the ability of both parties to communicate and transfer data over a network. The means of transmission depends on what is being sent and how you want that information delivered. At the lowest level, data is transmitted by using Internet Protocol (IP). There are two main points you need to know about IP. First, the packets are a fixed size, and second, you are not guaranteed delivery. If a packet fails, the protocol will not try to resend the data.

For a more controlled environment, Transmission Control Protocol (TCP) guarantees that the information will be delivered—and in the order it was sent, without errors. If a failure occurs, this protocol ensures the sender that it will make several more attempts at delivery. In addition, the size of the information being transferred can vary.

The next network layer is one built on top of TCP. *Hypertext Transfer Protocol (HTTP)* utilizes TCP, but adds a few more custom features. HTTP is a stateless protocol—meaning its data is not retained from one request to the next. After a request is made, the connection is closed. Because clients are not holding open connections to a server, the server can have more clients connect over a long period of time.

HTTP is also flexible in that it can transmit any file that conforms to the *Multipurpose Internet Mail Extension (MIME)*. MIME is an extension of the e-mail protocol used to allow the exchange of different kinds of data files over the Internet. HTTP was built in conjunction with HTML to enable users to access information through a web browser. Selecting a link or transmitting data from a form will generate an HTTP request to send to a web server whose address is defined by a URL.

The process to transmit the request is as follows:

1. An HTTP client or web browser makes a connection to a server.

2. The client initiates a request.

3. The server answers and sends a response to the client.

4. The connection is closed.

Figure 1.3 shows how the client makes a request for a GIF file to the server and the server responds with the appropriate information.

FIGURE 1.3   HTTP request/response communication

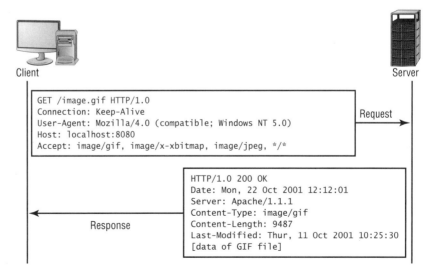

As Figure 1.3 illustrates, each response or request is made up of three parts: the definition line, the header section, and the body.

The Client Request

The client begins by making a connection with the server. Once linked, the client enters data and/or generates a request for information. If the HTML form contains data, the name/value pairs will be gathered and included with the request. The request will then be sent to the server, and the client will wait for a response. Figure 1.4 shows a sample request broken up by category.

FIGURE 1.4   Categorizing the request

Request line	POST /image.gif HTTP 1.0
Header (general)	Connection: Keep-Alive
Header (request)	Referer: http://example.com/search.html User-Agent: Mozilla/4.0 (compatible; Windows NT 5.0) Host: localhost:8080 Accept: image/gif, image/x-xbitmap, image/jpeg, */*
Header (entity)	Content-Type: application/x-www-form-urlencoded Content-Length: 23
Body	name=value&name=value&name=value

Request Line

The client initiates the transaction by connecting to an HTTP server. This request for information is sent with a line defining the HTTP method or action desired, the document address, and the protocol/version. The format of a request line is as follows:

Method   Request-URI   Protocol

For example:

POST   /index.html   HTTP/1.0

Aside from the POST method, there are many other method types, which we will discuss later, in the "Request Methods" subsection. For now, this line sends the server the information necessary to know what to do and where to do it, by using a defined protocol.

Header

The client might send additional information after the request line to help the server process the request. This information can consist of the host name, type of browser, language, file formats, and more. The header section usually contains client configuration details and specifics on the types of document formats that will be accepted in the response. Header information is sent line by line by using value pairs consisting of the header name and associated value. This pattern is very much like a `java.util.Map`.

The format of a header is as follows:

```
Keyword:          Value
```

For example:

```
User-Agent:       Mozilla/4.0 (compatible;Windows NT 5.0)
Accept:           image/gif, image/x-xbitmap, image/jpeg
Accept:           application/x-comet, application/msword
Accept:           application/vnd.ms-excel, */*
Host:             localhost:8080
Accept-Encoding:gzip, deflate
Accept-Language:en-us
Referer:          http://localhost:8080/servlets/index.html
Connection:       Keep-Alive
```

Notice that the `Accept` header can be defined multiple times.

In this example, you can see that the first key, `User-Agent`, identifies information about the client browser. The second key defines the type of files the client will accept, and the third provides more configuration information. Additional header tags can be utilized. Table 1.1 displays all the possible header tags for a request.

The header section is optional, but almost always included.

TABLE 1.1   Common Header Tags

Tag	
Accept	Specifies acceptable media types for the response
Accept-Charset	Indicates acceptable character sets for the response
Accept-Encoding	Restricts the content-coding acceptable for the response
Accept-Language	Defines all acceptable languages
Age	Indicates the age of a response body
Allow	Specifies methods that the resource defined by the URI can respond to
Authorization	Requests restricted documents
Cache-Control	Describes how proxies should handle requests and responses
Code	Specifies the encoding method for the body data
Content-Base	Resolves the relative URLs within the body of the document being returned
Content-Encoding	Identifies the encoding type applied to the body prior to transmission
Content-Language	Identifies the language of the response content
Content-Length	Identifies the length of the body measured in bytes
Content-Location	Identifies the actual location of the entity being returned
Content-MD5	A computing mechanism used to determine whether the body was modified during transmission
Content-Type	Identifies the type of data being returned

TABLE 1.1 Common Header Tags *(continued)*

Tag	
Expires	Indicates the date when the response should no longer be considered valid
From	Specifies the client e-mail address
Host	Identifies the host and port number the client is connected to
Last-Modified	Shows the date the returned content was last changed
Location	Redirects to a new location
Referer	Indicates the source from which the current request was generated
User-Agent	Identifies the browser's signature information
Warning	Identifies any additional risks associated with the response

Body

When there is a need to send additional information, a blank line is placed after the last header line, and then data can follow. The data being sent to the server from the client is usually included in the body when a POST action is defined.

An empty line is always included to separate the header and body information. If a body is not included, an empty line must still be included to signify the end of the request header.

The Server Response

After a connection is made with the server, the server looks at the first line to determine whether it can process the request. It then handles the request internally and generates a response. The response contains information about the success of the request, header information about the server, and an actual response, which might be an HTML page, a graphic, or some other MIME type. Figure 1.5 shows a response broken up by category.

FIGURE 1.5   Categorizing the response

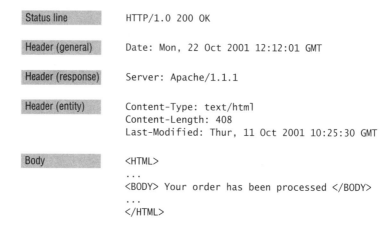

Status line	HTTP/1.0 200 OK
Header (general)	Date: Mon, 22 Oct 2001 12:12:01 GMT
Header (response)	Server: Apache/1.1.1
Header (entity)	Content-Type: text/html Content-Length: 408 Last-Modified: Thur, 11 Oct 2001 10:25:30 GMT
Body	<HTML> ... <BODY> Your order has been processed </BODY> ... </HTML>

Status Line

The server responds with a line that identifies the HTTP version it is using. The server attempts to utilize an HTTP version that most closely resembles that of the client. In addition, the server will send a status code to indicate the result of the request and a phrase to describe the code. The format of a status line is as follows:

Protocol   Status Code   Description

For example:

HTTP/1.0   200   OK

In this example, a code of 200 means that the request was successful and that the requested data will be provided after the headers.

Header

The response header is similar to the request header. It contains similar information as the header of the client request, except it pertains to the server. It tells the client about the server's configuration and data about the response.

For example, it might tell the client what methods are supported, request authorization, and/or give date information. The format is as follows:

Keyword: *Value*

For example:

Date: Mon, 22 Oct 2001 12:12:01 GMT
Server: Apache/1.1.1
Content-Type: text/html
Content-Length: 408
Last-Modified: Thurs, 11 Oct 2001 10:25:30 GMT

This example responds with the date the response is being sent, the type of server it was processed on, the format and length of the response, and the last date the content was modified.

Body

The body consists of the data the client requested. If the Content-Type is defined as text/html, then an HTML document will be sent in return. If the Content-Type is image/jpeg, then an image will be returned.

The server returns one response for each request. If a request comes in for an HTML page with an image, two responses will be sent in parallel. The browsers usually join the two to make it appear as if only one response was sent.

Request Methods

When a web server receives a request, it must first determine how to handle the information it receives. Looking at the request line answers this question. An HTTP method is the first element included. There are seven methods: GET, POST, PUT, HEAD, DELETE, OPTIONS, and TRACE. Each method serves a different purpose and demands a different type of response. Table 1.2 summarizes these action methods. We will go over the methods more thoroughly to ensure that you understand their differences and functionalities.

TABLE 1.2 Request Method Summary

Action	Description
GET	Retrieves a resource
POST	Transfers client information to the server
PUT	Provides a new or replacement document to be stored on the server
HEAD	Retrieves only the header information pertaining to the requested resource
DELETE	Removes a file from a specified URL
OPTIONS	Returns the supported HTTP methods of the server
TRACE	Returns the entire network route that the request took, from the client to the server and back

GET Method

A GET method is a request designed to retrieve static resources such as an HTML document or an image from a specific location on the server. When a client defines a GET action, they are most likely asking the server to return the body of a document identified in the request URI. When sending the request, the client might send additional information to the server to help process the request. The information will be transmitted in a query string attached to the URL.

The advantages of appending a sequence of characters to the URL are that the page can be bookmarked or e-mailed. Also, the data does not need to be sent from a form, thus removing one step from the process of retrieving the data.

There are disadvantages to transferring data via the URL as well. First, the client cannot send a large URL because most servers limit the URL string to about 240 characters. Second, because a GET request can be bookmarked, it is considered *idempotent*, which means the request can be safely repeated without necessarily consulting the user. Consequently, GET requests should not be used to cause a change on the server for which the client would be held responsible. Imagine a client who is ready to place an order at a website that uses a shopping cart. If the order request was processed by using a GET, then the order could be placed multiple times, causing several charges to be made against the client's payment method. The result could be an overcharged, irate customer.

Other types of GETs are as follows:

conditional GET   Returns a response only under specified circumstances. The request message header contains at least one of the following fields: If-Modified-Since, If-Unmodified-Since, If-Match, If-None-Match, or If-Range.

partial GET   Requests that only part of the entity be transferred. If a client already holds some of the data, and the data has not changed on the server, there is no need to retrieve the entity in its entirety. A partial GET must include a Range header field. This header enables the client to retrieve a section of data, rather than the entire entity. A partial GET can be used when an interrupt occurs and the client already has part of the entity in memory. There is no need to request bytes already received.

A common example of a GET request is made through search engine queries. The user enters the criteria for the information they want to be returned and then they select Search. In most cases, this triggers a GET request whereby the criteria is converted to a query string and added to the URL. In response, the web server will return static pages of related information. Let's examine this example in more detail.

Imagine you are accessing a search engine. The focus is set in a text field, and you are prompted to enter the details of your search. You type in your specifics and then click the Search button. A simple version of the HTML code would look like the following:

```
<HTML>
    <HEAD>
        <TITLE>The Famous Search Engine</TITLE>
    </HEAD>
    <BODY>
        <H1>Just ask </H1>
        <FORM ACTION='servlet/Search' METHOD='GET'>
```

```
          <P>Enter your critera:
          <INPUT TYPE='text' SIZE='40' NAME='criteria'>
          <INPUT TYPE='submit' VALUE='Search'> </P>
       </FORM>
       <!-- The page would contain more information -->
    </BODY>
 </HTML>
```

If you entered **Motorcycle** as your criteria and then pressed the Submit button, the browser would create a GET request that would look similar to the following code:

```
GET /servlet/Search/criteria=Motorcycle HTTP/1.0
User-Agent: Mozilla/4.0 (compatible; Windows NT 5.0)
Host: educationaledge.net
Accept: image/gif, image/x-xbitmap, image/jpeg, */*
```

The data from the form would be converted to a URL-encoded format and appear in the Address or Location field of your browser, along with the URL.

Go to: http://educationaledge.net/servlet/Search?criteria=Motorcycle

After the server receives and processes this request, it would send a response that resembles the following code:

```
HTTP/1.0 200 OK
Date: Sun, 16 Sep 2001 17:01:43 GMT
Server: HypotheticalServer/1.0
MIME-version: 1.0
Content-Type: text/html
Last-Modified: Wed, 17 July 2001 12:10:05 GMT
Content-Length: 6790

<HTML>
… <!-- Search results are formatted in the return page -->
</HTML>
```

After the response is sent, the browser would then display the new page for the user to view and access.

Although a search engine is a typical example of one use for a GET request, keep in mind that several other scenarios could prompt such a request. For example, you could use the GET to request any one of the following resources:

- A file or image

- Output from another language running on the server

- Results from a compilation

- Information from another hardware device—for example, a database query or video footage—accessible by the server.

At this point, we have exhausted all the details associated with the GET method. You are now ready to learn about the intricacies associated with the POST method.

POST Method

A POST method is a request designed for posting information to the server. If a client is looking to place an order or update a database with new information, the POST method is the best approach given the way it handles the data transfer.

Unlike a GET, the POST request transfers its data in the body of the actual HTTP request—the URL does not change. In fact, the exchange is invisible to the user. In addition, there are security provisions incorporated by both the client side and server side. The client's browser proves to be more secure because bookmarking or e-mailing the URL does not result in storing or communicating the data in the HTTP request—because it simply isn't present in the URL. On the server's end, the approach is more secure because the server's access log does not record the dynamic data that would be present when using a POST method. This also means that client actions are prevented from being repeated without the consent of the user. When transferring credit card information or updating a database, the POST method is the perfect solution. It performs the action once, and the information is safer because it is not displayed in the URL. There is yet one more advantage: the amount of data that is transferred can be very large, because the size of a request has no limitation.

There is one disadvantage you face with a POST request: it must be submitted from a form. Because of the way the data is encoded, a POST request cannot be transmitted from any other resource.

The next example uses a form to POST a request and generate a result. Let's say you access a website that requires you to register your login name and password. The HTML code would look something like this:

```
<HTML>
  <HEAD>
      <TITLE>Register NOW!</title>
  </HEAD>
  <BODY>
    <FORM ACTION='servlet/Register' METHOD='POST'>
      <P>Enter your login name: </P>
      <INPUT TYPE='text' SIZE='20' NAME='login'>
      <P>Enter your New Password: </P>
      <INPUT TYPE='password' SIZE='20' NAME='password'>
      <P>Re-enter your New Password:</P>
      <INPUT TYPE='password' SIZE='20' NAME='password2'>
      <BR><INPUT TYPE='submit' VALUE='Submit'>
    </FORM>
  </BODY>
</HTML>
```

If you entered a login name of **Delon**, a password of **ch1pDe3ign3r** (twice), and then hit the Submit button, the browser would generate a POST request to transfer the information to the server and retrieve the opening page to this site. The client request might look similar to the following:

```
POST /servlet/Register HTTP/1.0
User-Agent: Mozilla/4.75[en](Windows NT 5.0; U)
Host: educationaledge.net
Accept: image/gif, image/x-xbitmap, image/jpeg, */*

login=Delon&password=ch1pDe3ign3r&password2=ch1pDe3ign3r
```

The data from the form is converted to the URL-encoded standard and becomes a part of the entity body. Also, there must be a blank line between the header data and the body to notify the server to handle information from each part differently. After the server receives and processes this request, it might send a response containing the next page or a message:

```
HTTP/1.0 200 OK
Date: Sat, 18 Mar 2001 13:21:44 GMT
```

```
Server: HypotheticalServer/1.0
MIME-Version: 1.0
Content-Type: text/html
Last-Modified: Mon, 10 Mar 2001 11:16:15 GMT
Content-Length: 525

<HTML>
...
  <FORM>
    <H1> Press the button below to begin shopping </H1>
      <INPUT TYPE='submit' VALUE='Shop Now'>
  </FORM>
```

The request/response process would then begin again after the user selected the Shop Now button.

In general, a POST request provides a safer environment for requests that require clients to cause changes to a server resource. The need for security and the size of data being transferred will help define whether you should use a GET versus a POST request.

PUT Method

The PUT method is the complement to the GET method. Instead of getting static information, it requests to store static information. A PUT method asks the server to store the content body to the URI identified in the request line.

For example, imagine you have an HTML editor that you use to create web pages. You will likely want to use the editor to publish the document to a defined server. This can be done by using a PUT request. Let's say you create a simple HTML page that contains the phrase "United we stand!" The editor then has to provide a publishing option asking you for the destination of your transfer and (most likely) some authentication information. After providing the necessary information, you press a button (for example, an OK button), which triggers a request. The request might look something like the following:

```
PUT /test.html   HTTP/1.0
Connection: Keep-Alive
User-Agent: Mozilla/4.75[en](Windows NT 5.0; U)
Host: publish.com
```

```
Accept: image/gif, image/x-xbitmap, image/jpeg, */*
Content-Length: 150

<!DOCTYPE HTML PUBLIC "~//W3C//DTD HTML 3.2//EN">
<HTML>
  <BODY>
    <P>United we stand!</P>
  </BODY>
</HTML>
```

The server will store the entity body in the URI /test.html and likely respond with the following:

```
HTTP/1.0   201   Created
Date: Fri, 26 Oct 2001 16:02:15 GMT
Server: HypotheticalServer/1.0
Content-Type: text/html
Content-Length: 50

<HTML>
  <H1>The file was created.</H1>
</HTML>
```

If authentication fails, the server will send a response body to identify that authentication was denied and the user can try again with the correct information.

HEAD Method

A HEAD method is a request that is almost exactly like a GET. The only difference is that a HEAD request does not return the entity body. It returns the response line and headers only. Usually this type of request is used to verify a document's existence or properties. You could send a GET or a HEAD to see whether a document exists, and if it does not exist, both requests will return errors. If it does exist, then the response for a HEAD will be much smaller than that of a GET and consequently save you network bandwidth. The other reason to use HEAD is to learn about the properties of a particular resource. Remember, the response headers identify the document's size, type, and modification time.

Here are some examples of common uses for HEAD requests:

- By identifying the modification time, you can determine whether there is a need to update a cached version of the resource.

- The document size can let you deal with layout issues before retrieving the actual document. In fact, if it's very large, it gives you a chance to determine an alternate plan instead of waiting for it to be returned and then trying to figure out what to do about the data.

- The type of document can be essential if you are looking to support or view only certain kinds.

- The type of server can notify the client of special query features that might be available to produce a more precise request.

Do keep in mind that header information from the server is optional. Client requests shouldn't rely on non-default data from a specific header.

DELETE Method

The complement to the PUT method is the DELETE method. Whereas PUT enables you to place a file at a particular URL, the DELETE method enables you to remove a file from a particular URL.

A client request might read:

```
DELETE /graphics/badNews.gif HTTP/1.1
```

A server response might look like the following:

```
HTTP/1.0 200 OK
Date: Sat, 28 Oct 2001 21:10:05 GMT
Server: MyServer/1.0
Content-Type: text/html
Content-Length: 25
```

A server will likely ask for authorization before performing such a task, but if successful, a code of 200 will be returned.

OPTIONS Method

The OPTIONS method is used to return all supported HTTP methods on the server. It returns an Allow header and acceptable HTTP methods as values.

For example, if the server supports GET, HEAD, TRACE, and OPTIONS, part of the response will consist of the following:

```
Allow: GET, HEAD, TRACE, OPTIONS
```

If you are looking to assess the situation before attempting a call, the OPTIONS method is a good approach.

TRACE Method

When a request is sent, it passes through a series of proxy servers. During that journey, there is a chance that some of the headers have been changed. The TRACE method returns the request header values to the client to determine whether any changes took place. It is mainly used to help debug and perform an action similar to a traceroute. A *traceroute* is a Unix command that identifies all the locations or IP addresses that a request has utilized to get to its target address.

A solid understanding of all the HTTP request methods will help identify how a request maps to a servlet. In the next chapter, we will discuss the path of the request and how and what it does in the servlet.

Summary

In this chapter, we covered the details associated with the Servlet model. Specifically, we discussed:

- An overview of the J2EE model

- HTML form tags

- HTTP requests/responses

- HTTP methods: GET, POST, PUT, HEAD, DELETE, OPTIONS, and TRACE

So far, we have been focusing on the communication between the client, browser, and server. An HTTP request communicates with the browser and client, while the HTTP response communicates with the server and browser. We discussed the details associated with HTML, the language understood by browsers, and the HTTP protocol used to communicate the client's wants and data to the web server. These topics thoroughly covered exam Objective 1.2 and set us up to cover Objective 1.1. In the next chapter, we will discuss the path of the request and how it is handled within a servlet.

Exam Essentials

Be able to identify the functionality of the GET, POST, and HEAD methods. Each method is designed to retrieve information; it is how and what they retrieve that differentiates one from another. You should know what kind of information each request retrieves and how the information is retrieved.

Be able to identify the benefits associated with choosing to use a GET request. The GET method places its data in the URL, making it available for caching or e-mailing. If this data contains sensitive material, using this method could be a security risk. Because the GET method transfers its data in its URL, it does make the page easier to access. If used in the right circumstance, this can be a benefit.

Be able to identify the benefits associated with choosing to use a POST request. The POST method hides its data in the body of the request. This makes the page less accessible, which can be a good or bad factor depending on the task at hand. The POST request is also designed to send an error if the browser attempts to process the request more than once. This can be a benefit if you are performing a request by using a transaction that updates some resource on the server.

Be able to identify the benefits associated with choosing to use a HEAD versus a GET request. At times you might want to retrieve only the headers of a request to determine whether the resource exists or to determine the properties of the resource. In such cases, there is no need to retrieve the body of the request. Instead, a HEAD request becomes ideal. It returns only the header information provided by the server. A GET could accomplish the same tasks, but it would eat up wasted bandwidth.

Be familiar with browser controls and how they operate in relation to the GET, POST, and HEAD methods. Browsers use HTML to display components and capture their data. Each control stores specific data that is transferred when triggered. The default request of an HTML form is a GET request. It is often triggered with a submit button (other controls can trigger requests if customized by using JavaScript). It retrieves information but does not make modifications on the server side. A POST, on the other hand, is also triggered by similar controls, but it can make changes or process critical information on the server. A POST request is identified by specifying the METHOD='POST' attribute of the FORM tag. Both requests can return new HTML pages or new data to be rendered. A HEAD request simply returns the header information without making modifications to the current HTML page.

Key Terms

Before you take the exam, be certain you are familiar with the following terms:

CHECKED	partial GET
conditional GET	POST method
container	PUT method
controls	query string
DELETE method	request
Enterprise Information Systems (EIS)	response
Enterprise Java Bean (EJB)	Servlet model
form	servlets
GET method	SIZE
HEAD method	SRC
Hypertext Markup Language (HTML)	TRACE method
Hypertext Transfer Protocol (HTTP)	traceroute
idempotent	TYPE
Java Server Pages (JSPs)	Uniform Resource Identifier (URI)
MAXLENGTH	Uniform Resource Locator (URL)
Multipurpose Internet Mail Extension (MIME)	VALUE
NAME	web components
OPTIONS method	web server

Review Questions

1. Which HTTP method is used to store a resource on the server?

   A. GET

   B. POST

   C. PUT

   D. STORE

   E. HEAD

2. Given the following code, which request method will get invoked?

```
<HTML>
    <BODY>
        <FORM ACTION='servlet/Test'>
            <P>Enter the file you would like to Post:</P>
            <INPUT TYPE='text' SIZE='40' NAME='fileName'>
            <INPUT TYPE='submit' VALUE='Done'>
        </FORM>
    </BODY>
</HTML>
```

   A. PUT

   B. POST

   C. GET

   D. HEAD

3. Which of the following query strings is invalid? (Choose all that apply.)

   A. name=Michael&address=1234 Sunset Blvd.#301&state=CA

   B. name=Michael&address=1234+Sunset Blvd.+#301&state=CA

   C. name=Michael&address=1234+Sunset+Blvd%45
   +%23301&state=CA

   D. name=Michael&address=1234+Sunset+Blvd.+%23301&state=CA

4. Which of the following is false?

   A. The POST method request includes form data in the body of the request.

   B. The GET method includes form data in the URL when processing a request.

   C. The GET method transfers data in a more secure fashion.

   D. The POST method does not limit the size of data that can be transferred.

5. Which of the following tags is used to create a drop-down list?

   A. `<SELECT NAME='Choice' MULTIPLE></SELECT>`

   B. `<INPUT TYPE='select' NAME='choice'>`

   C. `<SELECT NAME='select'>`

   D. `<SELECT NAME='Choice'></SELECT>`

6. What character is used to separate the URI and query string in a GET request?

   A. &

   B. ?

   C. +

   D. =

7. Which of the following terms contains a request method, header information, and a body?

   A. HTTP request

   B. HTTP response

   C. HTTP protocol

   D. None of the above

8. Use the following code to answer this question, and assume that the user enters **myPassword** in the password control:

```
<HTML>
    <BODY>
        <FORM ACTION='servlet/Test'>
            <P>Enter your password:</P>
            <INPUT TYPE='password' SIZE='20' NAME='passwd'>
            <INPUT TYPE='submit' VALUE='Done'>
        </FORM>
    </BODY>
</HTML>
```

Which of the following name/value pairs will most likely be included in the request submitted for the code?

A. password=myPassword

B. passwd=**********

C. passwd=myPassword

D. password=**********

9. Which of the following tasks should not be performed by using a GET request? (Choose all that apply.)

A. Updating a database

B. Retrieving an image

C. Accessing a website

D. Sending credit card information

10. Which of the following HTML controls causes a request to be spawned when activated?

A. Input type='submit'

B. Input type='text'

C. Input type='radio'

D. Input type='password'

11. Which of the following request header tags is inaccurate?

    A. User-Agent: Mozilla/4.0 (compatible; Windows NT 5.0)
       Accept: image/gif, image/jpeg, image/jpeg,
       Accept: application/x-comet, application/msword
       Accept: application/vnd.ms-excel, */*
       Host: localhost:8080

    B. User-Agent: Mozilla/4.0 (compatible; Windows NT 5.0)
       Accept: image/gif, image/jpeg, image/jpeg,
       Host: localhost:8080

    C. User-Agent: Mozilla/4.0 (compatible; Windows NT 5.0)
       Accept: image/gif, image/jpeg, image/jpeg,
       application/vnd.ms-excel, */*
       Content-Type: text/html
       Host: localhost:8080

    D. None of the above

12. Which of the following is not a valid option for a GET request?

    A. To get a file or image

    B. To get results from a compilation

    C. To get information from another hardware device

    D. To get output from another program running on the server

    E. None of the above

13. How can you include a literal percent sign (%) within a query string?

    A. %

    B. 0025

    C. %25

    D. +

14. Which of the following elements is not included in a URL?

A. Protocol

B. Servername

C. Query string

D. Client IP

15. Which of the following is a valid INPUT TYPE?

A. SRC

B. hidden

C. SIZE

D. FORM

Answers to Review Questions

1. C.   A PUT method request is used to replace or store files on the server. The request URI identifies the location for the server to store the resource.

2. C.   If a method is not specified in a form, the browser will assign the GET method to the request by default.

3. A, B, D.   A query string must conform to the URL-encoded standard defined by RFC 1738. Characters that are non-alphanumeric are represented in a hexadecimal format (%XX). The first option is invalid because of the included spaces between Sunset and Blvd., and between ".·" and "#". Using the # character is illegal as well. The second option fails for similar reasons, and the last option is invalid because of the space placed before the name Michael.

4. C.   Because the GET method transfers data via the URL, its data can be bookmarked and saved for later use. This is far from secure. In addition, the data can be cached and processed multiple times without the client's approval. Again, these are features that are not secure if you are communicating sensitive data.

5. D.   The SELECT tag is used to create a control that enables the user to select an option from a drop-down list. If you include the MULTIPLE attribute, the control will look like a list, not a drop-down. Single selection is the default. Finally, the SELECT tag requires a closing tag, leaving the last option as the only correct response.

6. B.   The ampersand (&) is used to separate name/value pairs from one another. The plus sign (+) is used to fill blank space. The equal sign (=) is used to separate the name and value. This leaves the correct answer of a question mark (?). It is used to identify the beginning of the query string.

7. A.   An HTTP request begins with a request line, which defines the action that is being desired by the server. It can then contain a header and body.

8. C.   Visually, the password control alters the characters so they are not comprehensible. When they are sent, however, they appear in their normal text format.

9. A, D.   The GET method should not be used to make any modifications to the server (such as updating a database) or to send sensitive information (such as a credit card number). Because the information is present in the URL, this is extremely unsafe. In addition, the URL can be bookmarked and the request can be triggered multiple times without the knowledge of the client. Consequently, a GET request should not be used to perform transactions that would have negative effects if executed multiple times.

10. A.   A submit button generates a request from an HTML form. The other controls provide name/value data pairs to accompany the request.

11. C.   The Content-Type header tag is used to identify the type of data being returned. The first option is valid because multiple Accept tags are acceptable. You might think the third option is questionable due to the hard carriage return within the Accept declaration; however, the header request is valid. A hard carriage return is legal when listing header data.

12. E.   A GET request is used to get information from the server. All four options are valid types of data for a client to request via a call to GET.

13. C.   Literal symbols within a query string are denoted by using its Unicode value. The value is displayed by using the following notation: %XX. The final answer is invalid because a plus sign is used to represent a blank space.

14. D.   A URL contains all resources necessary to locate and communicate with its target source. The protocol defines the rules used to transmit information, while the servername is the domain name used for the server. Finally, the query string is the data transferred from the client to the server. A port can also be defined if the default 80 is not being used.

15. B.   The element SRC is an input attribute used to specify the location of the image control type. The SIZE element is also an input attribute. Its purpose is to identify the initial width of the control. The last option, FORM, is a tag used to encompass a variety of controls. The correct input type is hidden. These are controls that are not rendered, but whose values can be transmitted back to the server.

The Servlet Model

THE FOLLOWING SUN CERTIFIED WEB COMPONENT DEVELOPER FOR J2EE PLATFORM EXAM OBJECTIVES ARE COVERED IN THIS CHAPTER:

✓ **1.1 For each of the HTTP methods, GET, POST, and PUT, identify the corresponding method in the HttpServlet class.**

✓ **1.3 For each of the following operations, identify the interface and method name that should be used:**

- Retrieve HTML form parameters from the request
- Retrieve a servlet initialization parameter
- Retrieve HTTP request header information
- Set an HTTP response header; set the content type of the response
- Acquire a text stream for the response
- Acquire a binary stream for the response
- Redirect an HTTP request to another URL

✓ **1.4 Identify the interface and method to access values and resources and to set object attributes within the following three web scopes:**

- Request
- Session
- Context

✓ **1.5 Given a life-cycle method: init, service, or destroy, identify correct statements about its purpose or about how and when it is invoked.**

✓ **1.6 Use a RequestDispatcher to include or forward to a web resource.**

ow that you have a basic understanding of HTML triggers, the HTTP protocol, and servlet basics, the goal of this chapter is to give you a solid understanding of all the details associated with the objectives outlined for the Servlet model. So, in the following sections of this chapter, we will map the HTTP method directly to its servlet counterpart method and address the details associated with each method. The methods themselves rely heavily on the request and response objects passed in as arguments; consequently, we will show you how to extract information from the request and how to construct a suitable response.

After covering the request object in great detail, we will address the servlet life cycle handled by the container: its birth, through the `init()` method, its life, through the `service(...)` and `doXXX(...)` methods, and its death, through its `destroy()` method. Although this could conclude our discussion on the Servlet model, there is still one more possible action that can take place during the life of the servlet. Sometimes a servlet passes its request and response objects to another servlet to process. The `RequestDispatcher` interface provides two methods, `include(...)` and `forward(...)`, that make this action possible.

The Servlet Methods

The *Servlet model* is designed to allow small reusable server programs the ability to process a variety of requests from a client and then return a response efficiently. Depending on the HTTP request sent to the client, a specific servlet method will be assigned to handle the response. In this section, we will discuss the list of possible servlet methods that the container will invoke to handle an incoming request.

Until now, we have addressed how HTML tags use the HTTP protocol methods to send requests. Remember, a *request* is an object containing the client's intent, header information, and possible parameters. We haven't discussed how the HTTP protocol methods communicate with the servlet. Now, we will identify the specific mappings between HTTP methods and those in the HttpServlet class.

After a request is sent to a web server, the request line is parsed to determine the desired action. The HTTP method is then mapped to the associated servlet method. Because all HTTP servlets must extend the HttpServlet class, the servlets are guaranteed to have the appropriate method for the HTTP action. The Java Servlet Specification 2.3 states the following:

- GET requests are handled with a doGet(...) servlet method.

- POST requests are handled with a doPost(...) servlet method.

- PUT requests are handled with a doPut(...) servlet method.

- HEAD requests are handled with a doHead(...) servlet method.

First we'll present the commonalities among all the do*XXX* methods, and then we'll detail each one separately.

doXXX (...)

All corresponding HttpServlet request methods (do*XXX*) share the same signatures, parameters, and error handling. All methods behave similarly. They each take a request, process information, and return a response. As a result, the structure for these methods is similar; they take in the same parameters and throw the same exceptions.

Method Signature

As we have just stated, the structure for the HttpServlet request methods is standard. Each method is protected, meaning only classes within the same package or subclasses can access these methods. In addition, when they are overridden in your servlet, you can make them either protected or public. The return value is void because the response is sent by the container. A request and response object are provided via the parameters, and both the

ServletException and IOException are thrown in the event of transmission or streaming errors:

```
protected void doXXX(HttpServletRequest req,
                        HttpServletResponse res)
    throws ServletException, IOException
```

Parameters

By using the parameters passed in, you can access and create the necessary information to complete the requested task. *HttpServletRequest req* provides you a handle to the original request. By using this object, you get HTML parameters, header data, the method type, and date information. *HttpServletResponse resp* provides you a handle to construct a response. Remember, a *response* is an object that often contains header information and a possible body for the client to display.

Error Handler

Whenever information is transferred from point A to point B, a myriad of potential problems can occur. Sometimes those problems are a result of the network, and arise due to failures in the source or target system at runtime. Other times the problem is in the request or response object itself. The following list identifies the potential problems that can take place:

- If a content header cannot be handled, the container should issue an error message (HTTP 501 – Not Implemented) and discard the request. *5xx* error codes are usually reserved for server errors, and *3xx* and *4xx* error codes are reserved for application or container errors.

- If the request sent is incorrectly formatted, the do*XXX*(…) method will ignore any logic included in the method and simply return an HTTP 400 – Bad Request error message.

- If an input or output error is detected when the servlet handles the HTTP request, a java.io.IOException is thrown.

- If the HTTP request cannot be processed, a ServletException is thrown.

doGet (…)

The server indirectly calls the doGet(…) method when a GET request is sent. By overriding the HttpServlet's doGet(…) method in your servlet, you get a handle to the request to retrieve information about the call and then generate a response to return. The code for this signature is as follows:

```
protected void doGet(HttpServletRequest req,
                        HttpServletResponse res)
       throws ServletException, IOException
```

Like the GET action, the doGet(...) method is used to retrieve data. It is different in that instead of requesting the data, it actually performs the functionality necessary to get the data. It also is capable of sending a response back to the receiver.

The GET method should have the following characteristics:

Safe　This implies that the user cannot be held accountable for any side effects. For example, querying data has no side effects, whereas changing data does.

Idempotent　This means that the request can be safely repeated. Again, making a query is both safe and idempotent; buying a product online is not safe or idempotent.

A doGet(...) method is generally coded by using the following steps:

1. Reads the request data

2. Writes the response headers

3. Gets the response's writer or output stream object

4. Writes the response data

Before writing the response data, it is considered good practice to set the content type of the response to identify its format. For example, you could set it to text/html if the response output is written by using HTML tags, or text/plain if it's just simple text strings. This is especially important when using a PrintWriter object to return a response. In fact, setting the content type should be done before accessing the PrintWriter object. The container will write the headers before the body of the response is committed. Consequently, if you plan to modify the header information, it should be done prior to flushing a response body.

Another practice that is encouraged is to set the Content-Length header by using the response object to notify the container of the document size. This information enables the servlet container to use a persistent connection to return the response, which improves performance. By default, a container will set a response buffer size. If the content length fits inside that response buffer, then the container automatically sets its content length.

These issues aside, the doGet(...) is the best place to include logic for retrieving safe and idempotent requests. For tasks that don't require these precautions, but also request data, the doPost(...) is more suitable.

doPost (...)

The server indirectly calls the doPost(...) method when a POST request is sent. By overriding the HttpServlet's doPost(...) method in your servlet, you get a handle to the request to retrieve, update, or alter information and then generate a response to return to the client. The benefit of the POST action is that it enables the client to send one request with an unlimited amount of data to the web server. Data is more protected when using a POST (as opposed to a GET request), because it isn't blatantly visible or automatically cached. Processing credit card information is the prime example of when to use a POST request, which calls the doPost(...).

The code for this signature is written as follows:

```
protected void doPost(HttpServletRequest req,
                      HttpServletResponse res)
    throws ServletException, IOException
```

As for style, the doPost(...) is coded in a similar fashion to the doGet(...). It gets the request information, processes the data, and generates a response. In addition, the rules associated to constructing the response are the same.

The doPost(...) method is different from the doGet(...) in that it does not need to be safe or idempotent. In fact, most POST requests do have side effects, and the user should be held accountable. Let's say your user is purchasing stocks. That order should be processed in a doPost(...) method. This type of request is designed to prevent the user from repeating the same action because doing so could have such serious side effects.

In summary, the doGet(...) is the best place to include logic for retrieving safe and idempotent requests. For tasks that don't require these precautions, but also request data, the doPost(...) is more suitable.

doPut (...)

The server indirectly calls the doPut(...) method when a PUT request is sent. Usually a PUT request is made when the client is looking to place a file on the server. The process is written in the body of the doPut(...) method.

The following is how the code for doPut(...) should be written:

```
protected void doPut(HttpServletRequest req,
                     HttpServletResponse res)
     throws ServletException, IOException
```

Like the doPost(...), the doPut(...) does not need to be safe or idempotent. The actions taking place in this method can have side effects that hold the user accountable. Consequently, it is considered good practice to protect the URL from errors by saving a copy of the affected URL in a temporary directory or location.

Like an FTP request, the doPut(...) is effective in processing requests used to transfer data to a specific location.

doHead (...)

The server indirectly calls the doHead(...) method when a HEAD request is sent. A HEAD request is used when the client is interested in only the response header information. Prior to the Java Servlet Specification 2.3, an HTTP HEAD request called the doGet(...) method. It was designed to process the entire method but return only the header information from the response. The current release includes a doHead(...) method in the HttpServlet class for the developer to override. Now, the doHead(...) method is called without the need to process a body request.

The following shows how to define a doHead(...) method:

```
protected void doHead(HttpServletRequest req,
                      HttpServletResponse res)
     throws ServletException, IOException
```

Like the doGet(...), the doHead(...) should be written to be safe and idempotent. That is pretty easy to do because the doHead(...) usually contains only header information. The servlet specification includes this method to improve performance. Now, when the respective HEAD method is called, the headers can be set and the response returned. There is no need to process information for a body that will not be returned.

The next few methods are not directly mentioned in the objectives, but they can be potential options for some of the questions. A general understanding of these topics will help you find the correct answer during the exam.

doDelete (...)

The server indirectly calls the doDelete(...) method when a DELETE request is sent. A DELETE request is used to remove a document or web page from the server.

The method signature for doDelete(...) is as follows:

```
protected void doDelete(HttpServletRequest req,
                        HttpServletResponse res)
   throws ServletException, IOException
```

Like the doPost(...), this method does not need to be either safe or idempotent. Because the action of deleting can have serious effects, it's a procedure that you want the client to be held accountable for. For example, let's say that another company recently bought your company. As a result, you need to change the company's logo to represent a new image. You could make a request to DELETE the old graphic file and then make a request to PUT a new image in its place. As a precaution, it is considered good practice to save a copy of the old image in a backup directory or location.

doOptions (...)

The server indirectly calls the doOptions(...) method when an OPTIONS request is sent. An OPTIONS request is used to determine which HTTP methods the server or servlet supports. The request returns only header information. Most importantly, it returns a header tag called Allow and HTTP method values, which represent the doXXX methods available on the specified servlet.

The method signature for the doOptions(...) method is as follows:

```
protected void doOptions(HttpServletRequest req,
                         HttpServletResponse res)
   throws ServletException, IOException
```

Let's say your servlet overrides the doGet(...) and doPost(...) methods. An OPTIONS request will return the following header:

```
HTTP/1.0 200 OK
Allow: GET, HEAD, POST, TRACE, OPTIONS
Servlet-Engine: Tomcat Web Server/3.2.3
   (JSP 1.1; Servlet 2.2; Java 1.3; Windows 2000 5.0 x86;
   java.vendor=Sun Microsystems Inc.)
```

Now, you might be asking yourself why all those methods are available if you've overridden only the doGet(...) and doPost(...) methods. The reason is that if you override the doGet(...) method, by default, you also inherit the HEAD and TRACE methods. You don't have to override the doHead(...) and doTrace(...) methods, and the default execution will be performed. The OPTIONS method is available for every servlet, so this cannot be excluded.

There is generally no need to override this method unless the servlet implements methods beyond those implemented by HTTP 1.1. The default implementation is almost always sufficient.

doTrace (...)

The server indirectly calls the doTrace(...) method when a TRACE request is sent. A TRACE request is used to return the headers sent with the request to the client. It is usually used to help debug the servlet.

The method signature for the doTrace(...) method is as follows:

```
protected void doTrace(HttpServletRequest req,
                       Httpservletresponse res)
     throws ServletException, IOException
```

To understand how a trace works, let's walk through an example. Say you send out a request that contains the following information:

Request Line:

```
TRACE /greetings/servlet/Registration HTTP/1.0
```

The return response might look similar to this code sample:

```
HTTP/1.0 200 OK
Content-Type: message/http
Content-Length: 48
Servlet-Engine: Tomcat Web Server/3.2.3 (JSP 1.1;
    Servlet 2.2; Java 1.3.0; Windows 2000 5.0 x86;
    java.vendor=Sun Microsystems Inc.)

TRACE /greetings/servlet/Registration HTTP/1.0
```

The doTrace(...) method provides a trace for the request sent from the client to the servlet. If the request passes through a proxy, the request might get modified. The doTrace(...) method can return either the original, unmodified request or a modified request, if changes were made. As a final note, there is usually no need to override the doTrace(...) method because the functionality is already built into the default implementation.

Now that you have looked at each method, it is important to understand the details associated with the parameters that these methods utilize.

The Request

The request object provides the server with the client data necessary to process the request. This can include information about the header, client's host machine, form data entered by the client, and servlet. As the request object travels from client to server, it is wrapped by the `ServletRequest` interface to provide basic client information. It is then wrapped again with the `HttpServletRequest` interface to provide request information such as header data, cookies (which we will discuss later in this section), and other servlet-related items. Figure 2.1 demonstrates the path a request object takes and how it returns as a response.

FIGURE 2.1 The request/response path

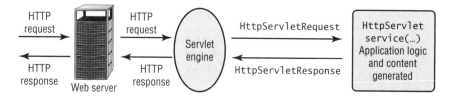

After the request object reaches the `service(...)` method, it will be passed to the appropriate HTTP request method. At that point, you can extract client information by using the request object handle passed to the appropriate HTTP request method. When taking the exam, you should be familiar with the method signatures, their purposes, and their associated interfaces. As a developer, knowing these methods will help you create robust servlets that contain the necessary details to accomplish your task. In this section, we will discuss the interfaces and methods available to extract and modify the request object.

ServletRequest and *ServletResponse* Interface

After the request is sent to the server, it is converted to a `ServletRequest` object, which contains the user-entered data, or parameters of the request. The container also creates a corresponding `ServletResponse` object to provide the receiver an object to transfer data back to the original source. These two objects are passed to the `Servlet` interface method `service(Servlet-Request req, ServletResponse res)`. A servlet can receive these objects because all servlets must implement an interface that extends the `Servlet` interface. Before these objects reach the actual servlet, they are cast to HttpServletRequest and HttpServletResponse objects, which include header and date information. Now these objects are ready to be passed to the service(...) method of the actual servlet object. Figure 2.2 displays the path.

FIGURE 2.2 The request process

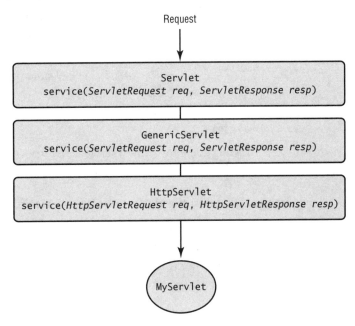

Parameters

The ServletRequest object gives you access to data often used to initialize a servlet. These methods are as follows:

- String getParameter(*String name*)
- Enumeration getParameterNames()
- String[] getParameterValues(*String name*)

These methods retrieve the values from the names assigned to the controls added to your HTML page. Look at the following code example:

```
<HTML>
    <BODY>
        <FORM ACTION=' servlet/GetData' METHOD='GET'>
```

```
            <P>NAME: <INPUT TYPE='TEXT' SIZE='25'
                name='firstName'></P>
            <P>Destination:
            <SELECT NAME='location'></P>
            <OPTION VALUE='California'>California
            <OPTION VALUE='Washington'>Washington
            <OPTION VALUE='New York'>New York
            <OPTION VALUE='Florida'>Florida
            </SELECT>
            <P><INPUT TYPE='submit' VALUE='GO!'></P>
        </FORM>
      </BODY>
    </HTML>
```

Listing 2.1 shows how a servlet can retrieve the values of these controls by using the getParameter(...) method.

Listing 2.1: Using the getParameter(...) Method

```java
import javax.servlet.*;
import javax.servlet.http.*;
import java.io.*;
import java.util.*;

public class GetData extends HttpServlet {

  protected void doGet(HttpServletRequest req,
                       HttpServletResponse res)
    throws ServletException, IOException {
      String enteredName = req.getParameter("firstName");
      Enumeration ctrlNames = req.getParameterNames();
      String[] states = req.getParameterValues("location");

      res.setContentType("text/html");
      PrintWriter out = res.getWriter();
      out.println("<HTML>");
```

```
out.println("<BODY>");
out.println("<P>Name entered: " + enteredName
    + "</P>");
out.println("<P>Control Names are: <BR>");

while(ctrlNames.hasMoreElements()) {
out.println((String)ctrlNames.nextElement() + "<BR>");
}

out.println("</P><P>The values selected are: ");
for (int i=0; i<states.length;i++) {
  out.println(states[i] + "<BR>");
}
out.println("</P></BODY>");
out.println("</HTML>");
out.close();
   }
}
```

When you run this servlet, you begin by accessing the window, shown in the following graphic:

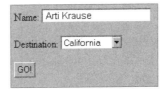

After you enter values into the form and select the GO! Button, a request is generated. This request is sent to the servlet and passes through the service(...) method to the doGet(...) method. Because the HttpServlet-Request has header information, it is aware that the action defined by the form is a GET request. Consequently, the doGet(...) method is called next. Within the doGet(...) method, you use the request object to retrieve the parameter names and values entered into the HTML form. You first get the value (Arti Krause) entered into the control called firstName. You then get the names of all the controls in the request: location and firstName.

Finally, you get the selected parameter (California) for the control named location. The following output is generated.

```
Name entered: Arti Krause

Control Names are:
location
firstName

The values selected are:
California
```

Within the doGet(...) method, the information is formatted and placed inside HTML tags, and into an OutputStream or PrintWriter extracted from the response. This response is then sent back to the browser to render the information.

The ServletResponse object provides methods that help you construct a response. These methods are as follows:

void setContentType(*String type*)

Before sending response information, you must notify the receiving application of the content type so it knows how to handle the response data. Because you are transmitting HTML text and the type is formatted as a MIME extension type, you set the content to text/html rather than just html.

The second step in developing a response is to extract a suitable stream to transfer the information:

ServletOutputStream getOutputStream()

This method provides a binary stream that enables you to transfer the data by using bytes.

Another approach is to transfer the data in character or Unicode format. A PrintWriter stream is used to write text:

PrintWriter getWriter()

While the servlet can extract the values from an HTML page by using the ServletRequest object, this object also enables the developer to set attributes for the request.

Attributes

An *attribute* is a name/value pair associated to a request. Either the container or developer of a servlet can set attributes. This action becomes useful when a servlet needs to communicate with another servlet. These attributes are available through the following methods:

- `Object getAttribute(String name)`
- `Enumeration getAttributeNames()`
- `void setAttribute(String key, Object value)`

Setting the attribute is similar to adding a value to a `java.util.Map` object. You define the key, a `String`, and then the associated object. In a later part of this chapter, we will cover request dispatching, where a servlet passes on part of the response development to another servlet. Before a request is dispatched to another servlet, the current servlet might want to pass along the request, a graphic image, a file, or just a value. This can be done by using the `setAttribute(…)` method. The receiving servlet can then access these values by calling `getAttribute(…)` and passing in the key name. If the key names are not known, the target servlet can get all names by using `getAttributeNames(…)`, and then extract the values by using the keys returned to request the specific value.

In an attempt to ensure a standard among vendors, the specification requires that each container predefines six attribute values when a request is generated. By using the key names defined in Table 2.1, you can access the request value assigned to each attribute.

TABLE 2.1   Predefined Request Attributes

Request Attribute	Type
`javax.servlet.error.status_code`	`java.lang.Integer`
`javax.servlet.error.exception_type`	`java.lang.Class`
`javax.servlet.error.message`	`java.lang.String`
`javax.servlet.error.exception`	`java.lang.Throwable`
`javax.servlet.error.request_uri`	`java.lang.String`
`javax.servlet.error.servlet_name`	`java.lang.String`

If you intend to forward the request to another servlet, you might want to change the value associated with a particular attribute. By using the `set-Attribute(...)`, you can accomplish this task by passing in the request attribute name and the new value.

In addition to attributes, the `ServletRequest` class is also used to acquire the originating locale of a servlet.

Internationalization

A locale identifies the country and language codes used by a system or server. When developing a servlet, you should consider the likelihood of someone else accessing your website from another country. If your site handles internationalization, the servlet could request the locale and generate a response based on the location of the originating client. The following two methods become useful for such a scenario:

- `Locale getLocale()`

- `Enumeration getLocales()`

The `getLocale()` method returns the preferred locale, also known as the `Accept-Language` header, that the client will accept. If the client fails to provide a header defining its locale, the method returns the default locale for the server.

Some systems might provide a list of acceptable locale headers. The `getLocales()` method returns all `Accept-Language` headers defined by the client in decreasing order. It starts with the most preferred locale and then lists the second preferred locale. As with the `getLocale()` method, if the client fails to provide a header, the server's default locale is returned instead.

Another option is to set the locale through the `ServletResponse` object. Syntactically, the method is as follows:

`void setLocale(Locale loc)`

The method changes the header value based on the `Locale` object passed as a parameter.

Besides customizing a response to meet the language needs of the client, your application may need to receive client information written in a different format. A `ServletRequest` object enables data encoding to help with this type of situation.

Data Encoding

When streaming information, you cannot be guaranteed that the data is coming from an International Organization for Standardization (ISO)

Latin alphabet. The character encoding value associated to a stream identifies how the characters are converted between raw 8-bit bytes and 16-bit Unicode characters. To read a request coming from a website that uses a different encoding mechanism requires that you change the character encoding value to a standard understood by the receiving system. Accessing and modifying these values can be done with the following methods:

- void setCharacterEncoding(*String env*)

- String getCharacterEncoding()

The setCharacterEncoding(...) method overrides the assigned encoding value to enable the servlet to read parameters or input from the request. The method does throw a runtime exception called java.io.Unsupported-EncodingException if the encoding mechanism is not valid.

WARNING   Keep in mind that this method must be called before any inquiries on the request are made.

The getCharacterEncoding() method is somewhat self-explanatory. It returns the name of the encoding value used by the request. If the request does not specify a name, the method returns null.

At this point, we have covered the important methods of the Servlet-Request object. We are now ready to analyze the methods in its subclass, HttpServletRequest. When the container casts the ServletRequest and ServletResponse objects to HttpServletRequest and HttpServlet-Response objects, respectively, additional functionality and information becomes available to the servlet.

HttpServletRequest and *HTTPServletResponse* Interfaces

The HttpServletRequest and HttpServletResponse objects provide methods that enable the developer to access and modify header and date information. Because these interfaces extend their respective Servlet-Request or ServletResponse interface, they also have access to the parameter methods discussed in the previous "Parameters" subsection.

The HttpServletRequest object gives you access to the request header, date, and method data. These methods are shown in Table 2.2.

TABLE 2.2 Request Methods

Method	Description
String getHeader(*String name*)	Returns the value of the specified header.
Enumeration getHeaders(*String name*)	Returns all values of the specified header.
Enumeration getHeaderNames()	Returns all header names.
int getIntHeader(*String name*)	Returns the value of the specified header as an int. If the header does not exist, a –1 is returned. If the value cannot be converted to an int, a NumberFormatException is thrown.
long getDateHeader(*String name*)	Returns the value of the specified request header as a long value that represents a Date object. This method is used with headers that contain dates, such as Last-Modified.
String getMethod()	Returns the HTTP request action name, such as GET or POST.

To really understand the results of these methods, let's look at an example. First we'll show you the request headers sent from the client to the server, then the results from the servlet. Here is an example of a header request:

```
GET /register/index.html HTTP/1.0
Date: Fri, 26 Oct 2001 17:12:10 GMT
User-Agent: Mozilla/4.75[en](Windows NT 5.0; U)
Accept: image/gif, image/x-xbitmap, image/jpeg, */*
Host: educationaledge.net
Accept-Encoding: gzip, deflate
Accept-Language: en-us
Connection: keep-alive
```

We've also included some sample code from a servlet to help you visualize how and what information is retrieved:

```java
public class HeaderServlet extends HttpServlet {

  public void service(HttpServletRequest req,
                      HttpServletResponse resp)
    throws ServletException, IOException    {

      String acceptValue = req.getHeader("Accept");
      Enumeration allValues = req.getHeaders("Accept");
      Enumeration headerNames = req.getHeaderNames();
      int numericValue = req.getIntHeader("Max-Forwards");
      long dateValue = req.getDateHeader("Date");

      String method = req.getMethod();

      super.service(req, resp);
  }
  // We've excluded the code to process the data so
  // you can focus on the methods and their result.
}
```

The result generated by each method is described here:

- getHeader("Accept") returns a single String containing image/gif, image/x-bitmap, image/jpeg, */*

- getHeaders("Accept") returns an Enumeration of String objects image/gif, image/x-bitmap, image/jpeg, */*

- getHeaderNames() returns all headers:

  - Date
  - User-Agent
  - Accept
  - Host
  - Accept-Encoding
  - Accept-Language
  - Connection

- getIntHeader("Max-Forwards") returns -1

- getDateHeader("Date") returns date in milliseconds since 1/1/70

- getMethod() returns GET

When more than one element is returned, it is stored in an Enumeration.

The HttpServletResponse object provides methods that enable the developer to modify header information. These methods are listed in Table 2.3.

TABLE 2.3 Response Methods

Method	Description
void setHeader(*String name*, *String value*)	Sets the value for a specific header name.
void setIntHeader(*String name*, *int value*)	Sets the integer value for a specific response header.
void setDateHeader(*String name*, *long date*)	Sets the date for a specific header. If one already exists, the new value will replace the old.
void setStatus(*int sc*)	Sets the return status code when there is no error. Some examples are SC_OK or SC_MOVED_TEMPORARILY.
void sendError(*int sc*)	Sends an error response to the client by using a specified status code. After a call to this method, the response is considered committed and should no longer be written to.
void sendError(*int sc*, *String msg*)	Sends an error response to the client by using the provided status code and a default HTML-formatted server error page containing the provided message.

TABLE 2.3 Response Methods *(continued)*

Method	Description
void sendRedirect(*String location*)	Sends a temporary redirect response to the client by using the specified redirect location URL. The location parameter can be a relative URL; before sending the response to the client, the container will convert the relative URL to an absolute URL. Exceptions: it throws IllegalStateException if the response was committed, and it throws IOException if an input or output exception occurs.

The following code snippet shows how these methods would be used:

```
protected void doGet(HttpServletRequest req,
                     HttpServletResponse res)
  throws ServletException, IOException {
    res.setContentType("text/html");

    res.setHeader("Server", "The SuperDooper Server/1.0")
    res.setIntHeader("Content-Length", 1029)
    res.setDateHeader("Last-Modified", 1003947922649);

    res.sendRedirect("http://otherserver.com:8090/
      index.html");
    ...
}
```

The response header, which would be sent to the URL defined by the sendRedirect method, would look similar to the following:

```
HTTP/1.0 200 OK
Date: Sat Oct 17 12:14:15 PDT 2001
Server: The SuperDooper Server/1.0
MIME-version: 1.0
Content-Type: text/html
Last-Modified: Wed Oct 24 11:27:15 PDT 2001
Content-Length: 1029
```

The status code from the setStatus(...) method is defined in the response line—200 and OK. This code was set by the servlet handling the redirect. As you can see, the name of the server can be customized as well as the last date of modification. The Last-Modified header is now set to the converted Date value, which is a long representing the number of milliseconds from January 1, 1970. Finally the Content-Length contains the numeric value we set by using the setIntHeader(...) method. Basically, the HttpServlet-Response interface provides the developer with methods to tailor and alter the data in the response headers.

Switching focus back to the HttpServletRequest, we will now look at ways to access path element information.

Path Elements

When a client attempts to locate a servlet, it searches through a specific path to reach its destination. The path itself, or the request URI, is generally composed of three important sections:

```
Request URI = contextPath + servletPath + pathInfo
```

Context Path

The *context path* is the first section of the path. It defines the *context* in which the servlet resides. Within a single Java Virtual Machine, several web applications might be running. For each web application, there is one context. All servlet classes within that web application will share that one context.

Here is the method signature:

```
public String getContextPath()
```

The rules for the context path are as follows:

- The path begins with a forward slash (/) but does not end with a forward slash (/).

- The path is an empty string, "", if the context is at the base of the web server's URL namespace.

Servlet Path

The *servlet path* identifies the mapped directory name associated to the actual servlet. Usually this consists of either the mapped servlet name or a mapped path to the servlet, but nothing more.

Here is the method signature:

```
public String getServletPath()
```

The rules for the servlet path are as follows:

- The path is an empty string if `url-pattern` matches a /* pattern.
- The path begins with a forward slash (/) in all other cases.

Path Info

The *path info* consists of extra path information between the servlet path and the query string.

Here is the method signature:

`public String getPathInfo()`

The rule for the path info is as follows:

- If path information does not exist, the method returns a `null`.

Now that you've reviewed these path elements, you can refer to the following table for a bit more detail. Table 2.4 displays examples of these three path types, assuming the context is defined as: `/games`.

TABLE 2.4   The Request Path Elements

Request Path	Path Elements
`/games/tictactoe/` `welcome.html`	Context path: `/games` Servlet path: `/tictactoe` Path info: `/welcome.html`
`/games/registration/` `StartServlet`	Context path: `/games` Servlet path: `/registration/StartServlet` Path info: `null`
`/games/Search/` `1234?query=Yamaha+R6`	Contex path: `/games` Servlet path: `/Search` Path info: `/1234`

Path Translations

If the developer is interested in accessing file system path information, they can do so through the `javax.servlet.ServletContext` by using the following method:

`String getRealPath(String path)`

The getRealPath(...) takes in a virtual path value and returns its absolute file path on the server. If, for example, you passed in index.html, the return string would represent the entire URL, such as c:\Java\jakarta-tomcat-4.0\webapps\test\index.html. The format of the URL is dependent on the platform. If a Unix server ran the request, it would format the root and slashes differently.

The virtual path is basically the URI without the path info or query string.

The other method used to translate virtual paths is available in the Http-ServletRequest interface:

String getPathTranslated()

This method takes the path info of the request and computes its real path. If there is no additional information between the servlet path and the query string, the method returns a null.

Finally, it is important to know that the container cannot translate or get the real path to a resource that is not directly accessible. For example, the resource might be located in a database or remote system that is not accessible locally, or an archive file (such as a WAR file). If the container cannot translate the virtual path, the method returns a null.

Cookies

The final topic of the request object that we will discuss is the cookie. When accessing web pages, the browser is often sent numerous cookies which are used to accept and store data. A *cookie* is a small data object sent to the browser by the servlet. It is made up of a name, a single value, and optional descriptive attributes, such as a version number and path information. When the user opts to accept the cookie, the browser typically saves the object and then sends the name and value of each cookie during each request. This technique is used to help manage servlet sessions. We'll discuss that in more depth in Chapter 6, "Session Management." Suffice to say, by using the getCookies() method of the HttpServletRequest interface, the developer can then extract the desired cookie attributes.

Cookie[] getCookies()

This method returns an array of all the Cookie objects contained within the request.

If the developer were then interested in sending a cookie to the browser, they could do so by calling the addCookie(...) method of the HttpServlet-Response interface.

The Session

Instead of relying on the client to accept cookies and the browser to cache the information locally, the Servlet model provides a *session object* as an alternative solution to maintaining client information past the life of a single request. An HttpSession object is created when a client makes its first request to an application. It provides a way to identify and store information about the user for an extended period of time. While a request and its attributes will cease to exist after its response is sent, a session, once created, will continue to exist until it either is manually terminated or times out. There are several methods that provide information or control over the life span of an javax.servlet.http.HttpSession object. They include:

- public long getLastAccessedTime()

- public int getMaxInactiveInterval()

- public void setMaxInactiveInterval(*int seconds*)

- public boolean isNew()

- public void invalidate()

The getLastAccessedTime() method returns the number of milliseconds since the birth of Unix, January 1, 1970, to the time the client made their last request. To get the number of seconds the container will allow between requests to keep the session active, invoke the getMaxInactiveInterval() method. If you would like to define this value in seconds, simply call the setMaxInactiveInterval(...) method. The isNew() method is used to notify the servlet of the client's session configuration. It returns a true value if the client does not know about the session or has not joined it yet. Joining a session means the client returns session tracking information sent by the server. If the client, however, refuses to join a session, then a new session is created for each request. This usually occurs when the web container uses only cookies for session tracking and the client refuses to accept cookies. The final method to consider regarding the life of the session is invalidate().

As the name suggests, it is used to manually terminate a session. It first unbinds all associated attribute objects and then prepares the session for garbage collection.

The attribute objects associated to a session usually consist of client information necessary to complete the entire transaction. Imagine a client who enters their name and address in one screen; then another screen needs that same information. Instead of repeatedly asking the client for the same information for each request made, the client's name and address can be stored to the session object and accessed by the servlet without the client. The methods associated to a session's attributes are as follows:

- `public void setAttribute(`*`String name, Object value`*`)`

- `public `*`Object`*` getAttribute(`*`String name`*`)`

- `public `*`Enumeration`*` getAttributeNames()`

- `public void removeAttribute(`*`String name`*`)`

The method `setAttribute(...)` binds the defined object to the session. By using the associated key name, you can retrieve the object with the `getAttribute(...)` method. If, however, you are looking to acquire all object names bound to the session, you will need to invoke the `getAttributeNames()` method. The Enumeration returned can be used to access all objects via the `getAttribute(...)` method. In addition to adding and accessing attributes, you can also remove them. By passing in the attribute name, the `removeAttribute(...)` method unbinds the attribute from the session.

The last session method you should be familiar with is the following:

- `public String getId()`

This method returns a string containing the unique identifier assigned to the particular session. One way to use the session ID is for storage of session information to a persistent data source. This is most useful when the session is transferred from one web container to another.

Although using sessions might seem as simple as adding and accessing attributes, there is more to managing them efficiently. Chapter 6, "Session Management," discusses the various ways to handle a session and the benefits from one approach versus another. For now, let's continue talking about servlet basics such as its life cycle.

The Servlet Life Cycle

A vendor who intends to provide server support for servlets must create a server application that adheres to the servlet specification. The specification calls for the server to maintain a container for specific tasks. Generally the container is a part of the web server; however, it can be an external entity. The *container* is responsible for managing the servlets contained within its environment. This means that the container determines:

- When a servlet is loaded and instantiated
- How to directly handle client requests or dispatch them to another resource
- When to take a servlet out of service

These stages of the servlet make up the *servlet life cycle*. Life-cycle management is a crucial strategy that all containers must implement successfully to be compliant. The life-cycle methods `init(...)`, `service(...)`, and `destroy()` are defined in the `javax.servlet.Servlet` interface, which all servlets must implement, either directly or indirectly. In this section, we will discuss the functionality of these methods and the circumstances in which they are affected.

Loading and Instantiating

A servlet can be instantiated when the container starts or when the container receives a request that needs to be serviced. Before instantiation, the container locates all the needed classes for the servlet and uses the standard `ClassLoader` to load the servlet class itself. There are no restrictions on where the files can be loaded—a local or remote file system or another network altogether is acceptable.

After a servlet is loaded, it is ready to be initialized so the servlet can be invoked when needed. The servlet is instantiated, and its default constructor is read. There is no reason to include a non-default constructor within a servlet, because it would never get called. This means that passing initialization parameters to the servlet must be done another way. After the constructor is read, the container creates an object called the *ServletConfig*. It contains name/value parameters defined from within a file (we will discuss the file later in this section). The ServletConfig object is passed to the Servlet interface method called:

```
public void init(ServletConfig config)
                            throws ServletException
```

When this method is called, it actually causes the Servlet's implementing class, GenericServlet, to invoke its version of the method. Because the init(…) method contains some configuration logic that is necessary for the servlet, it is important that the GenericServlet's init(ServletConfig config) method be processed before any other servlet method is called.

Initially, the servlet was designed to have users override the init(…) method that takes in a ServletConfig object and have the method make a call to super.init(config). Although this does work if you follow directions, it doesn't guarantee that the developer will make the parent call. Consequently, there is a convenience method provided called init() that takes no arguments. If you override the no-argument init() method, the container will automatically call the servlet's init(ServletConfig) method.

The container will then complete your servlet's init() method, which provides the servlet with an opportunity to initialize important resources.

The method within the servlet is as follows:

```
public void init() throws ServletException
```

Usually, all activities that are performed only one time during the life of the servlet are included in this method or the constructor. The init() method differs from the constructor in one major way: when the init() method is called, the container passes it a ServletConfig object. The init() method that developers override does not take in arguments; instead, you can gain access to the ServletConfig handle via the method getServletConfig(). Most importantly, this object provides the servlet access to initialization parameters which cannot be obtained via a non-default constructor (since it will never get invoked). Instead, these values are stored in a configuration file, most commonly referred to as the *deployment descriptor* (or *web.xml file*). As we will discuss in future chapters, every web application must have an associated XML file that defines several attributes of the application. These include listing servlets and any associated initialization parameters, security roles, transaction types, and application-wide initialization parameters. Instead of hard-coding servlet-specific parameters into the source code, you can use the

ServletConfig's method getInitParameter(*String* name) to obtain particular values from the web.xml file. These values can then be assigned to variables within the init() method. An alternative way to obtain a servlet's initialization parameters is by calling its own GenericServlet getInit-Parameter(*String* name) method. Regardless of approach, keep in mind that in order for changes to the web.xml file to take effect, the servlet or container must be restarted.

The following is a section of a sample web.xml file. We will show you how to define the parameters, and how to retrieve them from the init() method.

```xml
<web-app>
    <servlet>
        <servlet-name>CalendarServlet</servlet-name>
        <servlet-class>CalendarServlet</servlet-class>
        <init-param>
            <param-name>year</param-name>
            <param-value>2001</param-value>
        </init-param>
        <init-param>
            <param-name>taxrate</param-name>
            <param-value>.0725</param-value>
        </init-param>
    </servlet>
</web-app>
```

The CalendarServlet has two parameter value sets. The actual source code can access this information during the initialization phase. Again, let's look at a section of code from the servlet:

```java
public class CalendarServlet extends HttpServlet {
  int year;
  double rate;

  public void init() throws ServletException {
    ServletConfig config = getServletConfig();

    String yearParam = config.getInitParameter("year");
    year = Integer.parseInt(yearParam);
```

```
        String rateParam = config.getInitParameter("taxrate");
        rate = Float.parseFloat(rateParam);
    }
}
```

By using the `getInitParameter()` method of the `ServletConfig` object, you can access the value of the specified name passed in as an argument.

An additional benefit to the `ServletConfig` object is that it grants you access to the following information:

Servlet Context   By using the `getServletContext()` method, you can get a handle to this object, which provides the servlet with the means to communicate with the container. For example, by using the `ServletContext` object, the servlet can: access application-wide initialization parameters using the method `getInitParameter (String name)`, ask the container to get the MIME type of a file by using the method `getMimeType(String file)`, dispatch requests by using the method `getRequestDispatcher (String path)`, or write to a log file by using the method `log(String msg)`.

Servlet Name   By using the `getServletName()` method, you receive the name of the servlet instance. It is provided by either the deployment descriptor or its default class name.

Several problems can occur within the `init()` method that can prevent the servlet from entering service. Here are three such possible scenarios:

- The first scenario occurs when the `init()` method throws a `Servlet-Exception`. This usually happens if there is an initialization failure—for example, if the container fails to find the initialization parameters. Failure to initialize would cause the servlet to be released from the container.

- Another exception that can be thrown is an `UnavailableException`, which is a subclass of `ServletException`. This usually happens when you are looking to see whether a service is accessible—and it's not. If this particular exception is thrown, the container must wait a minimal time period before attempting to create and initialize a new instance of the servlet. There is no need to wait if a `ServletException` is thrown.

- The final situation occurs when the `init()` method does not return in a specified time period defined by the web server.

If no problems occur, the servlet is ready for the next phase of its life cycle: `service(...)`.

The `init()` method must complete successfully before the servlet can begin to receive requests. After that state is achieved, the servlet will either wait for a request to come through, or immediately begin processing any pending client requests.

Request Handling

After the `init()` method completes successfully, the `service(...)` method is next in line. Most often the container initializes servlets but waits for requests before activating the servlet. Yes, it is possible for the server to initialize, invoke, and cache a servlet without a request, but this process is less common. Usually the container waits to receive a request before doing anything with the servlet. When a request comes in, it is converted to a `Servlet-Request` object and passed to the `service(...)` method of the servlet. If the container receives an HTTP request, the object is cast to an `HttpServlet-Request` object and then passed to the specific servlet's `service(...)` method.

Here are the method signatures:

```
public void service(ServletRequest req,
                    ServletResponse res)
             throws ServletException, IOException
```

or

```
protected void service(HttpServletRequest req,
                       HttpServletResponse res)
               throws ServletException, IOException
```

The purpose of the `service(...)` method is to enable the servlet to respond to a request. If an HTTP request is sent, the `service(...)` method is responsible for dispatching the request to the appropriate `doXXX(...)` method.

Because servlets often run in multithreaded containers, developers should take threading issues into consideration if this method is overridden. It is quite likely that the same `service(...)` method will be accessed by multiple requests. In such cases, it is important to know how the container handles concurrent access. Does it pool its servlets or does it serialize requests and have them wait in a queue? From the developer's standpoint, you can implement the `SingleThreadModel` interface or synchronize access to all shared resources. These topics are covered in great detail in Chapter 8, "Thread-Safe Servlets."

The final detail of the `service(...)` method is its exceptions. Once again, the `ServletException` can be thrown if some error occurred while a request was processed. It is the responsibility of the container to clean up any partially generated code in such an event. Like the init(...) method, the service(...) method can also throw an UnavailableException, a subclass of the ServletException class. This usually occurs if the servlet is temporarily or permanently unable to handle the request. If the condition is permanent, the container removes the servlet from service and calls the destroy() method (which we discuss next) to release the instance. If, however, the lack of availability is temporary, the container might halt all requests to that servlet during that temporary period. If a request is refused, the container will send a response with a Retry-After header and a SERVICE_UNAVAILABLE(503) status. It is also possible that the container might treat all unavailability as permanent and remove all servlets from service when the UnavailableException is thrown.

Completion of the service(...) method results in a call to the servlet's appropriate doXXX(...) method. At that point, the servlet can either generate the response entirely on its own, or pass part or all of the responsibility to another servlet.

Request Dispatching

A common feature in web applications is the forwarding of a request from one servlet to another servlet for processing. This process is called *request dispatching*. The ServletRequest interface handles this process by providing a method that gives access to the RequestDispatcher object. That method is as follows:

RequestDispatcher getRequestDispatcher(*String path*)

The argument to the getRequestDispatcher(...) method is a string that describes the relative or absolute path of the ServletContext for which you are forwarding the request; basically, it's the receiving servlet's URI or URL. As a reminder, the ServletContext is the object used to communicate with the container.

If accessing the RequestDispatcher through a handle to the ServletContext object is more feasible, you can use the following method:

RequestDispatcher getNamedDispatcher(*String name*)

Because there is only one context per web application, there are some rules about where a request can be dispatched:

- The relative path cannot extend outside the current servlet context. To do so, you must use the getContext() method. It returns the absolute URL to the context requested.

- A servlet cannot dispatch a request to a context on another server.

The semantics of the path are as follows:

- If the path begins with a forward slash (/), it is considered relative to the current context.

- If the path contains a query string, the name/value pairs will be added to the receiving servlet's parameter list.

There is also a method for getRequestDispatcher(*String*) in the ServletContext interface. It was introduced in the 2.1 API and accepted only absolute URL paths for the string parameter. Because the ServletRequest version is more current (API 2.2) and accepts both relative and absolute paths, it is the preferred choice.

The getNamedDispatcher(*String*) method from the ServletContext interface enables the developer to get the RequestDispatcher for a resource by specifying its name rather than path. The name can be accessed in several ways: it can be hard-coded, in the web.xml file, or passed as an attribute of the method call. If the name of the servlet cannot be found, the method returns a null. Here, a code snippet depicts three different ways to obtain the RequestDispatcher:

```
//code snippet
public class ServletOne extends HttpServlet {
  public void doGet(HttpServletRequest req,
                    HttpServletResponse res)
    throws ServletException, IOException {
      String uri = "/servlet/ServletTwo";
      RequestDispatcher reqDis1 =
              req.getRequestDispatcher(uri);

      String name = "ServletTwo";
      RequestDispatcher reqDis2 =
          getServletContext().getNamedDispatcher(name);

      String query = "/servlet/ServletTwo?name=Roney";
      RequestDispatcher reqDis3 =
              req.getRequestDispatcher(query);
  }
}
```

The first two examples should return the same dispatcher. The third example simply shows how a query string can be attached to the URI. In order for these parameters to be sent with the request, the forward(*ServletRequest req, ServletResponse res*) or include(*ServletRequest req, Servlet-Response res*) method must be called. If the query string is not included in the URL used to access the RequestDispatcher, it can be acquired from the original request object and passed via the forward(...) or include(...) method.

include (...)

When dispatching a request to another resource, the calling servlet might want to retain control of the response. Here is the method signature:

```
public void include(ServletRequest req,
                    ServletResponse res)
    throws ServletException, IOException
```

The include(...) method enables the calling servlet to modify the response object before and after the call to the include(...) method. For example, let's take a look at a code sample from a servlet that communicates magic tricks to its audience:

```
...
public void doGet(HttpServletRequest req,
                  HttpServletResponse res)
  throws ServletException, IOException {
    res.setContentType("text/html");
    PrintWriter out = res.getWriter();
    out.println("<HTML><TITLE>Welcome to the Magic Show
    </TITLE></HTML>");
    out.println("<BODY>");
    out.println("Watch the video stream below: ");

    RequestDispatcher disp =
    req.getRequestDispatcher("/servlet/MagicVideo?video=1");
    disp.include(req, res);

    out.println("Tune in daily for a new trick");
    out.println("</BODY></HTML>");
}
...
```

In this example, the calling servlet simply provides the framework while the target servlet, MagicVideo, handles the video streaming. The target servlet cannot change the response status code or set headers; any attempt to make a change is ignored. The target can, however, process the request because it does gain access to the request object, via the include method. Here are the attributes that a target servlet can access when invoked through an include(...):

- javax.servlet.include.request_uri
- javax.servlet.include.context_path
- javax.servlet.include.servlet_path
- javax.servlet.include.path_info
- javax.servlet.include.query_string

Unfortunately, these variables are assigned values only if you access the target servlet by using the request object's getRequestDispatcher(...) method. The getNamedDispatcher(...) method leaves these values unset.

If it is necessary for the target servlet to have more control over the request, the forward(...) method proves to be more useful. The drawback is that any output from processing of the originating servlet after the forward(...) method is called is not displayed.

forward (...)

The forward(...) method is used to forward a request to another servlet. The originating servlet can perform some preliminary functions on the request and have another servlet generate the response. The act of having another servlet perform the task is invisible to the client.

Here is the method signature:

```
public void forward(ServletRequest req,
                    ServletResponse res)
       throws ServletException, IOException
```

Here is an example servlet that calls another servlet to generate a response:

```
import java.io.*;
import javax.servlet.*;
import javax.servlet.http.*;
```

```
public class PassMessageServlet extends HttpServlet {
  public void doGet(HttpServletRequest req,
                      HttpServletResponse res)
    throws ServletException, IOException {
      req.setAttribute("message", "Life is good");

      RequestDispatcher disp=
          req.getRequestDispatcher("/servlet/Test");
      disp.forward(req, res);
  }
}
```

Within the doGet(...), the PassMessageServlet uses the set-Attribute(...) method to store an element called message with a value of Life is good in the request. It then dispatches this request to a servlet called Test. Let's take a look at that code:

```
import java.io.;
import javax.servlet.*;
import javax.servlet.http.*;

public class Test extends HttpServlet {

  public void doGet(HttpServletRequest req,
                      HttpServletResponse res)
    throws ServletException, IOException {

      String theMessage =
          (String)req.getAttribute("message");
      res.setContentType("text/html");
      PrintWriter out = res.getWriter();
      out.println("<HTML>");
      out.println("<BODY>" + theMessage
                            + "</BODY></HTML>");
      out.close();
  }
}
```

The output for this example displays the message "Life is good."

The rules associated to a forward(...) call are as follows:

- The forward(...) method can be called only if output has not been committed to the client; otherwise, an IllegalStateException is thrown.

- The calling servlet can set headers and set status code information. But it must send the same request and response objects to the target.

- If the response buffer contains data that has not been committed, a call to forward(...) will clear the buffer before calling the service(...) method of the target servlet.

- The target servlet must send and commit its response before the forward(...) method can return.

In summary, the forward(...) method passes the response responsibility to the target servlet. The calling servlet can set attributes and access request information, but it cannot commit the response. Any response data defined before or after the forward will be ignored.

End of Service

The container can give life, and it can take it away. The longevity of a servlet's life is not defined. The container can keep a servlet alive for a few milliseconds, or the lifetime of the container. When the time comes to remove a servlet from service, the container calls the Servlet interface's destroy() method. Here is the method signature:

```
public void destroy()
```

This method is used to release all resources, such as threads or connections, and save any persistent data. A container might choose to remove a servlet before the system is shut down or as a measure to conserve memory resources. But before the destroy() method can be called, the container must wait for all threads running in the service(...) method to complete or time out. After a servlet is destroyed, and its destroy() method has been called, the servlet is ready for garbage collection. Consequently, the container cannot send any requests to that servlet. It would need to create a new instance.

Real World Scenario

The Exotic Bird Encyclopedia

Exotic Birds, Inc. has a website that provides users with the latest information on a wide range of bird species. Their website is designed to have the user first select the type of bird in question, and then to choose the topics of information they are interested in learning. The site offers information on personalities, habitat, nutrition, training tips, latest research, and related stories.

Because the application was developed with expandability in mind, a servlet for each topic was created. Each servlet retrieves specific information on its topic from an appropriate database source. The ResearchServlet is a prime example. In order to present the most accurate and current information on research studies, Exotic Birds, Inc. established an agreement with the National Zoo. Consequently, their ResearchServlet accesses the zoo's remote server to acquire its information. A main servlet links these individual servlets together by using a RequestDispatcher. After the client determines what information they are interested in, a request is sent to the server. The main servlet determines what topics are of interest and has the Request-Dispatcher invoke the appropriate servlets to generate and acquire the information. The main servlet then formats the response page and returns it to the client. The user can then see all the latest information to help them learn more about the specific bird they selected.

Summary

In this chapter, we covered the details associated with the Servlet model. Specifically, we discussed:

- HTTP-to-servlet method mapping: doGet(...), doPost(...), doPut(...), doHead(...), doDelete(...), doOptions(...), doTrace(...)

- Servlet request and response interface and method associations

- The servlet life cycle: init(), service(...), destroy()

- The include(...) and forward(...) methods of the Request Dispatcher class

We took foundation topics developed in Chapter 1 and connected them to the servlet. We traced the request from the client to the actual servlet. From the HTML trigger, the HTTP request is sent to the `service(...)` method of a servlet. The container either creates a new servlet for the request or activates an inactive servlet loaded into memory. After the servlet passes through the `service(...)` method, its action is determined and it is then sent to its associated do*XXX*(...) method. It is this method that processes the request or sends the request to another servlet for processing by using the `Request-Dispatcher`. After the servlet completes its task, a response might be sent, and the servlet is either destroyed or returned to an inactive state. The Servlet model effectively connects HTML code to server-side Java code.

Exam Essentials

Be able to identify the corresponding **HttpServlet** class methods for **GET, POST, and PUT** requests. The HTTP requests are directly mapped to methods in the `HttpServlet` class.

A GET request generates a call to the doGet(*HttpServletRequest req, HttpServletResponse res*) method.

A POST request generates a call to the doPost(*HttpServletRequest req, HttpServletResponse res*) method.

A PUT request generates a call to the doPut(*HttpServletRequest req, HttpServletResponse res*) method.

Be able to identify the interface and methods used to retrieve the request's HTML form parameters, initialization parameters, and header information. To retrieve HTML form parameters from a request, the `javax.servlet.ServletRequest` interface provides the following methods:

getParameter(*String name*)

getParameterNames()

getParameterValues(*String name*)

To retrieve a servlet's initialization parameter defined within the deployment descriptor, the `javax.servlet.GenericServlet` class provides the following method:

getInitParameter(*String name*)

To retrieve HTTP request header information, the `javax.servlet`
`.http.HttpServletRequest` interface provides the following methods:

> `getHeader(String name)`
>
> `getHeaderNames()`
>
> `getHeaders(String name)`
>
> `getDateHeader(String name)`
>
> `getIntHeader(String name)`
>
> `getMethod()`

The `javax.servlet.ServletRequest` interface provides the following
method used to obtain the content type:

> `getContentType()`

**Be able to identify the interface and methods used to set an HTTP response
header and content type.** The `javax.servlet.ServletResponse`
interface provides the following methods used to modify the header data:

> `setHeader(String name, String value)`
>
> `setIntHeader(String name, int value)`
>
> `setStatus(int sc)`
>
> `setDateHeader(String name, long date)`

The `javax.servlet.http.ServletResponse` interface provides the
following method used to modify the content type:

> `setContentType(String type)`

**Be able to identify the interface and methods used to acquire the binary or
text streams.** The `javax.servlet.ServletResponse` interface provides the `getOutputStream()` method to acquire a binary stream. The
`javax.servlet.ServletResponse` interface provides the `getWriter()`
method to acquire a text stream.

**Be able to identify the interface and methods used to redirect an HTTP
request to another URL.** The `javax.servlet.http.HttpServlet-`
`Response` interface provides the `sendRedirect(String location)`
method.

Be able to identify the interface and methods used to access values and resources, and set object attributes within a request. There are a variety of methods defined for a request object in the classes javax.servlet .ServletRequest and javax.servlet.http.HttpServletRequest. Earlier, we discussed how to get header, date, and parameter information. In addition to those methods, you need to be familiar with this list:

The first set of methods is used for getting and setting attributes. Attributes are data objects that can be associated to a request and retrieved by using a key.

getAttribute(*String name*)

getAttributeNames()

setAttribute(*String name, Object value*)

The next set of methods relates to path information:

getContextPath()

getServletPath()

getPathInfo()

For absolute paths, you can use the following methods:

getRealPath(*String path*)

getPathTranslated()

The following methods help determine regional information of the client machine:

getLocale()

getLocales()

Finally, it is important to be able to acquire more information from the client by using the following request method to retrieve cookies:

getCookies()

To add cookies to the response, use:

addCookie(*Cookie cookie*)

Be able to identify the life-cycle methods of a servlet—which indicate why, how, and when the servlet is invoked. The servlet container manages the life of the servlets contained within. It is important to understand when each servlet method is invoked and for what purpose. A servlet's life cycle methods consist of the following:

```
init()

service(HttpServletRequest req, HttpServlet-
Response resp)

doXXX(HttpServletRequest req, HttpServlet-
Response resp)

destroy()
```

Be able to identify how the include and forward methods of the Request-Dispatcher work. When there is a need to forward a task to another servlet for completion, the RequestDispatcher can handle the job. By acquiring the RequestDispatcher object from the servlet, you can use two methods to transfer duties: the include(...) method and the forward(...) method. The choice between the two methods depends strictly on what you are looking to have done and by whom.

Key Terms

Before you take the exam, be certain you are familiar with the following terms:

attribute	request dispatching
container	response
content type	ServletConfig
context	servlet life cycle
context path	Servlet model
cookie	servlet path
deployment descriptor	session object
path info	web.xml file
request	

Review Questions

1. Which of the following statements are false? (Choose all that apply.)

    A. The doHead(...) method in HttpServlet will execute the doGet(...) method if the doHead(...) method has not been overridden by the programmer.

    B. There is no doHead(...) method for a HEAD request.

    C. A GET request invokes the doHead(...) method and then the doGet(...) method.

    D. A HEAD request will return only the headers as a response.

2. Which of the following options define the full signature name for the servlet method associated with a POST request? (Choose all that apply.)

    A. protected void doPost(*HttpServletRequest req*, *HttpServletResponse res*) throws IOException, ServletException

    B. public void doPost(*HttpServletRequest req*, *HttpServletResponse res*) throws IOException

    C. public void doPost(*ServletRequest req*, *ServletResponse res*) throws IOException, ServletException

    D. private void doPost(*HttpServletRequest req*, *HttpServletResponse res*) throws IOException, ServletException

3. Which HttpServlet method should be used to publish a resource on the server?

    A. doGet(...)

    B. doOptions(...)

    C. doPost(...)

    D. doPut(...)

4. Which of the following is false?

   A. doGet(...) is for handling HTTP GET requests.

   B. doPost(...) is for handling HTTP POST requests.

   C. doPut(...) is for handling HTTP PUT requests.

   D. doHead(...) is for handling HTTP HEAD requests.

   E. None of the above.

5. What is the method declaration for the method used in the HttpServlet class that handles the HTTP POST request?

   A. doPost(*ServletRequest req, ServletResponse res*)

   B. servicePost()

   C. doPost(*HttpServletRequest req,*
            HttpServletResponse res)

   D. service(*HttpServletRequest req,*
            HttpServletResponse res)

6. Given the following request, what result would you expect from the subsequent method call?

```
GET /Register/index.html HTTP/1.0
Date: Fri, 26 Oct 2001 17:12:10 GMT
User-Agent: Mozilla/4.75[en](Windows NT 5.0; U)
Accept: image/gif, image/x-xbitmap, image/jpeg, */*
Host: educationaledge.net
Accept-Encoding: gzip, deflate
-------------------------
req.getHeader("Accept");
```

   A. A string representing image/gif, image/x-xbitmap, image/jpeg, */*

   B. A string array representing image/gif, image/x-xbitmap, image/jpeg, */*

   C. A string representing image/gif

   D. A string representing */*

7. Given a call to the following method, what response would you expect?

```
request.getDateHeader("User-Agent");
```

A. An IOException is thrown.

B. A DateFormatException is thrown.

C. An IllegalArgumentException is thrown.

D. A -1 is returned.

8. Which interface gives you access to the getParameterNames() method? (Choose all that apply.)

A. ServletRequest

B. ServletResponse

C. HttpServletRequest

D. HttpServletResponse

9. Which of the following methods must be both safe and idempotent? (Choose all that apply.)

A. doGet

B. doHead

C. doPut

D. doPost

10. Given the following code snippet, what output would you expect?

Calling servlet:

```
public void doGet(HttpServletRequest req,
                  HttpServletResponse res)
  throws ServletException, IOException {
      res.setContentType("text/html");
      PrintWriter out = res.getWriter();
      out.println("<HTML>");
      out.println("<BODY>Will you see the source?");
      out.println("</BODY></HTML>");
```

```
            RequestDispatcher disp=
                req.getRequestDispatcher("/servlet/Test");
            disp.forward(req, res);
            out.close();
    }
```

Target servlet:

```
    protected void doGet(HttpServletRequest request,
            HttpServletResponse response) throws
                    ServletException, IOException {
        response.setContentType("text/html");
        PrintWriter out = response.getWriter();
        out.println("<HTML><TITLE>The Test</TITLE>");
        out.println("<BODY>Will you see the target?");
        out.println("</BODY></HTML>");
        out.close();
    }
```

A. "Will you see the source?"

B. "Will you see the target?"

C. An `IllegalStateException` is thrown.

D. Nothing appears; the thread hangs.

E. Both "Will you see the source?" and "Will you see the target?" will appear.

11. Which of the following statements is true?

   A. If the target servlet does not commit or send its response, the calling servlet can still continue processing logic after the `forward(...)` call.

   B. Control does not return to the originating servlet after a `forward(...)` call is made.

   C. A `forward(...)` call will not continue to process until the target servlet commits or sends its response.

   D. None of the above.

12. Which of the following methods will enable you to get one or more values set by a request object?

A. getParameter(*String name*)

B. getAttribute(*String name*)

C. getAttributes()

D. getAllAttributes()

E. getAllParamters()

13. Given the following request URI, which option best describes the context path?

/cars/sportsCars/index.html

A. /cars

B. /cars/sportsCars

C. /sportsCars

D. Not enough information to determine the answer

14. Given the following request URI, where the context path is defined as /furniture and the servlet is called Search, which option best describes the result returned from the getPathInfo() method?

/furniture/tables/Search?type=kitchen

A. " "—empty string

B. /Search

C. /Search?type=kitchen

D. null

15. The ServletContext object can be directly accessed from which of the following objects? (Choose all that apply.)

A. HttpServlet

B. ServletRequest

C. ServletConfig

D. ServletResponse

Answers to Review Questions

1. B, C.   There is a doHead(…) method defined by the servlet spec. In 2.3, it is a protected method, which means you can include the method in your servlet code if you extend HttpServlet. This would result in a call to your servlet's doHead(…) method. The third option is false because a GET request does not invoke the doHead(…) method; it invokes the doGet(…) method instead.

2. A, B.   The doPost(…) method is defined in the HttpServlet class with a protected access modifier. When overriding a method, you can change the modifier to one that is more public. That eliminates the last option. The third option fails because the parameters passed are HttpServletRequest and HttpServletResponse. Finally, the first two answers are correct because you can override a method and throw fewer exceptions than that of your parent, or you could match the signature exactly.

3. D.   A PUT request is used to publish resources at a location on the server. This method calls its corresponding doPut(…) method in the servlet to help perform this task.

4. E.   As per the servlet spec 2.3, all methods described handle the HTTP request methods defined. Consequently, the answer is "None of the above."

5. C.   The doPost(…) method is called when an HTTP POST is submitted. The two arguments passed in are an HttpServletRequest and HttpServletResponse.

6. A.   The getHeader() method returns a string representation of the entire value. Consequently, all values are grouped into one string object. The method getHeaders() parses the values and returns them in an array.

7. C.   If the header value cannot be converted to a date, then an Illegal-ArgumentException is thrown.

8. A, C.   Because the HttpServletRequest interface extends Servlet-Request, it too has access to the getParameterNames() method.

9. A, B. Both the doGet(...) and doHead(...) methods should be written to be safe, meaning the user should not be held accountable if the request is processed. They should also be idempotent, which means no negative side effects should occur if the request is processed multiple times.

10. B. A forward(...) is used to forward responsibility to complete the response to another servlet. If the calling servlet adds data to the response buffer, the target servlet erases that information. Consequently, you see the output from the target response stream only.

11. C. A forward(...) call is a blocking method. This means the target servlet must commit or send its response before control can be returned to the forwarding servlet.

12. B. The first option fails because getParameter(*String name*) returns only a value associated to the parameter name passed. The getAttribute(...) method takes in a key string and returns a single value set by a request using the setAttribute(...) method.

13. D. The context path defines the path of the context for which the servlet resides. If the context is defined to be at the base of the web server's URL namespace, then the context is an empty string. If that is the case, then /cars/sportsCars represents the servlet path, and the context path is blank. If that is not the case, then /cars is the context path. Because you don't know where the context was defined, you have no choice but to select the last option.

14. D. The path info returned is the data between the servlet path and query string. Because the servlet is called Search and the query string begins immediately after, the method getPathInfo() returns null.

15. A, C. The ServletConfig interface has a method called get-ServletContext() that returns a handle to the ServletContext object. You can obtain a handle to this object through the Http-Servlet class as well. Its parent class, GenericServlet, also has the same method defined, getServletContext().

Chapter

3

Servlet Web Applications

THE FOLLOWING SUN CERTIFIED WEB COMPONENT DEVELOPER FOR J2EE PLATFORM EXAM OBJECTIVES ARE COVERED IN THIS CHAPTER:

✓ 2.1 Identify the structure of a web application and web archive file, the name of the WebApp deployment descriptor, and the name of the directories where you place the following:

- The WebApp deployment descriptor
- The WebApp class files
- Any auxiliary JAR files

✓ 2.2 Match the name with a description of purpose or functionality, for each of the following deployment descriptor elements:

- Servlet instance
- Servlet name
- Servlet class
- Initialization parameters
- URL to named servlet mapping

n order for an application to be accessible by a container, the many resources that make up the application must be strategically placed in a predefined directory structure. In this chapter, we will classify the various parts of a web application and identify where these parts must be placed. The directory layout is the key behind the container's ability to locate the data it needs.

Other configuration information is stored within a file specific to each web application. The container accesses this file to determine the purpose, location, and behavior of various resources. We will point out how to format this file and the tags used to communicate between the web application and the container.

Understanding a Web Application

It takes many pieces to make a final program that is accessible through the Web. These pieces, when grouped together, are referred to as the *web application*. A single application can consist of any or all of the following elements:

- Servlets
- JSP pages
- Utility classes
- Static documents
- Client-side Java applets, beans, and classes
- A standard configuration file (required)

A standard J2EE application can contain many servlets and/or JSP pages. The utility classes help execute these server programs, and the static documents provide a more aesthetic appeal to the client application. The client application might also incorporate other Java classes, such as business objects, or applets to help deliver the desired program. Finally, all web applications must contain a standard configuration file to help the server identify each object's purpose and structure.

In addition to informing the server about the details associated with each class, it is imperative that the web application be portable. If the application is placed on a new or different server, it should execute successfully with minimal administrative work. You can ensure successful execution by creating a standard directory structure and configuration file for a web application. All the server needs to do is use the directory structure to locate the application classes in their defined directories and then use the web application's configuration file to identify any configuration settings that need to be applied to needed resources. The server can then execute the application, and in the end, portability is achieved.

Understanding a Directory Structure

Grouping web application classes and files into a structured directory hierarchy provides the web server with a map to find the appropriate resource. This hierarchical structure is defined by the servlet specification but leaves the choice of implementation up to the vendor creating the container. While recommended by the specification, it is not required that all servlet containers adhere to this organizational pattern; however, in order for the servlet container to be certified by Sun, it must adhere to the servlet specification. The good news is that most servlet vendors choose to accept the defined format. More importantly, the exam will test your knowledge of the standard directory structure. In this section, we will discuss each layer of the hierarchy and the proper placement of each web application object.

The hierarchy is made up of three significant layers. The first is the context. It is one or more directories used to locate the web application associated to the client request. Within the context exists the /WEB-INF directory, which marks another layer. It contains several subdirectories that help organize class files and compressed Java files. The /WEB-INF directory also contains a document that maps all files and defines characteristics of the entire application. This layer is hidden from the client. This means the client cannot directly access files from within the /WEB-INF directory. The final layer is quite the opposite. Client-viewable files are located either in the context directory itself, or in the /classes directory which is located directly within the context. This includes welcome and error pages, graphic and audio files, and so forth.

The Context

A single web server can run multiple applications. Each application is usually contained within a directory called the root, or *context*. For example, you might have a chat servlet that is made up of multiple directories containing 20 classes and files. All those files and directories will be placed in one directory called /chatApp. The /chatApp directory is then defined as the context for this web application. The name of the created directory is arbitrary; however, the location of this directory is server dependent. The server determines how to point to the context.

The Tomcat reference implementation provides an automatic directory structure, whereby all directories placed inside the *tomcat-installation-directory*/webapps directory are automatically configured as web applications. Now, you are not forced to use this directory. You can point the context to another location, but that location must be defined in both the server and application configuration files. JRun, another web server by Macromedia, allows the developer to define the context by specifying the directory name or using a GUI wizard tool to specify the application directory. Basically, the location of the context can be customized.

The context itself is the root for a single web application.

Table 3.1 lists some context examples.

TABLE 3.1 Context Examples

Servlet	Path	Context
ChessServlet	webserver/webapps/chessApp	chessApp/
CalculatorServlet	myApps/calculatorApp	calculatorApp/
InstallServlet	/installApp	installApp/
MusicServlet	/	/

From this example, you can see that the parent directory can be any directory, as long as its location is communicated to the server. The context is a directory defined by the developer, and, again, its information must be mapped to the server.

A container should be configured to reject any attempt to deploy two web applications with the same context path.

When a request is sent from the client, the container must find the appropriate web application to handle the task. In doing so, the web application finds the longest context path that matches the start of the request URL. The container then locates the servlet by using the following mapping rules in the order shown.

Assuming that the "servlet path pattern" defines the request URL and the "incoming path" defines the longest context path match, the servlet container will try to find:

Exact mapping   All strings match exactly.

Here is an example of a match:

> Servlet path pattern: `/foo/bar`

> Incoming path: `/foo/bar`

Path mapping   The string begins with a forward slash (/) and ends with a forward slash and asterisk (/*). The longest match determines the servlet requested.

Here is an example of a match:

> Servlet path pattern: `/programs/wordprocessing/*`

> Incoming path: `/programs/wordprocessing/index.html`

> Incoming path: `/programs/wordprocessing/wp2.4/start.jsp`

Extension mapping   The string begins with an asterisk (*).

Here is an example of a match:

> Servlet path pattern: `*.jsp`

> Incoming path: `/catalog/order/start.jsp`

> Incoming path: `/catalog/form.jsp`

> Incoming path: `/test.jsp`

Default mapping   The container provides server content appropriate for the resource request, such as a default servlet. The string begins with a forward slash (/), and the servlet path is the requested URI minus the context path. The path info is null.

Here is an example of a match:

Servlet path pattern: /sport

Incoming path: /sport/index.html

Containers often have implicit mapping mechanisms built into their systems. For example, a container might have *.jsp extensions mapped to enable JSP pages to be executed on demand. The keynote is that explicit mapping by a web application or servlet takes precedence over implicit mapping.

Request mapping is case sensitive.

WEB-INF

For every web application, there must be a public directory called /WEB-INF. This directory contains the main files for the application that are not provided to the client by the container. For example, a graphics file would not be included here because that is something provided to the client. However, a servlet used to calculate data would be stored somewhere within the /WEB-INF directory structure.

Through the ServletContext object, which the servlet acquires by using the getServletContext() method, a servlet can access files and code in the /WEB-INF directory by using the following methods:

- *URL* getResource(*String path*)

- *InputStream* getResourceAsStream(*String path*)

Typically, these methods are used to include the output from other application resources into the current application. Either a URL or InputStream object is returned to the resource mapped in the path parameter. Basically, if an application developer wants to access another resource without exposing that file to the web client, they can do so by using these methods. There are three main categories for content in the /WEB-INF directory:

/WEB-INF/web.xml   The deployment descriptor.

/WEB-INF/classes   This directory contains all the server-side Java classes, such as servlet and utility classes.

/WEB-INF/lib   The /lib directory contains all necessary compressed Java files that are used for the web application. These files are referred to as *Java archive files* or *JAR files*. They can consist of servlets, JSPs, beans, and utility classes.

When loading classes from the /WEB-INF directory, the ClassLoader first loads from the /classes directory and then the /lib directory.

Web Application Archive File (WAR File)

When distributing a web application, it is convenient to deliver one file that contains all the necessary classes and resources utilizing the standard directory structure. A *web archive (WAR) file* is like a JAR in that it compresses all necessary classes and resources recursively in their directories into a single file. A JAR file is a compressed file used for a standard Java application and its related classes. A WAR file is a compressed file used for a standard web application and its related classes. The technique used to create a WAR file is the same as a JAR. You can create a WAR file by using the following command-line statement:

```
jar -cvf ShoppingCart.war *
```

Or you can extract a WAR file by using the following command:

```
jar -xvf ShoppingCart.war
```

Notice that the jar command is used to create and extract a WAR file. The second argument is a list of options telling the command what to do and how. Generally, you should be familiar with the basic options available after the minus sign. They are outlined in Table 3.2.

TABLE 3.2 WAR Options

Option	Definition
c	Create
x	Extract
t	Table of contents
v	Verbose
f	Target file

One of the first three options (c, x, or t) will be used to define the action. You are looking to either create (c) a WAR file, extract (x) the contents of the WAR file, or list the table of contents (t) from a specific WAR file.

The v (verbose) option is usually used to display the output of the command as it is taking place. The f (file) option denotes that the name of the WAR or JAR file will be defined in the next section of the command.

For additional options, refer to the following site: %JDK_HOME%/docs/tooldocs/ win32/jar.html or $JDK_HOME\docs\tooldocs\solaris\jar.html (where %JDK_HOME% and $JDK_HOME represent the path to the JDK installation directory).

The minus sign in front of the options is not mandatory. It is used only as a convention carried forward from Unix. The option tags can be placed in any order.

The third item in the previous command line is the name of the WAR file. It should end with a .war extension. Finally, if you are creating a file, the last item consists of a single directory or multiple directories, separated by spaces, which will be compressed into the WAR file.

Syntactically, the only difference between the two files types, a JAR and a WAR, is the extension. So why make two file types? Well, their purposes are very different. A JAR file is a compressed file containing resources and classes for a Java application. A WAR file is a compressed file containing resources and classes for a web application. The distinction is significant, in that the container is designed to look for different features for a WAR file than for a JAR file. In order for a container to execute a WAR file, the file should be placed in the server's default or configured directory used to hold all web applications.

Most servers provide a default directory for all WAR file applications. Placing a WAR file in this directory causes the server to automatically load the application into its context. Some vendors provide an additional feature, whereby they allow the placement of WAR files in another directory outside the default directory. Restarting the server will result in the loading of all WAR files from default and configured directories.

Because the WAR file contains all recursive directories needed to use the web application, starting with the context directory, the WAR file should be placed in the web server's application root directory-the one preceding the context.

When developing a web application, creating a WAR file might not be practical because classes need to be recompiled, reloaded, and tested. Usually the WAR file is created during the packaging and production stages of a project.

Client-Viewed Files

All files that the container can send to the client are located in the context or subdirectories other than the /WEB-INF or /META-INF directories.

The /META-INF directory is the *meta information* directory and contains, at a minimum, one file named MANIFEST.MF (the manifest file). The manifest file contains "meta" information pertinent to the classes that are included within the WAR/JAR file, such as digital signature information, version control information, and package sealing information.

Digital signature files are also located in the /META-INF directory, but have the extension of .sf, which stands for "signature file."

The default servlet starting page, usually referred to as `index.html`, is often located directly in the context directory. It is also common to have a graphics or images directory, which contains pictures to display on the web client, within the context directory. Here is a sample directory layout of the different files contained within a single web application:

```
webapps/test/index.html
webapps/test/instructions.jsp
webapps/test/comments.jsp
webapps/test/images/logo.gif
webapps/test/images/smileyFace.gif
webapps/test/WEB-INF/lib/testTabular.jar
webapps/test/WEB-INF/classes/com/
      spiderProductions/servlet/TestServlet.class
webapps/test/WEB-INF/classes/com/
      spiderProductions/util/Utilities.class
```

You can compress the files and directories of the `/test` context into a WAR file called `testApp.war`. The file will be placed in the root application directory as /webapps/`testApp.war`. The WAR file will contain everything from the test directory down.

 Real World Scenario

The Botanical Application

The Botanical Market in upstate New York has developed a thriving online business by selling a variety of rare herbs to the general population. Their website is simple, informative, and efficient. The developers focused their efforts on designing a web application that is portable because the company predicts future upgrades as their revenues grow.

In structuring the web application, the developers placed all static and JSP files in the context directory. Because they were accessing a database, which contained the inventory and order information, some servlets needed Java Database Connectivity (JDBC) calls. The drivers to the database were in JAR format, so they were placed in the *context*/WEB-INF/lib/ directory. The servlets, such as the HerbServlet, the OrderServlet, and the UserServlet, were placed in the *context*/WEB-INF/classes/ directory. After all pieces were placed in their appropriate locations, and the product was ready for production, the developers compressed the web application into a file called `HerbApp.war` starting at the context directory. That single file now resides in the current web server's default application directory.

The benefit of configuring the web application to meet the standard directory structure is that it will require very little administrative work to relocate the application to a new web server when the company chooses to upgrade. In an ideal setting, it should be as easy as moving the WAR file to the new server's application directory.

Using Deployment Descriptor Tags

A container can contain multiple web applications. But for each web application, there must exist only one *deployment descriptor*, also referred to as a `web.xml`. This file identifies and maps the resources for a single web application and is stored at the root of the `/WEB-INF` directory. Written in Extensible Markup Language (XML), the `web.xml` utilizes predefined tags to communicate resources and information for use by the web application. All commercial web servers will generate the `web.xml` file by using a GUI administration tool. Although this makes life a little easier for the developer, it is still the developer's responsibility to be able to understand the various tags and modify the file manually if changes or errors occur.

In this section, we will discuss the basic tags used to construct a `web.xml` file. We will then identify the tags used to map a request to a servlet and transition to tags that identify a servlet and its parameters. We'll start by showing you a complete `web.xml` (see Listing 3.1) and then discuss its tags and purpose in detail.

Listing 3.1: A Sample Deployment Descriptor

```
<?xml version="1.0" encoding="ISO-8859-01"?>

<!DOCTYPE web-app PUBLIC "-//SUN Microsystems, Inc.//
    DTD Web Application 2.3//EN" "http://java.sun.com/
    dtd/web-app_2_3.dtd">
```

```
<web-app>
    <display-name>Exotic Bird Encyclopedia</display-name>

    <context-param>
      <param-name>SEARCH_PATH</param-name>
      <param-value>/features/utilities</param-value>
    </context-param>



    <servlet>
        <servlet-name>Search</servlet-name>
        <servlet-class>SearchServlet</servlet-class>
        <init-param>
          <param-name>defaultType</param-name>
          <param-value>cockatiels</param-value>
          <description>default search value</description>
        </init-param>
    </servlet>

    <servlet-mapping>
        <servlet-name>Search</servlet-name>
        <url-pattern>/utilities/*</url-pattern>
    </servlet-mapping>

    <session-config>
        <session-timeout>60</session-timeout>
    </session-config>

    <mime-mapping>
        <extension>pdf</extension>
        <mime-type>application/pdf</mime-type>
    </mime-mapping>

    <welcome-file-list>
        <welcome-file>index.jsp</welcome-file>
        <welcome-file>index.html</welcome-file>
```

```
        <welcome-file>index.htm</welcome-file>
    </welcome-file-list>
</web-app>
```

This `web.xml` file begins by providing versioning information. The first tag, `?xml`, defines the version of the language being used. The character-encoding value is an ISO value and is defined as the Latin standard, which is used for American English countries. The `!DOCTYPE` line indicates the root XML element and the location for the *document type definition* (DTD) specification. A DTD is used to specify the structure of an XML document and to validate the document. The standard for a web application is to use the DTD spec provided by Sun Microsystems, which designates the `web-app` as the root element or tag. As you can see in the example, the servlets defined within the DTD will use the 2.3 or earlier spec. This information helps the container synchronize with the provided resources.

After the format tags have been defined, you are ready to begin mapping all resources to the web application. Because the DOCTYPE tag defines the root element as `web-app`, you are required to start with the `web-app` tag to open the form. Had the DOCTYPE indicated the root element as `web-app2`, then the XML document would begin with `web-app2`. In our example, all resources are defined between the opening `<web-app>` and closing `</web-app>` tags.

The first set of tags within the web application define parameters that are available to all servlets within the web application. By using the `ServletContext` method `getInitParameter(...)`, you can pass in the `param-name` and have the `param-value` returned within the servlet. Remember, the value is always represented as a `String`. Usually, the `context-param` specifies database drivers, protocol settings, and URL path information. Although these tags are important, they are not mandatory. Defining the servlets of the web application is most significant.

Basic Servlet Tags

To define a servlet, the XML document uses the opening `<servlet>` and closing `</servlet>` tags. All servlet-related characteristics are defined within these tags, such as the name, class, description, and parameters. When referring to the various servlets in an application, it is sometimes convenient to do so by using an alias name-a less technical name independent of the actual servlet name that follows the *XXX*Servlet naming standard.

```
<servlet>
    <servlet-name>Search</servlet-name>
    <servlet-class>SearchServlet</servlet-class>
</servlet>
```

In this example, we define the alias servlet name as Search, while the actual servlet class name is SearchServlet. This enables the servlet to be referred to by a name different from the actual servlet class name. Consequently, if you later changed the alias Search to a servlet class that had a completely different name, no additional changes to source code are necessary.

Initialization Parameters

For now, let's complete the servlet tag by looking at how to define servlet parameters:

```
<servlet>
    <servlet-name>Search</servlet-name>
    <servlet-class>SearchServlet</servlet-class>
    <init-param>
        <param-name>defaultType</param-name>
        <param-value>cockatiels</param-value>
        <description>default search value</description>
    </init-param>
</servlet>
```

Although a servlet can contain multiple parameters, they will always be embedded between a set of <init-param></init-param> tags. The init-param tag defines a name, value, and description for a variable that the outer servlet can access. In our example, the SearchServlet class can use the getInitParameter("defaultType") method, inherited from the GenericServlet class, to get the value cockatiels.

Remember the ServletRequest's getParameter(*String name*) method returns data acquired from the HTML request. The Servlet's getInit-Parameter(*String name*) method returns parameters defined within the web.xml file.

The description is optional but helps describe the variable's purpose. It is usually only valuable to GUI tools that will use the description to enable the user to know what to enter into the field. The closing `</init-param>` tag closes the information for the one parameter. If another parameter needed to be defined, a new set of `<init-param></init-param>` tags must be defined. Finally, the closing servlet tag, `</servlet>`, marks the end of specific information pertaining to the one servlet.

Mapping the URL to the Servlet

Before the servlet container can access a servlet's parameters, it must locate the servlet. When a container is started, it reads its server's configuration file (`.../conf/server.xml`) to determine the server configuration. The `server.xml` file can list different context paths using the `Context` tag. For example,

```
<Context path="/features" docBase="c:/projects/features">
</Context>
```

The `path` attribute points to the root directory (context) for a particular web application. The actual location of this context is expressed via the `docbase` attribute.

If mapping information is not included, the container will look to default directories defined by the server's deployment descriptor to find the specified servlet. For the reference web server implementation Tomcat, the default directory for all automatically loaded web applications is the directory called *tomcat-installation-directory*/webapps/.

Placing all web applications in a default directory is simple, but is not the most organized approach. A container that is running complex applications should be able to locate web applications in designated locations outside the default directory structure. By using the `Context` and `servlet-mapping` tags (which we will discuss next), you can place a servlet in a specific location and point the container to that location.

In order for the container to locate a servlet it must have information on the location and display rules of the following three items: the context, the code located in the `WEB-INF` directory, and the servlet's file. Let's look at each item specifically.

As was just described, the context is usually defined within the server's configuration file using both the path and docbase attributes. Next, we must consider the default servlet directory. This value is used in place of all files located within the WEB-INF directory. By default, Tomcat uses the term "servlet" within servlet URLs in place of explicitly defining the location of these hidden files.

Lastly, the servlet's fully qualified name is used to locate the servlet within the /classes directory. Because the fully qualified name can be long and cumbersome, each application's web.xml file may use optional servlet-mapping tags, which allow the developer to create an alias for the fully qualified servlet name. By including the servlet-mapping tags and defining a url-pattern, we can make the final modification. Consider the following code snippet:

```
<servlet>
  <servlet-name>SearchServlet</servlet-name>
  <servlet-class>com.kci.SearchServlet</servlet-class>
</servlet>

<servlet-mapping>
  <servlet-name>SearchServlet</servlet-name>
  <url-pattern>/search</url-pattern>
<servlet-mapping>
```

Let's take a look at how the URL of our SearchServlet can be altered depending on the deployment descriptor tags.

Basic URI http://localhost:8080/features/servlet/com.kci.SearchServlet

Using the **servlet-name** tag http://localhost:8080/features/servlet/SearchServlet

Using the **servlet-mapping** tag http://localhost:8080/features/search

The url-pattern tag is used to alter what the user sees and what the developer requests. Instead of relying on a directory provided by the server, you can provide the servlet with a more logical path structure. Based on the information provided, you, like the container, should be able to construct a URI for the following servlet.

```
context path = /car/engines  docBase=c:/projects
alias name = TurboRacer
```

```
servlet-name = com.eei.RaceCarServlet
url-pattern = /vehicles/fast
```

By utilizing the information, you should map the servlet to the following locations:

```
http://localhost:8080/car/engines/servlet/com.eei
   .RaceCarServlet
http://localhost:8080/car/engines/vehicles/fast/TurboRacer
```

The container takes the `url-pattern` (`/vehicles/fast`) that is associated with the servlet alias name (`TurboRacer`) and then maps that name to the actual servlet class (`com.eei.RaceCarServlet`).

Figure 3.1 breaks down the active location of the servlet graphically.

```
c://projects/car/engines/WEB-INF/classes/com/eei/
   RaceCarServlet.class
```

FIGURE 3.1   URL mapping

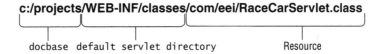

Session Configuration

After a request is mapped to a servlet, an `HttpSession` object is assigned to the client. Therefore, if there are 5000 user requests, the container will maintain 5000 `HttpSession` objects on the server. If a portion of those users is inactive, then the application is wasting memory resources. A timeout flag can be set two ways:

- Within the servlet code, in seconds, by using the `HttpSession` object's method, *setMaxInactiveInterval(int seconds)*

- Within the `web.xml` file, in minutes, by using the `session-config` tag.

The first approach utilizes servlet code to set the maximum number of seconds a request can remain inactive. The following code snippet demonstrates how this can be done:

```
...
public void doGet(HttpServletRequest req,
                  HttpServletResponse res)
```

```
        throws ServletException, IOException {
          ...
          HttpSession session = req.getSession();
          session.setMaxInactiveInterval(60);
          ...
      }
      ...
```

The downside to this approach is that when the number of seconds needs to be modified, the code itself must be recompiled. To solve this problem, you could use a deployment descriptor parameter value instead of hard-coding the number of seconds. Now, the question often asked is, "Why not use the second approach exclusively because it uses the deployment descriptor to define the value and exclude the code from the servlet?" A developer might opt to choose one approach over the other because the first applies the timeout value to a specific servlet, rather than the entire web application.

The second approach defines the maximum number of *minutes* all inactive HttpSession objects can exist through the web.xml file by using the session-config tag.

```
<session-config>
    <session-timeout>1</session-timeout>
</session-config>
```

Modifications to the web.xml file do not require the servlet to be recompiled. Instead, the container simply needs to be restarted and to reload the servlet. In both examples, we set the timeout amount to one minute. Ultimately, they both achieve the same end result-the code authorizes the container to remove the inactive session from memory after its time expires.

MIME Type Mappings

When transmitting information between the client and server, both parties need to know the format of the content being transferred. The Multipurpose Internet Mail Extension (MIME) type defines the format of the request or response. A MIME type is a String that defines the type and subtype: *type/ subtype*. Some common examples are text/html, text/plain, and image/gif.

When a servlet sends a response to a client, the browser needs to know how to render the information received. Consequently, the server can construct a response to notify the client of the MIME type, by using two different approaches:

- By using the HttpServletResponse's method: setContentType(...)

- By using the mime-mapping tag in the web.xml file for the web application

The first approach utilizes servlet code to set the MIME type of the response. The following code snippet demonstrates how this can be done:

```
...
public void doGet(HttpServletRequest req,
                  HttpServletResponse res)
  throws ServletException, IOException {
    ...
    res.setContentType("application/pdf");
    ...
}
...
```

Again, this applies the content type to a specific servlet. To apply the content type to all public files of a specific extension within an entire web application, you can use the mime-mapping tag. The following example demonstrates how the context will automatically associate the application/pdf MIME type with all files with the extension of .pdf:

```
<mime-mapping>
    <extension>pdf</extension>
    <mime-type>application/pdf</mime-type>
</mime-mapping>
```

After the client receives this response, it knows it must use a tool such as Adobe Acrobat Reader to interpret the .pdf response.

Welcome File List

When a website is accessed, the index.html file is usually the first page displayed. Typically this file is the default page for a website or a web application. In fact, if a client enters a URL path to a servlet, usually the web server will automatically change focus to point to the welcome page associated to the application. For example, if a user enters http://www.testWebserver.com/application, the site switches to http://www.testWebserver.com/application/index.html.

The `index.html` file is the default welcome page for servlets. Including the `welcome-file-list` tag in the `web.xml` file overrides the server defaults and enables the container to search for specified welcome pages. A list of welcome files can point the web server to alternative display pages.

```
<welcome-file-list>
    <welcome-file>index.jsp</welcome-file>
    <welcome-file>start.html</welcome-file>
    <welcome-file>go.html</welcome-file>
    <welcome-file>index.html</welcome-file>
</welcome-file-list>
```

The files listed within the `welcome-file-list` tag apply to the web application and its subdirectories. Let's take a look at an example. Imagine a company with a web application that resides in the root directory called `/SpiderInc.com`. Its subdirectories and files look similar to the following structure:

```
/SpiderInc.com
    |__index.html
    |__employees/
        |____index.jsp
```

When `SpiderInc.com` is accessed, the welcome page `index.html` is displayed by default. Now, when the `employees/` link is accessed, the user might be prompted for a login and password entry. After access is granted, a welcome page could be generated dynamically to acknowledge the user's name and information. The welcome page for the employee site is called `index.jsp`. In order for the container to associate the `index.jsp` file to the welcome page, the file `index.jsp` must be defined in the `web.xml` file with a `welcome-file` tag. This entry identifies additional filenames for the container to look for when searching for the welcome page for a site. In our example, the container will first look for `index.html`. If it can't find it in the `employees/` directory, it will look at the first filename in the `welcome-file` list and search for that file next. Because `index.jsp` is found, the container displays that page to the client. Without the XML entry, the container would fail to display the starting page because `index.html` is not available within the employees directory.

The specification does not address the order in which containers will access the welcome file list. Generally, most containers start with the first file in the list when searching for a welcome page.

Summary

In this chapter, we covered the details associated with the web application. We began by addressing the basic directory structure for a web application. Each resource should be placed in a specific location for the container to access its information when it is needed. Because the container doesn't always find direct matches for the files it is searching, we also covered the mapping rules a container will use to select the best fit. Finally, we described how to wrap up the entire application in a WAR file for production.

The second part of this chapter focused on identifying the most common deployment descriptor tags. The overall tag list is very large, and we covered only those that are general to the web application. Specifically, we addressed tags that apply to the entire application, such as the `Context`, `session-config`, `mime-type`, and `welcome-file` tags. In addition to those, we covered tags specific to the servlets contained within the web application itself.

The web application is made up of multiple pieces. It is important that the pieces are arranged logically and their purpose is identified to the server.

Exam Essentials

Be able to identify the required files for a web application.   A web application consists of a variety files from the following list:

Servlets (for example, `PlaceOrderServlet.class`)

JSP pages (for example, `Receipt.jsp`)

Utility classes (for example, `CalculateTotals.class`)

Static documents (for example, `welcome.html`)

Client-side Java applets, beans, and classes (for example, `OtherJavaFiles.jar`)

A standard configuration file (for example, `web.xml`)

Be able to identify the directory structure of a web application.   Each file should be placed in its associated directory. There are two main directories you should be familiar with: the context (or root) and the `/WEB-INF`. Files placed directly in the context are visible and accessible to the client. This is quite the opposite of files located directly in, or in subdirectories of, the `/WEB-INF` directory.

Be able to describe a WAR file. A WAR file is a single compressed file that contains all the contents of a web application. The same mechanisms used to compress Java applications into JAR files are used to compress web applications into WAR files. The main difference between the two files is the name, which identifies how the container should handle them. A WAR file signifies something very different to a web server than a JAR file.

Be able to discuss the most commonly used deployment descriptor tags. The deployment descriptor file, or `web.xml` file, contains a variety of tags that identify and characterize the resources within a single web application. Each XML tag communicates a specific meaning to the server.

Key Terms

Before you take the exam, be certain you are familiar with the following terms:

/META-INF	document type definition (DTD)
/WEB-INF/classes	exact mapping
/WEB-INF/lib	extension mapping
/WEB-INF/web.xml	Java archive (JAR) file
context	path mapping
default mapping	web application
deployment descriptor	web archive (WAR) file

Review Questions

1. Which of the following item(s) can be included in a web application? (Choose all that apply.)

   A. Servlets

   B. Utility classes

   C. Client-side beans

   D. An image file

2. Which of the following statements is true?

   A. It is mandatory that all servlet-compliant containers adhere to the structured directory hierarchy defined by the servlet specification.

   B. It is not mandatory or required that all servlet containers adhere to the directory structure defined by the specification.

   C. A servlet container does not need to adhere to the specification in order to be certified by Sun.

   D. None of the above.

3. Which of the following files could correctly define an entire web application?

   A. `chat.war`

   B. `chat.jar`

   C. `chat.xml`

   D. None of the above

4. Assume the context for the web application you are working with is defined as `/cars`. In which directory are you likely to find the file `index.html`?

   A. `/cars`

   B. `/cars/WEB-INF`

   C. `/cars/WEB-INF/resources`

   D. `/cars/META-INF`

5. Assume the context for the web application you are working with is /orderApp. In which directory are you most likely to find the single file Order.class?

   A. /orderApp

   B. /orderApp/WEB-INF

   C. /orderApp/WEB-INF/lib

   D. /orderApp/WEB-INF/classes

6. The <session-timeout></session-timeout> tag must be embedded in which outer tags?

   A. <web-app><session-config>HERE</session-config> </web-app>

   B. <web-app><servlet><servlet-config>HERE</servlet-config></servlet></web-app>

   C. <web-app>HERE</web-app>

   D. None of the above

7. Which of the following XML tags apply features to the entire web application, rather than to an individual servlet? (Choose all that apply.)

   A. mime-mapping

   B. init-param

   C. context-param

   D. session-config

8. Which of the following tags is used to identify the minimum amount of time a container must wait to remove an inactive HttpSession object?

   A. session-config-min

   B. session-timeout-min

   C. session-timeout-max

   D. session-timeout

   E. session-config

9. Which of the following methods is used to retrieve the value associated to the parameter name provided within the `init-param` tag?

    A. `getParameter(String name)`

    B. `getInitParameter(String name)`

    C. `getParameters()`

    D. None of the above

10. What is the return value of a method call to `getInitParameter-(String name)` if the name passed in is not found in the `web.xml` document?

    A. A `ServletException` is thrown.

    B. `null` is returned.

    C. A blank string is returned.

    D. The code will not compile.

11. Which opening tag is used to hold content-type mapping information for a response?

    A. `content-type`

    B. `mapping-type`

    C. `mime-mapping`

    D. `content-mapping`

12. In which directory are you likely to find the file `myServlet.jar`?

    A. `root/WEB-INF`

    B. `root/`

    C. `root/WEB-INF/lib`

    D. `root/META-INF/`

13. Which of the following statements is true?

    A. Request mapping is case sensitive.

    B. If mapping information is not included, the container will look to default directories defined by the server's deployment descriptor to find the specified servlet.

    C. Containers often have implicit mapping mechanisms built into their systems.

    D. All of the above.

Answers to Review Questions

1. A, B, C, D.   All of the objects defined can be included in a web application.

2. B.   Although it is recommended, it is not mandatory or required that all servlet containers adhere to the directory structure defined by the spec. However, to be Sun certified, a servlet container must meet the requirements of the specification.

3. A.   Although a JAR file contains compressed classes and resources for a Java application, a WAR file specifically contains these same types of files, but for a web application.

4. A.   The index.html file is forwarded to the web client. As a result, it cannot be located in either the /WEB-INF or /META-INF directories, or any of their subdirectories.

5. D.   All individual classes are located in the /WEB-INF/classes directory. If the class is compressed and converted to a JAR file, its JAR file needs to be placed in the /WEB-INF/lib directory.

6. A.   The session-timeout tag is used in conjunction with the session-config tag. It is not specific to a servlet, but rather applies to all servlets in the defined web application.

7. A, C, D.   The mime-mapping tag applies the MIME type for any file with the specified file extensions. The init-param is not a correct answer because it provides parameters for a specific servlet, unlike the context-param tag. This tag is general to all files in the web application. Finally, the last option is also correct because the timeout amount defined with the session-config tag applies to all HttpSession objects.

8. D.   The session-timeout tag identifies the number of seconds a container must wait before removing an inactive HttpSession object.

9. B.   The getInitParameter(*String name*) method, found in the ServletContext, ServletConfig, and FilterConfig interfaces as well as the GenericServlet class, is used to retrieve the value associated with the init-param tag.

10. B. When the string passed into the getInitParameter(*String name*) method cannot be matched to a param-name tag, null is returned.

11. C. The mime-mapping tag identifies the MIME type for files with the specified file extensions.

12. C. All Java archive files are read from the /lib directory, which is located inside /WEB-INF.

13. D. When matching URL names to their respective files or directories, the casing is important. This is best explained when trying to match Java files. A servlet called MyServlet.class is different from one called Myservlet.class. The next two options are true as well, because containers resort to default mapping techniques and are often built with implicit mapping mechanisms (as defined by the specification).

The Servlet Container Model

THE FOLLOWING SUN CERTIFIED WEB COMPONENT DEVELOPER FOR J2EE PLATFORM EXAM OBJECTIVES ARE COVERED IN THIS CHAPTER:

✓ **3.1 Identify the uses for and the interfaces (or classes) and methods to achieve the following features:**

- Servlet context init. parameters
- Servlet context listener
- Servlet context attribute listener
- Session attribute listeners

✓ **3.2 Identify the WebApp deployment descriptor element name that declares the following features:**

- Servlet context init. parameters
- Servlet context listener
- Servlet context attribute listener
- Session attribute listeners

✓ **3.3 Distinguish the behavior of the following in a distributable:**

- Servlet context init. parameters
- Servlet context listener
- Servlet context attribute listener
- Session attribute listeners

When defining a data element, you usually need to consider its life span, or *scope*. Depending on its placement, a parameter or attribute is accessible by various pieces of an application. In this chapter, we are going to provide a close look at how data is affected when it is stored at different levels of an application. The first level is global to all resources within the application, and it is known as the context. The second level exists during the life of a client's connection, and is commonly referred to as the session. Finally, we will conclude by addressing how data within these different areas is affected when the application is run in a distributed environment.

At all three levels, we will discuss how parameters and attributes can be accessed and manipulated. We will show you how either the context or session can respond to changes in its attributes by using specific listener interfaces. Specifically, we will discuss what happens when:

- The context or session is initialized or destroyed

- Attributes are added, removed, or replaced from a context or session

Our goal is to ensure a thorough understanding of how parameters and attributes are handled for each object. In addition, you must be familiar with the specific interfaces and generated events used to respond to changes in either one's life-cycle methods or attributes.

ServletContext

An application usually consists of many resources, such as multiple servlets, audio files, and static HTML files, to name a few. Maintained within the container, each resource is generally accessible to the others. However, sometimes the developer's desire is not to access another resource but rather to allow resources to share data. This can be accomplished using the `ServletContext` object. In this section, we will first discuss the details and methods associated with a `ServletContext` object. This includes how any servlet within an application can use its context to access the following:

- Initialization parameters passed through `web.xml`
- An `InputStream` to read data from a specified resource
- A `RequestDispatcher` object to transfer a request and response object
- Attributes shared by all resources

After you understand the value that a `ServletContext` adds to an application, we will shift gears and cover the various listener interfaces and event classes that can be used to respond to changes in a context's life cycle and attributes. The two interfaces we will discuss are:

- `ServletContextListener`
- `ServletContextAttributeListener`

The `ServletContext` is a critical object that helps glue all the pieces of an application together.

ServletContext **Methods and Attributes**

For each web application, there exists one `ServletContext` object contained within the application's `ServletConfig` object. The *context object* acts as a reference to the web application. When a servlet is initialized, the container provides it a handle to the context object for the servlet to communicate with the container. All servlets within the application use the single context object to access information about the container and server in which they reside. This information can then be displayed to the client and/or used to change or restrict servlet behaviors. For example, the context can be used to dispatch a request, write to a log file, or simply learn about the servlet version being supported. The context can be accessed by the servlet directly or indirectly. Because all servlets extend an implementation of the `GenericServlet` class, they have direct access to the following method:

ServletContext getServletContext()   This method returns the single context object associated with the entire web application. This method is originally defined in the `ServletConfig` interface, which the `GenericServlet` class implements.

For the most part, the context contains informative methods—methods that provide information about resource location, parameters, and attribute values managed by the container and server.

The current specification no longer provides handles to other servlets within the application. Those methods have been deprecated and return empty or null values. The only direct link that is currently provided by the context is a handle to the RequestDispatcher, to forward a task, and streams used to either write log information or read objects.

The context enables the developer or assembler to define values that apply to the entire web application. They can define either parameter values or attribute values.

Parameter values usually define the application's configuration information at deployment time. The value associated with the name is represented as a String; however, it can be converted to an appropriate object under the correct circumstances. For example, a parameter might provide a hidden file or image path and name that servlets might be interested in loading at some point, or it might simply provide an e-mail address to the application's webmaster. By using the context-param tag within the web.xml file, you can specify the name and value pair, as seen here:

```
<context-param>
    <param-name>picture</param-name>
    <param-value>/WEB-INF/graphics/image.gif</param-value>
</context-param>
```

The context-param tag must be placed at the start of the web-app tag. In other words, it can follow the <web-app> tag or its <description></description> tag only.

All servlets within the web application can access this filename by using the following methods available in the ServletContext class:

String getInitParameter(*String name*)   By passing in the name of the parameter, this method returns a string representation of the value. A null value is returned if the parameter doesn't exist.

Enumeration getInitParameterNames()   This method returns an enumeration of all names defined within the context-param tags. If there are none, the return value is empty.

The following code snippet shows how a servlet might access this parameter value:

```
public void doGet(HttpServletRequest req,
                  HttpServletResponse res)
    throws IOException, ServletException {
      ServletContext context = getServletContext();
      String pictureName =
            context.getInitParameter("picture");
      ...
}
```

After this information is acquired, you can use additional context methods to read in the actual object. Here are a few for you to consider:

URL getResource(*String path*)   This method returns a local or remote resource to the specified path. The path is viewed as relative to the context for the application and begins with a forward slash (/). If a resource cannot be mapped to the specified path, the method returns a null.

InputStream getResourceAsStream(*String path*)   This method creates an InputStream linked to a resource for the path parameter. The data within the InputStream can consist of a resource of any type or length.

String getMimeType(*String file*)   This method returns a string representation of the MIME type for the specified file.

RequestDispatcher getRequestDispatcher(*String path*)   This method returns the RequestDispatcher object to the resource specified by the path. It enables a current servlet to forward a request to the resource or to include the resource in a response.

Continuing our picture example, we are going to read in the image file to convert it to an ImageIcon object that we can use in an applet embedded within the client interface:

```
public void doGet(HttpServletRequest req,
                  HttpServletResponse res)
    throws IOException, ServletException {
```

```
ServletContext context = getServletContext();
String pictureName =
  context.getInitParameter("picture");
InputStream is =
  context.getResourceAsStream(pictureName);
byte[] array = new byte[1024];
is.read(array);
ImageIcon icon = new ImageIcon(array);
is.close();
}
```

After we access the actual path of the picture parameter, we use the getResourceAsStream(...) method to return to us an InputStream to read each pixel byte. To avoid a complex example, we've stipulated that the size of the image is always 1,024 bytes. The bytes are read into a byte array, and then that array is passed to the javax.swing.ImageIcon(...) constructor to create a graphical object that can be embedded in any swing component. A more convoluted but practical process would encompass reading in all the bytes without knowing the actual size beforehand. Our goal is to focus on the usage and rules of the ServletContext object.

Aside from providing read-only access to initialization parameters, the context also enables the servlet to read from and write to context attributes. Unlike parameters, attributes allow the passing of Objects rather than just Strings. Attributes are used to share common objects with various resources. Specifically, attributes are a way for the server to communicate information to the servlet. The server could make available statistics on the server load, or pass a handle to a shared resource pool, or provide other bits of information available at the server level. The only mandatory attribute a server must make available is the location of a private directory for the application's context. This value can be accessed through the javax.servlet.context.tempdir attribute. Needless to say, attributes can also be set by the user.

Let's say you are writing an application for a sushi restaurant called Kazumi. The owner specifically asked that the interface display the current lunch menu with the daily specials. Because these values are likely to change depending on the date, you will set them up as attributes.

Before we show you the code, let's address a few details. It's important to know that attributes can be defined within a web application by a servlet, or within the servlet container when the application is assembled or deployed. The names are usually defined by using the packaging structure to avoid overriding one another (for example, java.*, javax.*, com.sun.*, and so on).

Attributes are defined and stored by using get*XXX* and set*XXX* methods. Unlike parameters, they are not defined within a deployment descriptor.

All servlets within the web application can access these values and set them by using the following methods available in the `ServletContext` class:

void setAttribute(*String name, Object value*)   This method binds the specified object to the name for access by all resources within the web application.

Object getAttribute(*String name*)   This method returns the bound object to the name specified.

In the earlier specifications, it was not unusual to develop a servlet designed to prepare the context for all other resources. For example, instead of defining the attribute name and value through the web container, you could have a servlet take care of the task by using code similar to the following:

```
...
public void doGet(HttpServletRequest req,
                   HttpServletResponse res)
    throws ServletException, IOException {
      res.setContentType("text/plain");
      PrintWriter out = res.getWriter();

      ServletContext context = getServletContext();
      context.setAttribute("com.kazumi.specials.daily",
          "Unagi:2 pieces for $2");
      context.setAttribute("com.kazumi.date", new Date());

      out.println("The daily special is set");
}
...
```

In this example, the attributes are applied to the context by using the `setAttribute(...)` method. Later, we will discuss the `ServletContext AttributeListener` interface that was added in the 2.3 specification to enable a class to respond to attribute changes made to a context. For now, let's focus on the rules and concept. A servlet uses the `getAttribute()`

method to retrieve the stored attribute values. For example, you can now construct the part of the servlet that displays the menu with the defined daily special:

```
...
public void doGet(HttpServletRequest req,
                  HttpServletResponse res)
    throws ServletException, IOException {
        res.setContentType("text/html");
        PrintWriter out = res.getWriter();

        ServletContext context = getServletContext();
        String special = (String)
         context.getAttribute("com.kazumi.specials.daily");
        Date date = (Date)
         context.getAttribute("com.kazumi.date");

        DateFormat df =
         DateFormat.getDateInstance(DateFormat.MEDIUM);
        String now = df.format(date);
        out.println("<HTML>");
        out.println("<BODY>");

        out.println("<P> The special for " + now + " is: " +
                    special + "</P>");
        ...
        out.println("</BODY></HTML>");
}
```

By using the ServletContext's getAttribute(...) method, you can retrieve the object associated with the specified key name. The names themselves are either custom or defined within the servlet specifications. In Chapter 2, "The Servlet Model," we listed several predefined attribute key names created for request objects. These same names can be used to set values that apply to the entire context. Table 4.1 lists the predefined attribute names that are most likely used to set general messaging and exceptions for a ServletContext object.

TABLE 4.1 Attributes for *ServletContext*

Standard Attribute Name	Type
javax.servlet.error.exception_type	java.lang.Class
javax.servlet.error.message	java.lang.String
javax.servlet.error.exception	java.lang.Throwable

By using the setAttribute(...) method, you can pass the standard attribute name and its associated value. This enables developers to use a standard naming system for exceptions that occur at the context level.

There are several important distinctions between context parameters and attributes. The following are a few that you should be aware of:

- Parameters can be set only from within the container or the web.xml file. Attributes, however, can be set by the servlet or the container.

- Parameters return only Strings, whereas attributes allow key names to be associated with Objects.

- The lookup names used for attributes are either predefined or custom, but they should be defined by using a package structure. For example, the attribute name for error messages is javax.servlet.error .message.

In summary, the context utilizes parameters and attributes as a means of sharing information and objects with the resources of the web application. Initialization parameters are defined in the deployment descriptor and are accessible through the context. They provide configuration information in the form of String objects. Attributes, on the other hand, share objects with the application entities. Their name/value pairs can be set through the container or through the servlet using the context. They are less geared to providing information, and are more geared to providing resources.

Listener Interfaces and Event Classes

New to the 2.3 servlet specification are *listener* classes that help monitor the servlet context and session life cycle. The web container can be configured to notify listeners when a context is initialized or destroyed, when attributes are added or removed, or when a session is set to be passivated or activated. In this section, you will look at each listener interface and see when and how these listeners are used.

ServletContextListener

During the life of a web application, many resources are created and utilized by various entities such as servlets. When an application is created, it might be desirable to ensure that all servlets are provided a particular resource (for example, a database connection). When the application is destroyed, those resources might need to be removed as well. The addition of the `ServletContextListener` interface is designed to accomplish such tasks.

A class that implements the `ServletContextListener` interface must define two methods:

void contextInitialized(*ServletContextEvent e*) This method is called when the context is created. You are guaranteed that this method will complete before any requests are serviced.

void contextDestroyed(*ServletContextEvent e*) This method is called when the context is about to be destroyed. This method acts like a finalize method. It is used to clean up resources.

The most common example used to demonstrate the effectiveness of a `ServletContextListener` is the creation and removal of a single connection or a connection pool. A connection pool creates a defined number of connections to a database. Instead of allowing each client a continuous connection, the connections are borrowed from the pool when they are needed and returned after a task is completed. By checking connections in and out, the server can provide more clients database connectivity while utilizing fewer connections. The end result is a more efficient application. To create such an environment, the connections, or the pool, must be created before a request to a servlet can be processed. This can be done with a listener, as shown in Listing 4.1.

Listing 4.1: Using the ServletContextListener

```
package com.spiderInc;
import java.sql.*;
import javax.sql.*;
import javax.naming.*;
import javax.servlet.*;
```

```
public class ConnectionPoolHandler
      implements ServletContextListener {

  public void contextInitialized(ServletContextEvent e) {
    ServletContext context = e.getServletContext();
    String dbName = context.getInitParameter("Database");
    PooledConnection con;

    try {
      InitialContext ic = new InitialContext();
      con = (PooledConnection)ic.lookup("java:comp/env/
        jdbc/" + dbName);
    } catch (Exception ex) {}

    context.setAttribute("con", con);
  }

  public void contextDestroyed(ServletContextEvent e) {
    ServletContext context = e.getServletContext();
    PooledConnection con =
        (PooledConnection)context.getAttribute("con");
    try { con.close(); } catch (Exception ex) {}
  }
}
```

When the web application begins, the contextInitialized(...) method
is invoked and must complete before any requests can be forwarded to a servlet. It is the perfect place to initialize any variables that will be shared by other
resources. Before this particular web application can begin, you must first
create a connection pool to a particular database. To allow for database flexibility (meaning you can change the database without recompiling the
application code), you define the actual database name in the container as
a parameter. By using the getInitParameter ("Database") method, you
retrieve the database name to then look up its associated pool using the
Java Naming and Directory Interface (JNDI). The exam does not test you
on lookup techniques or JNDI, so we won't go into it in detail. Basically,
you access a connection pool defined within the container by using the

lookup(...) method. After you acquire a connection pool, you set that object as an attribute for all servlets to access.

When the web application is shut down, the contextDestroyed(...) method will be called. The preceding example uses the context to get the object associated with the attribute name con. The bound PooledConnection object is returned and then closed.

Here is a code snippet showing how a servlet could use the attributes to accomplish database tasks:

```
public class QueryServlet extends HttpServlet {
    public void doGet(HttpRequestServlet req,
                      HttpResponseServlet res)
      throws IOException, ServletException {

        ServletContext context = getServletContext();
        PooledConnection con =
          (PooledConnection)context.getAttribute("con");
        Connection connection = con.getConnection();
        Statement stmt = connection.createStatement();


    }
}
```

The QueryServlet uses the context to get the attribute value for con. After a handle to the connection pool is returned, a connection is checked out from the pool. A statement is created, and then a query can be sent to the database. From this example, you can see that the ServletContextListener serves its purpose in initializing all necessary data before a servlet request is invoked.

In addition to understanding *how* a context is initialized, it is also important to understand *when* a context is likely to be initialized and removed. The most obvious time a context is created or destroyed is when the container first starts up the application or closes it down. However, during the container's life, a web application can be stopped and reloaded if necessary. For example, you might need to switch the application to a backup database for maintenance purposes. Changes would be made to point the application to the right database, and the container should provide mechanisms to reload the application dynamically. Your listener would get the new ServletContext and change the connection information by reinitializing the database connection through the defined initialization parameters.

We've discussed how to create a listener and when it will be invoked, but the final piece is linking the listener to the container. The container is made aware of a listener through the deployment descriptor. By using the listener tags, you identify which listeners are associated with the application. Continuing with our example, let's take a look at how the `ConnectionPoolHandler` is defined within the `web.xml` file:

```
<listener>
    <listener-class>
        com.spiderInc.ConnectionPoolHandler
    </listener-class>
<listener>
```

When the `web.xml` file is read, the server creates an instance of the listener class. By using introspection, it determines what listener interface the class implements and registers it accordingly. The order in which event classes are listed defines the order they will be invoked. The servlet 2.3 specification mandates that the container complete instantiations of the listener classes in the application prior to executing the first request for the application. As a result, these tags should appear before the servlets are declared in the `web.xml` file.

All event listener classes use the same listener tag.

There is no need to make a method call such as add*XXX*`Listener`. By using reflection, the server handles the registration between it and the listener.

It is mandatory that the web container create an instance of all listener classes and register them for event notification before the first request for the application is processed. Also, the container must maintain a handle to the listener until the last request is made for the application.

ServletContextEvent

When the container creates or destroys a context, it generates a `Servlet-ContextEvent` object that contains a reference to the actual `ServletContext`. An *event* is simply an object that holds data about an activity that took place.

Usually, it has only `get` methods to access information about the object. For the `ServletContextEvent` class, the following method is available:

ServletContext getServletContext() This method returns a handle to the application's `ServletContext`.

The `ServletContextListener` is notified when a change is made to the context for the web application. In order for the listener to respond, it most likely needs access to the actual context.

ServletContextAttributeListener

The attributes of a context are shared by all servlets in the web application. After a servlet gets an attribute, it is quite likely that another servlet will change the value of that attribute by calling `setAttribute(...)`. To ensure application-wide consistency, receiving notification of any changes to the attributes would be beneficial. The `ServletContextAttributeListener` provides the solution. An implementing class must define the following methods:

void attributeAdded(*ServletContextAttributeEvent e*) This method is called when an attribute is added to the context.

void attributeRemoved(*ServletContextAttributeEvent e*) This method is called when an attribute is removed from the context.

void attributeReplaced(*ServletContextAttributeEvent e*) This method is called when an existing attribute value is changed.

The specific method of a `ServletContextAttributeListener` will be called depending on the attribute action. The server locates this listener through the deployment descriptor. Similar to the `ServletContextListener`, the class name must be defined by using the `listener` tags. By using reflection, the server will determine the implementing interface and know to call this class when attribute values are changed.

When a change occurs to an attribute, the listener might want to know which attribute was changed and then respond. For example, a servlet might change the context database attribute. The `ServletContextAttributeListener`'s `attributeReplaced(...)` method would be called. The listener could then disconnect from the old database, get the new value, and reconnect to the new database.

ServletContextAttributeEvent

The `ServletContextAttributeEvent` class extends the `ServletContext-Event` class and adds two methods to acquire the name and value of the attribute that has changed. In addition to the `getServletContext()` method, the following methods are available:

`String getName()` This method returns the name of the attribute being created, replaced, or removed.

`Object getValue()` This method returns the value of the attribute being created, replaced, or removed.

HttpSession

While the context provides servlets access to the container's data, a *session* provides servlets access to the actions of each user utilizing the site. An application is made up of many pieces. A significant piece is a session object. An `HttpSession` object is created when a user sends its first request to an application. The object is maintained on the server end and can be configured to track each action the user takes while at the site. Remember, with HTTP, each request/response transaction creates a new object. The session connection is separate. After a session connection is established, it exists until a user is idle for a specified time period. This period is defined within either the deployment descriptor or the server. During the life of the session, the user is likely to make multiple requests while transferring information to the server. The user information can be stored in the session to eliminate the need to resend the information to the server.

A shopping cart provides the perfect example of how sessions work. Imagine that a client accesses a site that enables registered users to purchase music CDs. From the time the user logs in to the time they place their order and check out, a session exists and stores the data of the entire transaction. The following example walks you through the process. Figure 4.1 shows how the first request, a login, causes the container to create an `HttpSession` for that user with the information sent by the client.

FIGURE 4.1 The creation of a session object

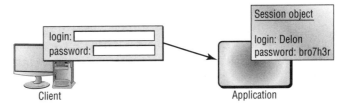

The session is created and is written to store the information sent by the client request. As the session continues to persist with each additional request, the user begins to shop. If the user finds a CD of choice, they can add it to their cart. This information can then be stored in the session object for checkout purposes. Figure 4.2 shows how the session object tracks the transactions the user makes.

FIGURE 4.2 Creating session data

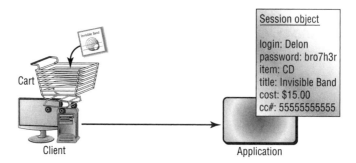

After the user is ready to check out, they send a request to the application. The application can use the information stored by the session to verify the order before finalizing the transaction. Figure 4.3 shows how the session data is used to communicate the order to the client.

FIGURE 4.3 Using session data

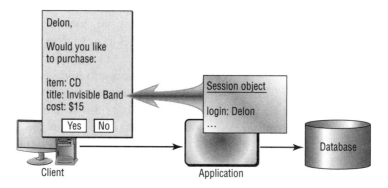

The session information is used to verify the order before the information is written to a database. When the user is finished, all necessary data can be written to the appropriate storage locations and the session is removed.

The HttpSession object does not automatically track user actions. Capturing and storing the information is the responsibility of the developer. When a servlet receives a request, it can use the HttpServletRequest class to access the current session or create a new one:

HttpSession getSession(*boolean value*)   This method gets the current session for the request. A true parameter creates a new session object if one does not already exist.

After a servlet has a handle to the session object, it can use the methods within the HttpSession class to manipulate the session's data. Some of those methods are as follows:

Object getAttribute(*String name*)   This method returns the object associated with the specified name. For example, a session can hold objects, such as a bean, for the user.

void setAttribute(*String name, Object value*)   This binds an attribute object to a key name.

void removeAttribute(*String name*)   This removes the bound object and name from the session based on the specified name.

To make servlets more robust and flexible, listener interfaces have been added to the session object. These interfaces enable servlets to monitor and respond to the creation or removal of a session, or to a change in its attributes. Next, we will take a close look at the various session listener classes, their uses, and benefits.

HttpSessionListener

HttpSessionListeners are notified when a session is created or destroyed. Let's say you have a brokerage application that closely monitors the user's every action to validate the purchase or sale of stocks. To prevent any customer disputes, the brokerage writes each action to a hard disk while the customer is logged in. As soon as a session becomes active, you want to make a new and unique file for that customer. Your listener could perform the necessary steps when it receives notification that a new session has been added to the server. These are the methods that an implementing class must define:

void sessionCreated(*HttpSessionEvent e*)   This method is called when a session is created.

void sessionDestroyed(*HttpSessionEvent e*) This method is called to identify that a session has been invalidated.

The following is a code example of the scenario we have just discussed:

```
public class HttpSessionHandler
                 implements HttpSessionListener {
    public void sessionCreated(HttpSessionEvent e) {
      HttpSession session = e.getSession();
      File file= new File(session.getId());
      session.setAttribute("trackingFile", file);
    }
    public void
    sessionDestroyed(HttpSessionEvent e) {
      HttpSession sess = e.getSession();
      File file =
        (File)sess.getAttribute("trackingFile");
      ServletContext context = sess.getServletContext();
      Connection con =
      (Connection)context.getAttribute("dbConnection");
      // use connection to write file to database
      file.delete();
    }
}
```

In the previous code example, it's important to note that we use the `session.getId()` method to create a file object. This approach guarantees the creation of a unique file for each session based on the session name. Basically, no two sessions can overwrite each other. The servlet can use the `HttpServletRequest` object to get the session and access the file. A description of the request can then be logged to the file for future documentation. See the following sample code:

```
public class BuyStockServlet extends HttpServlet {
    public void doGet(HttpServletRequest req,
                     HttpServletResponse res)
      throws IOException, ServletException {
        HttpSession sess = req.getSession();
        File temp =
            (File)sess.getAttribute("trackingFile");
```

```
                  FileWriter fw = new FileWriter(temp);
                  Enumeration enum = req.getParameterNames();
                  while(enum.hasMoreElements()) {
                      fw.write(req.getMethod());
                      String name = (String)enum.nextElement();
                      String[] values =
                        req.getParameterValues(name);
                      for(int k=0; k<values.length; k++) {
                          fw.write(values[k]+" ");
                      }
                  }
              }
          }
```

After the servlet accesses the session object, it can get the file attribute. It wraps the File object in a FileWriter and filters through the request data to then write it to the file. When the session is invalidated, the Http-SessionListener is notified and the sessionDestroyed(...) method is called to then write the file to a database.

HttpSessionEvent

When a session is created or destroyed, an HttpSessionEvent object is instantiated to store a handle to the actual session:

HttpSession getSession()   This method returns the HttpSession object.

Because multiple clients can access a site at one time, the listener will be called each time a new session is created. The getSession() method returns the session for the session object created or destroyed.

HttpSessionAttributeListener

In an effort to monitor the client's actions, you can utilize the HttpSession-AttributeListener interface to receive notification when a client session's attributes are changed. This enables you to write code that automatically generates a response to changes in their information or wants. By defining the following methods, the implementing `HttpSessionAttributeListener` class is notified when an attribute is added, removed, or replaced:

void `attributeAdded(HttpSessionBindingEvent e)` This method is called after an attribute is added to a session.

void `attributeRemoved(HttpSessionBindingEvent e)` This method is called after an attribute is removed from a session.

void `attributeReplaced(HttpSessionBindingEvent e)` This method is called after an attribute is replaced within a session.

The attributes represent the data or model of a session object. When a session's data is changed, another response or reaction might be appropriate. For example, imagine a web application that provides the user with a ticker tape listing the stocks of the NASDAQ stock exchange. When a user logs into this site, a session is created. They then have the option to select a particular ticker for more detailed information on that stock. By selecting a stock, they are actually adding themselves to an alias list that is notified when changes to the stock occur. Let's say a user clicks on the symbol XLNX. This action causes a stock object with that symbol to be added to their session ID. The addition of a stock object attribute can trigger the creation of an `HttpSessionBindingEvent` and a call to the `attributeAdded(...)` or `attributeReplaced(...)` method of the `HttpSessionAttributeListener`. These methods could then access the session ID and get the user's name and e-mail address in order to add them to a notification list for up-to-date information about changes to the stocks defined within their stock object. The process might occur in the following fashion:

1. The user begins by selecting XLNX from the listed ticker:

    1. SUNW 20.4   ORCL 32.5 IBM 59.7 XLNX 35.4 QCOM 60.7

2. The symbol is added to the client's Session Object:

```
Session Object
UserName = Joe
UserEmail = Joe@eei.com
Stock = stockList // This is a List object that contains
    //all selected stocks.
                  // In this case, it contains XLNX.
```

3. The HttpSessionAttributeListener is notified:

```
public class HttpSessionAttributeHandler
              implements HttpSessionAttributeListener{
  public void attributeAdded(HttpSessionBindingEvent e) {
    HttpSession session = e.getSession();
    String email=
      (String)session.getAttribute("UserEmail");
    ArrayList stockList = (ArrayList)e.getValue();
    Iterator iter = stockList.iterator();
    while(iter.hasNext()) {
        String symbol = (String)iter.next();
        ServletContext context
              = session.getServletContext();
        Connection con = (Connection)
              context.getAttribute("Connection");
        // Write email address and symbol to database
        // if they don't already exist.
    }
  }
  public void attributeRemoved(HttpSessionBindingEvent e)
        {}
  public void attributeReplaced(HttpSessionBindingEvent e)
        {}
}
```

The user selects the symbol XLNX, which creates a Stock attribute whose value is a cumulative list of all symbols selected during the session. Assuming this is the first symbol selected, the addition of a new attribute prompts the server to notify the HttpSessionAttributeListener by calling its attributeAdded(...) method. By using the HttpSessionBindingEvent object, we are able to get the value of the new attribute and use the connection acquired from the context to then write the e-mail address and symbol to a database. Another servlet can query the database and e-mail interested parties about latest news when information about the symbol changes. In general, this listener acts as a mediator to respond to session attribute changes.

It is important to remember that a session can continue to exist after a transaction is complete. The user might still want to start a new transaction. When this happens, attributes can be replaced or removed.

Attribute changes to a `ServletContext` or an `HttpSession` object can occur concurrently. Because containers are not required to synchronize the listener notifications, it is possible to have one notification corrupt the data of another. Consequently, the developer must maintain the integrity of the attribute values when coding the listener classes.

HttpSessionBindingEvent

When an action takes place with respect to a session's attributes, an `HttpSessionBindingEvent` object is created. The `HttpSessionBinding-Event` class extends the `HttpSessionEvent` class and adds methods to access attribute information. This object stores a handle to the session, the attribute name, and the attribute value. The methods are as follows:

`HttpSession getSession()`   This method returns a handle to the session object.

`String getName()`   This method returns the name bound to or unbound from the session.

`Object getValue()`   This method returns the value that has been added, removed, replaced, not bound, or unbound from the session.

The event is either passed to an `HttpSessionAttributeListener` or `HttpSessionBindingListener`.

HttpSessionActivationListener

The `HttpSessionActivationListener` is used to maintain sessions that migrate from one server to another. When a session is about to be moved to a new server, it is passivated, or made inactive. After the session is on the new server, it is brought back to life and activated. The implementing interface is notified during both these events. This provides an opportunity to save or store data across Java Virtual Machines (JVMs). A listener must implement the following methods:

`void sessionDidActivate(HttpSessionEvent se)`   This method is called right after the session is activated. At this point, the session is not yet in service.

void sessionWillPassivate(*HttpSessionEvent se*)   This method is
called when a session is about to be passivated. At this point, the session
is no longer in service.

Let's say you have a web application that stores customer transaction information to a file. Due to the success of the application, the developers designed
a distributed environment by pooling multiple computers together to efficiently
handle resource usage. When one server is bombarded with hits, sessions are
moved to a new server, where more resources might be available. Now, if a
session is moved to a new server with a new JVM, the file that was originally
written to is no longer available. An HttpSessionActivationListener
ensures the data integrity of a session. When the session is about to be passivated, sessionWillPassivate(...) is called. This method could be used to
read the contents of the file into the session object. When the session is transferred over, sessionDidActivate(...) is called. This method could be used to
read the content from the session and write it to a file on the new server. Here
is a code sample illustrating this example:

```
public class HttpSessionActivationHandler
  implements HttpSessionActivationListener{
    public void sessionDidActivate(HttpSessionEvent e){
      HttpSession ses = e.getSession();
      try {
        File f = (File)ses.getAttribute("file");
        byte[] fileByteArray = new byte[(int)f.length()];
        FileInputStream fr = new FileInputStream(f);
        fr.read(fileByteArray);
        ses.setAttribute("file", fileByteArray);
        fr.close();
      } catch (IOException ignore) {}
    }
}
    public void sessionWillPassivate(HttpSessionEvent e){
      HttpSession ses = e.getSession();
      try {
        byte[] byteFile = (byte[])ses.getAttribute("file");
        FileOutputStream fs =
            new FileOutputStream("NewFile.txt");
```

```
            fs.write(byteFile);
            fs.close();

            ses.setAttribute("file", new File("NewFile.txt"));
        } catch(IOException ignore) {}
    }
}
```

An `HttpSessionActivationListener` is registered in the deployment descriptor by using the listener tag. The process is almost exactly the same as with other listeners. To enable the session to transfer to another server, all target servers must mirror the original server. The listener must be defined in the `web.xml` file for all possible servers. Remember, the activation method and passivation methods will probably be called on different systems.

HttpSessionBindingListener

When a session attribute is added, removed, or replaced, the `HttpSession-AttributeListener` is notified. The `HttpSessionBindingListener` is very similar in that it is notified when an object is bound to or unbound from a session. The difference between the two listeners is based on whether you would like to handle the event change from the session's perspective or from the object's perspective:

- The `HttpSessionAttributeListener` looks at all objects added to the session. It manages all attribute changes for the session.

- The `HttpSessionBindingListener` lets the object know when it is bound (added) to or unbound (removed) from the session so it can directly respond to the event.

 When a session times out or is invalidated, objects are unbound from the session. `HttpSessionBindingListener` is notified and `HttpSessionAttribute-Listener` is not.

The implementing class must define the following methods:

void valueBound(*HttpSessionBindingEvent event*)   This method identifies the session and notifies the object that it is being bound to a session.

void valueUnbound(*HttpSessionBindingEvent event*) This method identifies the session and notifies the object that it is being unbound from a session.

A mail application could greatly benefit from this listener because it could disconnect from the mail server when the session was invalidated.

 Real World Scenario

EEI's Mail Application

In an attempt to offer employees the ability to check their company e-mail while off site, Educational Edge, Inc. (EEI) created a web mail application. Soon after the program was released, however, a problem began to occur: the technical department was consistently notified that users were having problems logging back into the system after their sessions timed out.

Apparently, employees were logging into the application and then letting it sit idly until their session was invalidated. The application was not designed to close the connection on a timeout, and unfortunately the destruction of the session did not automatically close network connections. If a user tried to log back into the application, they were unable to establish a connection because the old one was not yet closed. To ensure the integrity of users' mail, most mail applications do not allow users to have multiple sessions alive. Consequently, the connection had to be manually closed within the application code.

The developers worked on a new version that created an HttpSession-BindingListener object. In the valueUnbound(...) method, the connection was closed and the problem resolved. It is also important to note that the HttpSessionBindingListener is usually implemented in one of the main servlet classes, and not in a class written specifically as a listener. In this manner, the mail servlet class would know when it was bound to or unbound from the session and could respond accordingly. In general, this listener is most effective when resources need to be cleaned up or established as a result of objects being bound to and unbound from a session.

In general, event listener classes are used to respond to changes made to the servlet context and HTTP sessions. They are instantiated and registered in the web container when the application is being deployed. An application can have multiple listeners for each event type and the order of invocation can be specified within the container. When the application is shut down, the container will first invalidate a session and invoke session listeners and then invoke context listeners to close the application.

Distributable Environment

A *distributable* environment, also known as *clustering*, utilizes multiple back-end servers to distribute processing responsibilities. This technique promotes efficiency and dependability. With multiple servers to handle requests, the application can manage a large number of simultaneous requests on different systems. When one machine crashes, requests can be redirected to another server to keep the application alive.

The benefits seem to warrant that all systems be configured to run in a distributed environment. This, however, is not the case. Designing a robust system is more complicated than creating an application that runs on one system. In addition, more multiple servers are costly. The hardware and software prices for the servers increase the cost of the application almost twofold for each additional layer or cluster. The question is whether the cost is worth the performance benefits. Unfortunately, the performance benefits are enjoyed only under extreme loads. If the application doesn't receive a lot of hits and the current system can handle the requests, there is no need to forward or transfer loads to different resources. Now, if the system has high visibility and is accessed heavily, the cost is negligible compared to the benefits gained from a dependable system. Imagine the profits lost from a system that is not accessible. Also, the increased processing speed could bring in larger profits that would pay for the costs of a robust system and then some.

If you choose to create a distributed system, you should keep some design considerations in mind. The application is no longer run on one JVM; there is no longer one servlet context or one servlet instance. As a result, some rules must be considered when developing the application.

First, variables must be handled differently. In fact, instance and static variables should be avoided. Imagine a servlet that stores a counter to measure how many times it is accessed during its lifetime. If the counter is an instance or static variable, the following applies:

Instance variable   The variable will measure only the number of times that specific instance is accessed. Each servlet will generate a different value.

Static variable The variable is shared among all instances—within the same JVM. In a distributed environment, the static variable cannot be accessed by another JVM.

Keep in mind that the server might create multiple instances of a servlet for pooling, threading, or reloading purposes.

To prevent problems, the variable could be stored to an external resource, such as a database, and accessed by each servlet instance to update and access the value. If the variable applies to the session, it can be set as an attribute rather than a variable.

Second, the `ServletContext` should not store state. Remember, a context provides the servlet access to the server and container information. Multiple JVMs mean there are multiple contexts, and their data will differ depending on location. When a session is transferred to another server as a part of resource management, the servlet context is left behind and a new context is created. Again, the data you would consider storing in a context should also be placed in an external resource such as a database.

Third, `HttpSession` objects must also be handled with distribution in mind. Because a session might be migrated between different systems, all associated objects must be transferable. For example, an object that implements `java.io.Serializable` makes it portable. If an object contains data that cannot be transferred—for example, `Thread` objects—the session will not be activated in its correct form when it attempts to come alive on the new server.

Fourth, files should also be handled differently. In a distributed environment, you are not guaranteed the location of the servlet. Consequently, it is preferable and more reliable to access files by using a path relative to the context, rather than the server. The encouraged approach is through the `getResource(...)` method of the `ServletContext`: `getServletContext()` `.getResource(String path)`. Because the file is packaged with the application, it is accessible from the same location (the relative path to the application's context directory) regardless of the server.

Finally, threading must be considered. *Synchronization* is a locking mechanism used to ensure that data cannot be accessed by multiple requests. The only problem is that synchronization applies to only one JVM. Synchronization cannot be guaranteed in a distributed environment.

Deployment Descriptor

Developing an application to run in a distributable environment requires careful consideration of how to handle attributes and path information. Writing code that deals with such issues is the first step in enabling your application to run between multiple systems. The second step is to modify the web.xml file to include a tag indicating that the application is suited for such an environment.

Marking the deployment descriptor enables the server to deploy the application across multiple back ends. This is done by placing an empty <distributable/> tag between the file's description and context-param tag.

Without this empty tag, the application is non-distributable by default. The addition of the tag indicates the possibility for the application to be split.

```
<web-app>
    <description >    </description>
    <distributable/>
    <context-param>   </context-param>



</web-app>
```

Marking an application distributable does not guarantee that the application will be split between multiple systems. It indicates only that the application is *capable* of being split between multiple machines.

Distributed Containers

At this point, we've discussed how to write an application that can run on more than one server and how to modify the web.xml file to notify the server of the potential environmental behaviors. Now you're ready to look at the different kinds of container types available to manage distributed applications.

There are four types of container support. It's important to understand the different types in order to know what behaviors to expect. A complex application that performs multiple operations and is likely to receive many concurrent hits might require a more robust server, whereas a simple application that displays sport statistics might require only a simple server. The type of container selected is heavily dependent on the amount of thread-safety you are looking to obtain. Table 4.2 displays the functionality options.

TABLE 4.2 Container Support

	Clustering	Session Migration	Session Failover
Type 1			
Type 2	X		
Type 3	X	X	
Type 4	X	X	X

Each container has its own set of distinctive features, which in turn produces variation in each session. The following list describes the four containers in greater detail:

Type 1   This container does not support clustering and is usually a stand-alone application that ignores all distributed information. The stand-alone Tomcat server falls in this category.

Type 2   Non-session requests are randomly distributed, whereas session-related requests are tied to their originating server. The session is tied to a particular host. Because sessions are not transferred, they can contain data that is nontransferable. The disadvantages of this container are as follows:

Sessions cannot be migrated to an underutilized server.

A crash will also result in a broken session.

Type 3   In addition to the features defined in the type 2 containers, a type 3 enables sessions to be migrated to underutilized servers to improve load balancing. The specification guarantees that the session will migrate only between requests. This feature prevents concurrency issues. Because session migration is a feature, the session's data must be transferable.

Type 4   This container builds on type 3 and adds the capability to duplicate the contents of a session. When an individual component crashes, the user's session is not necessarily destroyed because the data can be saved and transferred.

Generally, `ServletContext` and `HttpSession` are associated with the JVM servicing the session requests. Because distributed containers are not required to propagate either object to another JVM, you cannot rely on this functionality if the container simply states that it is compliant with the 2.3 specification.

The final important note is to understand how listener classes are handled in a distributed environment. Basically, there is one listener class instance per listener class defined in the deployment descriptor per JVM. If a session is transferred to another server, the application in the new environment should contain a separate listener instance to handle session events.

Filters

In photography, a single image can be changed greatly by the filter used to capture the picture. One filter might soften edges, while another might enhance the color contrast by hardening edges. Another might add the date and author signature to the photo. These alterations do not change the fundamental image; instead, they provide subtle enhancements. Generally speaking, a filter is often a thin layer of some sort that provides subtle changes to a particular object. In this example, the object is a picture.

In the Java world, a filter can be applied to one or more servlets/JSPs or application files. Imagine that a client selects an image in JPEG format and sends it to a servlet to modify. If the servlet can handle only TIF files, a filter can be used to handle the conversion before the servlet even accesses the image. Another example of filter use is to compress the response output stream to improve bandwidth utilization. The filter could use the request headers to check whether the client (browser) supports compression, and if so, wrap the response object with a custom writer or output stream object that handles compression. The stream would then eliminate unnecessary bits and transfer content at a faster rate. Filters can be used to encrypt or decrypt data, to log and audit activity, and to trigger events. The options are endless.

Filters are covered in the exam. Currently, the topic is not listed as an exam objective, but you can expect to find a few questions about this subject matter. Consequently, in this section, we will discuss how a filter fits into the servlet life cycle and all the elements necessary to create a functional and effective filter.

The Life Cycle

A *filter* is an object that can transform a request or modify a response. It can preprocess a request before it reaches a servlet and it can postprocess a response after it leaves a servlet. Figure 4.4 displays how the filter intercepts the request and response objects.

FIGURE 4.4 The filter life cycle

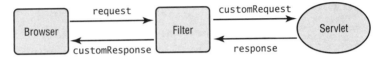

Before a request reaches a servlet, a filter can intercept the request and examine its contents. Besides examining the request, the filter can modify either the request headers or the request data by customizing the request. It does this by wrapping its own request object around the original request. After the filter completes its task, it then forwards the newly customized request to the servlet.

The servlet will then perform its tasks and potentially generate a response. In such a case, the response can be caught by the same or a different filter. After the filter intercepts the response, it can modify the response headers or response data by again wrapping a filter response object around the original response to create a customized object. This customized object is then sent to the client.

When a filter intercepts a response object, it cannot alter the output stream information if the output stream was closed by the servlet. As a result, you are encouraged to have a servlet `flush()` a stream rather than `close()` it.

In simple terms, the process is as follows:

1. A client sends a request.

2. The filter intercepts the client's request.

3. The filter examines and can modify the request headers and request data by using its own custom request to wrap around the intercepted request object.

4. The filter propagates the request to the servlet.

5. The servlet generates a response and flushes it.

6. The filter intercepts the response.

7. The filter can modify the response headers and response data by using its own custom response to wrap around the intercepted response object.

8. Once complete, the filter sends the newly filtered response to the client.

The Filter

Filters are quite easy to create. The difficulty lies in the logic used to manipulate the content. To create a filter, you must follow three simple steps. The filter class must:

1. Implement the appropriate interface

2. Define its methods

3. Be declared within the deployment descriptor

Creating the Filter

All filters must implement the `javax.servlet.Filter` interface. This interface defines three abstract methods that are called during different points of the filter's life cycle. They include:

- `public void init(FilterConfig config)`

- `public void doFilter(ServletRequest req, ServletResponse resp, FilterChain chain)`

- `public void destroy()`

When a filter is activated, the first method that is called is `init(FilterConfig config)`. This method is used to prepare or initialize the filter for service. The method is passed a `javax.servlet.FilterConfig` object, which contains deployment descriptor information and a handle to the application's context. This object can be used to:

- Retrieve the filter name defined within the deployment descriptor

- Retrieve the initialization parameters defined within the deployment descriptor

- Return a reference to the `ServletContext` object associated with the request or response

Most commonly, the logic within the init(...) method consists of saving a local instance of the FilterConfig object for later use. If the filter requires access to parameters before it completes the initialization process, the FilterConfig object can then be used to get the information by using the getInitParameter(*String name*) method.

After the init(...) method completes, the doFilter(*ServletRequest req, ServletResponse resp, FilterChain chain*) method is called. This method represents the body of the filter. It handles any conversions, processing, or alterations that must be done before the request object is accessed by the servlet or after the response object is sent from the servlet. To accomplish its task, the filter can use the ServletRequest object to invoke methods such as setAttribute(...) to change the request characteristics. Header data can also be accessed or changed by casting the request to an HttpServletRequest object (assuming it is passed to an HttpServlet). Similarly, a parallel process can be followed to alter the ServletResponse object.

A filter should be written to accomplish a particular task related to the request or response. It should not be written to accomplish *many* tasks. Instead, if the task is complex it should be broken down, with a single filter written to accomplish each sub-task. These filters can be chained together to complete the complex task.. Chaining filters means one filter calls the next. The process is managed by using the FilterChain handle passed to the Filter object's doFilter(...) method. A FilterChain is an object provided by the servlet container. Its purpose is to invoke the next filter in the chain, or if the calling filter is the last filter in the chain, to invoke the resource (for example, the client or servlet) at the end of the chain. Access to this object enables one filter to be chained to another. The interface has one method: doFilter(*ServletRequest req, ServletResponse resp*). If the filter uses another filter, the current filter can call chain.doFilter(req, resp), passing the current request and response object to the next.

The last method called is destroy(). This method is called by the web container to indicate that the filter will be removed from service. If the filter uses other resources, you might want to deallocate memory to prepare the filter object for garbage collection.

Let's consider the following example. Imagine you have a website that utilizes hundreds of servlets, which contain information that has copyright restrictions. Instead of manually inserting the legal statement at the end of each page, a filter class can be added to take care of this task. Listing 4.2 provides the code necessary to create such a filter.

Listing 4.2: Creating a Filter to Append

```
package data;

import java.io.*;
import javax.servlet.*;
import javax.servlet.http.*;

public class CopyrightFilter implements Filter {

    private FilterConfig config;
    String year;

    public void init(FilterConfig config)
        throws ServletException {
            this.config = config;
            year = config.getInitParameter("date");
    }

    public void doFilter(ServletRequest req,
        ServletResponse resp,FilterChain chain)
        throws IOException, ServletException {
        chain.doFilter(req, resp);
        PrintWriter out = resp.getWriter();
        out.println("<BR>Copyright &copy; " + year +
            " All legal rights are reserved.");
        out.flush();
    }

    public void destroy() {}
}
```

Defining the Deployment Descriptor

After the filter is created, it must be added to the deployment descriptor in order for the container to place the filter into service and to know when to invoke the appropriate filter with the right servlet. The first set of tags that must be included are filter-name and filter-class. The filter-name tag is used to provide a general name for the filter. The name is linked to the actual class name defined within the `filter-class` tags. Another tag, `init-param`, is optional. It is used to pass initialization parameters to the filter. The following code snippet shows the use of these tags:

```
<filter>
    <filter-name>copyrightFilter</filter-name>
    <filter-class>data.CopyrightFilter</filter-class>
    <init-param>
        <param-name>date</param-name>
        <param-value>2002</param-value>
    </init-param>
</filter>
```

The next step required is to map the filter to the appropriate servlets or JSPs. You have two options. The first approach links the filter to a single servlet (assuming you are using this filter on an actual *servlet*) by using the `servlet-name` tag, as shown in the following code sample:

```
<filter-mapping>
    <filter-name>sampleFilter</filter-name>
    <servlet-name>myServlet</servlet-name>
</filter-mapping>
```

The second approach offers more flexibility. It links the filter to a URL pattern. This enables the developer to apply the filter to a group of servlets, JSPs, or any static content. Using the `url-pattern` tag, you can identify the files or types of files to which the filter is to be applied. The following code uses the filter example we discussed to append the copyright statement to all pages that end with `.jsp`:

```
<filter-mapping>
    <filter-name>copyrightFilter</filter-name>
    <url-pattern>/*.jsp</url-pattern>
</filter-mapping>
```

There is an order to which the container processes `filter-mapping` tags. Filters using the `url-pattern` tags are processed first, in the order they appear in the deployment descriptor; then the `servlet-name` tag filters are run—again, in the order they appear in the deployment descriptor.

The `filter` and `filter-mapping` tags must be defined before any servlet tags. Listener tags are defined in this same region.

Summary

This chapter focused on features that are associated with or handled by the container. We began by explaining the purpose of a `ServletContext` object and how it links the application to the container. By using the object's initialization parameters, the application components can acquire configuration information from the container. Another feature of the context is its capability to store attribute values. These values are set in either the container or the servlet code. Attributes enable objects to be bound to the context. We then discussed the two listener interfaces used to receive notifications of changes to the context: the `ServletContextListener`, which is notified when the context is created or destroyed, and the `ServletContextAttributeListener`, which is notified when an attribute is added, removed, or replaced.

The next major topic was `HttpSessions`. Sessions hold transaction data that is captured while a client accesses the application for a period of time. Attributes are used to get and set information into the session object that is stored on the server end. By using session objects, the application can reduce the need to cache long-term data or have clients repeat data transmissions. Four listeners exist for session objects: The `HttpSessionListener` is notified when a session is created or destroyed. Like the context, there exists an `HttpSessionAttributeListener` that is notified when attributes are added, removed, or replaced. The `HttpSessonActivationListener` is used for notification when a session is being moved between systems. It receives an `HttpSessionEvent` when the session is activated or passivated. The final listener is the `HttpSessionBindingListener`, which notifies a specific object when it is being bound to or unbound from the session. It passes an `HttpSessionBindingEvent` that provides methods for access to the session handle, and the name or value for the attribute being bound to or unbound from the session.

Next we discussed the necessary considerations for an application that exists within a distributable environment. We pointed out how some containers offer this flexibility and some do not. If the application can be distributed, a few concepts should be incorporated into the servlet code. The context should avoid maintaining state because a new context is associated with a session if the session is moved to a new system. When a session is moved, only listeners on the system where the session resides will be notified of changes. Attributes or external resources are usually better ways to store object data.

As for the deployment descriptor, all listeners are defined by using the `listener` tag and the `listener-class` tags. The container uses reflection to determine which listener the class actually implements. The order in which the listeners are defined is the order they will be invoked, unless the application is closing. In that case, the session listeners are called first, and then the context.

Exam Essentials

Be able to identify the important characteristics of the ServletContext initialization parameters. Initialization parameters are used to define configuration data that applies to the entire web application. The methods used to access the parameters are available in the ServletContext class. Those methods are as follows:

```
String getInitParameter(String name)
Enumeration getInitParameterNames()
```

Be able to identify the important characteristics of the ServletContext-Listener. The ServletContextListener is notified when a context is created or destroyed. An implementing class must define the following two methods:

```
void contextDestroyed(ServletContextEvent sce)
void contextInitialized(ServletContextEvent sce)
```

When an event occurs, the listener receives a ServletContextEvent object that defines the context. By using the ServletContextEvent, you can get the actual context using the getServletContext method.

Be able to identify the important characteristics of the ServletContext-AttributeListener. A context attribute is used to bind objects to a web application. By using the ServletContext's get and set methods, you can define attributes:

```
Object getAttribute(String name)
void setAttribute(String name, Object value)
```

The ServletContextAttributeListener is notified when a context attribute is added, removed, or replaced. An implementing class must define the following methods:

```
void attributeAdded(ServletContextAttributeEvent scab)
void attributeRemoved(ServletContextAttributeEvent scab)
void attributeReplaced(ServletContextAttributeEvent scab)
```

Be able to identify the important characteristics of the Session-AttributeListener. The SessionAttributeListener is notified when a session attribute is added, removed, or replaced. An implementing class must define the following methods:

```
void attributeAdded(HttpSessionBindingEvent se)
void attributeRemoved(HttpSessionBindingEvent se)
void attributeReplaced(HttpSessionBindingEvent se)
```

Be able to identify the WebApp deployment descriptor element names that declare the ServletContext initialization parameters. ServletContext initialization parameters are defined either directly in the container or in the web.xml file by using the following tags:

```
<context-param>
    <param-name></param-name>
    <param-value></param-value>
</context-param>
```

The context parameter is defined before the servlets in the web.xml file.

Be able to identify the WebApp deployment descriptor element names that declare the ServletContextListener, ServletContextAttribute-Listener, and HttpSessionAttributeListener. All event listeners use the same deployment descriptor tags. They are as follows:

```
<listener>
    <listener-class>com.MyServletContextHandler
        </listener-class>
</listener>
<listener>
    <listener-class>com.MyServletContextAttributeHandler
        </listener-class>
</listener>
```

Distinguish the behavior of servlet context initialization parameters in a distributable environment. In a distributable environment, the servlet context should avoid maintaining state. Instead, data should be stored and accessed through an external resource such as a database. Because the parameters are defined in the container or the web.xml file, you cannot be guaranteed that each system will be configured exactly the same.

Distinguish the behavior of the **ServletContextListener**, the **Servlet-ContextAttributeListener**, and the **SessionAttributeListener** in a distributable environment.   An event listener instance is mapped directly to the listener defined within the deployment descriptor in a particular JVM. In a distributable environment, the listener must exist on the server system to ensure attribute and context integrity. A JVM on one system cannot notify a listener on another system. Consequently, the listener must be located on the target server in order to receive context or session events.

Key Terms

Before you take the exam, be certain you are familiar with the following terms:

clustering	listener
context object	scope
distributable	session
event	synchronization
filter	

Review Questions

1. Which of the following is false regarding `ServletContextListeners`? (Choose all that apply.)

    A. They are notified when a servlet context is initialized.

    B. They are notified when a servlet context is loaded.

    C. They are notified when a servlet context is destroyed.

    D. They are notified when a context attribute is added.

2. Which of the following statements is false?

    A. The `FilterChain` object is used to call the next filter or servlet.

    B. Filters can alter the attributes of the `ServletContext` for the servlet it is filtering.

    C. A filter can perform behavior before and after a servlet is invoked.

    D. A `Filter` object can be applied only to servlets and JSPs.

3. Which of the following deployment descriptor tags is used for listing context initialization parameters?

    A. param-name

    B. context-param

    C. context-name

    D. context-attribute

    E. None of the above

4. Which of the following methods returns an enumeration of all initialization parameters and their values?

    A. getInitParameterNames()

    B. getInitParameterValues()

    C. getInitParameters()

    D. None of the above

5. Which of the following interfaces is called when a context is destroyed?

A. ServletContextDestroyedListener

B. HttpServletContextListener

C. ServletContextListener

D. HttpSessionActivationListener

6. Which of the following methods is called when a context is initialized?

A. contextInitialized(ServletContextEvent e)

B. contextInitial(ServletContext e)

C. contextInitialize(ServletContext e)

D. contextInitialize(ServletContextEvent e)

7. Which of the following statements is false?

A. The contextInitalized(...) method is called when a web application's context is created.

B. The contextInitialized(...) method does not need to complete for servlet requests to be processed.

C. The contextInitialized(...) method is used to initialize data shared by all servlets in the application.

D. You can have more than one ServletContextListener object per application.

8. A session can be created under which of the following circumstances?

A. When the container starts

B. When a request is first sent to a servlet

C. When a response is sent back to a client

D. When a client accesses the index.html file of a website

9. Which of the following listeners is invoked when a session is created?

   A. HttpSessionAttributeListener

   B. HttpSessionBindingListener

   C. HttpListener

   D. HttpSessionListener

10. Which of the following events enables you to retrieve the name and value of an attribute?

    A. HttpSessionEvent

    B. HttpEvent

    C. HttpAttributeEvent

    D. HttpSessionAttributeEvent

    E. HttpSessionBindingEvent

11. Which of the following listeners is called after a session is passivated?

    A. HttpSessionListener

    B. HttpSessionActivationListener

    C. HttpSessionPassivateListener

    D. None of the above

12. Which of the following statements is true?

    A. The listener tag is used to define all context and session listeners.

    B. The listener interface name must be defined within the deployment descriptor.

    C. The HttpSessionActivationListener must be defined within the originating server only.

    D. The listener-name tag is used to define the name of the listener class.

13. How are listeners registered to the server?

    A. The servlet must call the server's add*XXX*Listener and pass a reference to the listener.

    B. The interface-name tag is used to list the associated interface in the deployment descriptor.

    C. The server uses reflection to determine which listener interface is associated with which class.

    D. None of the above.

14. Which of the following interfaces is notified when a session times out?

    A. HttpSessionListener

    B. HttpSessionAttributeListener

    C. HttpSessionBindingListener

    D. HttpSessionActivationListener

15. Which of the following statements is false?

    A. There is one listener instance per listener class defined in the deployment descriptor.

    B. Containers are required to propagate the servlet context and session events to other JVMs.

    C. In a distributed environment, the ServletContext objects should avoid maintaining state.

    D. Attribute listeners for the context and session objects can be invoked concurrently.

Answers to Review Questions

1. B, D.   A ServletContextListener is notified under two conditions: when the context is initialized and destroyed. The ServletContext-AttributeListener handles attribute notification. Finally, a context is not loaded; it is created.

2. D.   When declaring a filter in the deployment descriptor, you must identify which resources the container must associate with the filter. The url-pattern has no limitations, and in fact, the filter can be called before any static file. In such cases, you can add content but can't remove or change existing content because you do not have access to that information.

3. B.   The <context-name></context-name> tags are used to define the name of a context initialization parameter. The <context-value></context-value> tags are used to define the value of a context initialization parameter. Finally, the <context-param></context-param> tags are used to list a context initialization parameter.

4. D.   The only option that is a valid and existing method is getInit-ParameterNames(). Unfortunately, this method does not return parameter names and values; instead, it returns a listing of all the names. This enables the servlet to then filter through each name to get the desired value.

5. C.   The contextDestroyed(ServletContextEvent e) method of the ServletContextListener interface is invoked when a context is about to be destroyed. The method allows resource cleanup before the context is removed from memory.

6. A.   A ServletContextEvent object is passed to the context-Initalized(...) method when the context is first created.

7. B.   When the context for a web application is created, the context-Initialized(...) method is, in fact, invoked. The method *must* complete before any servlet requests can be processed, because the data is shared by all servlets. Finally, there is no limitation on the number of listener objects you can have. The server will simply invoke all listeners that apply.

8. B.   A session is associated with a particular user. Consequently, a session cannot be created without a client. When a request is sent, the servlet can use the `getSession(boolean)` method to either access the current session or create a new one.

9. D.   An `HttpSessionListener` defines two methods: `session-Created(…)` and `sessionDestroyed(…)`. The `sessionCreated(…)` method is invoked when a client session is created.

10. E.   An `HttpSessionEvent` gives you access only to the session. To gain access to the name and value associated with an attribute, use the `HttpSessionBindingEvent` object. The other classes listed do not exist.

11. D.   The `HttpSessionActivationListener` is called before a session is passivated. There isn't much that can be done after the session is disabled, so no listener is notified in that circumstance.

12. A.   All listeners are defined by using the listener tag in the deployment descriptor. The server uses reflection to determine which listener to apply the class toward. As for `HttpSessionActionListeners`, the implementing class must be defined in all servers that have access to the server. The listener class is defined with the tag `listener-class`, not `listener-name`.

13. C.   The server interrogates the class defined within the listener tag and uses reflection to determine the listener interface that the class utilizes. The server, not the servlet, handles the association between the listener and server.

14. C.   When a session is invalidated through a timeout, the `HttpSession-BindingListener` for that object is notified to identify the object is being removed or unbound from the session.

15. B.   Compliant containers are not required to handle distributable applications. Consequently, it is not mandatory that containers forward context or session events to other JVMs.

Chapter

5

Handling Exceptions

THE FOLLOWING SUN CERTIFIED WEB COMPONENT DEVELOPER FOR J2EE PLATFORM EXAM OBJECTIVES ARE COVERED IN THIS CHAPTER:

✓ **4.1 For each of the following cases, identify correctly constructed code for handling business logic exceptions, and match that code with correct statements about the code's behavior:**

- Return an HTTP error using the `sendError` response method
- Return an HTTP error using the `setStatus` method

✓ **4.2 Given a set of business logic exceptions, identify the following:**

- The configuration that the deployment descriptor uses to handle each exception
- How to use a `RequestDispatcher` to forward the request to an error page
- Specify the handling declaratively in the deployment descriptor

✓ **4.3 Identify the method used for the following:**

- Write a message to the WebApp log
- Write a message and an exception to the WebApp log

In an ideal world, all applications could run without encountering problems. In reality, however, applications have little control over user input or environmental effects. Consequently, all programs, especially those that are networked, can falter. With this in mind, developers must take a proactive approach toward error handling when developing code. The code must anticipate potential problems, notify the client, log the issue, limit damage, and offer recovery alternatives. In this chapter, we will discuss the various ways to handle common application errors. They include:

- How to notify the client of errors or status changes

- How to use and create error pages

- How to log messages

- How to define servlet exceptions

Problem Notification

No matter how well an application is written, problems will always occur. Outside factors are constantly changing and can cause connections to be broken, files to be moved, or invalid user data to be entered. Under such circumstances, *exceptions* provide a way to resolve, log, and communicate the problem.

When a problem occurs within a servlet, the developer must decide how the application should proceed. Should it return an error and continue? Or should it return an error page and stop the execution of the application? If an error page is returned, who will develop it–the server or the application?

How will the application locate a custom error page? These are the questions a developer must answer and consider when writing efficient servlets.

In this section, we will cover the methods and procedures necessary to set error codes and return error pages. But before we discuss the more advanced methods of error handling, let's look at the basic approach. Imagine a site that requires the user to select an item from a list. Each element in the list represents a separate file that exists elsewhere. If that file cannot be located, we might have a problem. Listing 5.1 provides HTML code for a form containing such a list. The image that follows is the HTML output generated from the code.

Listing 5.1: index.html

```
<HTML>
  <BODY>
    <FORM ACTION='servlet/InventoryServlet' METHOD='GET'>
      <P>Select the desired inventory list:</P>
        <SELECT NAME='inventoryList'>
        <OPTION VALUE='/inventory/Shampoos.html'>
            Shampoo List
        <OPTION VALUE='/inventory/Conditioners.html'>
            Conditioner List
        <OPTION VALUE='/inventory/Products.html'>
            Products List
        </SELECT>
        <P><INPUT TYPE='submit' value='GO!'
                        name='button'>
      </P>
    </FORM>
  </BODY>
</HTML>
```

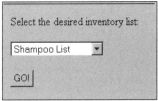

After the user selects an item, the form triggers a request to the InventoryServlet and attempts to retrieve the file associated to the selected item. Listing 5.2 displays the servlet's code.

Listing 5.2: InventoryServlet.java

```java
import java.io.*;
import javax.servlet.*;
import javax.servlet.http.*;

public class InventoryServlet extends HttpServlet {
  protected void doGet(HttpServletRequest req,
                       HttpServletResponse res)
    throws ServletException, IOException {

    res.setContentType("text/html");
    PrintWriter out = res.getWriter();
    String filePath = req.getParameter("inventoryList");
    String theFile="";
    try {
        theFile=getFile(filePath);
    } catch(FileNotFoundException e) {
        out.println("File not found");
    }
    out.println("<HTML><BODY>");
    out.println("<P> The File content is: " +
        theFile +  "</P>");
    out.println("</BODY></HTML>");
  }
  public String getFile(String path)
    throws FileNotFoundException {
    String theFile="";
    try {
        InputStream is =
         getServletContext().getResourceAsStream(path);
        BufferedReader br =
         new BufferedReader(new InputStreamReader(is));
```

```
          String temp = br.readLine();
          while (temp != null) {
             theFile += temp + '/n';
             temp = br.readLine();
          }
          while (br != null) {
                theFile += br.readLine() + '\n';
          }
     } catch (Exception e) {
          throw new FileNotFoundException();
     }
     return theFile;
   }
}
```

If the file cannot be found, a FileNotFoundException is caught, whereby you write a String message to the output stream writer explaining what went wrong. In this simple example, the page continues to execute, and the error message merely appears before the response content. The following image displays the resulting output.

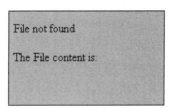

Notice that the message is incorporated with the output stream data. Although the page serves its purpose of informing the client, it isn't the most aesthetic or flexible approach.

sendError

Instead of simply sending debugging messages to the browser to display, it might be more appropriate to return an error page. Web servers are able to generate default error pages if and when a particular error is sent. In this section, we will discuss how to send an error and content to the web server for an automatic error page response.

The HttpServletResponse class provides a *sendError(...)* method that gives the developer an opportunity to set an error status code for the response header and enables the servlet to replace the response body with a server-specific page explaining the error. The method signature is as follows:

```
public void sendError(int sc)
public void sendError(int sc, String msg)
```

The first parameter is an integer value defining the error code for the type of problem that occurred. The second parameter is a String object used to provide a custom message to the server-generated error page. The message parameter is ignored if a custom error page is provided for the passed-in status code. We will discuss that in more detail in the "Error Pages" section.

Back to our example: instead of writing to the output stream when an error occurs, you can now set the sendError(...) status and message to the response object, as shown here:

```
...
try {
    theFile=getFile(filePath);
} catch(FileNotFoundException e) {
    res.sendError(res.SC_NOT_FOUND,
        "The name of the file that could not be found is: "
        + filePath);
}
...
```

The provided error page is server dependent, but usually includes the error code and an explanation. Depending on the error, the message entered in the sendError(...) method might or might not be included in the automatically generated page. The image might look similar to the following graphic.

Not Found (404)

Original request: /application/servlet/Search

Not found request: /application/servlet/Search

If the error code is changed to 410 or SC_GONE, the following output appears. Notice how this page includes the sendError(...) message.

Error: 410

Location: /application/servlet/Search

The name of the file that could not be found is: /inventory/Shampoos.html

Remember, the server has the choice to include or exclude the message. For some errors it might include the message, and for others it might not. When using the sendError(...) method, three things should happen:

- An error response is sent to the client by using the specified status code.

- The servlet's response body is replaced with an HTML-formatted server error page containing the specified message.

- The content type is set to text/html, leaving cookies and other headers unmodified.

A response is committed after it is sent to the client. When the sendError(...) method is used, the response is considered committed and should no longer be written to. If the response is already committed and sendError(...) is called, an IllegalStateException should be thrown. Unfortunately, not all vendors or versions follow this standard. For example, iPlanet 4.x breaks this rule; however, it is supported by iPlanet 6.x.

If a condition occurs that is not a problem, but just a status notification, you can use the setStatus(*int statusCode*) method to modify the response header. This topic is covered next.

setStatus

The HttpServletResponse class provides a setStatus(...) method that gives the developer an opportunity to set a status code in the response object. This value can be used to notify the client when there is no error for the response header, whether or not an error occurred while processing the request. The method signature is as follows:

```
public void setStatus(int statusCode)
```

This method sets the status by using a specified number or constant SC_*XXX* value defined in the HttpServletResponse class. The coding preference, however, is to use the constant value rather than hard-coding a number.

There is a fine difference between the setStatus(*int statusCode*) method and the sendError(*int errorCode*) method: the setStatus(...) method does not generate an automatic error response page, whereas sendError(...) does. In fact, if you use setStatus(...) to define an error, then the servlet is completely responsible for generating the response. The body can be text based, a generated image, or anything else appropriate. If an error page is not configured, a server-dependent Page Not Found message will appear. Later we will discuss how to create custom error pages.

Stylistically, setStatus(...) should be used for non-errors, such as SC_OK or SC_MOVED_TEMPORARILY, whereas sendError(...) should be used for errors that are a part of the 400 and 500 series. A *non-error* is a flag that does not indicate a critical problem.

When setStatus(...) is called to define a non-error, the status code is set and the servlet code continues to process. When setStatus(...) is called to define an error, the status code is set and an error page is sought in response. If one is not found, a server-dependent Page Not Found message will appear.

Here is some sample code that shows how the setStatus(...) method should be used:

```
...
try {
    theFile=getFile(filePath);
    res.setStatus(res.SC_OK);
} catch(FileNotFoundException e) {
    res.sendError(res.SC_NOT_FOUND);
}
```

If all goes well, the status is set to SC_OK; if not, a server-generated error page is created and sent to the client.

The setStatus(...) method is also useful when you have a servlet that takes a long time to process. If written correctly, the servlet can be designed to provide the client with intermittent updates on the state of the activity. If, for example, a reload is required, a message notifying the client could be sent.

A call to the setStatus(...) method does not commit the response, but it does cause the container to clear the response buffer (causing any previous response body information to be erased). As a result, this method should be called early in the development of a response. In addition to erasing the response body, the container will also set the `Location` header but preserves cookies and other headers. If the response is already committed, calls to `setStatus(...)` are ignored.

Error Pages

Until now, we have relied on default error pages or raw text sent to the output stream writer as means of conveying problems to the client. There are a few more error page options worth discussing. There are three types of error pages:

- Server-generated pages

- Static custom pages

- Dynamic custom pages

The default behavior of `setStatus(...)` and `sendError(...)` generates an error page formatted by the server. In this section, we will address how static and dynamic custom pages can be created and what their associated benefits are. We will also cover how request dispatching can be used to pass error-handling responsibility to another servlet.

Static Error Page

A *static error page* is usually an HTML-formatted page that contains a response to the occurring problem. Its information explains the problem, but does not change. A status code is associated to the page through the deployment descriptor.

For example, imagine that you created an error page called `404.html`. It could be as simple as the following:

```
<HTML>
    <BODY>
        This is my error page for code: 404
    </BODY>
</HTML>
```

By using the `error-page` tag, you could cause the status code value of 404 to display your page `404.html`.

```
<web-app>
    <error-page>
        <error-code>
            404
        </error-code>
        <location>
            /errors/404.html
        </location>
    </error-page>
</web-app>
```

The `error-code` tag defines the status code for the problem. The `location` tag defines the error file and its path. The value for the `location` tag must begin with a forward slash (/) and it must refer to a resource within the context. The following image shows the custom error-page output.

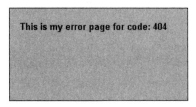

It is important to know that entries in the `web.xml` file will override the default server configuration error pages. If either `sendError(404)` or `setStatus(404)` is called, the file `404.html` located in the `/errors` directory of the context directory will appear. The benefit of static error pages is that they provide standardized error responses for the entire application.

Dynamic Error Page

For a more flexible page response, you can create a *dynamic error page*. Dynamic pages enable the message, the page, or the data to change depending on the set error code. Instead of using HTML pages, a servlet could be written to handle errors. The server provides two servlet attributes to help accomplish this task:

javax.servlet.error.status_code returns an `Integer` object defining the error status code.

javax.servlet.error.message returns a `String` message, usually defined by the second argument passed to the `sendError(...)` method.

A general-purpose error page must be defined within the `location` tag. Here is sample code for `web.xml`:

```
<web-app>
...
    <error-page>
        <error-code>
            404
        </error-code>
        <location>
            /servlet/ErrorServlet
        </location>
    </error-page>
...
</web-app>
```

One dynamic page or servlet could be used for multiple error-codes; however, each error code must be specified in the `web.xml` file. Also, each error code must have its own `<error-page>` `</error-page>` element entry.

Instinctively, you might have thought to reference the `ErrorServlet` by using the following path: `/contextDir/WEB-INF/classes/ErrorServlet`. This, however, will not work because of permissions. Remember, you cannot directly reference files within the `/WEB-INF` directory. For Tomcat, servlet classes can be accessed from the `/servlet` directory.

For iPlanet and JRun, you can configure the servlet so the path `/servlet/ErrorServlet` points to the default directory name `/servlet` under the context root. These servers do not automatically map the `/servlet` directory to the `/WEB-INF/classes` directory.

Listing 5.3 shows a sample servlet that generates a static error page when invoked.

Listing 5.3: Custom Error Servlet

```
import java.io.*;
import javax.servlet.*;
import javax.servlet.http.*;
```

```
public class ErrorServlet extends HttpServlet {
  public void doGet(HttpServletRequest req,
                    HttpServletResponse res)
   throws IOException, ServletException {
    res.setContentType("text/html");
    PrintWriter out = res.getWriter();

    Integer code =(Integer)req.getAttribute
                    ("javax.servlet.error.status_code");
    String msg =(String)req.getAttribute
                    ("javax.servlet.error.message");
    out.println("<HTML>");
    out.println("<BODY>");
    out.println("<H1>" + code + "</H1>");
    out.println("<H2>" + msg + "</H2>");
    out.println("</BODY></HTML>");
  }
}
```

When sendError(...) or setStatus(...) is called for an error, an instance of ErrorServlet will extract the status code and message from the method call. It will then display that information in a custom error page.

Going back to our earlier example in which we attempt to locate the file /inventory/Shampoos.html, let's assume we are unable to do so, and as a result create a message explaining which file could not be found. Using the javax.servlet.error.status_code variable, we determine which error was sent. If a message was passed we use the javax.servlet.error.message variable to determine its value. If we wanted to be robust we would ensure this value was not equal to null before adding it to our page. For learning purposes, this works just fine. Assuming the user calls sendError(...) passing the int res.SC_NOT_FOUND, with the message generated from Listing 5.2, the following servlet-generated page will appear when the Shampoo List option is selected.

404

The name of the file that could not be found is: /inventory/Shampoos.html

Problem accessing /application/servlet/Search

This response page is simple, but shows you how dynamic pages can be generated. You can create a more complex page that monitors error trends to locate weaknesses in the system or application in addition to generating error pages.

A dynamic page uses the `web.xml` file to locate an error servlet associated to a defined `error-code`. If, however, your servlet would like to pass an error to a specific servlet to handle, given a situation rather than an error code type, you would need to use a `RequestDispatcher`. We will discuss this technique next.

Passing the Error

A servlet can handle its own errors or it can pass off the responsibility to another servlet to handle. The *RequestDispatcher* can be used to forward a request to an error page:

```
...
try {
    theFile=getFile(filePath);
} catch(FileNotFoundException e) {
    String display = "/servlet/ErrorServlet";
    RequestDispatcher dispatcher =
        req.getRequestDispatcher(display);
    dispatcher.forward(req, res);
}
...
```

We have shown you how a basic `RequestDispatcher` works in Chapter 2, "The Servlet Model." When used for error handling, however, it is important to know what information the target servlet can access.

When a call to `sendError(...)` is made, the system sets the values for the variables:

`javax.servlet.error.status_code`

`javax.servlet.error.message`

However, this is not the case with errors handled by the `RequestDispatcher`. By forwarding the responsibility to the `RequestDispatcher`, the calling servlet must set the error attributes. Otherwise, the output will result in `null` values, as shown here.

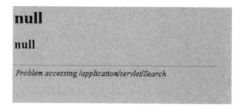

After the code is changed to define the error attribute values, the output will display the expected information, as shown after the following code snippet.

```
...
try {
    theFile=getFile(filePath);
} catch(FileNotFoundException e) {
    req.setAttribute("javax.servlet.error.status_code",
            new Integer(405));
    req.setAttribute("javax.servlet.error.message",
            "Custom message: The file was not found");
    String display = "/servlet/ErrorServlet";
    RequestDispatcher dispatcher =
            req.getRequestDispatcher(display);
    dispatcher.forward(req, res);
}
...
```

405

Custom message: The file was not found

Problem accessing /application/servlet/Search

In summary, errors can be passed off to other servlets by use of the `RequestDispatcher`. Because the `web.xml` file is not used by the processing servlet, the error attributes must be set prior to forwarding the request. Next we will address how to track these errors by logging messages.

Logging Messages

The sendError(...) method is designed to communicate errors or problems to the client. This user-friendly description isn't always beneficial to the developer when the intent is to debug the situation. The GenericServlet class offers two methods that enable the servlet to write its errors to a log file for further inspection:

public void log(*String msg*) writes an error message to the servlet log file.

public void log(*String msg*, *Throwable t*) writes an error message and Throwable object, which contains a stack trace of the exception, to the servlet log file.

The log file provides a way to track the servlet's actions by displaying detailed descriptions of the problems. The following example attempts to locate a file that cannot be found. When the exception is caught, the name of the file and a stack trace are written to the log file for future investigation. A *stack trace* is the computer path taken to arrive at the current problem.

```
...
try {
    theFile=getFile(filePath);
} catch(FileNotFoundException e) {
    log("The following file could not be found: "
            + filePath, e);
    res.sendError(res.SC_NOT_FOUND);
}
...
```

The location and format of the log file is server dependent. The reference implementation, Tomcat, provides a /logs directory that stores a servlet.log file with all the messages logged by the application's servlets. At a minimum, each log usually includes the registered name of the servlet and the associated time stamp for when the error took place.

Reporting Messages

Reporting a stack trace message to the client is a bit more difficult than simply executing a System.out.println(*e.printStackTrace()*) statement.

In fact, that statement won't compile, because the `printStackTrace()` method returns a `void`. To pass an error message to a client, the `sendError(...)` method must be called. But before it can be passed a message, you must capture the trace and write it to a `PrintStream` or `PrintWriter`. The `Throwable` class provides methods that extract the trace; they include:

void printStackTrace() prints a `Throwable` object to a standard output stream.

void printStackTrace(PrintStream p) prints a `Throwable` object to a specified print stream.

void printStackTrace(PrintWriter p) prints a `Throwable` object to a specified print writer.

Using the exception handle within a catch block, you can write the trace to a stream or writer. Its data must then be converted to a `String` (possibly using the `BufferedWriter` class's `write(String s, int off, int len)` method) and passed to the `sendError(...)` method. The information will then be displayed as part of the error page message.

Servlet Exceptions

When a method throws an exception, the developer has two choices: the servlet can either catch the exception or throw it to the server to handle. When a server catches an exception, it has complete freedom to handle the problem in the way it deems appropriate. It could automatically log the exception, it could pass the client a message, it could call `destroy()` on the servlet and reload it, or it could do something else completely different.

The server cannot be expected to catch all exceptions. Specifically, the specification states that those exceptions handled by the server must subclass `IOException`, `ServletException`, or `RuntimeException`.

It is common for the server to handle these types of exceptions, as they can affect the life cycle of the servlet. For example, if a servlet's `service(...)` or do*XXX*(...) method literally throws the `ServletException` due to corruption, the server knows the best way to respond to the problem and notify the client. Generally, the server handles all `RuntimeExceptions` (or any subclass such as `NullPointerException` or `ClassCastException`). Because runtime exceptions indicate problems in logic evident during the interpretation phase, only the server can catch them.

It is not mandatory for a `RuntimeException` to be declared in a method's signature.

Now that we have discussed ways for a servlet to handle exceptions, we will provide a closer look at the type of exception objects the servlet can throw. The first is a `ServletException`, which indicates that a serious problem occurred. The second is an `UnavailableException`, which notifies the client that a servlet is not available. The last is a custom exception page for known exceptions to send to the client. This feature enables developers to provide custom exception pages for exception handling.

ServletException

A `javax.servlet.ServletException` is thrown by a servlet to indicate a general servlet problem has occurred. The `ServletException` class sub-classes the `Exception` class and has four constructors:

`ServletException()` is the default constructor that creates a basic servlet exception used to provide a more descriptive name of the problem.

`ServletException(String message)` constructs a servlet exception with the specified message.

`ServletException(Throwable rootCause)` constructs a servlet exception with a `Throwable` object containing a stack trace of the root problem.

`ServletException(String message, Throwable rootCause)` constructs a servlet exception with a specified message and a `Throwable` object containing a stack trace of the root problem.

When an exception occurs, the developer might want to catch the exception and throw it back to the calling thread with a different name. For example:

```
...
try {
    is.read();
} catch (IOException e) {
    throw new ServletException(e);
}
...
```

The ServletException acts as a wrapper to provide a more relevant exception name to the caller. Now, after the ServletException is caught, the getRootCause() method can be called to return the Throwable object. This method returns the Throwable object that contains a trace identifying the original problem and source. If the exception was created without a Throwable object, null is returned.

UnavailableException

The javax.servlet.UnavailableException is a subclass of the ServletException class. An UnavailableException is thrown to indicate a servlet is either temporarily or permanently unavailable:

Permanently unavailable   The servlet throwing the exception cannot recover from the error until some action is taken. Usually, the servlet is corrupt in some way or not configured properly. Generally, the servlet should log both the error and the actions needed to correct the problem.

Temporarily unavailable   A servlet cannot handle the request for a period of time due to some system-wide problem. For example, there might not be sufficient memory or disk storage to handle requests, or a third-tier server might not be accessible. Some of these problems are self-correcting, and others might require a system administrator to take corrective action.

A servlet that throws an UnavailableException that is permanent is removed from service, and a new servlet instance is created to handle further requests. If a new instance cannot be created, an error will be sent to the client.

When a servlet is unavailable, the server will return a response containing an SC_SERVICE_UNAVAILABLE(503) status code to notify the client of the situation. The response will also include a Retry-After header with an estimated time of unavailability.

If either a temporary or permanent UnavailableException is thrown during the init(...) method, the service(...) method will never be reached. Instead, the server will try to initialize a new instance either immediately or after the defined period of time.

The UnavailableException class has two constructors:

UnavailableException(*String msg*) constructs an exception with a descriptive message indicating the servlet is permanently unavailable.

UnavailableException(*String msg, int seconds*) constructs an exception with a descriptive message indicating the servlet is temporarily unavailable for an estimated amount of time.

When the exception is temporary and an estimated time cannot be provided, the specification encourages developers to provide a negative value for the second argument. Do keep in mind that the time is only an estimate. After the exception is thrown, the component catching the exception can use the following methods to learn more about the problem:

int getUnavailableSeconds() returns the number of seconds the servlet expects to be temporarily unavailable.

boolean isPermanent() returns a boolean indicating whether the servlet is permanently unavailable.

 Real World Scenario

Planning for Error Handling

You are hired to participate in the development of a large web-based banking application. Your role is to ensure that all potential errors are handled in a manner that meets security and customer standards. The company's network is spread through the West Coast and maintains four servers in different locations.

Recently you were notified that each system will be managed by a separate group and is likely to have a different web server running the application. This, of course, means you cannot rely on one server to handle errors because the behavior of each server is likely to differ. This consideration definitely affects how the errors will be handled.

The bank is a franchise, which means the differences between each branch must appear seamless to the customer. When a problem occurs, it must be handled the same way in all branches. The client should see the same message and expect the same results.

Because you cannot rely on the consistent behavior of each server, you decide to develop a single ErrorServlet class that would handle all potential errors. This single ErrorServlet class would display the common message to the client and perform any necessary logging to the log files. This solution would alleviate much of the work required to create individual error pages and would provide more maintainable code while satisfying the client requirements.

Exception Pages

We have established that a server can choose to handle an exception in the fashion it deems appropriate. The developer, however, can control the look and content of the error page used to notify the client of server-handled exceptions. Using the web.xml file and custom error pages, a web application can specify the exception page to display when a specific exception is thrown. Earlier, we showed you how to display error pages for a particular error code. Now we will show you how to display an exception page for a particular exception type.

This sample code from the web.xml file shows how a static or servlet page can be used when a specific exception is thrown:

```
...
<error-page>
    <exception-type>
        javax.servlet.UnavailableException
    </exception-type>
    <location>
        /servlet/DynamicErrorDisplay
    </location>
</error-page>
...
```

When the UnavailableException is thrown, the server will locate the DynamicErrorServlet and display its contents to the client.

The exception-type must include the fully qualifying package name. Otherwise, the exception will be handled in its default manner.

By using error attributes, you can construct a dynamic servlet to handle various exception types. Although the system might provide default values for some of these attributes, the developer can also set their definitions at some point within the application and share them with other servlets depending on the definition scope. Table 5.1 lists the error attributes.

TABLE 5.1   Error Attributes

Attribute	Type	Explanation
`javax.servlet.error.status_code`	`java.lang.Integer`	The status code
`javax.servlet.error.exception_type`	`java.lang.Class`	The exception class
`javax.servlet.error.message`	`java.lang.String`	The error message
`javax.servlet.error.exception`	`java.lang.Throwable`	The exception object
`javax.servlet.error.request_uri`	`java.lang.String`	The URI of the request processed by the servlet where the error occurred
`javax.servlet.error.servlet_name`	`java.lang.String`	The logical name of the servlet

The `javax.servlet.error.exception` is new to the 2.3 specification. By providing the `Throwable` object, the message and type can be extracted, thereby making `javax.servlet.error.message` and `javax.servlet.error.exception` type redundant. The two attributes are still included to ensure backward compatibility.

Listing 5.4 is a simple servlet that demonstrates how the attributes are used to generate a generic error page. This code creates a basic error page with the message associated with the exception and the location of the error.

Listing 5.4: Dynamically Generated Error Page

```
import java.io.*;
import javax.servlet.*;
import javax.servlet.http.*;
```

```
public class DynamicErrorDisplay extends HttpServlet {
  public void doGet(HttpServletRequest req,
                    HttpServletResponse res)
   throws ServletException, IOException {
   res.setContentType("text/html");
   PrintWriter out = res.getWriter();

   String message = null;

   Throwable t =
   (Throwable)req.getAttribute("javax.servlet.exception");

   if (t != null)
       message = t.getMessage();

   out.println("<HTML>");
   out.println("<BODY>");
   out.println("<H1>" + message + "</H1>");
   out.println("<I>Error accessing "
                          + req.getRequestURI() + "</I>");
   out.println("</BODY></HTML>");
  }
}
```

Using the getAttribute(*String name*) method, we extract the most current Throwable reference. We then extract the associated message to incorporate the information in the response page.

Summary

In this chapter, we covered the various ways to handle errors. When a problem occurs, you can catch the exception and handle the error by doing one of the following:

- Printing a message to the client
- Providing a server-generated error page to the client

- Providing a custom-generated page to the client
- Dispatching the request to another servlet to handle the error

Printing a message to the client requires a little work but does not ensure a consistent response to an error. The second approach is the simplest because you rely on the server to handle the error and generate the page. The specification does not mandate how the server should handle errors or exceptions, so once again you have the problem of inconsistency in a distributed environment. The third and fourth options require more work to develop the error and exception pages; however, you are guaranteed consistency among servers.

Finally, this chapter focused on the exceptions thrown by the servlet. The ServletException is thrown when a general servlet problem occurs. The UnavailableException is thrown when a servlet is either temporarily or permanently unavailable.

Exam Essentials

Be able to identify correctly constructed code for handling logic exceptions and their behavior.   When a method "throws" an exception, the calling thread can either try to catch the exception or pass the responsibility to its calling thread. If a thread decides to "pass the buck," it should wrap the exception and log its path so the thread that finally handles the error knows the originating source.

Be able to return an HTTP error by using the sendError response. When using the response object, you can invoke the sendError(...) method by passing the status code and a message. Assuming the output is not committed, this causes the server to generate an error page with the information provided.

Be able to return an HTTP error by using the setStatus method. By using the response object, you can invoke the setStatus(...) method by passing in the status code. This call does not automatically generate an error page; instead you must provide a static or dynamic page in the web.xml file for a response. Generally, this method should be used only for setting the status of non-errors.

Identify the configuration that the deployment descriptor uses to handle each exception. For all error pages, you should use the error-page tags. If the page identifies a code, error-code is used to identify the value. If, however, the page identifies an exception, the tag is exception-type. The location of the file is found by using the location tag. Location values must begin with a forward slash (/) and cannot identify servlets from within the /WEB-INF directory.

Know how to use a RequestDispatcher to forward a request to an error page. The RequestDispatcher can be used to forward handling of the error to another servlet. If this procedure is followed, then attributes must be set prior to the dispatch. The deployment descriptor must provide the mapping necessary to locate the error handling servlet. It is then up to the target servlet to handle the problem.

Identify the method used to write a message and an exception to the WebApp log. The GenericServlet class offers a log(...) method used to pass a custom message, or a custom message and Throwable object, to a server-specific log file.

Key Terms

Before you take the exam, be certain you are familiar with the following terms:

dynamic error page	ServletException
exceptions	stack trace
non-error	static error page
permanently unavailable	temporarily unavailable
RequestDispatcher	unavailableException
sendError	

Review Questions

1. Which of the following calls will cause an error page to be automatically generated by the server? (Choose all that apply.)

   A. `response.setStatus(404);`

   B. `request.setStatus(request.SC_NOT_FOUND)`

   C. `response.sendError(response.SC_NOT_FOUND)`

   D. `response.sendError(404, "Couldn't find file");`

2. Which of the following methods is not a legal way to handle an exception?

   A. `catch (Exception e){`
   ```
           String display = "/servlet/ErrorServlet";
           RequestDispatcher dispatcher =
           req.getRequestDispatcher(display);
           dispatcher.forward(req, res);}
   ```

   B. `catch (Exception e) {`
   ```
           out.println("Problem");
      }
   ```

   C. `catch (Exception e) {}`

   D. `catch (Exception e) {`
   ```
           res.sendError(400, "Problem");
      }
   ```

   E. None of the above

3. Errors can be handled in which of the following approaches? (Choose all that apply.)

   A. `RequestDispatcher`

   B. `sendError(...)` method

   C. `sendStatus(...)` method

   D. `setError(...)` method

4. Which of the following statements is false?

   A. A servlet can write its errors to a log file.

   B. A servlet can write its errors to a client.

   C. A servlet can write its errors to a custom file.

   D. None of the above.

5. Which of the following methods are used to pass an error message to the client?

   A. log(*String msg*)

   B. log(*String msg, Throwable t*)

   C. sendMessage(*String msg*)

   D. sendError(*int code, String msg*)

   E. sendError(*String msg, Throwable t*)

6. In which of the following classes or interfaces will you find the log method for a servlet?

   A. Servlet

   B. GenericServlet

   C. ServletResponse

   D. HttpServletResponse

7. Which of the following approaches enables a servlet to pass the error to another servlet to handle?

   A. log

   B. sendError

   C. RequestDispatcher

   D. setStatus

8. Given the following servlet: /*context*/WEB-INF/classes/Servlet-Error.class, which of the following paths best provides access to the servlet from the location tag in the deployment descriptor?

A. /*context*/WEB-INF/classes/ServletError.class

B. /*context*/WEB-INF/classes/ServletError

C. servlets/ServletError

D. /servlet/ServletError.class

E. None of the above

9. Which of the following is not a legal error attribute?

A. javax.servlet.error.status_code

B. javax.servlet.error.exception_type

C. javax.servlet.error.exception

D. javax.servlet.error.uri

10. Which of the following exceptions is thrown when a servlet cannot be accessed temporarily?

A. ServletException

B. UnavailableException

C. UnaccessibleException

D. FailureException

11. Which of the following methods is used to return the Throwable object of a ServletException?

A. getThrowable()

B. getRoot()

C. getRootCause()

D. getThrowableObject()

E. getSource()

12. Which of the following methods are used to pass an error to another servlet to handle by using the `RequestDispatcher`? (Choose all that apply.)

    A. `process(ServletRequest req, ServletResponse res)`

    B. `include(ServletRequest req, ServletResponse res)`

    C. `forward(ServletRequest req, ServletResponse res)`

    D. `processError(ServletRequest req, ServletResponse res)`

13. Which of the following statements is false?

    A. The seconds defined within an `UnavailableException` represent an estimated value.

    B. A server can handle an unavailable request by returning a SC_ SERVICE_UNAVAILABLE status code.

    C. A server can handle an unavailable request by returning a header `Retry` with the end time of unavailability.

    D. None of the above.

14. Which of the following are most likely legal `location` values given a servlet called `TestServlet` and an HTML file called `Test.html`? (Choose all that apply.)

    A. `Test.html`

    B. `/Test.html`

    C. `/context/WEB-INF/classes/TestServlet`

    D. `/servlet/TestServlet`

15. Which of the following is not a legal error attribute?

    A. `javax.servlet.error.status`

    B. `javax.servlet.error.exception_type`

    C. `javax.servlet.error.message`

    D. `javax.servlet.error.servlet_name`

Answers to Review Questions

1. C, D.   When `sendError(...)` is called, the server will generate an automatic error page for the specified status code. You can pass in either the status code integer value only or the code plus a message.

2. E.   You can catch an exception by forwarding the request to a `Request-Dispatcher`, by printing a message to the response `OutputStream`, by ignoring the exception, or by having the server generate an error page.

3. A, B.   An error can be forwarded to another servlet through the `RequestDispatcher` to handle a problem. The `sendError(...)` method is also useful in that it has the server generate an error page. The other methods are not legal methods.

4. D.   The first three options are true. By using the `log(...)` method, a servlet can write its errors to the server-specific log file. To write the error to the client, the servlet uses the `sendError(...)` method. If a servlet created its own file, it could then write to that file when problems occur. This process isn't used, but is possible.

5. D.   The log method is used to write errors to the web application's log file. To communicate with the client, the `sendError(...)` method is used. Its first argument is always an `int` to identify the code type; the second argument is a `String` defining the message.

6. B.   The `log(...)` method is used to write errors to the web application, not back to the client. Consequently, the response object is not used. The `Servlet` interface includes only life-cycle and access methods. This leaves the `GenericServlet` class as the answer.

7. C.   The `RequestDispatcher` enables a servlet to pass the responsibility of handling an error to another servlet. When an error is passed, the attributes for the request are not set.

8. E.   Files located within the `/WEB-INF` directory cannot be accessed directly. In addition, files defined within the `location` tag must begin with a forward slash (`/`). The fourth option fails as well because you do not include the `.class` extension.

9. D.   The last attribute is actually `javax.servlet.error.request_uri`. It is used to return the URI of the request processed by the servlet where the error occurred.

10. B. When a servlet is either temporarily or permanently unavailable, the UnavailableException is thrown.

11. C. The getRootCause() method returns the Throwable object of the exception. It returns null if one is not included.

12. B, C. The forward(...) method is used to have another servlet handle the response, while the include(...) method allows another calling servlet to modify the response object before and after the call. The target servlet can pass the responsibility back to the calling servlet to commit the response.

13. C. The server usually sends back a header called Retry-After. There is no header called Retry.

14. B, D. All location values must start with a forward slash. In addition, you cannot access a servlet directly from its /WEB-INF directory. Instead, you can access the servlet from the server-specific directory structure.

15. A. The attribute for the status code is actually javax.servlet.error.status_code.

Session Management

THE FOLLOWING SUN CERTIFIED WEB COMPONENT DEVELOPER FOR J2EE PLATFORM EXAM OBJECTIVES ARE COVERED IN THIS CHAPTER:

✓ **5.1 Identify the interface and methods for each of the following:**

- Retrieve a session object across multiple requests to the same or different servlets within the same WebApp
- Store objects into a session object
- Retrieve objects from a session object
- Respond to the event when a particular object is added to a session
- Respond to the event when a session is created and destroyed
- Expunge a session object

✓ **5.2 Given a scenario, state whether a session object will be invalidated.**

✓ **5.3 Given that URL rewriting must be used for session management, identify the design requirements on session-related HTML pages.**

Imagine having a conversation with a person who was unable to remember what you just said. At first, you might find this interesting; however, soon your amusement would turn to irritation as they continually asked you to repeat yourself. This is the scenario servlets would encounter if their data could not be temporarily cached during a conversation with a web application. When a client accesses a web application, they often supply information that will be used by the application at a later period during the conversation. If this information could not be retained, the application would need to ask for the information again. This is both time-consuming and inefficient. A servlet's session object is used to resolve this issue. Sessions provide various ways to monitor and maintain client data. In this chapter, we will address how to:

- Track a client's session

- Change a session's data

- Respond to the creation or destruction of a session object and its attributes

- Invalidate a session

Knowledge of how the session works will help you manage a session object more efficiently. We will begin by discussing the various ways to track a session.

Tracking Sessions

When a client interacts with a server application, that client is likely to make multiple requests to achieve a particular goal. Because the HTTP protocol is stateless, it closes its connection after each request. Consequently, client data stored within a request is available for only a short period of time.

For a client object with a longer lifespan, a session is used. A *session object* is usually created when a client makes its first request to an application. It is unique to a client and can exist longer than a single request or even longer than the life of a client. It is an object used to track client-specific data for the duration of the conversation or a specified period of time. What distinguishes one session from another is its unique ID. In fact, the container uses this ID to map an incoming request to the correct session object, which in turn is associated to a particular client. The actual client information can be transferred by using one of three session processes:

- Using hidden form fields

- Rewriting the URL

- Using cookies

Our focus in this section will be to discuss the many ways to maintain a session object. We will begin by addressing how to transfer a session ID by using a form attribute type called `hidden`.

Using Hidden Form Fields

Transferring information between an HTML form and a servlet can be done in several ways. The most basic procedure is to transfer information back and forth as data values. A form can contain fields with client-cached values passed between each request. Because this information does not need to be visible to the client, it is marked by using a field type of `hidden`.

Imagine the following web application scenario:

1. A login screen is displayed.

2. The user enters their login name and password.

3. The servlet verifies the information and returns a web page for the client to utilize the company's services.

4. The new page stores the client's login name from the previous servlet. This information is not visible to the client, but is needed for checkout purposes.

By using *hidden HTML values*, you can store client data between servlets to use at a later date. The following HTML code produces the login screen used for this scenario:

```
<FORM ACTION='servlet/CarServlet' METHOD='POST'>
  <P>Enter your: </P>
```

```
<P>Login <INPUT TYPE='text' SIZE='18' NAME='login'></P>
<P>Password <INPUT TYPE='password' SIZE='15'
                    NAME='pwd'></P>

<P><INPUT TYPE='submit' VALUE='GO!' NAME='button'> </P>
</FORM>
```

After the user enters their login name and password, they trigger the request by clicking the submit button. The servlet then verifies the information and constructs a response containing the client's information. The following code shows this process. (Pay particularly close attention to the bold text. It highlights how hidden values are transferred.)

```
public class CarServlet extends HttpServlet {
  public void doPost(HttpServletRequest req,
                     HttpServletResponse res)
    throws ServletException, IOException {
    String login = req.getParameter("login");
    String pwd = req.getParameter("pwd");
      ...
    //verify login and password with database
    //Use database to get customer information like
    //their firstName, lastName, address

    Customer cust = db.getCustomer(login);
    String firstName=cust.getFirstName();
    String lastName=cust.getLastName();
    String address=cust.getAddress();

    res.setContentType("text/html");
    PrintWriter out = res.getWriter();
    ...
    //generate HTML form containing car characteristics
    ...
    out.println("<FORM ACTION=
            'CheckOutServlet' METHOD='POST'>");
```

```
        out.println("<INPUT TYPE='hidden' NAME='loginName'
                VALUE='"+ login + "'>");
        out.println("<INPUT TYPE='hidden' NAME='firstName'
                VALUE='" + firstName + "'>");
        out.println("<INPUT TYPE='hidden' NAME='lastName'
                VALUE='" + lastName + "'>");
        out.println("<INPUT TYPE='hidden' NAME='address'
                VALUE='" + address + "'>");
        ...
        out.println("<INPUT TYPE='submit' VALUE='CheckOut'>");
    }
}
```

The CarServlet creates an HTML form response containing four hidden
values. Each value is assigned a specific piece of client information. By press-
ing the submit button, the user triggers a request to check out. This request
is sent to the CheckOutServlet, which retrieves hidden values by using the
ServletRequest method getParameter(*String name*).

```
    public class CheckOutServlet extends HttpServlet {
        public void doPost(HttpServletRequest req,
                            HttpServletResponse res)
            throws ServletException, IOException {

            String loginName = req.getParameter("loginName");
            String address = req.getParameter("address");
            res.setContentType("text/html");
            PrintWriter out = res.getWriter();
            out.println("<HTML><BODY>");
            out.println("<P> Thanks for your order " +
                            loginName + "</P>");
            out.println("<P> Your invoice will be mailed to:
                    </P>");
            out.println("<P><I>" + address + "</I><P>");
        }
    }
```

Figure 6.1 shows the hidden value output.

FIGURE 6.1 Hidden value output

Hidden values provide a way to transfer data to the server in a manner that prevents the client from modifying the information directly. Typically, the client does not even know the data is being sent back and forth. The disadvantages to this approach are as follows:

- Tracking each hidden value in each servlet can become tedious. Unfortunately, as the session persists and information increases, passing hidden data back and forth can become taxing.

- The session can persist only through dynamically generated pages. If there is a need to display static, e-mail, or bookmarked documents, the session will be lost.

- Hidden value transfers are the least secure method of maintaining information between pages. Because HTTP transfers all data as clear text, it can be intercepted, extracted, and manipulated. If someone were watching the transmission between client and server, they could easily read information such as the login ID and password.

Although there are many disadvantages, it is a simple approach that can be used when you are communicating a small amount of noncritical information.

Rewriting the URL

Anonymous session tracking can also be done by using a technique called URL rewriting. This approach to session tracking is used when clients do not accept cookies (we'll talk about cookies in the next section). *URL rewriting* is a methodology that associates a session ID to all URL addresses used throughout the session. Using the ID, a developer can map client-related data to the session object for that client. The ID is temporarily stored until the session has ended. After the session has ended, the ID and related data are discarded. Keep in mind that it is important for the session ID to have a standard name that all containers can recognize. The specification defines that name as `jsessionid`. A standardized name enables the container to associate requests to their session objects stored on the server.

"Rewriting" the URL to contain the session ID enables any related servlet to extract previously tracked data. There are two methodologies used to rewrite a URL. One approach is to manually adjust the URL to include the session ID, and the second approach is to use provided API methods to encode the URL. We will cover both techniques in detail.

Manual URL Rewriting

Manually rewriting a URL can be done by physically adding the ID to the constructed URL. How the ID is stored and accessed from within the URL can vary. Table 6.1 lists several ways to rewrite the URL.

TABLE 6.1   URL-Rewriting Approaches

URL	State
`http://localhost:8080/servlet/` `MyServlet`	Original
`http://localhost:8080/servlet/` `MyServlet/567`	Extra path information
`http://localhost:8080/servlet/` `MyServlet?jsessionid=567`	Add parameter
`http://localhost:8080/servlet/` `MyServlet;jsessionid=567`	Custom change

The first example in Table 6.1 shows the original path. The second approach adds the session ID to the path directly. This approach works on all servers, but isn't very effective when other information must also be added to the path of the URL. The third approach adds the ID as a parameter. To avoid naming collisions and guarantee automatic mapping, the session ID must be called `jsessionid`. The last approach uses a custom, server-specific change that works for servers that support this technique. However, even custom approaches are required to name the parameter jsessionid.

In this section, we will show you how to rewrite the URL by adding a session ID to the URL path. But first, let's talk about how the ID is generated. The goal is to derive a value that is completely random and not shared. The Remote Method Invocation (RMI) API provides several methods that help develop such a method. The common procedure is to create a method that does the following:

```
public static String generateSessionID(){
    String uid = new java.rmi.server.UID().toString();
    return java.net.URLEncoder.encode(uid);
}
```

The UID class is used to create a unique identifier on the host system generating this value. For further complexity, the value is converted into MIME-type format by using the URLEncoder's encode(*String uid*) method. Fundamentally, the goal is achieved; when called, this method generates a unique ID that can be used by a session on the existing system.

Now you're ready to learn how to "rewrite" the URL to contain the session ID. We'll begin by revisiting the URL structure:

```
Request URL = contextPath + servletPath + pathInfo +
query string
```

Given a request URL of /games/Chess, you can break the pieces into their defined categories:

Context path: /games

Servlet path: /Chess

Path info: /null

Query string: /null

If you had a session ID with the value 567, that ID could be incorporated into the URL by adding it to the path info section, as follows:

```
/games/Chess/567
```

Literally, this can be done by concatenating the session ID to the ACTION value's URL. For example:

```
out.println("<FORM ACTION='/games/Bingo/"
        + sessionID + "' METHOD='POST'>");
out.println("<INPUT TYPE='submit' VALUE='Bingo'>");
```

Let's say the current servlet that is running is called /games/Overview. On the page, there is a button with the text "Bingo." When the button is pressed, the current URL is switched to /games/Bingo/567. This new servlet page provides the session ID within the URL, which enables the developer to extract any data stored from previously accessed servlets. To access the session ID, use the HttpServletRequest method getPathInfo(). This method returns extraneous information between the servlet and the query string. The new servlet can then use utility classes to retrieve data associated with the session ID. Generally, you would expect to have a utility class for writing data and its associated session ID to a location. The class should also provide functionality to retrieve the client data based on a unique session ID. You might expect the class to contain methods similar to those listed here:

```
Import java.sql.*;
public class SessionIDUtility {
    public static String generateSessionID(){
        String uid = new java.rmi.server.UID().toString();
        return java.net.URLEncoder.encode(uid);
    }
    public static void writeSessionValue(Connection con,
            String sessionID, String name, String value) {
        // write record to database for the provided
        // sessionID
    }
    public static String[] getSessionValues(
            Connection con, String sessionID) {
        //returns the values associated to the provided
        //sessionID
    }
    public static Object getSessionValue(
            Connection con, String sessionID, String name) {
        // returns the Object associated to the name
        // for a particular session ID
    }
}
```

Given these methods, a servlet could save current data and retrieve it from any other servlet accessed during the session. Figure 6.2 shows a simple application that begins by asking the user for their name. A session ID is generated to store the name for other servlets in the application to access. When the user selects a game of choice, the new servlet accesses the session information by retrieving the ID and then getting the user's name. The application should appear as shown in Figure 6.2.

FIGURE 6.2 Sample URL-rewriting application

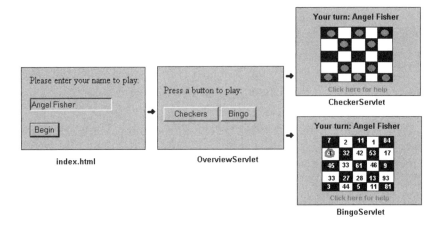

The first image is a simple HTML page that asks the user for their name. When the Begin button is pressed, the /games/OverviewServlet is accessed and displays two game options. Before we go into the functionality details, take a look at the source code for these files. Listing 6.1 displays the HTML code necessary to launch the initial program.

Listing 6.1: index.html

```
<HTML>
    <HEAD><TITLE>Welcome to the Game Center</TITLE></HEAD>
    <BODY>
        <FORM ACTION='servlet/OverviewServlet'
            METHOD='POST'>
        <P>Please enter your name to play: </P>
        <P><INPUT TYPE='text' SIZE='20'
                            NAME='name'></P>
        <P><INPUT TYPE='submit' VALUE='Begin'
                            NAME='button'></P>
```

```
        </FORM>
      </BODY>
    </HTML>
```

The file `index.html` simply provides a form for the user to submit their name. When a request is triggered, the `OverviewServlet` is invoked. The code for this class is shown in Listing 6.2.

Listing 6.2: OverviewServlet.java

```java
import javax.servlet.*;
import javax.servlet.http.*;
import java.io.*;
import java.util.*;
import java.sql.*;

public class OverviewServlet extends HttpServlet {

    public void doPost(HttpServletRequest req,
                        HttpServletResponse res)
      throws ServletException, IOException {
      String name = req.getParameter("name");
      String sessionID =
        SessionIDUtility.generateSessionID();
      Connection con = (Connection)
        getServletContext().getAttribute("Connection");
      SessionIDUtility.writeSessionValue(con,
        sessionID, "name", name);

      res.setContentType("text/html");
      PrintWriter out = res.getWriter();
      out.println("<HTML><BODY>");
      out.println("<H1>The Game Center</H1>");
      out.println("<P>Press a button to play:</P>");

      out.println("<FORM ACTION=' CheckersServlet/" +
        sessionID + "' Method='POST'>");
```

```
        out.println("<INPUT TYPE='submit' VALUE=" +
          "'Checkers'></FORM>");
        out.println("<FORM ACTION='/games/BingoServlet/" +
         sessionID + "' Method='POST'>");
        out.println("<INPUT TYPE='submit' VALUE='Bingo'>");
        out.println("</FORM></BODY></HTML>");
   }
  }
```

Listing 6.2 shows how the servlet prepares to rewrite the URL. First, the user's name is acquired, and then a unique session ID is generated for that particular user. A preassigned connection is accessed from the ServletContext and used to write the session ID and name to a local database. Finally, the page is generated with each button linked to a different URL including the session ID. If the user selects Bingo, they will access the BingoServlet. Listing 6.3 displays the code for this class.

Listing 6.3: BingoServlet.java

```java
import javax.servlet.*;
import javax.servlet.http.*;
import java.io.*;
import java.util.*;
import java.sql.*;

public class BingoServlet extends HttpServlet {
   public void doPost(HttpServletRequest req,
                        HttpServletResponse res)
      throws ServletException, IOException {
        String sessionID = req.getPathInfo();
        String userName="";
        if (sessionID == null) {
           // Redirect the user back to the login screen.
           // If a session ID is null, it indicates the
           // user has not logged into the system.
        }

        Connection con = (Connection)
          getServletContext().getAttribute("Connection");
```

```
    userName = (String)SessionIDUtility.getSessionValue(
      con, sessionID, "name");

    res.setContentType("text/html");
    PrintWriter out = res.getWriter();
    out.println("<HTML><BODY>");
    out.println("<H1>Your turn: " + userName +
              "</H1>");
    // generate the bingo game


    out.println("For help, click " +
      "<A HREF='Help/'+ sessionID +
      "?rules=Bingo'>Click here for help</A>");
    out.println("</FORM></BODY></HTML>");
  }
}
```

Listing 6.3 shows how the servlet accesses the session ID from the URL path by using the request method getPathInfo(). Remember, this method returns the path information listed after the servlet path and before the query string. A connection to the associated database is acquired, and the session ID is used to extract data associated with the current user. After the name value is obtained, it is incorporated into the Bingo page. Finally, a hyperlink is used to provide help; it too contains the session ID value, in case the Help servlet needs the session-related user data.

Using Methods to Encode the URL

Instead of manually generating a session ID and physically adding it to the URL, the API provides methods that manage the task for the developer. The HttpServletResponse class offers the following two methods:

- public String encodeURL(java.lang.String url)

- public String encodeRedirectURL(java.lang.String url)

The encodeURL(...) method rewrites the specified URL to include a session ID if needed. If one is not needed, the method returns the original URL. An unchanged URL can result from a server that does not support URL rewriting or from a server that has the feature turned off. As for the semantics of how the URL is encoded, that feature or technique is server-specific. In general, it is good practice to have all URLs emitted by a servlet run through this method to ensure application-wide access to the session ID.

The second method is similar to the first in that it, too, encodes the passed-in URL by adding the session ID. It differs, however, in when it is used. At times there is a need for a servlet to temporarily redirect a response to a different location. This is done by using the `HttpServletResponse`'s method `sendRedirect(String url)`. Before calling this method, the URL should be encoded by using a method specifically designed to handle URL encoding for a redirected response: `encodeRedirectURL(String url)`. The reason for using a different method is that a redirect URL is different from a normal URL. For a *redirect URL*, all non-ASCII values must be converted to their hexadecimal values; this includes ampersands and equal signs. For a normal URL, the ampersands and equal signs do not need to be converted to hexadecimal format. This distinction is critical and necessary for the `sendRedirect(...)` method to work. The following is an example of a rewritten URL:

```
http://localhost:8080/servlet/OverviewServlet;
jsessionid=4347
```

To encode links in your URL, you must make slight modifications to the HTML code. Here is an example of how to rewrite the URL to include an encoded URL in a form:

```
String urlSession = res.encodeURL("servlet/OveriewServlet");
out.println("<FORM ACTION='" + urlSession + "'" +
                " METHOD='POST'>");
out.println("<INPUT TYPE='submit' VALUE='Exit'>");
out.println("</FORM></BODY></HTML>");
```

If your intent is to encode a URL for a link, you simply include an encoded `String` instead of the standard URL:

```
out.println("Click " +
  "<A HREF='"+ res.encodeURL("servlet/OverviewServlet") +
  "'>here</A>");
```

In order for the container to encode the URL with a session ID, three conditions usually exist:

- The browser supports URL encoding.

- The browser does not support cookies.

- The session tracking feature is turned on.

When using the encodeURL(...) method, the session ID is stored as a path parameter. As such, you must call req.getPathInfo() to retrieve the ID value.

You can also access the ID by calling req.getSession() to acquire a handle to the actual session object (assuming one exists). Using the session instance, the ID value can then be accessed by calling session.getId(). This object is covered in more detail in the upcoming "Using the HttpSession Object" section.

The servlet can also use the following HttpServletRequest methods to learn more about the methodology used to generate the ID, as well as its validity:

- public boolean isRequestedSessionIdFromCookie()
- public boolean isRequestedSessionIdFromURL()
- public boolean isRequestedSessionIdValid()

These methods validate the session object and its place of origin. If the session is not valid, the servlet can redirect the user to a new screen to log in again. If the session ID was obtained from the URL, the servlet might opt to perform a different task than if it was obtained from a cookie.

Using Cookies

Another way to perform session tracking is through persistent cookies. Remember, a *cookie* is an object containing small amounts of information sent by a servlet to a web browser, then saved by the browser, and later sent back to the server. Because the cookie's value can uniquely identify a client and maintain client data, using cookies is an optimal way to track sessions.

A cookie is created by using two parameters: a name and a value. The constructor is as follows:

public Cookie(*String name, String value*)

Unlike a hidden value, which must exist in all servlet pages, a cookie is added to the servlet's response object and is propagated to all servlets accessed during the session.

The servlet specification mandates that the name of the value used to track the session for a cookie must be called JSESSIONID.

The ID name must be all uppercase when used within a cookie, but lowercase when used in URL rewriting.

A cookie can be added to an HttpServletResponse object in the following way:

```
Cookie cookie = new Cookie("JSESSIONID", "567");
res.addCookie(cookie);
```

If another servlet is interested in accessing this information, it can call the getCookies() method of the HttpServletRequest class:

```
public Cookie[] getCookies()
```

Using our example from the preceding "Rewriting the URL" section, you can create a cookie to add the session ID. Listing 6.4 demonstrates how to use cookies to rewrite the OverviewServlet.

Listing 6.4: Using Cookies with the OverviewServlet

```
import javax.servlet.*;
import javax.servlet.http.*;
import java.io.*;
import java.util.*;

public class OverviewServlet extends HttpServlet {
    public void doPost(HttpServletRequest req,
                        HttpServletResponse res)
      throws ServletException, IOException {
      String name = req.getParameter("name");
      String sessionID =
          SessionIDUtility.generateSessionID();
      Cookie cookie = new Cookie("JSESSIONID",
                                    sessionID);
      res.addCookie(cookie);
```

```
res.setContentType("text/html");
PrintWriter out = res.getWriter();
out.println("<HTML><BODY>");
out.println("<H1>The Game Center</H1>");
out.println("<P>Press a button to play:</P>");

out.println("<FORM ACTION='/games/Checkers'" +
                    " Method='POST'>");
out.println("<INPUT TYPE='submit'" +
                " VALUE='Checkers'></FORM>");
out.println("<FORM ACTION='/games/BingoServlet'" +
                " METHOD='POST'>");
  out.println("<INPUT TYPE='submit' VALUE='BINGO'>");
  out.println("</FORM></BODY></HTML>");
    }
}
```

The BingoServlet can then use its request object to get all the cookies associated with the session. The modified code would look similar to Listing 6.5.

Listing 6.5: Using Cookies with the BingoServlet

```
import javax.servlet.*;
import javax.servlet.http.*;
import java.io.*;
import java.util.*;
import java.sql.*;

public class BingoServlet extends HttpServlet {
    public void doPost(HttpServletRequest req,
                        HttpServletResponse res)
        throws ServletException, IOException {
      String sessionID;
      String userName;
      Cookie[] cookies = req.getCookies();
      if (cookies != null) {
        for (int i=0; i<cookies.length; i++) {
            String id = cookies[i].getName();
```

```
if(id.equals("JSESSIONID")) {
    sessionID = cookies[i].getValue();
    break;
    }
  }
}
Connection con =
  getServletContext().getAttribute("Connection");
userName =
  (String) SessionIDUtility.getSessionValue(
      con, sessionID, "name");
res.setContentType("text/html");
PrintWriter out = res.getWriter();
out.println("<HTML><BODY>");
out.println("<H1>Your turn: " + userName +
          "</H1>");
// generate the bingo game

out.println("For help, click " +
  "<A HREF='Help/?rules=Bingo'>" +
  "Click here for help" +
  "</A>");
out.println("</FORM></BODY></HTML>");
    }
  }
```

In this example, we get all the cookies associated with the request. We filter through each cookie until we come across the one called JSESSIONID. By using the assigned ID, the doPost(...) method can then use the get-SessionValue(...) method within the SessionIDUtility class to get the user's name. In our example, we could have just added the user's name to the cookie. Instead, we opted to show you the approach using a session ID value because a session usually contains more than one data element. Notice that the hyperlink to the Help servlet no longer contains the ID value within its URL. When the Help servlet is invoked, it will receive the existing session cookies within its request object.

The final and most convenient way to handle session data is to pass an HttpSession object, which implicitly contains the client's data, back and forth between all session-related servlets.

Using the *HttpSession* Object

Previously, we discussed ways to track the session object between client/server requests, where each example (cookie or URL rewriting) used a database for persistent storage of session data. In this section, the HttpSession object replaces the database for persistent storage, and uses one of the methods previously discussed to propagate the session ID.

Internally, the container determines the method used to transmit the session ID between the client and server (whether it used cookies or URL rewriting).

The servlet creates an HttpSession object to maintain data for the entire duration of a transaction. Assuming the client's browser supports session management, an HttpSession object is created when the client first accesses a web application. Data can then be written to or retrieved from this object.

It is important to understand that a session exists only within its original context. For example, if a servlet uses the RequestDispatcher to forward its request to another application, a new session is created that is different from the calling servlet.

To access a session object, use the HttpServletRequest method:

`public HttpSession getSession()`

The method returns the HttpSession object tied to the client requesting the current servlet. If the object does not exist, the getSession() method will automatically create a new HttpSession instance.

The other method used to access a session object is as follows:

`public HttpSession getSession(boolean create)`

This method differs from the previous version in that it requires a boolean value:

- A true value creates a new session object if one does not already exist.
- A false value prevents a session object from being created if one does not exist.

A false value is really what distinguishes this method from its overloaded getSession() method. Instead of creating a new session without further validation, the developer might want to redirect the user back to a login page before a session is created. Once created, the session object will continue to accumulate stored data until the session is terminated.

Data is stored to an HttpSession object as attributes:

```
public void setAttribute(String name, Object value)
```

The setAttribute(...) method binds a Java object to a specified key name. Another servlet can then use the HttpSession object and access its data by using the following method:

```
public Object getAttribute(String name)
```

The getAttribute(...) method uses the key name to find and return the associated object.

Once again, let's revisit the OverviewServlet in Listing 6.4 to see how this approach changes the code. See Listing 6.6.

Listing 6.6: Using an HttpSession Object with the OverviewServlet

```
import javax.servlet.*;
import javax.servlet.http.*;
import java.io.*;
import java.util.*;

public class OverviewServlet extends HttpServlet {
    public void doPost(HttpServletRequest req,
                       HttpServletResponse res)
      throws ServletException, IOException {
        String name = req.getParameter("name");

        HttpSession session = req.getSession();
        session.setAttribute("name", name);

        res.setContentType("text/html");
        PrintWriter out = res.getWriter();
        out.println("<HTML><BODY>");
        out.println("<H1>The Game Center</H1>");
        out.println("<P>Press a button to play:</P>");

        out.println("FORM ACTION='/games/Checkers'" +
                    " MethodMETHOD='POST'>");
```

```
            out.println("<INPUT TYPE='submit' VALUE='" +
                          "Checkers'></FORM>");
            out.println("<FORM ACTION='/games/BingoServlet'" +
                          " MethodMETHOD='POST'>");
            out.println("<INPUT TYPE='submit' VALUE='Bingo'>");
            out.println("</FORM></BODY></HTML>");
    }
}
```

Using the session object is both a clean and convenient approach to storing client data. The actual session instance is stored at the web application level, whereby each ServletContext maintains its own pool of HttpSession objects.

Remember, each application has one ServletContext, and each context has multiple sessions for each client that accesses the application.

Retrieving the attributes is as easy as adding them. Listing 6.7 is the BingoServlet modified to use the session object either to redirect the user back to a login screen (if the session object is null) or to extract client data.

Listing 6.7: Using an HttpSession Object with the BingoServlet

```
import javax.servlet.*;
import javax.servlet.http.*;
import java.io.*;
import java.util.*;

public class BingoServlet extends HttpServlet {
    public void doPost(HttpServletRequest req,
                        HttpServletResponse res)
                throws ServletException, IOException {

        HttpSession session = req.getSession(false);
        if(session == null) {
            ServletContext sc =
                getServletConfig().getServletContext();
```

```
              RequestDispatcher disp =
                sc.getRequestDispatcher("/servlet/
                    LoginServlet");
              disp.forward(req, res);
              return;
          }

          String userName =
            (String)session.getAttribute("name");

          res.setContentType("text/html");
          PrintWriter out = res.getWriter();
          out.println("<HTML><BODY>");
          out.println("<H1>Your turn: " + userName +
                    "</H1>");
          // generate the bingo game
...
          out.println("For help, click " +
            "<A HREF='Help/?rules=Bingo'>" +
            " Click here for help</A>");
          out.println("</FORM></BODY></HTML>");
      }
  }
```

The preceding example demonstrates two ideas. The first is how a servlet can redirect a request to a login screen if a session does not exist. The second is how a servlet within the same context automatically receives session data acquired from previous servlets. This is shown by using the getAttribute(...) method. The key value name is passed as a parameter to access its associated object. Remember, the name value was set by the OverviewServlet.

Adding an attribute is as easy as removing one. To unbind an attribute, call the method:

```
public void removeAttribute(String name)
```

After this method is invoked on an attribute, it is no longer accessible by any servlet within the application.

The final method of interest is the one that enables a servlet to list all the attributes associated with the current session:

```
public Enumeration getAttributeNames()
```

The getAttributeNames() method returns an Enumeration object of all current attributes. If a session has no attributes, a null value is returned.

Sometimes there is a need to respond to changes to a session's attributes. The servlet API provides several session listener classes designed specifically for this purpose.

HttpSessionBindingListener

By implementing the HttpSessionBindingListener, your application can be notified when an object is bound or unbound to a session object. The interface has two primary methods that must be defined:

- valueBound(*HttpSessionBindingEvent event*)

- valueUnbound(*HttpSessionBindingEvent event*)

The valueBound(...) method is called before the object is made available through the getAttribute(...) method. In contrast, the value-Unbound(...) method is called after the object is no longer available via the getAttribute(...) method of the HttpSession interface. The listener is passed an HttpSessionBindingEvent, which contains the session object, the name, and the value of the object either bound or unbound to the session.

Both methods are public and have a void return value.

HttpSessionListener

By implementing the HttpSessionListener, your application can be notified when a session is created or destroyed. The interface has two primary methods that must be defined:

- sessionCreated(*HttpSessionEvent event*)

- sessionDestroyed(*HttpSessionEvent event*)

As intuition would suggest, the sessionCreated(...) method is called after the session is produced. In contrast, the sessionDestroyed(...) method is called to notify the application that the session was invalidated. Each method provides a handle to the HttpSessionEvent object. This instance provides access to the session object.

Both methods are public and have a void return value.

To register session listeners to the container, you must include the listener tag in the web.xml document. For example:

```
<listener>
    <listener-class>
        ConnectionPoolHandler
    </listener-class>
</listener>
```

The container determines the type of listener defined and then establishes an abstract link between the session and the listener. When changes occur to the session, the appropriate listener is notified.

For a more detailed explanation of these two listeners, review the discussion on HttpSession listeners in Chapter 4, "The Servlet Container Model."

So far, we have covered how to create and maintain sessions by using several approaches—as well as how to respond to session changes. It is now time to discuss how sessions are invalidated.

Invalidating Sessions

A session can be invalidated in multiple ways. It can expire automatically, after a specified or default period of inactivity, or a servlet can explicitly invalidate a session through method calls. Before learning about these options, it is important to understand the effects on the application and client when a session is nullified. Basically, all the attribute data is lost. If you want to retain session information after it is invalidated, it should be stored to an external resource such as a database or a long-term cookie. For example, say you have a user who has a login name and password stored to a database. When they log into the system, a session is created and data is added to monitor their activity. After they log off or a session is about to be terminated, the data can be stored to that user's name or account in a database for later retrieval. Brokerage firms are known for using this approach as a means of justifying their user's transactions.

Logically, you would expect a session object to terminate when the client is done with an application. You would expect this to occur when the client leaves the site, terminates the browser, or simply walks away from the application for a period of time. Unfortunately, the application is not notified when such occurrences take place because of the nature of the HTTP protocol.

The HTTP protocol is stateless, and by design will close the connection after each request to the server. As a result, an application is not notified after each connection is closed.

Because the server cannot distinguish the intent of the client, the server will keep the session alive during inactive periods for a default period. To change that default time, the web.xml document can be modified to identify the number of minutes the server will keep the session alive during inactive periods.

The `session-config` tag holds all configuration tags for the application's session. The `session-time` tag defines the number of inactive minutes a session will exist before the server terminates the object. The following is sample code for the web.xml file used to change the default termination period:

```
<web-app>
    ...
    <session-config>
        <session-timeout>
            15
        </session-timeout>
    </session-config>
</web-app>
```

The servlet specification requires that the timeout value be specified in whole numbers. Some servers allow the use of negative values to indicate that sessions should not be terminated. The server's documentation will provide more details on this capability.

A second approach to modifying the life of a session is to have individual servlets define the inactive time period before a session is destroyed. The `HttpSession` interface provides the following methods:

- `public void setMaxInactiveInterval(int secs)`
- `public int getMaxInactiveInterval()`

These methods allow fine-grained control. Instead of applying a time period to the entire application, you can set the time to specific servlets. The benefit of this approach is that you can customize the timeout period per user or after certain activities have taken place, such as a lengthy database lookup.

WARNING Notice that the time is measured in seconds rather than minutes.

The getMaxInactiveInterval() method returns the value set. If the set method is not used and the time is set by using the session-timeout tag, the getMaxInactiveInterval() method will return the timeout value defined within the web.xml file.

The third approach is pretty abrupt. The HttpSession interface provides the following method:

```
public void invalidate() throws IllegalStateException
```

After a handle to the session is obtained, the invalidate() method can be called to close the session and unbind all associated objects. If the session is already invalidated, then an IllegalStateException object is thrown.

Now that we've covered how to end a session, it is important for you to understand the best practices associated to a session's timeout period. Given specific scenarios, you should know whether a session object would be invalidated sooner versus later. Table 6.2 breaks down the strategies.

TABLE 6.2 Session Invalidation Strategies

Type	Example	Session Time-out Periods	Explanation
Secure web applications	Online banking	Shorter	Prevent imposters from invading abandoned systems.
Resource-intensive applications	Database connections	Shorter	Enable servers to reclaim or release resources quickly.
Non-resource-intensive applications	No database connections	Longer	Maximize convenience rather than focusing on server scalability.

TABLE 6.2   Session Invalidation Strategies *(continued)*

Type	Example	Session Time-out Periods	Explanation
Shopping cart applications	Stores	Longer	A timeout might cause client to forget original items.
Applications that cache database information	News sites	Depends	Shorter period results in a larger cache. Longer sessions cause the database lookup to process more slowly.

Determining how an application should manage a session is achieved by balancing convenience, user security, and server efficiency. A site that logs a user off too quickly could become incredibly inconvenient for users who need to take short breaks from a transaction to check e-mail or take a phone call. For security purposes, however, you don't want to keep certain sessions open for extended periods of inactivity. Imagine a bank web application that stores the user's login and account information in a session. If the data remains available while the user has stepped away from the application for an extended period of time, there is greater risk of fraud. Finally, efficiency should be considered. A client session might be using resources that are "expensive" to the system, such as a database connection. The longer this object is maintained, the slower the application and server might run. In such cases, sessions should not have long inactive periods.

 Real World Scenario

Detailed Session Management

Investments, Inc. is interested in providing their customers with online access to their investment accounts. The application must enable users to place orders, purchase stocks, and sell stocks. All clients will need to establish secure login accounts to access their private information. As a consultant, you are asked to design a session strategy that will best meet the company's security needs and provide client convenience.

One of the biggest concerns of the company is to ensure that decisions made by the client can be validated. A partnering company recently had a client claim they did not intend to purchase a particular batch of stocks. Because the company did not maintain every procedure taken by the client, they could not prove the client was responsible for their own error.

To minimize complexity, you have decided to utilize the session object provided by the servlet API. Whenever the user triggers an event, all entered information and trigger options are written to the session. Because security is a huge priority, inactive periods are kept to a minimum. If the user is in the middle of a transaction and has to leave the application, they would prefer to log in again rather than risk the corruption of their account.

Finally, you must consider when to store the information to a database. Normally, the session data is removed after the object is removed. To retain it for legal purposes, you want to write the session data to a database before the session is terminated. To ensure that the data is written before the session is invalidated, you create an HttpSessionListener. After the session is destroyed due to inactivity or the user logs out, which would cause a call to session.invalidate(), the listener is notified and the sessionDestroyed(*HttpSessionEvent e*) method is called. By using the HttpSessionEvent, you can retrieve a handle to the session object to extract all the data and write it to a database. The end result is an application that provides security and a legal trail.

Summary

In this chapter, we covered the various ways to manage a session object. We began by discussing the ways to monitor or handle session data; those processes are as follows:

Method 1: Hidden values

```
out.println("<INPUT TYPE='hidden'" +
                "NAME='mailingAddress'" +
                "VALUE='" + address + "'>");
```

Method 2: URL rewriting

```
out.println("<FORM ACTION='BingoServlet/' + sessionID +
                    "' METHOD='POST'>");
```

or

```
String urlSession = res.encodeURL("servlet/MyServlet");
out.println("<FORM ACTION='" + urlSession + "'" +
                    " Method='POST'>");
out.println("</FORM></BODY></HTML>");
```

Method 3: Cookies

```
Cookie cookie = new Cookie("JSESSIONID", "567");
res.addCookie(cookie);
```

Method 4: Sessions

```
HttpSession session = req.getSession();
```

We then addressed ways to invalidate a session and the associated strategies. Here are the three ways to invalidate a session:

- `<session-config><session-timeout> 60 </session-timeout></session-config>`

- `HttpSession.setMaxInactiveInterval(...)`

- `HttpSession.invalidate()`

Finally, we discussed the circumstances in which you should provide long versus short inactive periods for a session.

Exam Essentials

Be able to identify the interface and methods for a session object retrieved across multiple requests to the same or different servlets within the same WebApp. The HttpServletRequest class provides a getSession() method that returns an HttpSession object for the specific client.

Be able to identify the interface and methods to store and retrieve objects to and from a session object. The HttpSession interface provides a setAttribute(*String name*, *Object value*) method to store an object and a getAttribute(*String name*) to retrieve a bound object.

Be able to respond to an event when a particular object is added to a session. When an object is added to a session object and implemented, HttpSessionBindingListener is notified and its valueBound(*Http-SessionBindingEvent e*) method is called. When an object is removed, the listener's valueUnbound(*HttpSessionBindingEvent e*) method is called.

Be able to respond to an event when a session is created and destroyed. An implementation of the HttpSessionListener will enable your application to receive notification of when a session object is created or destroyed. The interface contains a sessionCreated(*HttpSessionEvent e*) and sessionDestroyed(*HttpSessionEvent e*).

Be able to identify the interface and methods to expunge a session object. The HttpSession interface provides the invalidate() method to terminate a session object.

Identify the most common ways a session object can be invalidated. A session can be invalidated three main ways. One is by modifying the web .xml file to define a default timeout period by using the session-timeout tag. The second process is to specifically modify the session's timeout period by using the setMaxInactiveInterval(*int sec*) method. The third approach is to call invalidate() on the HttpSession object.

Given that URL rewriting must be used for session management, identify the design requirements on session-related HTML pages. URL rewriting is a way to transfer the session ID or data by including it in the URL. The generated HTML pages must include the URL link plus the session ID, either directly or encoded by using the encodeURL(*String url*) or encodeRedirectURL(*String url*) method.

Key Terms

Before you take the exam, be certain you are familiar with the following terms:

cookie	redirect URL
hidden HTML values	session object
HttpSession	URL rewriting

Review Questions

1. Which of the following best describes an example of URL rewriting?

   A. `out.println("<INPUT TYPE='hidden' NAME='name' VALUE='BillyBob'>");`

   B. `out.println("<FORM ACTION='servlet/TestServlet/ BillyBob' METHOD='POST'>");`

   C. `HttpSession session = req.getSession();`

   D. `session.addAttribute("name", "BillyBob");`

   E. None of the above

2. Which interface provides the method `getSession()`?

   A. `ServletRequest`

   B. `ServletResponse`

   C. `HttpServletResponse`

   D. `HttpServletRequest`

3. Which of the following methods is used to store objects into a session object?

   A. `setData(String name, Object obj)`

   B. `setDataAttribute(String name, Object obj)`

   C. `setAttribute(String name, String obj)`

   D. `setAttribute(String name, Object obj)`

4. Which of the following methods is used to expunge a session object?

   A. `end()`

   B. `destroy()`

   C. `invalidate()`

   D. `kill()`

5. Which of the following is not a valid methodology for session management?

   A. Cookies

   B. HttpSession objects

   C. Hidden values

   D. ServletContext object

6. The session-timeout tag defines the number of inactive _____ a session will exist before being terminated.

   A. Milliseconds

   B. Seconds

   C. Minutes

   D. Hours

7. Which of the following statements is invalid?

   A. The session timeout value determines how long a session lasts.

   B. A session is associated with a client.

   C. The setMaxInactiveInterval(…) method is used by the servlet via the HttpSession object.

   D. If a session timeout is not set, the server will terminate sessions by using a default time value.

8. What is the recommended timeout period that a shopping cart application should have?

   A. Short

   B. Medium

   C. Long

   D. Doesn't matter

9. Which of the following best describes what is returned when the `getMaxInactiveInterval()` method is called?

   A. The default inactive timeout period, in minutes, for a session to exist before termination.

   B. The number of seconds an inactive session can exist when using the `setMaxInactiveInterval(int sec)` method.

   C. The default inactive timeout period, in seconds, for a session to exist before termination.

   D. It depends on how the server or application handles the session timeout period.

10. Which of the following is not a valid way to change the inactive period of a session before the server terminates the session?

   A. `<session-timeout>60</session-timeout>`

   B. `setMaxInactiveInterval(500)`

   C. `<session-config>30</session-config>`

   D. Do nothing

11. Which of the following methods is used to retrieve a bound session object?

   A. `getBoundObject(String name)`

   B. `getData(String name)`

   C. `getSessionObject(String name)`

   D. `getAttribute(String name)`

12. Which of the following is an example of URL rewriting by using the `encodeURL(String url)` method? (Choose all that apply.)

   A. `http://localhost:8080/servlet/play;jsessionid=567`

   B. `http://localhost:8080/servlet/play`

   C. `http://localhost:8080/servlet/play?jsessionid=567`

   D. None of the above

13. Which of the following methods is called when an object is removed from a session object?

   A. valueUnbound(*HttpSessionEvent e*)

   B. valueUnBound(*HttpBindingSessionEvent e*)

   C. valueUnbound(*HttpSessionBindingEvent e*)

   D. valueUnBound(*HttpSession e*)

14. Which of the following statements is true?

   A. The valueBound(...) method is called before the object is made available through the getAttribute() method.

   B. The valueBound(...) method is called after the object is made available through the getAttribute() method.

   C. The valueBound(...) method is called at different times depending on the server's preference.

   D. None of the above

15. Which of the following listeners is called when a session is destroyed?

   A. HttpSessionBindingListener

   B. HttpSessionListener

   C. HttpSessionChangedListener

   D. SessionListener

Answers to Review Questions

1. **B.** URL rewriting consists of adding data to the URL. The receiving servlet can then extract the additional information to utilize the data.

2. **D.** A session is reliant on HTTP transactions. Because the application's communication with the client is through the `HttpServletRequest` interface, and the session is not transmitted back to the client, the session object is obtained via the `HttpServletRequest` interface.

3. **D.** The `setAttribute(String name, Object obj)` method binds an object with a related key name to the session object. The other methods are all illegal.

4. **C.** The `invalidate()` method terminates the associated session and then unbinds any objects bound to it.

5. **D.** The `ServletContext` is associated with the web application, not with the individual client session. Consequently, data stored to the context is not unique to a client.

6. **C.** The timeout tag defines the minimum number of minutes of inactivity that can pass before a session can be inactive before being terminated by the server.

7. **A.** A session timeout value tells the amount of time the session will stay alive only during an inactive period, not its entire life.

8. **C.** Because a client usually collects multiple items in a cart, a short-lived inactive period could cause problems and irritation to the user. This could result in a loss of business because the user might not want to return or might forget what they already selected.

9. **D.** Depending on how the session timeout period is set, the `getMaxInactiveInterval()` method will return the number of seconds that the inactive session will exist before termination.

10. **C.** The `session-config` tag requires the `session-timeout` tag to define the number of minutes a session can be inactive. As for doing nothing, the server usually has a default inactive period defined automatically.

11. **D.** The `getAttribute(String name)` method returns the object bound to the session by using the associated name reference.

12. A, B.   The encodeURL(*String url*) method encodes the specified URL by including the session ID in it. If encoding is not needed, the method returns the URL unchanged.

13. C.   The valueUnbound, lowercase *b*, method is called when an object is unbound from the session object. An HttpSessionBindingEvent is passed to the method containing the session object, and the name and value of the object removed can be gathered from this event object.

14. A.   The servlet specification mandates that the valueBound(...) method should be called before the object is made available through the getAttribute() method.

15. B.   The HttpSessionListener is called when a session is created and destroyed.

Secure Web Applications

THE FOLLOWING SUN CERTIFIED WEB COMPONENT DEVELOPER FOR J2EE PLATFORM EXAM OBJECTIVES ARE COVERED IN THIS CHAPTER:

✓ **6.1 Identify correct descriptions or statements about the security issues:**

- Authentication, authorization
- Data integrity
- Auditing
- Malicious code
- Website attacks

✓ **6.2 Identify the deployment descriptor element names, and their structure, that declare the following:**

- A security constraint
- A web resource
- The login configuration
- A security role

✓ **6.3 Given authentication type: BASIC, DIGEST, FORM, and CLIENT-CERT, identify the correct definition of its mechanism.**

As computer technology advances, the number and type of services available over the network increases. Convenience, however, has a price. The transfer of critical information creates business vulnerabilities that many wish to overlook. For numerous companies, the one area that requires the most attention receives the least: security. Security is a crucial aspect of any application that exchanges privileged information. In this chapter, we will address the basic weaknesses a system faces and identify key elements that should be considered to create a secure system and limit exposure to outside threats.

Security Issues

Most people find entertainment in sports, movies, talking, and other benign activities. However, many individuals receive amazing satisfaction and gratification from invading computer systems and either corrupting or capturing vital data. These individuals, known as *hackers* or *attackers*, thrive on system vulnerabilities. Utilizing various hacker tools, they are often able to scan systems to locate holes through which they can enter and attack. For many it's a game, and with others it's for more personal reasons, such as revenge. Regardless of the motives of potential attackers, securing your web application should be a priority to ensure the integrity of your data and application. This process begins by implementing the four basic security principles:

- Authorize
- Authenticate

- Provide data confidentiality

- Monitor access

In addition to these principles, we will also discuss the following security concerns:

- Malicious code

- Website attacks

Authentication and Authorization

The onset of the Internet caused network security to become a huge concern. When Java first hit the market, it was known as the Internet language. It marketed applet development as the product that provided a secure environment for clients accessing unknown sources over the Internet. However, restricting applet access to the client system was not a successful solution to security. Instead, other means of protection were needed to enable authorized access without limiting functionality.

The Java language has matured since its creation and now offers several technologies to authenticate and authorize an outside user for access to a server application. The concern is no longer focused on the applet client, but rather a J2EE client (servlet or JSP) attempting to access an enterprise application.

Figure 7.1 provides a visual representation of these two approaches to security: the client-server approach, in which the aim is to secure the client, and the J2EE approach, in which the aim is to secure the server.

FIGURE 7.1   Security strategies

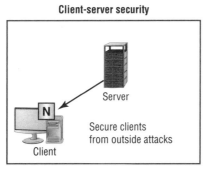
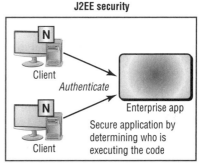

When a client requests information, the server has no way of determining who is making the request. The client's IP address fails to define the user because that user can attempt to access a server from various computers. In addition, it is easy for a user to falsify their IP address to disguise their identity. Consequently, the server must determine the client via user authentication and authorization, which we'll explain in just a moment.

Our focus is on J2EE security and the processes used to protect the web application from false or unwanted clients. *Authentication* is the process whereby the client supplies credentials to prove their identity. Most often proof is provided via a password. Other examples include the swipe of a card or digital certificates, and one day perhaps even retinal scans or fingerprints.

Each user within a secure system is mapped to an identifier, also known as a *principal*. A principal is usually recognized by their user ID when logging into a system. The `conf/web.xml` file is then used to associate principals with one or more *roles*. Roles are given privileged access to certain parts of the web application (again through definitions in the `conf/web.xml`). Roles will be discussed in a bit more detail in the "Auditing" section. Authorization is the process whereby a principal is given privileged access due to his or her role.

Java Authentication and Authorization Service

With the introduction of the Java Authentication and Authorization Service (JAAS) API, authentication can be handled by utilizing pluggable modules configured to authenticate by using something as simple as a username and password or something more complex—for example, a SmartCard reader. JAAS offers an enterprise application a variety of services for authentication on the back end. As vendors standardize this API, you will see more and more applications using complex pluggable modules rather than developing basic authentication and authorization code. JAAS is bundled in the Java Developer Kit 1.4 or available separately at the Sun website.

Data Integrity

Access control fails if others can gain access to password or authentication information as it is transmitted over the network. Encrypting information protects data and provides another level of security. The protocol called Secure Sockets Layer (SSL) was developed to use public key cryptography to encrypt communication between the client and server. A *public key* is an encryption scheme, either generated by software or issued by a third party, used to encode or decode information. Sitting between the HTTP and TCP/IP protocol, SSL encrypts the data to prevent hackers from acquiring confidential information. Anyone attempting to intercept the data transfer will simply encounter indecipherable nonsense.

Two main security concerns are solved when using public key cryptography. The first is confidentiality. Because the data is encrypted, you are guaranteed privacy. The second is integrity. As long as the information can be decoded properly by the intended recipient, you can be fairly sure that the data was not tampered with during transmission.

Auditing

Auditing users is a way of ensuring that users who log in successfully access only those resources that are appropriate to their role. The servlet security model is *role-based*. This means that users are assigned to roles, such as Manager, Employee, or Guest. Each role is assigned certain privileges, and access is granted to roles rather than users. To determine whether to provide a client with access to a given resource, the server:

1. Discovers which roles are available

2. Checks to see which roles are allowed

3. Checks to see whether the user is assigned to any available roles

Notice that security evolves around the role rather than the user. By using a server-specific tool, users are mapped to particular roles. The granularity of permissions can be defined at a finer level. By using the tool or the deployment descriptor, you can specify the method permissions for each role as well.

Access for each role can be denoted in two ways: through declarative security or programmatic security.

Declarative Security

Declarative security uses the deployment descriptor to specify which resource a role can access. The advantage of this approach is that implementing security is independent of source code; when security changes must be made, there is no need to recompile or make changes to the code.

By including the `security-constraint` tag in your `web.xml` file located in the `/WEB-INF` directory, you can define each resource and the roles that have access. Here is an example of how to restrict a particular directory to users that have the role of Administrator.

```
<security-constraint>
    <web-resource-collection>
        <web-resource-name>
            Admin area
        </web-resource-name>
        <url-pattern>
            /admin/*
        </url-pattern>
    </web-resource-collection>
    <auth-constraint>
        <role-name>
            Administrator
        </role-name>
    </auth-constraint>
</security-constraint>
```

The `web-resource-name` tag defines the human-language name for the resource, and `url-pattern` identifies the location of the resource. Within the `security-constraint` tag, you can then define which roles have access to the identified resources by using the `auth-constraint` tag. Do keep in mind that you can list more than one `role-name` within the authorization group.

Users and roles are usually mapped to an *access list* stored by the server. Sometimes it's a simple file containing each user's login name, password, and role. Other times it's stored as a database with encrypted employee information.

When discussing BASIC authentication later in this chapter, we will go into more detail on user mapping and show you how Tomcat manages user role information.

Programmatic Security

At times declarative security is not specific enough. You might need to limit access within a particular method based on a user. This kind of granularity requires security to extend itself to the method source code, which is done by using *programmatic security*. Within a method such as doGet(...), you might want to determine who is making the request and then, based on the result, determine whether to execute a particular response.

There are three Java methods within the javax.servlet.HttpServlet-Request class that provide information about the user making a request:

String getRemoteUser() returns a String of the username used to log in to the website.

boolean isUserInRole(String role) indicates whether the user accessing the servlet is assigned to the passed-in role.

Principal getUserPrincipal() returns a java.security .Principal object representing the user who is logged in.

Here is an example of how programmatic security can filter activity based on the user:

```java
import javax.servlet.*;
import javax.servlet.http.*;
import java.io.*;
import java.util.*;

public class AccessServlet extends HttpServlet {
    public void doGet(HttpServletRequest req,
                      HttpServletResponse res)
       throws ServletException, IOException {

        res.setContentType("text/plain");
        PrintWriter out = res.getWriter();

        String username = req.getRemoteUser();
        if (username == null) {
           out.println("You are not logged in.");
        } else if ("Mary".equals(username)) {
           out.println("Hello Mary,
                   glad you can join us");
        } else {
           out.println("Hello " + username);
        }
```

```
                out.close();
        }
}
```

Depending on who makes a GET request, the message returned is different. Mary gets the most personal message, whereas general users simply get a basic "Hello." If a user is not logged in, getRemoteUser() returns null. This example has Mary assigned to the role of GeneralUser. With this said, the deployment descriptor would look like the following:

```
<security-constraint>
    <web-resource-collection>
        <web-resource-name>
            AccessServlet
        </web-resource-name>
        <url-pattern>
            /serlvet/AccessServlet
        </url-pattern>
    </web-resource-collection>
    <auth-constraint>
        <role-name>
            GeneralUser
        </role-name>
    </auth-constraint>
</security-constraint>
```

All users assigned to the role of GeneralUser have access to the AccessServlet. Within the servlet, we use programmatic security to deliver a different message depending on the user. Each tag will be thoroughly discussed in the BASIC authentication section.

As you can see, declarative and programmatic security can be used together. The downside of defining security measures within code is that changes to security will result in the need to recompile the code.

Malicious Code

In the technical world, the term *malicious code* is synonymous with *virus*. Unfortunately, many people thrive on developing software that locates system vulnerabilities to attack. Sometimes the code is kind enough to simply overflow a particular folder with messages of love, but at other times viruses have been known to wipe out entire hard drives. There are no flags or method calls that can protect your system against these types of assaults. One solution is the use of antivirus software. Antivirus software is critical in keeping your system safe from potential code attacks. Simply installing the software is not enough. Staying current is most important. Because new viruses are being developed every day, the software must be updated on a regular basis. The goal is to stay one step ahead of the attacker.

Website Attacks

When establishing a website, assume the site will be attacked. Even if the information isn't critical, hackers often use other people's systems for the sole purpose of hiding their trail. By bouncing from machine to machine, they can arrive at a destination with a trail too difficult to trace. One form of protection against hacker activity on your system is the utilization of a firewall.

Firewalls block network traffic by limiting access to most ports and unauthorized users. Once again, the firewall requires the client to provide proper authorization to enter the system. Unfortunately, firewalls are not foolproof in that there are ways to bypass security by impersonating an authorized user.

Another tactic to help prevent attacks is the installation of intrusion detection tools. There are a number of tools you can use to detect attackers. Packet sniffers, for example, enable you to view all the traffic on your network. If any activity looks odd, you can use your firewall to block the intruder.

At a minimum, a protected system requires firewalls, intruder detection, and antivirus software. All these preventive techniques can succeed only if user authentication isn't compromised. In the next section, we will discuss the different ways to authenticate a user.

Authentication Types

The web container provides four authentication techniques to determine client validity:

BASIC authentication requires the client to provide a user login name and password in order to access protected data.

FORM authentication adds a bit of elegance to logging in. It enables an application to request authorization by using a customized HTML page.

DIGEST authentication provides a little bit more security in that it encrypts the login name and password to prevent others from acquiring this privileged information while it travels over the network.

CLIENT-CERT authentication stands for client certificate. This approach requires the client to provide a digital certificate containing information about the issuer, signature, serial number, key type, and more. Basically, it is a complex object used to identify the client.

In this section, we'll show you how each technique is used to authenticate users that want to gain access to the web application.

BASIC

The simplest form of authentication is known as HTTP basic authentication, or BASIC. As its name indicates, an application utilizing this form of certification asks for basic information, such as the user's login name and password. The data is then transferred to the server by using BASE64 encoding for validation. The good news is that this process is easy to implement; the bad news is that it doesn't offer much security beyond authenticating the client. If intercepted, the username and password could easily be decoded by running a simple BASE64-decode on the data. If a website provides information that is not critical for an exclusive group, BASIC could be an option.

When a user attempts to access information protected in this fashion, the browser will automatically display a dialog box requesting the user's login name and password. This process is automatic and cannot be customized.

You must identify within the deployment descriptor the code requiring protection, the type of authentication, and who is to gain access. When the client attempts to access this code, a dialog box similar to the image in Figure 7.2 appears.

FIGURE 7.2 BASIC authorization dialog

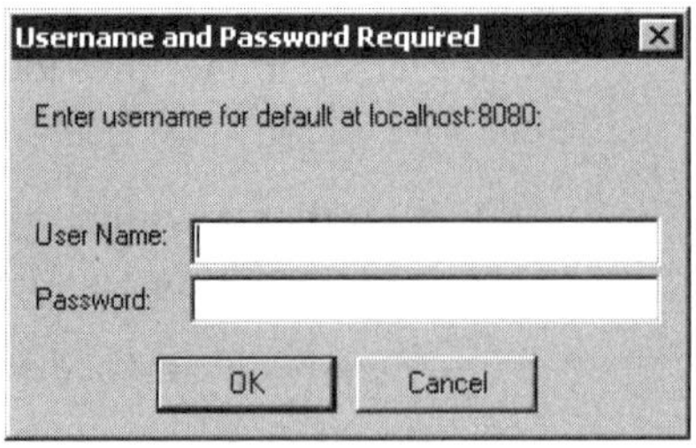

One of the benefits Java offers is the ability to define security outside the application source. There is no need to recompile Java code when security options are changed. When using servlets, the security permissions are defined within the web.xml file. Before discussing the needed XML elements, we begin by looking at a simple servlet:

```java
import javax.servlet.*;
import javax.servlet.http.*;
import java.io.*;
import java.util.*;

public class PrivateServlet extends HttpServlet {
    public void doGet(HttpServletRequest req,
                      HttpServletResponse res)
      throws ServletException, IOException {

        res.setContentType("text/plain");
        PrintWriter out = res.getWriter();

        out.println("You are accessing" +
            "private information");
    }
}
```

This servlet serves no other purpose but to print a message. Our goal is to restrict access to this servlet to a small group of privileged users. To accomplish this task, we must modify the web.xml file to include our security requirements. There are three groups to include, and their order is critical: security-constraint, login-config, and security-role.

The *security-constraint* Element

The first tag group that must be defined is <security-constraint></security-constraint>. These tags are critical in that they define what code is protected. The following sample shows what elements are included within this constraint:

```xml
<security-constraint>
  <web-resource-collection>
    <web-resource-name>
        SecretProtection          <!-- name for tool-->
```

```
    </web-resource-name>
    <url-pattern>
        /servlet/PrivateServlet <!--protected servlet-->
    </url-pattern>
    <url-pattern>
        /servlet/Secret
    </url-pattern>
    <http-method>
        GET                         <!-- protected http method -->
    </http-method>
    <http-method>
        POST
    </http-method>
    </web-resource-collection>
    <auth-constraint>
        <role-name>
            broker                  <!-- role with access -- >
        </role-name>
        <role-name>
            administrator
        </role-name>
    </auth-constraint>
</security-constraint>
```

Within the security-constraint, there are two sub-elements:

- web-resource-collection

- auth-constraint

The web-resource-collection element defines three important features of the protected code:

> The **web-resource-name** is the name used by a tool to reference the servlet. The name must be specified even if a tool is not used.

> The **url-pattern** indicates the URL pattern to the source code requiring protection. If alias names are used to reference servlets, those too should be included.

The **http-method** indicates all HTTP methods that should have restricted access. If no HTTP method is specified, then all methods are protected.

Remember: the methods defined within the http-method element apply to all servlets defined by the url-pattern element.

The auth-constraint element defines any number of roles that can have access to the protected code. Remember, all users belong to roles. For example, a user with a login of Bob14 can belong to the broker and employee roles. This information is usually defined within a server-specific access list or database. Tomcat uses the conf/tomcat-users.xml file to characterize each group. The file might look similar to the following:

```
<tomcat-users>
  <user name="Mandy"  password="secret" roles="broker" />
  <user name="Tim21"  password="secret"
                      roles="administrator" />
  <user name="Bob14"  password="secret"
                      roles="broker, employee" />
</tomcat-users>
```

The *login-config* Element

The second tag group is defined within the <login-config></login-config> tags. It is here that the type of container authentication is defined. The following sample shows what elements are included within this constraint:

```
<login-config>
  <auth-method>
      BASIC      <!--BASIC, DIGEST, FORM, CLIENT-CERT -->
  </auth-method>
  <realm-name>
      Default             <!-- Optional, used for BASIC -->
  </realm-name>
</login-config>
```

Within the login-config tags, there are two sub-elements:

- auth-method
- realm-name

The auth-method element is used to define authentication types of basic, digest, form-based, and client-side certificates. Specifically, the methods must be defined as BASIC, DIGEST, FORM, or CLIENT-CERT. Keep in mind that these method types are case sensitive.

The realm-name element is used by the BASIC authentication to identify a specific area of a website. For example, if there is a member area of the website, this value might be "Members Area."

The *security-role* Element

The final basic security tag group is defined by the <security-role> </security-role> tags. Within these elements are defined roles the application might use to limit access. Generally, this listing is beneficial to tools because they provide the application assemblers or deployers a list of roles to select from to assign to methods.

```
<security-role>
    <description>
        Represents all fulltime employed individuals.
    </description>
    <role-name>
        employee
    </role-name>
</security-role>
```

Within the security-role tags, there are two sub-elements:

- role-name

- description

The role-name tag is required and defines available roles for the application to utilize. The description tag, as the name implies, provides a description of the particular role being listed.

In summary, BASIC authentication requests client authentication when a request for protected data is made. To set up this process, the web.xml file must be configured to include security-constraint information, which defines what data is protected, and login-config data, which defines the type of authentication the container should implement, and it must define the available roles by using the security-role tag.

FORM

In an attempt to provide more elegance to the art of validating users, form-based authentication is available. Rather than rely on the browser's default pop-up dialog to request the user's login name and password, the application can provide its own custom form to request this information. The benefit to the form approach is aesthetic. Essentially you can guarantee that all users, regardless of which browser they use, will see the same login screen (possibly with the company's logo displayed).

Several requirements are necessary to ensure that the custom form communicates correctly with the server's access list:

- The form method must be POST

- The action or URL must be defined as j_security_check.

- The attribute for the username must be j_username.

- The attribute for the password must be j_password.

Utilizing these values enables the server to access the correct attributes given the standardized names. Let's take a look at a simple custom form. We'll call it Login.html:

```
<HTML>
  <BODY>
    <FORM ACTION='j_security_check' METHOD='POST'>
    <P>Welcome to my custom login screen!</P>
    <P>Name: <INPUT TYPE='text' NAME='j_username'
                                 SIZE=15></P>
    <P>Password: <INPUT TYPE='password' NAME='j_password'
                                 SIZE=15></P>
    <P><INPUT TYPE='submit' VALUE='OK'></P>
    </FORM>
  </BODY>
</HTML>
```

As you can see, each name is defined by the standard rules and results in a custom form that can be used for login purposes. See Figure 7.3.

FIGURE 7.3 Custom authentication form

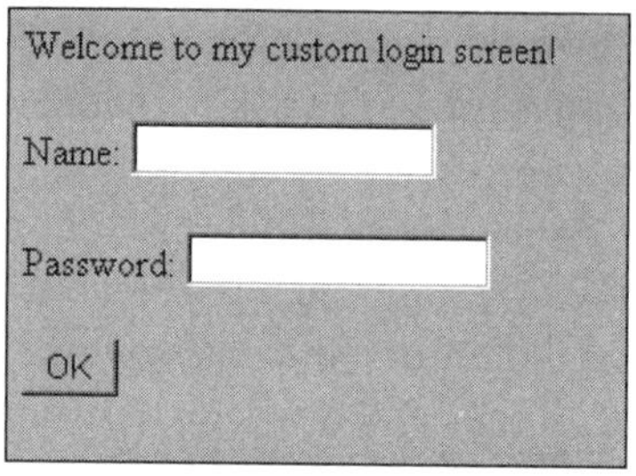

If the user attempts to log in but fails, you can no longer rely on the browser's error dialog box. Consequently, when creating a login form, you must also create an error form. Once again, we will keep it very simple and define the following `Error.html` page:

```
<HTML>
   <BODY>
      You failed to log in successfully.
      Hit the "Back" button to try again.
   </BODY>
</HTML>
```

On their own, the `Login.html` and `Error.html` pages are not linked—meaning that when the user presses the OK button, there is no direct connection to the error page. Instead, the two pages "communicate" via an intermediary. Basically, when someone tries to log in, the server verifies authenticity of the client by using `j_username` to get the username and then using `j_password` to get the password. If there is a failure, the server must be able to find the error form to display. The connection between the code and server is made within the `web.xml` file. Once again, you need to make modifications to this document to inform the server of the name and whereabouts of the login and error pages used during FORM authentication.

The one area that changes is within the `login-config` tags. In addition to identifying the type of authentication, you must also define the location for the custom login page and custom error page:

```
<login-config>
    <auth-method>
        FORM
    </auth-method>
    <form-login-config>
```

```
    <form-login-page>
        /Login.html
    </form-login-page>
    <form-error-page>
        /Error.html
    </form-error-page>
  </form-login-config>
</login-config>
```

Within the `login-config` tags, you not only define the type of authentication, but if it is of type FORM, then you include a sub-element group called `form-login-config`.

The *form-login-config* Element

Fundamentally, this tag is used to help the server locate the forms to display during appropriate times. The two sub-elements are as follows:

- `form-login-page`
- `form-error-page`

As their names indicate, the `form-login-page` tag defines the login page that should be used when a request for protected code is made. This page is displayed instead of the default login dialog box used with BASIC. Similarly, the `form-error-page` defines the error page that will be displayed if authorization is denied.

Customizing your login and error page displays is fairly easy. The trick is to follow the naming conventions within your login pages and modify the deployment descriptor to locate those files.

DIGEST

As we have said, one of the greatest security limitations of BASIC authentication is that information is transferred over the network in simple BASE64-encoded text. Someone snooping the line can easily capture a client's username and password to gain access to the site. DIGEST adds an extra layer of security when authenticating the user. Instead of transferring the password, the server creates a *nonce*, a random value that is unique. An example of a nonce could be the client's IP address followed by a time stamp and some random data. It might look something like this:

```
127.0.0.1:86433665446:dujehIIJRTGDKdkfj
```

The server sends the nonce to the client, and then things get interesting. The client uses a secure encryption algorithm to create, or hash, a digest. A *digest* is a one-directional, encrypted value that represents data. In this case, the digest consists of the nonce, username, and password. Figure 7.4 shows the simple process used to generate a digest.

FIGURE 7.4 Creating a digest

After the digest is generated, the client sends the digest back to the server. The server then uses the nonce it sent originally and the username and password on file to generate a digest on its end. The server compares the digest sent by the client to the one generated locally. If they match, the client can access the protected resource. If not, access is denied.

If the client is valid. Figure 7.5 illustrates the process.

FIGURE 7.5 The DIGEST process

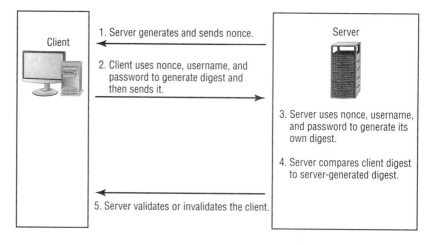

The nonce is critical in that it protects against attackers who intercept the hash value and intend to reuse it at a later date. Because the nonce contains a time stamp and a random value, the request will most likely time out and be removed from the server at a later time, causing the client's request to be invalidated.

Unix administrators are familiar with password encryption. Often passwords are stored in a secure file. However, if someone manages to gain administrative access, they can view this information. Because passwords are considered extremely sensitive and critical data, the OS encrypts them so even the administrator cannot know these values. If an attacker captures the hashed password/digest, they will not have access to the user. Instead they will need to guess various passwords and generate a digest to see whether there was a match. This is because a digest is considered a one-way transformation of data.

Most browsers implement DIGEST authentication in their own manner, making it difficult to set up and use. If it were easier, HTTP authentication could widely provide useful low-level security.

CLIENT-CERT

HTTPS client authentication, or CLIENT-CERT, is the strongest form of authentication. HTTPS is HTTP over Secure Socket Layer (SSL). Instead of simply providing a username and password, the client must provide that information in addition to a personal certificate for authorization to access the server.

A *client certificate* is an encrypted object, known as a signature, personalized with data for a particular person. It provides a secure way to authenticate users communicating over a network. Instead of simply logging into a system and providing a password, which can be decrypted, the user provides a certificate that can be read only by using a special key. Client certificate technology is composed of two pieces: a digital signature and a digital certificate.

A *digital signature* is an object that associates an individual with a particular piece of data. It adds one more level of security to a digest. Not only is it providing authentication, but it also links the user to the data. This means that the request cannot be intercepted, re-signed, and sent by an imposter without the server realizing the error.

Keys are a critical part of understanding how the validation process occurs. Prior to any login attempts, the client generates two keys. The first is a *private key* that holds the individual's authentication code and is stored in a secure location, on a SmartCard or in a file. It should be known and accessed only by its owner. The second is a *public key* given to all receivers to validate the authenticity of the user attempting to log in. When using servlets, the server stores all public keys of users who can access the system in a database or Lightweight Directory Access Protocol (LDAP) directory server. Then when a client tries to access a protected site, they are prompted to provide a user-name and password. When transmitting this information, a digest is generated along with a digital signature by using the client's private key. The digest is then sent to the server, which uses its public key to unlock the signature. If the public key is a forgery and not part of the key pair used by the private key, the signature will not unlock, and the user is invalidated. Figure 7.6 demonstrates the process.

FIGURE 7.6 Digital signatures

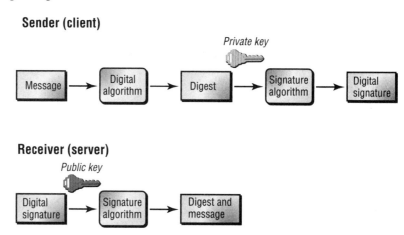

Digital signatures provide integrity by guaranteeing that the data hasn't changed since it was signed. Basically, it is impossible for an attacker to re-create the signature with a new set of data without access to the user's private key. Any alteration of data invalidates the digital signature. In addition, a digital signature also provides authentication because after someone signs something, they cannot deny having done so.

Scenarios that were previously threatening pose no or little threat when using certificates. Here are some potential scenarios:

- If the object is retrieved during its commute to its destination by an unauthorized receiver, that person will be unable to extract its infor-mation because they lack the key.

- Because the certificate also has a time stamp associated with it, a retrieved certificate is invalidated after a period of lapsed time; thus it cannot be forged during future login attempts.

- Obtaining a stolen public key serves no purpose because although it allows you to verify the person sending the certificate, it does not grant you access to the system they are attempting to access.

Unfortunately, digital signatures are not 100 percent safe. When a public key is delivered to a user, there is a possibility that an attacker will acquire this value. You cannot be certain your public key belongs to the client intended unless the key was transferred in an absolutely secure environment. A common problem is known as man-in-the-middle attacks. Someone places themself between the client and server and manages to intercept the authentication and pose as a valid user. If they manage to intercept and alter the public key, then they can configure the public key to recognize a false signature. The goal is to prevent them from manipulating the public key maintained at the target site. One solution to protecting a public key during its transfer is to encrypt communication or use direct connections; the other is to use digital certificates.

Digital certificates attach identity to a public key. They act like a driver's license or passport in that they prove you are who you claim to be. A certificate contains your public key and some additional information signed by a third party's private key. Companies such as VeriSign and Thawte, known as a *certificate authority (CA)*, sell certificates to individuals to enable them to sign their public key. Usually a certificate contains the information outlined in Table 7.1.

TABLE 7.1 Certificate Information

Information	Description
Version	Version of the certificate (v1, v2, v3). Each version contains different attributes.
Serial number	Integer value unique to the CA issuing the certificate.
Signature algorithm	Algorithm used to sign the certificate.
Subject	Whom the certificate is issued to. This item can include a common name, organization or organizational unit, the organization's location, state, and country.

TABLE 7.1 Certificate Information *(continued)*

Information	Description
Subject public key	Public key of the certificate. This is the most important piece.
Signature	Signature signed by the CA.

If a single attribute is changed, the certificate is invalidated. When information needs to be altered, the CA needs to reissue a new certificate.

Instead of sending a public key to intended recipients, you transfer a certificate. If the certificate is intercepted and altered, the certificate and the key within are invalidated. Consequently, the man-in-the-middle technique fails to compromise the client or server. Of course, there is room for certificate corruption. If the certificate authority is not reliable, they can create forged certificates, allowing attackers to act as imposters.

For the most part, client certificates provide the most security but do require the most work. When data transactions are critical and security is essential, a client certificate ensures authentication, authorization, data integrity, and confidentiality. By designing a site where the client must initially provide a certificate and then a digest with each request, you can be almost fully assured that the client is who they say they are and the data they are sending is in its original form.

 Real World Scenario

When Security Is a Priority

You have just been hired to work on securing a website managed by the government. Fairly confidential information is available on this site for officials to access while off site. Your role is to ensure that only authorized users are granted access and to protect the information from malicious attacks.

Due to the sensitive nature of the information, high security is a priority—which means that BASIC, FORM-based, and DIGEST authentication are not options. Mandating certificates becomes the primary option. Each user's private key can be stored on a SmartCard; however, that limits usage to systems that have readers for this device. For systems without this mechanism, you could provide users a CD-ROM containing their authentication information.

Because most browsers fail to automatically support client authentication, you must develop the code to handle the security measures. As a precautionary measure, this machine should be separate from the main system, and at a minimum a firewall would sit between the two. Multiple firewalls between layers of systems and security clearance will further secure the system against harmful attacks. The systems should also be audited regularly to look for unauthorized activity. By using advanced tracking tools, you can notify appropriate members when security breaches are made. Because of the multiple layers of the system, the intruders likely can be stopped before accessing critical information. Utilization of the above security precautions allows the system to be well defended from unauthorized users yet accessible to its intended audience.

Deployment Descriptor Tags

In this chapter, we've discussed almost a third of all the deployment descriptor tags the exam will cover. Now that you've read about each piece separately, we want to provide a final sample of how security is handled as a whole within the web.xml file. See Listing 7.1.

Listing 7.1: Web.xml-Authentication

```
<web-app>
    <servlet>
        <servlet-name>
            secret
        </servlet-name>
        <servlet-class>
```

```
            SalaryServlet
        </servlet-class>
    </servlet>

    <security-constraint>
        <web-resource-collection>
            <web-resource-name>
                SecretProtection
            </web-resouce-name>
            <url-pattern>
                /servlet/SalaryServlet
            </url-pattern>
            <url-pattern>
                /servlet/secret
            </url-pattern>
            <http-method>
                GET
            </http-method>
            <http-method>
                POST
            </http-method>
        </web-resource-collection>
        <auth-constraint>
            <role-name>
                manager
            </role-name>
        </auth-constraint>
    </security-constraint>

    <login-config>
        <auth-method>
            FORM
        </auth-method>
        <form-login-config>
            <form-login-page>
                /Login.html
```

```
                </form-login-page>
                <form-error-page>
                    /Error.html
                </form-error-page>
            </form-login-config>
        </login-config>
    </web-app>
```

Part of your success on the exam depends on your knowledge of each tag, its order, and its purpose. Table 7.2 lists all the tags used for security in the deployment descriptor.

TABLE 7.2 Security Tags

Element	Description
security-constraint	A general element that defines protected resources and roles.
web-resource-collection	A general element that defines the protected resources.
web-resource-name	The human-language name used to reference the protected resource.
url-pattern	The location of the protected resource.
http-method	The methods that the defined roles can access. If no http-method is defined, the default implicitly lists all HTTP methods.
auth-constraint	A general element that defines all roles with access to the protected resources.
role-name	The name of the group with access.
login-config	A general element that defines login configuration information.
auth-method	The type of authentication used by the application.

TABLE 7.2   Security Tags *(continued)*

Element	Description
form-login-config	A general element that defines the configuration information pertaining to forms used in FORM authentication.
form-login-page	The location and file used to display a custom authentication page.
form-error-page	The location and file used to display a custom error page.

Summary

In this chapter, we covered the key elements a developer should consider to ensure security for their application. Depending on the degree of security needed for the web applications you're running, you should consider the following security principles:

- Authorization
- Authentication
- Data integrity
- Auditing (access control)

You should consider each principle and aim for measures which provide a balance between security, and convenience for you and the users.

Servlet containers offer four types of authentication used to ensure different levels of security:

BASIC   The most simple and least secure is HTTP basic authentication. It requests the user's login name and password and transmits the data in a simple encoded format.

FORM   To avoid using the browser's authentication dialog, you can use form-based authentication. This process enables you to customize your authentication and error pages to suit your website.

DIGEST   Added security can be achieved through HTTP digest authentication. Instead of transmitting your password over the network, a digest is submitted between client and server.

CLIENT-CERT   The last type discussed is HTTPS client authentication. It offers the most security and provides the most guarantees by requiring clients to have a private key and a corresponding certificate in order to be authenticated.

To enable security in the application, modifications to the web.xml file are required. Several tags are used to identify the resources that are protected, the location of those resources, the type of authentication used, the methods that can be accessed, and the roles a user must belong to for privileged access.

Exam Essentials

Be able to describe the security issues associated with authentication and authorization.   Validating the user is a critical measure that you must consider for most applications. Not only must the client claim to be a particular user, but they must also provide evidence, such as a password or certificate, to prove their identity. Once authenticated, their roles will define what files they are authorized to access.

Be able to describe the security issues associated with data integrity. When information is transferred over the network, there is potential for interception. Without some form of encryption or security measures, an attacker can intercept the data prior to its arrival for storage or to make alterations before sending it back on its way.

Be able to describe the security issues associated with auditing.   Rather than allowing all users access to all resources, it is important to establish roles, which enforce authorized utilization of protected resources. Auditing user access helps ensure security by limiting access to protected areas.

Be able to describe the security issues associated with malicious code. Code that is sent with the intent to do harm is considered malicious code. The most common form is known as a virus. To avoid such attacks, antivirus software is recommended to screen incoming data. If the code is coming from within, authorizing each user is a way to place responsibility on the source.

Be able to describe the security issues associated with website attacks. Again, there is a great possibility that attackers will want to infiltrate a website for the purpose of gathering or destroying information. Authenticating the user makes this option a little more difficult, but firewalls are a must as well. They shield critical information from the end user or the attacker.

Be able to identify the deployment descriptor element names and their structure for a security constraint.   The `security-constraint` tag is used to define protected resources and which roles have access to those areas. It contains two main sub-elements: `web-resource-collection` and `auth-constraint`.

```
<security-constraint>
    <web-resource-collection>
    </web-resource-collection>
    <auth-constraint>
    </auth-constraint>
</security-constraint>
```

Be able to identify the deployment descriptor element names and their structure for a web resource.   Protected resources are referenced by the `web-resource-collection`. Within this tag are sub-elements called `web-resource-name`, used to define the name of the protected resource; `url-pattern`, used to define the location of the protected resource; and, optionally, `http-method`, used to define the HTTP methods that should have restricted access.

```
<web-resource-collection>
    <web-resource-name>
    </web-resouce-name>
    <url-pattern>
    </url-pattern>
    <http-method>
    </http-method>
</web-resource-collection>
```

Be able to identify the deployment descriptor element names and their structure for login configuration.   The `login-config` tag is used to define authentication rules for the application. The sub-element `auth-method` identifies the type of authentication. If it is of type FORM, then you must also include the `form-login-config` tag to define the custom login and error pages.

```
<login-config>
    <auth-method>
    </auth-method>
    <form-login-config>
        <form-login-page>
        </form-login-page>
        <form-error-page>
        </form-error-page>
    </form-login-config>
</login-config>
```

Be able to identify the deployment descriptor element names and their structure for a security role.   Access is granted to protected resources based on roles. The `auth-constraint` tag uses the `role-name` tag to define which roles have access to the protected resources of the application.

```
<auth-constraint>
    <role-name>
    </role-name>
</auth-constraint>
```

Be able to identify the correct definition of BASIC authentication.   HTTP basic authentication relies on the default authentication dialogs of the browser to request the user's login information.

Be able to identify the correct definition of DIGEST authentication. HTTP digest authentication uses a message digest in place of transferring the user's password.

Be able to identify the correct definition of FORM authentication.   HTTP form-based authentication enables the application to provide its own authentication and error page.

Be able to identify the correct definition of CLIENT-CERT authentication. HTTPS client authentication requires the client to have a private key and corresponding certificate in order to authenticate with the server.

Key Terms

Before you take the exam, be certain you are familiar with the following terms:

access list	hackers
attackers	keys
authentication	malicious code
authorization	nonce
certificate authority (CA)	packet sniffers
client certificate	principal
declarative security	private key
digest	programmatic security
digital certificate	public key
digital signature	role-based
firewalls	

Review Questions

1. Which of the following services would most likely utilize a retinal scan?

   A. Auditing

   B. Authentication

   C. Access control

   D. Data confidentiality

2. Which of the following best describes a principal?

   A. Manager

   B. 8yb3x

   C. bjohnson

   D. Employee

3. Which of the following is not an authentication technique used by a web container?

   A. BASIC

   B. DIGEST

   C. FORM

   D. CLIENT-CERTIFY

4. A public key fails to ensure which of the following?

   A. Confidentiality

   B. Integrity

   C. Authentication

   D. All of the above

5. Which of the following XML tags is appropriate for defining code that is to be protected?

    A. `security-constraint`

    B. `auth-constraint`

    C. `user-data-constraint`

    D. None of the above

6. Which of the following authentication types cannot be used for the `auth-method` element?

    A. BASIC

    B. DIGEST

    C. CERT

    D. FORM

7. When using FORM authentication, your form writes to which of the following URLs?

    A. `/servlet`

    B. `j_security`

    C. `j_security_source`

    D. `j_security_check`

8. Which of the following values is used to define the name for a user login while using FORM authentication?

    A. `j_username`

    B. `j_userlogin`

    C. `j_loginname`

    D. `j_user`

9. Which of the following HTTP methods must be used in FORM authentication?

    A. GET

    B. POST

    C. PUT

    D. HEAD

10. Which of the following deployment descriptor tags are used to identify the HTML page used when authentication fails in FORM authentication?

A. `<form-failed></form-failed>`

B. `<form-authentication-failure></form-authentication-failure>`

C. `<form-error></form-error>`

D. `<form-error-page></form-error-page>`

11. Which of the following deployment descriptor tags encompasses the `form-login-page` and `form-error-page` tags?

A. `<form></form>`

B. `<form-config></form-config>`

C. `<form-login-config></form-login-config>`

D. `<form-authenticate-config></form-authenticate-config>`

12. Which of the following authentication types uses a private key?

A. BASIC

B. DIGEST

C. FORM

D. CLIENT-CERT

13. Which of the following statements is false?

A. A certificate can be bought from a third-party vendor.

B. Certificates contain client information and their public key.

C. CLIENT-CERT stands for HTTPS Client authentication.

D. Most browsers support CLIENT-CERT.

14. Which of the following key terms is used to define a random value generated by the server for authentication purposes?

    A. Nonce

    B. Digest

    C. Certificate

    D. Digital signature

15. Which of the following devices is not a recommended place to store a private key?

    A. A public file

    B. A database

    C. A SmartCard

    D. A secure file

Answers to Review Questions

1. B.   Authentication is a service that requests the principal user to provide proof of their identity. A retinal scan is a very secure form of evidence used in high-security companies and government agencies.

2. C.   A principal is defined as a user. "bjohnson" represents a login name recognized by the system. Usually the principal is associated with a group such as Manager or Employee.

3. D.   The last answer is incorrect. The fourth method for authentication is CLIENT-CERT, which uses a Secure Socket Layer (SSL) to verify the user.

4. C.   A public key encrypts data to provide confidentiality. If it can be decoded accurately, then integrity is ensured. Authentication, however, is not proven by using public keys.

5. A.   Within the `security-constraint` tag, you can define which roles have access to the identified resources by using the `auth-constraint` tag.

6. C.   Client certificates are defined with the name CLIENT-CERT.

7. D.   The standardized name `j_security_check` must be defined as the action for a login screen used in FORM authentication.

8. A.   To ensure that the server retrieves the correct name when requesting the password, you must define its name as `j_username` when using FORM authentication.

9. B.   The form must `POST` a request to the server.

10. D.   The `form-error-page` tag is used to define the error page for the server to display when authentication fails.

11. C.   The `form-login-config` tag contains the two sub-elements: `form-login-page` and `form-error-page`.

12. D.   Client certificates require the client to provide a key and certificate to prove their identity.

13. D. Unfortunately, HTTPS Client authentication, or CLIENT-CERT, is the most secure form of authentication but the least supported. Configuring HTTPS Client authentication is highly server-dependent. Although many servers do not support HTTPS authentication, J2EE servlet containers do.

14. A. A nonce is a random value generated by the server and sent to the client to accompany a digest of the user's username and password.

15. A. A public file is definitely not a recommended place to store a private key. If others can access your private key, they can impersonate you and cause a lot of havoc.

Thread-Safe Servlets

THE FOLLOWING SUN CERTIFIED WEB COMPONENT DEVELOPER FOR J2EE PLATFORM EXAM OBJECTIVES ARE COVERED IN THIS CHAPTER:

- ✓ **7.1 Identify which attribute scopes are thread-safe:**
  - ▪ Local variables
  - ▪ Instance variables
  - ▪ Class variables
  - ▪ Request attributes
  - ▪ Session attributes
  - ▪ Context attributes

- ✓ **7.2 Identify correct statements about differences between the multithreaded and single-threaded servlet models.**

- ✓ **7.3 Identify the interface used to declare that a servlet must use the single thread model.**

Threads seem to be a topic that most developers wish to avoid but can't. In a single-threaded environment, ensuring the integrity of a Java class is as easy as making all instance variables private and providing public accessor or mutator methods. In a multithreaded environment, achieving a "thread-safe" application is a bit more complex. Ensuring application integrity is a difficult task when multiple users have the ability to access and alter the same information simultaneously. When multiple clients concurrently access a single object's data, the application becomes vulnerable to several negative conditions. Those conditions include: object state corruption (the data produced is inaccurate), production of unreliable results (based on inaccurate data), race conditions (more than one thread is competing for data access before the data even exists), and, finally, deadlock (threads are left idle, unable to move forward). To avoid such situations, it is critical for developers to consider the importance of an object's state and how it is handled.

When developing for a multithreaded environment, threading issues cannot be avoided. Servlets are intrinsically *multithreaded*. This means a single instance can be accessed by more than one thread. Because servlets, by their nature, are designed for multiple users, creating a thread-safe environment is a vital key to the success of the application. In this chapter, we will discuss the various ways to handle data and their related threading issues. We will also address the significant differences between a single versus multithreaded model.

Variables and Attributes

Servlets offer a variety of options for storing data. The important points to learn from this chapter are how various data elements are stored and how they are affected by threads. Each variable or attribute provides a different level of scope, which affects access by the user or users. Here is a list of the data types we will discuss in depth in this section:

Local variables   Short-term values that are often used as loop iterators

Instance variables   Data that persists for the life of the servlet, shared by all concurrent users

Class variables   Data that exists for the life of the servlet, is shared by all concurrent users, and is declared static

Request attributes   Data passed to other servlets invoked by the `RequestDispatcher`

Session attributes   Data that persists through all future requests for the current user

Context attributes   Data shared by all servlets that persists for the life of the application

With regard to variables, (as opposed to attributes), concern for thread safety should be applied only to instance and class variables. Here's why: All threads share the same heap, and the heap is where instance variables are stored. When multiple threads are accessing the same instance variable, there is potential for data corruption, because more than one thread can access that same instance variable. Class variables have a similar problem; they are stored within the same Java Virtual Machine (JVM) method area. This means multiple threads can use the same class variables concurrently. In summary, because all threads share the same heap and the same method area, there is potential for data corruption with regard to multiple threads having access to class and instance variables.

Local variables, method parameters, and return values are quite different. These variables reside on the Java stack. The JVM awards each thread its own Java stack. Because each thread has its own set of local variables, method parameters, and return values, there is no need to worry about multi-threaded access. Table 8.1 identifies each variable discussed and indicates whether it is architecturally designed to be thread-safe.

Now that you have a general understanding of how threads affect the different variables, we will discuss how to avoid problems with each variable type.

TABLE 8.1 Which Variables Are Thread-Safe

Variable Type	Thread-Safe
Class	No
Instance	No
Local	Yes
Parameter	Yes
Return	Yes

Local Variables

Local variables are defined within the body of a method. This limits the variable's scope to the life of the method, leaving little or no threading issues to worry about. Each requesting thread that accesses a servlet's method is assigned a new local variable. Consequently, each individual thread accesses its own local variable(s). Listing 8.1 provides a simple example of a servlet using a local variable.

Listing 8.1: Using Local Variables

```
import javax.servlet.*;
import javax.servlet.http.*;
import java.io.*;
import java.util.*;

public class LocalVariableServlet extends HttpServlet {

    public void doGet(HttpServletRequest req,
                      HttpServletResponse res)
       throws ServletException, IOException {
         int count=0;

         res.setContentType("text/plain");
         PrintWriter out = res.getWriter();
```

```
            count = (int)Math.round(Math.random());
            out.println("Count = " + count);
        }
    }
```

Listing 8.1 creates a new count variable for each thread accessing the doGet(...) method. A random value is generated and rounded to the nearest integer value. It is then assigned to the count variable to finally print to the response output stream. Figure 8.1 provides a visual representation of how four threads accessing LocalVariableServlet obtain their own count variable. By design, local variables are thread-safe.

FIGURE 8.1 Clients obtain their own local variable

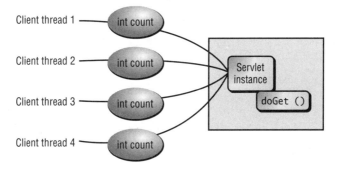

Instance Variables

Instance variables are defined within the class body and are separately assigned to each instantiated object. However, because servlets are often instantiated by the container and service multiple requests, it is likely that many threads will access the same servlet instance and its variables. This behavior defies the basic threading rule, which states that more than one thread should not access the same object. Breaking this rule can result in data corruption if not handled correctly.

Understanding the servlet life cycle helps clarify *why* instance variables are susceptible to concurrency issues. A servlet is initialized either when the web container first starts up or when the servlet is called for the first time. Once created, the instance is stored for client access. Each client accessing the servlet invokes the same instance. This means the client will view and modify the same instance variables as the previous client. Listing 8.2 defines a count variable that is incremented when each thread makes a GET request to the InstanceVariableServlet class.

Listing 8.2: Using Instance Variables

```
import javax.servlet.*;
import javax.servlet.http.*;
import java.io.*;
import java.util.*;

public class InstanceVariableServlet extends HttpServlet{
    int count=0;

    public void doGet(HttpServletRequest req,
                      HttpServletResponse res)
      throws ServletException, IOException {

        res.setContentType("text/plain");
        PrintWriter out = res.getWriter();

        count++;
        out.println("Count = " + count);
    }
}
```

The problem with utilizing instance variables is that when two threads invoke the same servlet, they can corrupt each other's data. Thread A could cause count to increment to 1, but before it prints the count value, thread B could gain access to the instance and cause count to increment to 2. After control is returned to the first thread, the output will display 2 rather than the correct value, 1.

Unlike local variables, instance variables are shared among all accessing threads. See Figure 8.2.

To protect against data corruption, shared data must be accessed by only one thread at a time. Solving this problem requires utilizing the lock associated with the instance. By wrapping non-thread-safe code in a *synchronized* code block, you force the requesting thread to acquire the instance lock in order to gain access to the code block. For example:

```
synchronized(this) {
    count++;
    out.println("Count = " + count);
}
```

FIGURE 8.2 Clients share the instance

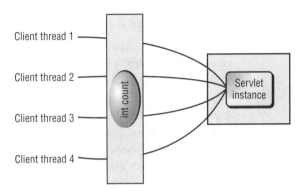

After a thread obtains the object's lock, it accesses the synchronized code block and holds on to the lock until exiting the code block. Other threads attempting to enter the same block are forced to wait until the lock is relinquished by the first thread, as seen in Figure 8.3.

FIGURE 8.3 Accessing the instance in turns

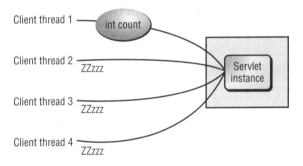

By synchronizing the instance variable data, you protect against another thread corrupting shared data. However, from a stylistic point of view, there are a few more concepts to consider. Synchronizing code can cause:

- Reduction in performance

- Deadlock

- Increased resource utilization

Blocking other threads comes with a price. While a thread waits for a lock, it is inactive and not productive. The result is a reduction in performance.

Another consideration is the potential for deadlock. Sometimes locking too much information can prevent the application from moving forward.

Consider a scenario with two threads: The first thread gains access to a synchronized block and attempts to accomplish a task. A second thread attempts to enter the same code block but is forced to wait because it lacks the lock. The first thread, however, encounters a problem. It is unable to execute code because it is waiting on results from the second thread—and the second thread can't provide any results because it is waiting for the lock to be relinquished. Ultimately, both threads are at a standstill. To minimize the possibility of deadlock, you should synchronize only that code absolutely requiring protection.

The final issue concerning locks is the overhead required to transfer the lock between object and thread. Again, utilizing resources to swap objects between threads can slow down the application or server.

Listing 8.3 shows how to prevent data corruption and keep performance high.

Listing 8.3: Using the Instance Variable Safely

```
import javax.servlet.*;
import javax.servlet.http.*;
import java.io.*;
import java.util.*;

public class InstanceVariableServlet extends HttpServlet{
    int count=0;

    public void doGet(HttpServletRequest req,
                      HttpServletResponse res)
      throws ServletException, IOException {

        res.setContentType("text/plain");
        PrintWriter out = res.getWriter();

        synchronized(this) {
            count++;
            out.println("Count = " + count);
        }
    }
}
```

This solution works best if there is a need to protect shared data. Another option is to make the variable *immutable*. This means the variable is final and cannot change. Without the ability for change, there is no chance of corrupting the value. Of course, this option wouldn't work in this scenario, but it is another consideration.

In summary, instance variables are not considered thread-safe and should be avoided if possible. If utilizing an instance variable is unavoidable, then sensitive code should be carefully synchronized to prevent multiple threads from distorting the data.

Class Variables

Class variables, or static variables, are shared among all instances of a servlet. It is a misconception to think a server will create only one instance of a particular servlet. The truth is, the server can create a new instance of the same servlet for each registered `servlet-name` defined. Within the `web.xml` file, a single servlet can be registered under multiple names. The following code demonstrates how this is done:

```
<web-app>

  <servlet>
    <servlet-name>First</servlet-name>
    <servlet-class>ClassVariableServlet</servlet-class>
  </servlet>
  <servlet>
    <servlet-name>Second</servlet-name>
    <servlet-class>ClassVariableServlet</servlet-class>
  </servlet>
  <servlet>
    <servlet-name>Third</servlet-name>
    <servlet-class>ClassVariableServlet</servlet-class>
  </servlet>

</web-app>
```

Notice that the `ClassVariableServlet` can be referenced by the name `First`, `Second`, or `Third`. The server can, in fact, create an instance for each referenced name if necessary. Consequently, any class or static variable defined in the `ClassVariableServlet` is shared among all instances. Listing 8.4 demonstrates how the servlet monitors the number of instances and how its variables are affected.

Listing 8.4: Using Class Variables

```java
import javax.servlet.*;
import javax.servlet.http.*;
import java.util.*;
import java.io.*;

public class ClassVariableServlet extends HttpServlet{
  int count;

  static HashMap instances = new HashMap();
  static int classCount;

  public void doGet(HttpServletRequest req,
                    HttpServletResponse res)
    throws ServletException, IOException {
      res.setContentType("text/plain");
      PrintWriter out = res.getWriter();

      count++;
      out.println("Since loading, the " +
          req.getServletPath() +
          " instance has been accessed " +
          count + " times.");

      instances.put(this, this);
      out.println("There are currently " +
          instances.size() + " instances.");

      classCount++;
      out.println("Across all instances, the " +
                  "ClassVariableServlet class has been " +
                  "accessed " + classCount + "times.");
  }
}
```

This code is made up of three important parts. The first is an instance variable that is monitored and incremented by each reference or instance. The second part is a java.util.HashMap used to count the number of instances maintained by the server. Each reference is added by using the put(...) method, and duplicates are ignored. The final important piece is the class variable called `classCount`. It measures the number of times the `ClassVariable-Servlet` is accessed among all instances.

The output generated from this servlet will differ with each request, and as each instance is created and accessed. The first time this servlet is run, it will have been accessed once with only one instance created. However, if the servlet is reloaded, the result shown in Figure 8.4 will occur.

FIGURE 8.4   A single instance

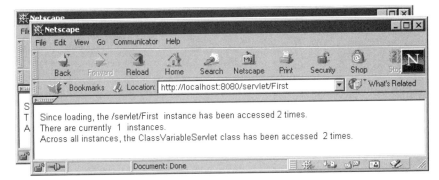

When the browser reloads the servlet, the doGet(...) method is accessed again, causing both instance and class variables to increment. Notice that a reload does not cause a new instance to be created. You can expect the same behavior if another thread accesses the /servlet/First servlet.

Now let's consider a different scenario. If a new thread attempts to access the same servlet but uses the reference /servlet/Second, the output shown in Figure 8.5 will result.

FIGURE 8.5   A second instance

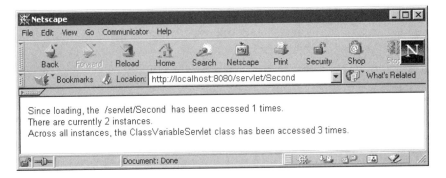

The server creates a new instance of the `ClassVariableServlet` and its instance variable is accessed only once. The variable `classCount`, however, is accessed for a third time: first when `/servlet/First` was accessed, then on its reload, and now by `/servlet/Second`.

Our final image drives home the difference between an instance versus class variable. Figure 8.6 shows how a third thread accessing `/servlet/Third` causes the values to change.

FIGURE 8.6   The third instance

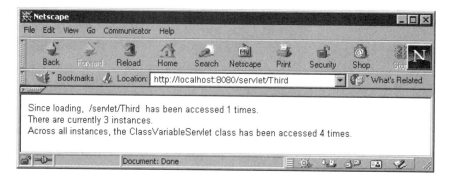

Once again, a new instance is created. While the instance variable is accessed for the first time, the class variable has now been incremented four times.

For each registered name, a servlet can have unique `init` parameters. Consequently, multiple instances of the same servlet can have different initialization attributes.

Now that we have established how class variables work, we can focus on how they behave when accessed by multiple threads. Basically, class or static variables are shared among all instances of the servlet, which makes them vulnerable to threading issues. In a multithreaded application, static variable behave the same way instance variables do. Both allow multiple users to access the data simultaneously. If a method alters either variable type and is accessed by one thread, a second thread could call that same or a different method, altering the variable simultaneously. The end result is a corrupt value.

The solution to class variable threading issues is the same as the one used for instance variables: simply synchronize critical data or make the variables immutable. These actions can protect against problems generated from multiple access.

Request Attributes

When a servlet attempts to use another servlet to process part or all of a response, a `RequestDispatcher` is used. The originating servlet sends both the request and response to the target servlet for further execution. However, prior to transmission, objects can be associated with the request. These objects are called *request attributes*. The `setAttribute(String name, Object obj)` method of the `ServletRequest` interface allows additional information to be associated with the request object. Once the request object contains all its necessary information, one of the following methods of the `RequestDispatcher` interface is invoked to transfer part or all of the control to the target servlet:

The forward(...) method   The `forward(HttpServletRequest req, HttpServletResponse resp)` method causes the servlet engine to "forward" control of the HTTP request internally from your current servlet to another servlet or JSP or static file. The target resource is responsible for generating or delivering the response.

The include(...) method   The `include(HttpServletRequest req, HttpServletResponse resp)` method means you "include" the result of another resource, such as a servlet, JSP, or HTML page, inside the response. The calling servlet then regains control of the response for further modifications.

For a detailed discussion on the `RequestDispatcher`, refer to Chapter 2, "The Servlet Model."

Manually handling servlet-to-servlet communication would be a difficult task to manage, especially in a multithreaded environment. The `RequestDispatcher` object is designed to streamline the process and ensure that concurrency problems do not occur. Listing 8.5 shows a basic servlet dispatching a request to another servlet called `TargetServlet`.

Listing 8.5: A Simple RequestDispatcher Servlet

```
import javax.servlet.*;
import javax.servlet.http.*;
import java.io.*;
import java.util.*;
import javax.swing.*;

public class CallingServlet extends HttpServlet {

    public void doGet(HttpServletRequest req,
                      HttpServletResponse res)
        throws ServletException, IOException {

        ImageIcon icon = new ImageIcon(
            getInitParameter("icon"));

        req.setAttribute("logo", icon);
        String display = "/servlet/TargetServlet";
        RequestDispatcher dispatcher =
            req.getRequestDispatcher(display);
        dispatcher.forward(req, res);
    }
}
```

In this example, the calling thread begins by requesting an icon defined within the web.xml file. Remember, the return value can actually differ depending on the reference name mapped to this servlet instance. After the icon is obtained, it is associated with the request object by using the setAttribute(...) method. The path for the target servlet is then defined and must be relative to the servlet context for the application. A RequestDispatcher to the TargetServlet is acquired. Finally, both request and response objects are forwarded to the target source.

To dispatch a request to a resource *outside* the current servlet context, you must use the ServletContext.getRequestDispatcher(*String path*) method.

Control is returned to the calling thread when using the `forward(…)` or `include(…)` method; however, with the `forward(…)` method, no further modifications to the response can be made.

With a basic understanding of how the `RequestDispatcher` transfers control to another servlet, the fundamental question of whether its request attributes are thread-safe must be answered. Amidst the chaos of request dispatching, the request attributes are actually thread-safe. The imagery of control transferring between multiple servlets, while multiple threads are accessing the original caller, might seem confusing; however, some fundamental rules prevent problems from occurring in this environment.

The logic rests on two critical points:

- Dispatched requests must run in the same Servlet engine, JVM, and Thread as the servlet.

- Dispatcher parameter values are not shared among threads within a single JVM

The container creates the `RequestDispatcher` object to wrap around the target servlet (or another server resource). This dispatcher must run within the same servlet engine, JVM, and thread as the target servlet. Consequently, the `RequestDispatcher` oversees and manages the transfer of control.

When dispatched, a single thread moves between the source and the target servlet. Because the attributes are linked to the request object, any other thread accessing the dispatcher code will be assigned its own thread and therefore cannot affect the attributes of first dispatched thread.

The second point builds on the first: request parameters are not shared. Each request dispatch causes the calling thread to separately store its set of request attributes on the heap. Consequently, if one thread modifies its attributes, it will not affect other dispatch threads.

Ultimately, the `RequestDispatcher` ensures that the integrity of the data will not be compromised. Figure 8.7 demonstrates the process.

FIGURE 8.7 Thread-safe request parameters

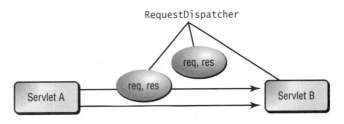

The RequestDispatcher acts like a traffic manager in a multithreaded world. It routes traffic from point A to point B while making sure no collisions occur. Without the dispatcher, it would be difficult to avoid concurrency problems as parameters are passed between servlets. Because request attributes are designed for utilization with the RequestDispatcher, you can be assured they are thread-safe.

Session Attributes

When a user accesses an application, their short-term data can be tracked by using a session object. The object comprises temporary client information referred to as *session attributes*. A session begins when the developer creates an HttpSession object for the client. That can happen when the client visits the first or subsequent pages of the application. The session ends either when the developer terminates their access or after an elapsed time period. Because a session is created by the container and associated with each client through its request object, threading is handled internally and is quite safe.

A servlet uses the HttpServletRequest method getSession() to retrieve the current session. That value should be stored in a local variable to avoid concurrency issues. After the session object is obtained, the servlet uses the setAttribute(*String name, Object obj*) method of the HttpSession interface to store client information, and the getAttribute(*String name*) method to retrieve data. Listing 8.6 shows how a servlet sets client attributes to the session.

Listing 8.6: Using Session Attributes

```
import javax.servlet.*;
import javax.servlet.http.*;
import java.io.*;
import java.util.*;

public class SessionServlet extends HttpServlet {

    public void doGet(HttpServletRequest req,
                      HttpServletResponse res)
      throws ServletException, IOException {
```

```
HttpSession session = req.getSession();
session.setAttribute("userName",
  req.getRemoteUser());

res.setContentType("text/plain");
PrintWriter out = res.getWriter();
out.println("Welcome " +
  session.getAttribute("userName"));
  }
}
```

The session is retrieved dynamically from the current request object. Because of Java's design, you are guaranteed that the request parameter is directly threaded to the current client. As a result, the session returned is also the session associated with the client accessing this code. Any attributes added or acquired fall under the same category and are thread-safe. Once the variable is local to a method, there is no threat of data corruption from intercepting threads due to local variable threading rules. Figure 8.8 provides a visual representation of how session objects and their attributes are linked directly to the client thread.

FIGURE 8.8 Sessions linked to the client

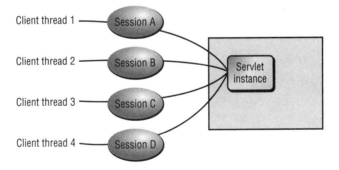

Fundamentally, each client operates on its own session object. By design, adding session attributes is thread-safe.

Context Attributes

As discussed in Chapter 2, the ServletContext is an object that provides global data to an entire application. This global data is referred to as *context attributes*. If a servlet needs to acquire the port number used to access the main database, it would invoke the `getServletContext()` method to first get a handle to the application's context. It then would call the `getAttribute(String name)` method, using the key name, to return the desired port number.

Remember not to confuse attributes with parameters. Parameters are defined within the deployment descriptor, and return only String values associated to a key name. Attributes, on the other hand, return a value of type Object to its associated key.

Context attributes are shared by all servlets and JSPs within the web application. Generally, servlets use the `ServletContext`'s `getAttribute(...)` method to read context data, and rarely use the `setAttribute(...)` method to define the values.

Before a servlet can get an attribute it must first be set. This is usually done by another servlet. Let's assume another servlet executes the following code:

```
context.setAttribute("driver",
        "oracle.jdbc.driver.OracleDriver");
context.setAttribute("databaseProtocol",
        "jdbc:oracle://dbServer1:1521");
```

This would enable any servlet within the web application to get the attribute driver or databaseProtocol .

Listing 8.7 displays a basic servlet using the `ServletContext` to retrieve a context attribute for the database driver needed to establish a database connection.

Listing 8.7: Using Context Attributes

```
import javax.servlet.*;
import javax.servlet.http.*;
import java.io.*;
import java.util.*;
import java.sql.*;
```

```
public class ContextServlet extends HttpServlet {

    public void doGet(HttpServletRequest req,
                      HttpServletResponse res)
       throws ServletException, IOException {

        res.setContentType("text/plain");
        PrintWriter out = res.getWriter();

        ServletContext context = getServletContext();
        String driver =
            (String)context.getAttribute("driver");
        try {
            Class.forName(driver);
            Connection con = DriverManager.getConnection(
                context.getAttribute("databaseProtocol") +
                "CustomerListDB");
            ...
        } catch (ClassNotFoundException e) {
            out.println("Unable to load driver");
        } catch (SQLException e) {
            out.println(e.getMessage());
        }

    }

}
```

This code demonstrates the use of context attributes in a simple way. How threads are handled is another story. Because all application resources have access to the data within a context, a modification made by one thread will affect all other threads. If thread A calls setAttribute(...) and changes the value of the driver attribute, thread B will access the new driver when getAttribute("driver") is called. So, as you can see, problems arise if during the implementation of the setAttribute(...) method, another thread calls setAttribute(...) on the same name. If the method setAttribute(...) is not synchronized, there is potential for concurrency problems. Most server applications offer a synchronized setAttribute(...) method; however, it is not mandated, nor is it guaranteed.

So in summary, we can say context attributes can be thread-safe only if the setAttribute method is synchronized.

Single-Threaded Servlets

One solution to preventing threading problems within servlets is to limit the number of threads that can access a single servlet to one. This can be done by having the servlet implement the *SingleThreadModel* interface. There are no methods that must be implemented. Instead, the interface is used as a flag to notify the container how to handle the servlet life cycle. As per the API specifications, a servlet that implements the `SingleThreadModel` is "guaranteed" to allow only one thread access to the `service(...)` method at a time. This guarantee is achieved by the container either synchronizing access to the single servlet instance or maintaining a pool of servlet instances. The latter approach is more common. Containers can be configured to create multiple servlet instances per a single registered name. Figure 8.9 shows this graphically.

FIGURE 8.9   How the `SingleThreadModel` affects instances

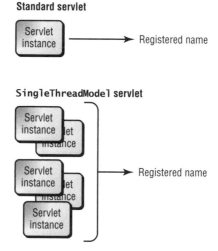

As a request comes in, the container provides an available instance from the pool. When resources run out, the container can either make the current thread wait or produce another instance. The benefit of this model is that each thread has access to its own instance variables for the servlet. This means instance variables are now thread-safe without the need to synchronize. One problem solved.

Unfortunately, threading issues extend beyond instance variables. Class variables are not protected by the `SingleThreadModel` interface. Because class variables are shared among all instances, including those registered by the same name, a method that changes their value can cause data corruption. Imagine the following scenario. Thread A begins by using its personal instance to access the doGet(...) method. The doGet(...) method makes a change to a class variable. If thread B comes into the picture, it also uses its own instance to call the same doGet(...) method. Both threads could modify the class variable and cause the other to work using an inaccurate value. Figure 8.10 clarifies the process.

FIGURE 8.10   Class variables with the SingleThreadModel

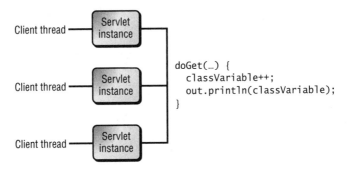

The image shows three instances accessing the same class variable. Implementing the SingleThreadModel interface fails to solve threading problems with class variables. The solution? Synchronization.

Although the SingleThreadModel seems to be the fast and easy solution, it is not encouraged practice. The interface manages to make a single servlet thread-safe, but fails to apply that to the entire system. A positive and a negative still result in a negative. The encouraged alternatives are to synchronize methods or use external resource pools.

Single versus Multithreaded Servlets

When one thread accesses a Java class, there is little concern for corruption. Servlets, however, are different. By design, even single-threaded servlets can provide room for data errors. Generally, a container will create an instance of the servlet by calling its constructor and init() method. The servlet will then persist until additional requests are made. With the implementation of the `SingleThreadModel` interface, each request will either wait in turn to access the instance's `service(...)` method or get its own unique instance of the registered servlet. Instance variables are protected, but shared resources are still not thread-safe.

Multithreaded servlets must use synchronized blocks to protect data that can be concurrently accessed. In summary, Table 8.2 identifies the differences between single-threaded and multithreaded servlets.

TABLE 8.2 Thread-safe?

Data Element	Normally Thread-safe?	Synchronized	`SingleThreadModel`
Local variables	Yes	N/A	N/A
Instance variables	No	Yes	Yes
Class variables	No	Yes	No
Request attributes	Yes	Yes	Yes
Session attributes	Yes	Yes	Yes
Context attributes	Depends	Yes	Depends

 Real World Scenario

Ways to Handle Multiple Threads

A local university has hired you to help design their website used to run courses online. Each course is designed to have a maximum of 100 students enrolled at a time. Although the majority of each class will consist of static pages containing information, the application must also provide testing, discussion, and homework areas. These areas will be designed by using servlets and will also be accessible to all students.

The problem is that multiple students can access a servlet—for example, the TestServlet—and corrupt other students' access. To avoid creating a mess, there are two solutions. The first is to have the servlet implement the SingleThreadModel interface. Given the server used, this option will cause the container to create a pool of instances. This approach ensures that each student uses their own servlet instance, with its own instance variables to process the exam. The second option is to process the servlet in its normal state and define the students' answers as session attributes. The downside of this approach is that if the student leaves their system for an extended period of time, the session will time out and they will need to start over. There are many ways to solve a problem. Depending on the server's capabilities and performance issues, one approach will outweigh another.

Summary

In this chapter, we discussed the various threading issues associated with a variety of data elements. When multiple threads access a servlet, its instance and class variables are vulnerable to corruption. Local variable and method parameters are safe due to the design of the JVM. To protect data against possible corruption, synchronized code blocks can be placed around calls to modify the data. By forcing threads to obtain the object's lock for access, you prevent multiple threads from simultaneously altering critical data.

Another solution to threading issues is to have the servlet implement the SingleThreadModel interface. As discussed in this chapter, this can solve some of the problems, but can still leave you with the need to synchronize shared data. The other option is to make variables immutable. It's one solution, but not practical.

In conclusion, the following suggestions can be made: In place of instance variables, session attributes provide a safer way to handle data in a multithreaded environment. If applicable, context attributes can provide more thread safety than class variables.

Exam Essentials

Be able to identify which of the following variables and attributes are thread-safe: local variables, instance variables, class variables, request attributes, session attributes, and context attributes.   It is important to know how each variable and attribute is affected by multiple client access. Instance and class variables are especially prone to concurrency issues. Local variables and session/request attributes are thread-safe. Context attributes can be corrupted, but their design makes that unlikely.

Be able to identify correct statements about the differences between multithreaded and single-threaded servlet models.   The multithreaded model allows more than one client request to access a single instance. If variables are synchronized, concurrency problems can be avoided. The single-threaded model is designed to have only one request access an instance at a time. Although this seems to solve all threading problems, it doesn't. Synchronization is still necessary on certain variables or attributes.

Be able to identify the interface used to declare that a servlet must use the single-thread model.   The `SingleThreadModel` interface guarantees that a request will access its own servlet instance. Although this option offers some thread safety, it does not protect the entire application from threading issues.

Key Terms

Before you take the exam, be certain you are familiar with the following terms:

class variables	multithreaded
context attributes	request attributes
immutable	session attributes
instance variables	`SingleThreadModel`
local variables	synchronized

Review Questions

1. Which of the following code samples defines a class variable?

   A.
   ```
   public class MyServlet extends HttpServlet {
       public void doGet(HttpServletRequest req,
                           HttpServletResponse res)
         throws ServletException, IOException {
         int count=0;
         ...
       }
   }
   ```

   B.
   ```
   public class MyServlet extends HttpServlet {
       static int count = 0;
       public void doGet(HttpServletRequest req,
                           HttpServletResponse res)
         throws ServletException, IOException {
         ...
       }
   }
   ```

   C.
   ```
   public class MyServlet extends HttpServlet {
       int count;
       public void doGet(HttpServletRequest req,
                           HttpServletResponse res)
         throws ServletException, IOException {
         ...
       }
   }
   ```

   D. None of the above

2. Which of the following data elements are considered thread-safe?

   A. Local variables

   B. Static variables

   C. Class variables

   D. Instance variables

3. Which of the following statements best describes how to protect against data corruption?

    A. Synchronizing only shared data

    B. Synchronizing all servlet methods

    C. Synchronizing the `doGet()` or `service()` method

    D. Making all instance and class variables immutable

4. Identify the data element used to transfer control with a `RequestDispatcher`.

    A. Instance variable

    B. Request attribute

    C. Session attribute

    D. Dispatcher attribute

5. Request attributes are associated with which of the following?

    A. The request object

    B. The `RequestDispatcher`

    C. All instances of the servlet

    D. The current servlet

6. Which of the following cannot be created from multithreaded access?

    A. Corrupt data

    B. Synchronized blocks

    C. Deadlock

    D. Unreliable return values

7. Which of the following statements is true?

    A. To access a synchronized block, a thread must obtain the object's lock.

    B. After a synchronized block is accessed, other threads can access the code if they have a higher priority.

    C. You can synchronize an entire method or just its parameters.

    D. An object's lock is relinquished after the method is complete.

8. Under most circumstances, which of the following data types exists for the life of the current user?

   A. Local variables

   B. Class variables

   C. Session attributes

   D. Request attributes

9. What methods must be defined when the `SingleThreadModel` interface is implemented?

   A. `public void run()`

   B. `public void synchronize(Object lock)`

   C. `public void block()`

   D. None of the above

10. Which of the following items are located on the Java stack? (Choose all that apply.)

    A. Instance variables

    B. Local variables

    C. Method parameters

    D. Class variables

11. Poor use of synchronization can result in which of the following problems? (Choose all that apply.)

    A. Reduction in performance

    B. Thread termination

    C. Deadlock

    D. Increased resource utilization

12. Which of the following statements is true?

    A. A container can create only one instance per servlet class.

    B. A requesting thread receives a handle to a servlet instance from the container.

    C. A container will create only one instance per a servlet's registered name, under all circumstances.

    D. A container is likely to create a pool of instances of a particular servlet if it does not implement the `SingleThreadModel` interface.

13. Which of the following statements is most likely false?

    A. A separate `RequestDispatcher` is only associated with each request object.

    B. Request attributes are indirectly linked to the `RequestDispatcher` object.

    C. A `RequestDispatcher` manages threading issues associated with the request attributes of each request object.

    D. The `RequestDispatcher` is a wrapper for the target servlet.

14. Which of the following statements are false? (Choose all that apply.)

    A. Context attributes are shared by all threads.

    B. Context attributes can be set within the deployment descriptor.

    C. Context attributes cannot be set by using a `setAttribute(String name, Object obj)` method.

    D. There is never a need to synchronize when making modifications to context attributes.

15. The API specification makes which of the following guarantees when a servlet implements the `SingleThreadModel`?

    A. It guarantees that no two threads will access the same request method.

    B. It guarantees that no two threads will access the same `service(...)` method.

    C. It guarantees that no two threads will access the same instance.

    D. It guarantees that no two threads will access the same variables.

Answers to Review Questions

1. B.   Class variables are defined by using the `static` keyword and are located under the class definition.

2. A.   Local variables are placed on the stack. Because each thread is provided its own stack, there is no chance for another thread to access this value.

3. A.   Synchronizing large blocks of code should be avoided to protect against performance hits. Consequently, only shared data should be locked. As for making all instance and class variables immutable, well, that isn't always a feasible option.

4. B.   The `RequestDispatcher` manages requests that are sent to other server resources. Each request can be composed of additional objects defined as request attributes.

5. A.   Request attributes are linked to the request object and managed by the `RequestDispatcher`. The dispatcher, on the other hand, is linked to the servlet context.

6. B.   Synchronized blocks are created by developers to prevent threading issues. The other options can result from multiple threads accessing the same servlet.

7. A.   A thread must obtain the object's lock to read synchronized code blocks. After the lock is held by one thread, all others must wait until the lock is relinquished—this occurs when the original thread exits the synchronized code block. Finally, you cannot synchronize parameters.

8. C.   A session object is created when a client first accesses a website. During the life of the session, data is added and will continue to persist for the life of the current user or until the session times out.

9. D.   The `SingleThreadModel` interface is a flag interface with no methods. It is used by the container to determine the type of life cycle for the servlet.

10. B, C.   Both local variables and method parameters are stored on the Java stack. Each request is provided its own stack to prevent threading problems. Instance variables are stored in the heap, which is shared by all threads. Finally, class variables are stored in the method area, making them accessible by all threads as well.

11. A, C, D.   If code is not synchronized correctly, negative effects can result. Performance can decline, resource utilization can increase, and threads can freeze. Threads, however, will not terminate.

12. B.   The first option is incorrect because a container usually creates one instance per registered name. The third option is inaccurate because a container can create more than one instance per registered name if the servlet implements the `SingleThreadModel`. Finally, pooling is, in fact, an option when the `SingleThreadModel` interface is implemented. This leaves the second option. When a request is sent to the container, it is up to the container to provide a servlet instance to the requesting thread.

13. A.   The `RequestDispatcher` object can be obtained in two ways. One way is through the `Request` object, and the other is through the `ServletContext` object. Consequently, it is not tightly coupled with the request object.

14. B, C, D.   There is a `setAttribute(String name, Object obj)` method within the `ServletContext` class. Although it isn't used much, it is still available. Because context attributes are shared by all threads, modifications to their values can require synchronization if the `setAttribute(...)` method is not synchronized. B is false because context parameters are defined in the deployment descriptor, not attributes.

15. B.   The API states:

> "If a servlet implements this interface, you are guaranteed that no two threads will execute concurrently in the servlet's service."

Basically, the server can either synchronize the `service(...)` method for that one instance, or it can create a pool of instances and allocate a handle when a request is made. Although the third option is a possibility, it is not guaranteed.

Java Server Pages (JSPs)

THE FOLLOWING SUN CERTIFIED WEB COMPONENT DEVELOPER FOR J2EE PLATFORM EXAM OBJECTIVES ARE COVERED IN THIS CHAPTER:

✓ **8.1 Write the opening and closing tags for the following JSP tag types:**

- Directive
- Declaration
- Scriptlet
- Expression

✓ **8.2 Given a type of JSP tag, identify correct statements about its purpose or use.**

✓ **8.3 Given a JSP tag type, identify the equivalent XML-based tags.**

✓ **8.4 Identify the page directive attribute, and its values, that:**

- Import a Java class into the JSP page
- Declare that a JSP page exists within a session
- Declare that a JSP page uses an error page
- Declare that a JSP page is an error page

✓ **8.5 Identify and put in sequence the following elements of the JSP page life cycle:**

- Page translation
- JSP page compilation
- Load class

- Create instance
- Call jspInit
- Call jspService
- Call jspDestroy

✓ **8.6 Match correct descriptions about purpose, function, or use with any of the following implicit objects:**

- request
- response
- out
- session
- config
- application
- page
- pageContext
- exception

✓ **8.7 Distinguish correct and incorrect scriptlet code for:**

- A conditional statement
- An iteration statement

✓ **9.1 Given a description of required functionality, identify the JSP page directive or standard tag in the correct format with the correct attributes required to specify the inclusion of a web component into the JSP page.**

✓ **10.1 For any of the following tag functions, match the correctly constructed tag, with attributes and values as appropriate, with the corresponding description of the tag's functionality:**

- Declare the use of a JavaBean component within the page.
- Specify, for jsp:useBean or jsp:getProperty tags, the name of an attribute.
- Specify, for a jsp:useBean tag, the class of the attribute
- Specify, for a jsp:useBean tag, the scope of the attribute

- Access or mutate a property from a declared JavaBean.
- Specify, for a `jsp:getProperty` tag, the property of the attribute.
- Specify, for a `jsp:setProperty` tag, the property of the attribute to mutate, and the new value.

✓ **10.2 Given JSP page attribute scopes: `request`, `session`, `application`, identify the equivalent servlet code.**

✓ **10.3 Identify techniques that access a declared JavaBean component.**

One of the goals of the J2EE model is to have each task or role handled separately. By eliminating dependencies, each component becomes reusable, extensible, and manageable. This same philosophy carries over to the Java Server Page (JSP) model. Generally speaking, the Internet's history began with a scripting language called Common Gateway Interface, more commonly known as CGI. CGI provided client-server communication but failed to efficiently handle security, multithreading issues, extensibility, logging capabilities, and other enterprise-related features. This opened the door to servlet technology. Servlets replaced CGI by using Java technology to communicate between the client and application. A servlet intercepts a browser request and executes it on the server by mixing dynamic content with static content generated by HTML. Although servlets provide a Java solution to communication, they still closely link Java and HTML code. JSPs, on the other hand, provide a solution to this level of dependency. As per the JSP specification, JSPs "enable the separation of dynamic and static content." Because JSPs are built on top of servlets, they focus on the presentation while the servlet focuses on the content. In this chapter, we will discuss the design behind this technology and how to implement it correctly.

The JSP Model

To be a first-rate servlet developer, you must be a strong Java programmer. In addition, you should also have decent HTML and design skills to generate elegant graphical responses. In an ideal world, people could accomplish both tasks with proficiency. In a realistic world, however, those who develop the front end, or *presentation layer*, are strong in graphic design and are in a separate group from business logic programmers who develop the middle or back end of an application. This fact makes superior servlet development difficult. The solution to this predicament is to add another technology to servlets to help share the task. This design is known as the *JSP model*. Unlike servlet developers, a good JSP developer simply needs to be strong in design and front-end development. The need to know Java can be left to the servlet programmer. By separating the design developer from the Java developer, you enable a single individual to master the presentation layer while another masters the middle, or business logic, layer.

The JSP model relies on two main objectives. The first is to allow and encourage the separation of the presentation layer from Java code. The second objective is to enable developers to author web pages that have dynamic content, with maximum power and flexibility. By mere design, the second objective is met. As for the first—well, it is still possible to include Java code inside JSP files. The "separation" is encouraged and possible, but not mandatory. Figure 9.1 illustrates how the priorities of each technology differ.

FIGURE 9.1 Servlet design versus JSP design

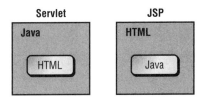

A servlet is Java code with HTML embedded within, whereas a JSP is HTML code with embedded Java. Creating an inverse model enables each developer to focus on their own area of expertise. Let's compare the code necessary to generate a "Hello World!" greeting by using a servlet versus a JSP; see Figure 9.2.

Figure 9.2 proves a developer needs to fully understand Java to write a servlet, whereas a JSP developer's strength is in HTML. Both files generate the same output; "Hello World!" will appear in the top-left corner of the browser. To ensure this result, all JSP pages must be saved by using the `.jsp` extension. In addition, the file (that is, `hello.jsp`) must be placed in either the server's document root or the application's context path.

FIGURE 9.2 Servlet code versus JSP code

HelloServlet.java

```
import javax.servlet.*;
import javax.servlet.http.*;
import java.util.*;

public class HelloServlet extends HttpServlet {
    public void doGet(HttpServletRequest req,
                      HttpServletResponse res)
      throws ServletException, IOException {

        res.setContentType("text/html");

        PrintWriter out = res.getWriter();
        out.println("<HTML>");
        out.println("<BODY>");
        out.println("Hello World!");
        out.println("</BODY>");
        out.println("</HTML>");
    }
}
```

hello.jsp

```
<HTML>
  <BODY>
    Hello World!
  </BODY>
</HTML>
```

Most vendors who support servlets also provide JSP support. The reference implementation for JSPs is called Jasper. It is embedded within the Tomcat server.

The naming standard for JSP pages suggests that all filenames should be identified with an initial lowercase letter.

Next, we will discuss how JSPs work.

JSP Life Cycle

The first time a client makes a request, the JSP engine captures the request and loads the appropriate .jsp page. It then creates a special servlet from the Java Server Page to execute the page's content. Listing 9.1 shows the wrapper class source code generated by an Apache server to execute the hello.jsp page. (The actual code may very among servers.)

Listing 9.1: JSP to Servlet Code for hello.jsp

```
import javax.servlet.*;
import javax.servlet.http.*;
```

```java
import javax.servlet.jsp.*;
import org.apache.jasper.runtime.*;

public class hello$jsp extends HttpJspBase {

  static {}
  public hello$jsp() {}

  private static boolean _jspx_inited = false;

  public final void _jspx_init()
    throws org.apache.jasper.runtime.JspException {}

  public void _jspService(HttpServletRequest request,
                          HttpServletResponse  response)
    throws java.io.IOException, ServletException {

    JspFactory _jspxFactory = null;
    PageContext pageContext = null;
    HttpSession session = null;
    ServletContext application = null;
    ServletConfig config = null;
    JspWriter out = null;
    Object page = this;
    String  _value = null;

    try {
      if (_jspx_inited == false) {
        synchronized (this) {
          if (_jspx_inited == false) {
            _jspx_init();
            _jspx_inited = true;
          }
        }
      }
    _jspxFactory = JspFactory.getDefaultFactory();
```

```
    response.setContentType(
      "text/html;charset=ISO-8859-1");
    pageContext =
      jspxFactory.getPageContext(
        this, request, response,"", true, 8192, true);
    application = pageContext.getServletContext();
    config = pageContext.getServletConfig();
    session = pageContext.getSession();
    out = pageContext.getOut();

    // HTML // begin
[file="/jsp/checkbox/checkresult.jsp"from=(0,0);to=(7,0)]
    out.write("<html>\r\n<body>\r\n
Hello World!\r\n</body>\r\n</html>\r\n");
    // end

  } catch (Throwable t) {
    if (out != null && out.getBufferSize() != 0)
        out.clearBuffer();
    if (pageContext != null)
        pageContext.handlePageException(t);
  } finally {
    if (_jspxFactory != null)
        _jspxFactory.releasePageContext(pageContext);
  }
 }
}
```

As you can see, the JSP engine dynamically generates all the necessary servlet logic to provide functionality for the presentation layer. The "Hello World!" string is written to the output stream defined within the service method.

Later, when we discuss implicit objects (bold objects within the code), you might want to refer back to this example to see exactly where and how these variables are defined.

A fundamental servlet rule is that all servlets must implement the `javax.servlet.Servlet` interface. Standard servlets extend `javax.servlet.http.HttpServlet`, which indirectly implements the `javax.servlet.Servlet` interface. A servlet converted from a JSP must follow the same directive. The difference, however, is that the extending class is a container-specific implementation. Figure 9.3 diagrams the inheritance/implementation hierarchy.

FIGURE 9.3 Servlet inheritance hierarchy

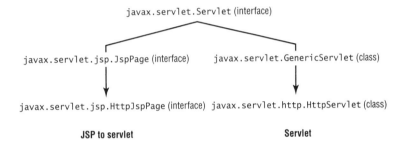

All servlets converted from a JSP must utilize the `javax.servlet.jsp.JspPage` interface. It contains two important methods:

void jspInit() is invoked when the first request is made to initialize the JSP.

void jspDestroy() is invoked by the container to clean up resources—for example, when the container shuts down, or when the generated servlet is unloaded from memory.

To provide additional functionality, a declaration can be used to override both these methods within the JSP. Declarations are covered in the next section, "JSP Elements."

Next, let's look at the interface `javax.servlet.jsp.HttpJspPage`. It adds the most important method:

void _jspService(*HttpServletRequest request, HttpServletResponse response*) captures every JSP request. (The `_jspService(...)` method is to the JSP as the `service(...)` method is to the servlet.)

WARNING The implementation for this method is generated by the container and should *not* be overridden.

The servlet produced is stored on the server for future needs. Initially, the first client who accesses the JSP page will experience a delay, known as the *first-person penalty*. This delay results from the time required to generate and compile (or translate) the JSP into a servlet. Figure 9.4 illustrates the life-cycle process.

FIGURE 9.4 JSP life cycle

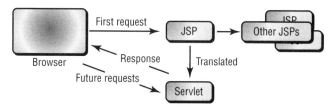

Specifically, a JSP goes through the following process before it can be utilized: When a client first makes a request for a JSP, the container determines whether one currently exists. The container uses an internal list that maps the name of each .jsp page with its compiled .class file. If a reference does not exist, the .jsp page is translated to Java servlet code and a .java file is created. The container then compiles the code, generating a .class file, and loads it into memory. An instance is created, and then the servlet's init() method is invoked. At that point, the _jspService(...) method is next in line. The request and response are passed to the _jspService(...) method to complete execution. JSPs do not have doXXX() methods.

If a servlet for the JSP already exists, the container will determine whether the page needs to be regenerated or recompiled. Based on server settings, the container might regenerate the JSP if a timeout occurred since the last generation. A time-stamp change to the JSP page will also cause an update to the servlet.

Finally, if the server decides to discard the generated servlet, it calls the servlet's destroy() method, which drops the reference to the servlet and sets it up for garbage collection.

The process is as follows:

1. Translate the page (.jsp to .java).

2. Compile the JSP page (.java to .class).

3. Load the class.

4. Create the instance.

5. Call `jspInit()` when the page is first initialized.

6. *Call `_jspService(...)` for every request made to the JSP.

7. Call `jspDestroy()` when the JSP is destroyed by the server.

*All future requests are serviced by the servlet (assuming no changes are made to the JSP).

Now that you understand the general ideas and life cycle behind Java Server Pages, we will focus on the rules and semantics associated with building these powerful pages.

JSP Elements

A JSP page is made up of a variety of tags and elements. Some elements include pieces of Java code, while others transfer control to another object to carry out an intended task. In this section, we will cover acceptable scriptlet techniques used to incorporate Java expressions, variables, methods, code blocks, or conditional statements within a JSP page. Again, the JSP page places priority on web design by making HTML the primary focus, but it still allows the use of Java code in a scripting format. It is a feature and available, but not always encouraged.

Values assigned to JSP elements are case sensitive.

This section covers the following element types:

- Hidden comment
- Declaration
- Expression
- Scriptlet
- Directive

Hidden Comment

A *hidden comment* identifies text that should be ignored by the JSP container. Hidden comments are usually used to explain behavior or to comment out JSP code.

JSP Syntax

```
<%-- comment --%>
```

XML Syntax

None

Example

```
<HTML>
<HEAD><TITLE>A Comment Example</TITLE></HEAD>
<BODY>
<H2>Sample Comments</H2>
<%-- this comment is not included in the response --%>
</BODY>
</HTML>
```

Text written within hidden tags is not included in the response body. Instead, the information is used to help the developer understand and utilize the source code more effectively.

Declaration

A *declaration* declares Java variables or methods that future Java code can access within the JSP page.

JSP Syntax

```
<%! declaration; [declaration;]+    %>
```

Example

```
<%! int k=0;
    int a, b, c;
    Color redColor = new Color(255, 0, 0);
    private static final String MESSAGE="Hello";

    public String getMessage() {
        return MESSAGE;
    }
%>
```

XML Syntax

```
<jsp:declaration>
    declaration; [declaration;]+
</jsp:declaration>
```

Example

```
<jsp:declaration>
    int k=0;
    int a, b, c;
    Color redColor = new Color(255, 0, 0);

    private static final String MESSAGE="Hello";

    public String getMessage() {
        return MESSAGE;
    }
</jsp:declaration>
```

Any declaration that is valid within the Java programming language is valid within the declaration JSP elements. This includes multiple declarations as well as variable declarations combined with method declarations. The use of the `static` keyword has the same effect as declaring a static variable in a Java class—the value is shared by all instances of the class. On a more general note, you must first declare a variable before using it in future code snippets or scriptlet code (we will discuss the latter shortly, under "Scriptlets").

Consider the following rules when writing declarations:

- You can declare static or instance variables, new methods, or inner classes.

- Each variable declaration must end with a semicolon.

- Variables and methods available through import statements are accessible without requiring additional declarations.

- After declaring a variable or method, the information is available to subsequent Java code.

- Declarations usually contain code that would go outside the servlet's `_jspService(...)` method.

The methods `jspInit()` and `jspDestroy()` can be implemented within a declaration. These methods are called by the servlet's `init()` and `destroy()` methods. The JSP, however, cannot override the servlet's `init()` and `destroy()` methods because they are declared final by the background servlet.

Expression

An *expression* is a valid statement of logic used within a JSP page. It indicates a variable or method invocation whose resulting value is written to the response output stream. Because all expressions are computed and converted to `String` objects, they are most commonly used to provide dynamic `String` information to the response body.

JSP Syntax

```
<%= expression %>
```

Example

```
The file you accessed is <%= array.length %>
bytes in length.
Your randomly selected number is:
<%= Math.round(Math.random()*100) %>.
```

XML Syntax

```
<jsp:expression>
    expression
</jsp:expression>
```

Example

```
The file you accessed is <jsp:expression>
array.length </jsp:expression> bytes in length.
Your randomly selected number is: <jsp:expression>
Math.round(Math.random()*100) </jsp:expression>.
```

When an expression element is encountered, the expression itself is

1. Evaluated

2. Converted to a `String` object

3. Inserted into the response output stream

The output generated from an expression is similar to the results that you would receive from an `out.println(...)` statement.

Because Java code is now being used as a scripting language, there are a few rules that apply. Consider the following:

- Expressions are generally not terminated with a semicolon. (Some servers do not require a semicolon; others do).

- They are evaluated from left to right.

- They can be composed of more than one part or expression.

The ternary operator provides an example of how multiple expressions can exist within a single expression:

```
<%= (boolean evaluation) ?
    (true expression) :
    (false expression)
%>
```

Scriptlet

A *scriptlet* is a code fragment used within a JSP page. It can consist of multiple statements, made up of variable declarations, code blocks, and conditional and iterative statements. Conditional statements consist of `if`, `if/else`, and `switch` blocks, and iterative statements are represented by `for`, `while`, and `do` loops.

When a scriptlet is translated to the servlet, it is placed within the `_jsp-Service(...)` method. Consequently, static blocks cannot be defined within a scriptlet.

JSP Syntax

```
<% code fragment %>
```

Example

```
<%
  String rate = request.getParameter("taxRate");
  int value;
  try {
    value = Integer.parseInt(rate);
  } catch (NullPointerException e) {
%>
```

```
<%@ include file="error.html" %>

<%
   }
%>
```

XML Syntax

```
<jsp:scriptlet>
   code fragment;
</jsp:scriptlet>
```

Example

```
<jsp:scriptlet>
  String rate = request.getParameter("taxRate");
  int value;
  try {
      value = Integer.parseInt(rate);
  } catch (NullPointerException e) {
</jsp:scriptlet>

<jsp:directive.include file="error.html" />

<jsp:scriptlet>
   }
</jsp:scriptlet>
```

The logic for a scriptlet is embedded within the body of the JSP servlet's _jspService(...) method. This means the logic is executed with each request. In addition, all implicit objects (which we will discuss in the upcoming section, "Implicit Objects") are available to the scriptlet. If the scriptlet generates output, it is buffered in the out (JspWriter's) object, which is then sent to the client.

Scriptlets provide a way to include fragmented Java code to help generate a response. A scriptlet differs from a declaration in that the text can be broken up into pieces. For example, an if block can be defined within a scriptlet tag. Without completing the else block, you can insert a different JSP tag to perform a particular behavior. You can then conclude the else block with a final scriptlet. Within the scriptlet, you can include the following tag types:

- Declaration (variable, method, class)

- Expression (valid variable or method invocation)

- Any implicit or explicit object declared with a `jsp:useBean` element

- Any valid scripting language statement

Not only is it important for you to know what you can include within a scriptlet, but the objectives require you to distinguish between correct and incorrect iteration and conditional scriptlet code.

Statements

When writing either iteration or conditional statements within a scriptlet, you should be concerned with two factors. The first is how curly braces are handled, and the second is how code is interpreted within and outside the scriptlet block.

The rules for using curly braces within a scriptlet are the same as those used within a regular Java application.

- Conditional or iteration statements require braces if more than one line of code within the body must be evaluated.

- Opening braces can appear on the statement's declaration line or later.

- All opening braces must have a matching closing brace.

There is no difference between writing a conditional statement or an iterative statement. The rules that apply are standard to the Java language. When a JSP is precompiled, the server reads in the JSP and creates a servlet. All scriptlet statements are placed within the servlet *as is*, without modification. Consequently, anything legal in a normal block is legal within a scriptlet.

The following code demonstrates acceptable scriptlet code:

```
<% if(true)  %>
     Life is great!
<% else { %>
     Life is tough.
     But will get better.
<% } %>
```

The code snippet translates to the following Java code:

```
if(true)
    out.println("Life is great!");
else {
    out.println("Life is tough.");
    out.println("But will get better.");
}
```

Text outside the scriptlet is automatically written to the output stream. However, text within the scriptlet tags must be valid Java code. For example, the following example fails:

```
<% for(int i=0; i<5; i++){
    To be or not to be.
  } %>
```

An error is generated because a `String` cannot simply exist within a code block. Utilizing the appropriate rules, the next example succeeds:

```
<% for(int i=0; i<5; i++) { %>
do something else
<%  out.println("i is equal to: " + i ); %>
<% } %>
```

Any text or scriptlet code between the braces is part of the `for` loop and will be evaluated the number of times specified within the `for` loop iteration block. In the previous example, "do something else" will print five times, along with the statement about the value of `i`.

Scriptlets are a quick and dirty way to provide functionality. Unfortunately they enable you to write sloppy code that obscures the distinction between the presentation (HTML) and business logic (Java code). The recommended alternative is to use JavaBeans or custom tags. They require more work to write and access, but provide greater flexibility and clarity with the code design. We will cover these topics later in this chapter and in the next.

Directive

A *directive* enables a JSP page to control the overall structure for the translation phase of the servlet. Directives provide global information independent of a specific request. Some examples include incorporating classes or other files, and defining page characteristics. The three types of directives are as follows:

- The `include` directive
- The `page` directive
- The `taglib` directive

We will discuss each directive in detail by describing its purpose and how it is defined in JSP and XML syntax.

The *include* Directive

The `include` directive includes a static file in a JSP page.

JSP Syntax

```
<%@ include file="relativeURL" %>
```

XML Syntax

```
<jsp:directive.include file="relativeURL" />
```

Example

include.jsp:

```
<HTML>
<BODY>
The quote for the day is:
"<%@ include file="dailyQuote.jsp" %>"
</BODY>
</HTML>
```

dailyQuote.jsp:

```
<%! public String generateQuote() {
        String quote=null;
        // accesses file to get a quote
        return quote;
    }
%>
<%= generateQuote() %>
```

This code displays the following in the page:

The quote for the day is: "Never regret."

The purpose of an include directive is to insert a file in a JSP page when it is translated. The types of files consist of a JSP page, HTML file, XML document, or text file. The process of including a file in your current JSP page is referred to as a *static* include. This means the text of the included file is added to the JSP page. This process is somewhat literal, meaning that a file that contains interpretive tags, such as <HTML></HTML>, will be literally included in the file.

The contents of the file specified with this directive are preprocessed, and the resulting output is placed in the original JSP page. When the preprocessor encounters any static text (<HTML> </HTML>), the preprocessor is supposed to generate out.println("\r\n<HTML> </HTML>") statements. The resulting output is then captured by the compiler and inserted into the original JSP page.

If the included file is a JSP page, the JSP elements are translated and included in the JSP page. After the include file is translated, the translation process continues with the original JSP.

A container can behave in different ways when handling include files. Depending on the JSP container, you might expect:

- The JSP page to be recompiled if the include file changes

- The include file to be opened and available to all requests, or to have security restrictions

The value for the file attribute is relative, which means the path consists of the URL minus the protocol, port, and domain name. Some examples include:

- error.jsp

- temp/buyNow.html

- /beans/generateReceipt.jsp

When the relative path starts with a forward slash (/), the path is relative to the JSP application's context. If the relative URL starts with a directory or filename, the path is relative to the JSP page.

The *page* Directive

A *page directive* defines attributes that apply to an entire JSP page.

JSP Syntax

<%@ page *ATTRIBUTES* %>

A page directive is used to provide information to the JSP page. Consequently, many attribute values are used to define data for the page. Table 9.1 lists all page directive attributes, their descriptions, and their default values.

TABLE 9.1   page Directive Attributes

Attribute	Description	Default Value
language	Defines the scripting language used in scriptlets, declarations, and expressions in the JSP page.	java
		Legal value for the JSP 1.2 spec
extends	Delineates the fully qualified name of the superclass for the Java class in the JSP page.	package.class
import	Identifies the classes available to the scriptlets, expressions, and declarations in the JSP page. A comma is used to separate the multiple imports. The following packages are implicitly imported:	package.class
	java.lang.*	package.*
	javax.servlet.*	package.class, package.class
	javax.servlet.jsp.*	
	javax.servlet.http.*	

TABLE 9.1 page Directive Attributes *(continued)*

Attribute	Description	Default Value
session	Defines whether the client must join an HTTP session to use the JSP page. true refers to the current or new session, whereas false indicates that you cannot use a session object, but you can still use beans, as long as they are not part of a session object.	true
buffer	Used by the out object to handle output sent from the compiled JSP page to the browser.	8kb
autoFlush	Indicates whether to automatically flush the buffer after it is full. If set to false, an exception will be thrown when the buffer overflows. A false value cannot be used when the buffer is set to none.	true
isThreadSafe	Defines whether the JSP page is thread-safe. A true value means that concurrent client requests to the JSP page will not cause corruption. This is usually done through synchronization within the JSP page. A false value means the container must send client requests one at a time.	false
info	Declares a text string accessible from within the servlet.	Custom to the container
errorPage	Describes the pathname to the page used to display error messages when exceptions are raised.	relativeURL

TABLE 9.1 page Directive Attributes *(continued)*

Attribute	Description	Default Value
isErrorPage	Defines whether the JSP page is an error page. A true value allows the exception object to be used within the JSP page. A false value indicates that you cannot use the exception object in the JSP page.	false
contentType	Defines the MIME type and character encoding that the JSP page uses for the response.	text/html; charset= ISO-8859-1
pageEncoding	Identifies the character encoding used for the JSP response.	ISO-8859-1

Example

```
<%@ page import="java.io.*, java.util.*" %>
<%@ page language="java" pageEncoding="ISO=8859-01" %>
```

XML Syntax

```
<jsp:directive.page pageDirectiveAttribute [+
    pageDirectiveAttribute] />
```

Example

```
<jsp:directive.page errorPage="error.jsp"
    extends="java.awt.Color" isThreadSafe="true" />
```

The attributes apply to the entire JSP page and any static include files. The combination of the two is referred to as a *translation unit*.

The following rules apply to the page directive:

- You can use the page directive more than once in a translation unit.

- You can use a page attribute only once in a translation unit, except for import. (The import statement operates similarly to Java code.)

- A page directive can be placed anywhere within the JSP page or included files. (It is good practice to place it at the top of the JSP page.)

The *taglib* Directive

A *taglib directive* defines a tag library and prefix for the custom tags used in the JSP page.

JSP Syntax

```
<%@ taglib uri="URIForLibrary" prefix="tagPrefix" %>
```

Example

```
<%@ taglib uri="http://www.company.com/tags"
    prefix="public" %>
<public:loop>
...
</public:loop>
```

XML Syntax

None

The `taglib` directive enables custom tags to be included in a JSP page. The first attribute defines the tag library, whereas the second specifies the tag prefix. The `taglib` must be defined before the use of a custom tag. Although there can be more than one `taglib` directive defined, the prefix must be unique.

There are two attributes to consider. The Uniform Resource Identifier, or `uri`, describes the set of custom tags associated with the `prefix` tag. The `prefix` is the name that precedes the custom tag name. Empty prefixes are illegal, and the following prefixes cannot be used because they are reserved by Sun Microsystems: `jsp`, `jspx`, `java`, `javax`, `servlet`, `sun`, and `sunw`.

Knowing the different attributes and syntax rules related to the four types of scripting tags can be a bit confusing. Table 9.2 organizes each tag and identifies its major features.

TABLE 9.2 JSP Elements

Standard Tag	JSP Syntax	XML Syntax	Attribute	Purpose
Hidden	`<%-- comment --%>`	None	None	Comments
Directive	`<%@ include %>`	`<jsp:directive.include | jsp:/directive.page />`	file	Control and define JSP structure before translation

TABLE 9.2 JSP Elements *(continued)*

Standard Tag	JSP Syntax	XML Syntax	Attribute	Purpose
Directive *(cont.)*	`taglib`		`uri`, `prefix` (`language`, `extends`, `import`, `session`, `buffer`, `autoFlush`, `isThreadSafe`, `info`, `errorPage`, `isErrorPage`, `contentType`)	
	`page`			
Declaration	`<%! declaration %>`	`<jsp:declaration>` `</jsp:declaration>`	None	Declare variables and methods
Scriptlet	`<% scriptlet %>`	`<jsp:scriptlet>` `</jsp:scriptlet>`	None	Code fragment
Expression	`<%= expression %>`	`<jsp:expression>` `</jsp:expression>`	None	Variable or method invocation

The exam requires you to know the JSP syntax, meaning the opening and closing tags, and XML syntax of each tag. In addition, you must understand the purpose of each and how it is used.

Implicit Objects

Java code embedded within a JSP tag has access to many of the same objects available to a servlet. These are referred to as *implicit objects*. Some examples include the `HttpServletRequest` object, known as *request*, or the `ServletContext`, known as *application*. Currently the container provides nine predefined variables with specified names that JSP-embedded Java can utilize. In this section, we will cover each predefined variable, its purpose, and functionality:

The application object   The *application object* is of the ServletContext data type. It provides a set of methods to communicate with the container. There is one context per web application, which means the application object can access the entire application. This is known as application scope. In general, separate contexts or applications do not share variables.

In addition, the application variable is often used to acquire parameter values from the context-param XML tag. This tag is used to initialize variables from the deployment descriptor level. It is the same convenience you are granted with a servlet, just made available to a JSP page. The following example demonstrates the process.

The web.xml file might look something like the following:

```
<context-param>
    <param-name>paramName</param-name>
    <param-value>paramValue</param-value>
</context-param>
```

Within the JSP or scripting code, you could access this information by making the subsequent call:

```
application.getInitParameter("paramName");
```

These variables are analogous to creating static global variables for your web application.

The pageContext object   The *pageContext object* provides the JSP with information about the current request, also known as its *page attributes*. These include any parameters, or handles to the session, request, context, or outputStream object. The javax.servlet.jsp.PageContext abstract class provides the following convenience methods to access other implicit objects from the pageContext:

- getOut()
- getException()
- getPage()
- getRequest()
- getResponse()

- getSession()

- getServletConfig()

- getServletContext()

It also provides methods for forwarding, inclusion, and error handling:

- forward(Stringurl)

- include(Stringurl)

- handlePageException(Throwable t)

Because the pageContext object provides a single point of access, it is also an ideal location to set attribute values for sharing data with all other application components.

It has a page scope, which means the object can be accessed only directly, through the _jspService(...) method.

The config object   The *config object* is of the ServletConfig data type. It enables the container to pass information to the JSP page before it is initialized. The scope of the config object is limited to the page.

An object limited to the page scope is bound to the javax.servlet.jsp .PageContext abstract class. This means the current JSP page is placed inside the PageContext as long as the JSP page is responding to the current request. Using the PageContext's implicit object, pageContext, you can access the config attributes, such as all the namespaces or other classes associated with the current JSP page, through the get-Attribute(*String name*) method.

The request object   The *request object* initiates the _jspService(...) method upon a client's call. When created, the request object generates header information, such as cookies, the intent or type of request, such as a GET or POST, and possible parameters passed by the client.

The request object is bound to the ServletRequest interface, meaning its data is accessible through the getAttribute(*String name*) method. It is designed, however, to support method calls to an implementation-specific subclass of javax.servlet.ServletRequest, such as HttpServletRequest.

It has a request scope, which implies that the object's reference exists as long as the request is alive. Technically, a new request object is created for the client request and destroyed when a response is generated. Even if a forward(...) or include(...) is performed, the request object is still in scope.

The response object   The *response object* is an instance of the implementation-specific subclass of the javax.servlet.ServletResponse interface, often known as HttpServletResponse. Unlike servlets, it enables HTTP status codes and headers in the JSP to be changed after output has been sent to the client. This is due to the output stream being buffered (assuming the page directive buffer attribute is not set to none).

The response object has a page scope, which means it is bound to the PageContext and can be accessed directly within the _jspService(...) method—a period more commonly referred to as the life of the current request.

The session object   When a client makes a request, a session is automatically created to maintain client information. This object is referenced by the *session object* and is available as long as session=false is not defined with a page directive. By using the getAttribute(*String name*) method, you can retrieve data stored in an object by passing in a specified name.

As of the servlet 2.2 specification, the getValue(*String name*) method is deprecated and replaced with the getAttribute(*String name*) method.

This object has a session scope, which means it exists for the life of the session and is bound to the PageContext. A session object is usually useful for getting a unique ID associated with the entire transaction. For security reasons, the current specification allows only for the retrieval of the sessionID that is associated with the client request and passed to the PageContext to make it available to the JSP. Previously, you could get a list of sessions or a session by using an ID. This approached proved to be less secure.

The out object   The *out object* is used to write response information to the client. It is of the class javax.servlet.jsp.JspWriter, which is a buffered version of the java.io.PrintWriter class. The buffered size can be configured by using the buffer attribute in the page directive. For example:

```
<%@ page buffer="16kb" %>
```

The page object The *page object* is similar to the this keyword in Java. It represents an instance of the servlet generated by the JSP page for the current request. The page object exists for future use when another language can be specified by using the language attribute of the page directive. Until then, it isn't used much. When used in the future, it is important to know it has a page scope.

The exception object The *exception object* is an instance of the java .lang.Throwable class. It represents the uncaught Throwable object that results in the error page being invoked. Let's say an uncaught exception is encountered during request processing—for example, a RuntimeException; you could use the implicit exception object within the error page to print out a stack trace.

If you use the errorPage attribute of the page directive, the exception object is not available to that page. Only the error page itself can access the exception object.

This object has page scope and can be used to help debug your code. The following snippet demonstrates how:

```
<%@page isErrorPage="true" %>
...
<%= exception.getMessage(); %>
```

In the code example, the error page prints a message associated to the exception object. The exam requires that you know the functionality of each implicit object, its data type, and its scope. Table 9.3 lists the characteristics of each object.

TABLE 9.3 Implicit Objects and Their Scope

Implicit Object	Data Type	Scope
application	javax.servlet.ServletContext	Application
config	javax.serlvet.SerlvetConfig	Page
request	javax.servlet.http.HttpServletRequest	Request
response	javax.servlet.http.HttpServletResponse	Page

TABLE 9.3 Implicit Objects and Their Scope *(continued)*

Implicit Object	Data Type	Scope
session	javax.servlet.http.HttpSession	Session
pageContext	javax.servlet.jsp.PageContext	Page
out	javax.serlvet.jsp.JspWriter	Page
page	java.lang.Object	Page
exception	java.lang.Throwable	Page

All implicit objects exist within a defined scope. The scope attribute defines where the object can be referenced and when the reference is removed. Each scope can be summarized in the following way:

Application scope   Objects with an *application scope* are available for the life of the application. All components assigned to this range have access to peer components within the same context. Figure 9.5 provides a visual representation of the access area of an object with application scope.

FIGURE 9.5 Application scope

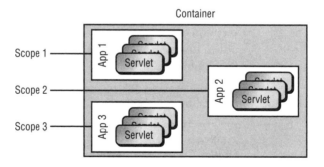

Page scope   An object with a *page scope* is available only within the current page. It can be accessed directly within the _jspService(...) method or indirectly with any custom methods (provided there is a method that returns a handle to the object) of the originating JSP page. Figure 9.6 demonstrates how the config object, which has a page scope, is available within its original page, but uses a new config instance when a request is transferred to a new page.

FIGURE 9.6   Page scope

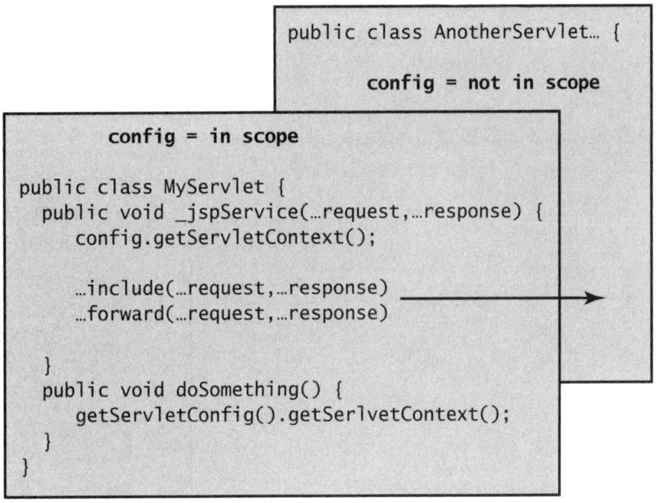

```
                              public class AnotherServlet… {

                                  config = not in scope

            config = in scope

   public class MyServlet {
     public void _jspService(…request,…response) {
       config.getServletContext();

       …include(…request,…response) ————————————————→
       …forward(…request,…response)

     }
     public void doSomething() {
       getServletConfig().getSerlvetContext();
     }
   }
```

Request scope   An object with a *request scope* is accessible from all pages processing the same request. This includes dispatched requests. If a request is transferred by using either of the RequestDispatcher methods include(…) or forward(…), the component is *in* scope. Figure 9.7 shows how an object with a request scope (for example, the request object) is still in scope after a dispatch occurs.

FIGURE 9.7   Request scope

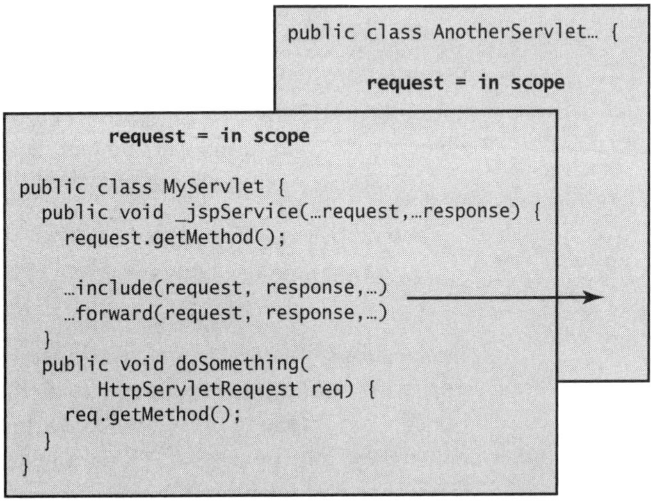

```
                              public class AnotherServlet… {

                                  request = in scope

            request = in scope

   public class MyServlet {
     public void _jspService(…request,…response) {
       request.getMethod();

       …include(request, response,…) ————————————————→
       …forward(request, response,…)

     }
     public void doSomething(
         HttpServletRequest req) {
       req.getMethod();
     }
   }
```

Session scope   Objects with a *session scope* are available for the life of the session. Until the session is closed manually or automatically due to a method call or a timeout, components can exist and share data. Figure 9.8 displays the available range for an object with a session scope.

FIGURE 9.8   Session scope

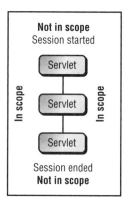

It is also important to understand the life cycle of implicit objects in order to know how and when to use them. We have covered four scriptlet formats, which include:

Expression <%= ... %>   Expressions are evaluated at HTTP processing time or when the HTTP server processes the request. Expressions are left unprocessed until the buffer is written out to the client, meaning all implicit objects have been initialized and are available.

```
<%= locateClient(request) %>
```

Scriptlet <% ... %>   Scriptlets are executed at request-processing time and embedded within the _jspService(...) method. This means all implicit objects have been initialized and can be accessed directly.

```
<%
  out.print("Tomorrow or the next life," +
    "whichever comes first");
%>
```

Declarations <%! ... %>   Declarations are initialized when the JSP's jspInit() method is invoked. Its methods, however, are available outside the _jspService(...) method. In order to access implicit objects, either they must be passed as a parameter or there must be an available servlet method which provides a reference to the instance.

```
<%!
  public String locateClient(HttpServletRequest req) {
    ServletConfig config = getServletConfig();
    return req.getRemoteHost();
  }
%>
```

Directive <%@ ... %>   Directives are invoked at translation time. When another page is included into the current page, its contents are inserted in the _jspService(...) method. The code for the included file is added to the code of the calling JSP page, right where the include directive is placed. Consequently, all the implicit objects are available to the code of the included page. Consider the following example:

```
jspMain.jsp
<HTML>
<BODY>
<%@ include file="second.jsp" %>
</BODY>
</HTML>


second.jsp
<HTML>
<BODY>
<%= request.getRequestURI() %>
</BODY>
</HTML>
```

Implicit objects are a key feature to providing a JSP with all the functionality available to a servlet. For greater functionality, a JSP can use "actions" to invoke a behavior.

Actions

Aside from displaying HTML and invoking scripts within your JSP page, you might want to pass certain tasks off to another servlet or JSP to handle. You might even want to use a JavaBean to set or get property values useful to the application, or maybe include some sort of plug-in within the web page. These tasks can be realized by using actions. *Actions* are Java tags that affect the runtime behavior of the JSP. In this section, we will go through each of the following actions by discussing its purpose and syntax, and providing examples:

- jsp:include
- jsp:forward
- jsp:plugin
- jsp:param
- jsp:useBean
  - jsp:setProperty
  - jsp:getProperty

jsp:include

A servlet can transfer a request to another resource to manage the response by using the RequestDispatcher. JSPs have this same functionality. Instead of acquiring a handle to the dispatcher, the tag jsp:include, or the *include action*, is used to temporarily transfer control and allow another resource access to the current request and response objects. This tag enables you to include either a static or dynamic resource. If static, the content of the resource is included in the JSP page. If dynamic, the request is sent and returned with a result included in the JSP page. After the action is finished, the JSP container continues to process the rest of the JSP page.

An included page can access only the JspWriter object. It cannot set headers or set cookies. Calls to related methods will be ignored.

Syntax
```
<jsp:include page="relativeURL" />
```
   or
```
<jsp:include page="relativeURL" flush="true|false" >
   <jsp:param name="parameterName"
      value="parameterValue">
</jsp:include>
```

Example

```
<jsp:include page="/header.jsp"/>
<jsp:include page="/greeting.jsp">
    <jsp:param name="username" value="chessMaster" />
</jsp:include>
```

Inclusion is processed at request time. Each attribute is evaluated and parameters set, if necessary. The include tag has three attribute types that can be used:

The **page** tag defines the relative URL of the target source. To include multiple pages within a page, you must provide a separate jsp:include action for each.

The **param** tag identifies any parameter values that need to be passed to the target.

The **flush** tag is equal to either true or false. A true value signifies that the page output is buffered and flushed prior to being returned to the original JSP. A false value means the buffer is not flushed. The default value is false.

In JSP 1.1, a bug within a provided JSP library class caused an error to generate if the flush attribute was not specified or had a value of false. Developers were required to specify the flush=true attribute to avoid receiving an error.

An include can be used in two ways. The first is as a directive with a file attribute to "include" a static file at *compile time*. The second approach is via an action. An include action uses the page attribute to incorporate another file's output, either static or dynamic, in the response at *request time*.

jsp:forward

Like the jsp:include, the *forward action* transfers control of the current request handler to a specified resource. The target source is then responsible for generating the response. Similar to the RequestDispatcher's forward(...) method, all buffered output is cleared when the request/response object is sent. If the output has already been flushed, the system throws an exception.

The target source can be quite flexible. It can be an HTML file, another JSP page, or a servlet, assuming all share the same application context as the forwarding JSP page. After a forward action is invoked, execution of the current page is terminated.

Any lines after the `jsp:forward` block are not processed.

Syntax

```
<jsp:forward page="relativeURL" />
```

or

```
<jsp:forward page="relativeURL" >
    <jsp:param name="parameterName"
        value="parameterValue">
</jsp:forward>
```

Example

```
<%
if(session.getAttribute("checkOut").equals("checkOut"))
    { %>
    <jsp:forward page="/processReceipt.jsp"/>
<% } %>
```

You can pass parameters to the target source by using the `param` tag, making it a dynamic resource. The `name` attribute defines the parameter, and the `value` is either a case-sensitive literal `String` or an expression that is evaluated at request time.

The following rules apply to the output stream associated to a `jsp:forward` action:

- If the page output is buffered, the buffer is cleared prior to forwarding.

- If the page output is buffered and the buffer was flushed, an attempt to forward the request will result in an `IllegalStateException`.

- If the page output was unbuffered and anything has been written to it, any attempt to forward the request will result in an `IllegalStateException`.

jsp:plugin

When creating web applications, you might need to include Java plug-in software to enhance the graphical or functional behavior. The *plugin action*, defined as `jsp:plugin`, displays or plays an applet or bean in the browser. The plug-in is either built into the browser or downloaded from a specific URL.

Syntax

```
<jsp:plugin
    type="bean|applet"
    code="classFileName.class"

    [optional attributes]
    <jsp:params>
        <jsp:param name="paramName" value="paramValue" />
    </jsp:params>
    <jsp:fallback> text message for user
    </jsp:fallback>
</jsp:plugin>
```

The `jsp:plugin` element is made up of four parts: mandatory attributes, optional attributes, the `jsp:params` tag, and the `jsp:fallback` tag.

Mandatory attributes indicate the type of plug-in component and its class name. Table 9.4 lists the mandatory attributes for the `jsp:plugin` action.

TABLE 9.4 `jsp:plugin` Mandatory Attribute List

Attribute	Description
type	The type of object the plug-in will execute. Your choices are bean or applet. There is no default value for this attribute.
code	The class filename. You must include its .class extension.

Optional attributes help locate the code, position the object within the browser window, and specify any URL to download plug-in software. Table 9.5 lists the optional attributes for the `jsp:plugin` action.

TABLE 9.5 jsp:plugin Optional Attribute List

Optional Attribute	Description
codebase	The class file directory or path to the directory for the Java class. If a directory is not specified, the JSP page or path is used instead.
name	The name of the bean or applet instance.
archive	A list of pathnames for files that will be preloaded. Each file is separated by a comma.
align	The position of the plug-in output within the web page. Your choices are bottom, top, middle, left, or right.
height	The initial vertical pixel measurement of the plug-in output. Not required, but some browsers will not require a height of 0.
width	The initial horizontal pixel measurement of the plug-in output. Not required, but some browsers will not allow an object of 0 height.
hspace	The number of pixels to the left and right of the plug-in output.
vspace	The number of pixels on the top and bottom of the plug-in output.
jreversion	The Java Runtime Version required to run the plug-in. The default value is 1.2.
nspluginurl	The URL where the plug-in can be downloaded from Netscape Navigator.
iepluginurl	The URL where the plug-in can be downloaded from Microsoft Internet Explorer.

The jsp:plugin **action has two sub-elements:**

jsp:params allows parameter names and values to be passed to the object.

jsp:fallback displays a text message for the user if the plug-in cannot be started. If it manages to start, but the bean or applet cannot, then a pop-up dialog appears to explain the problem.

Example

```
<jsp:plugin type="bean" code="AnimatedLogoBean.class"
     codebase="com/eei/company"
     name="logo"
     archive="companyAdds.jar"
     align="top"
     height="50"
     width="150"
     hspace="5"
     vspace="5"
     jreversion="1.2">
  <jsp:params>
      <jsp:param name="message" value="On the edge of
          technology" />
  </jsp:params>
  <jsp:fallback>
      <p>Sorry, but the Plug-in could not be started.
      </p>
  </jsp:fallback>
</jsp:plugin>
```

The preceding example displays an animated logo within a company's website. Although almost all attributes are used, they are not required. After the JSP page is translated and invoked, the plug-in will be processed and embedded in the web page displayed for the client.

jsp:param

A *param action* is used to provide a name/value pair to a servlet. It is used in conjunction with the jsp:include, jsp:forward, and jsp:params actions. A translation error occurs if the element is used elsewhere. New values take precedence over existing values and are scoped within the include or forward page.

Syntax

For a single parameter:

`<jsp:param name="parameterName" value="parameterValue" />`

Example

`<jsp:param name="ssn" value="555-55-5555" />`

There are two mandatory attributes associated with the `param` action. The first is called `name`. It is the name or key for the parameter. The second attribute is `value`. It defines the value of the attribute.

jsp:useBean

A powerful feature of Java Server Pages is the ability to incorporate Java-Beans within a page. The JSP tags handle the HTML, while the beans handle the Java logic. The clean separation makes for better readability, maintainability, and extensibility. It can be accomplished by using the *useBean action*. By definition, a *JavaBean* is simply a class that contains private data with accessor and mutator methods. These methods perform all the necessary business logic to arrive at the appropriate result. In addition, they have the ability to have their attributes changed dynamically. Through reflection, the container can determine which attributes are visible and changeable. JSPs benefit from this inclusion because a bean can perform a distinct task and make the resulting information available to the JSP page through an accessor method.

The benefit of using a JavaBean over a standard Java class is that with a bean, the container can be triggered to set bean properties by using parameter values from the client's request. For example, if a JSP `request` object contains a parameter of `taxRate`, and the bean has a method called `setTaxRate(float txr)`, the server will invoke the method passing the attribute value.

The trigger that causes the server to set parameters is an action called `jsp:setProperty`. When this action is used with the `property` attribute set to an asterisk (*), the server links parameter data with the servlet's data. We will discuss this action in the section called "`jsp:setProperty`."

Through introspection, the server can dynamically update the bean so the JSP page can access the attribute information without having to call `request.getParameter(String name)`.

Syntax

```
<jsp:useBean id="beanInstanceName"
   scope="page|request|session|application"
{
    class="package.class" |
    type="package.class" |
    class="package.class" type="package.class" |
    beanName="{package.class | <%= expression %>}"
       type="package.class"
}
{ /> | </jsp:useBean> }
```

Attributes

You can use several attributes to define how the server should use or locate the bean:

id   Specifies the name of the bean. If a bean scope extends beyond the current page, it can be saved. The key used to acquire the bean instance is the `id` name. If the bean instance does not exist, a new bean is created. This variable is case sensitive. The name must be unique within the translation unit. Duplicate IDs will result in a fatal translation error.

scope   Specifies the extent of the bean's visibility. There are four options to choose from: `page`, `request`, `session`, or `application`.

page scope   The bean variable is stored as an instance variable. Within the page, the bean is used once and then destroyed. You can use the bean within the JSP page or any of the page's static `include` files. This means files acquired via the `include` directive are within scope, while pages acquired from the `include` action are not in scope.

request scope   The bean instance is stored as a request attribute. This means the bean can be used from any JSP page processing the same request. Whereas a page scope ends at the onset of a `jsp:forward` action, a request scope keeps the bean alive through `jsp:forward` and `jsp:include` actions. When the response is returned, the bean is destroyed.

session scope   The bean instance is stored as the user's `session` attribute. Consequently, the bean exists across the entire session. If the client disconnects, the bean will be made available when the client reconnects. By default, the `session` attribute is `true`. For this reason, it is not necessary to include the session attribute for a session object to be created. If a JSP is defined to not participate in a session via the `<%@ page...%>` directive, and attempts to, a fatal transaction error will occur.

application scope   The bean instance is stored as a servlet context attribute and is therefore available to the entire application.

class   Specifies the class name of the bean. When the bean is constructed, the server uses the fully qualifying class name to generate the instance. If the bean already exists, the class name is not necessary.

type   Defines the class type used to cast the bean to its appropriate data type. When the object is retrieved from a particular scope, it is returned as a generic object. The bean is then cast to the class type defined. If the type is not defined, the value defaults to the same type as that defined by the class variable. If they do not match, a `ClassCastException` is thrown. By providing a `type` attribute without `class` or `beanName` attributes, you can give a local name to an object defined in another JSP page or servlet.

beanName   Replaces the `class` attribute to create the bean instance. This value is passed as a parameter to the `java.beans.Beans.instantiate(...)` method to create the instance. It enables developers to dynamically create the bean, because the attribute can accept a request-time attribute expression as a value.

It is not valid to provide both `class` and beanName.

Example

```
<jsp:useBean id="tax" class="com.eei.TaxBean"
scope="application" />
```

The `jsp:useBean` action attempts to first locate an instance of the bean. If unsuccessful, a new bean will be created from a class or serialized template. The following steps are taken to process the bean:

1. An attempt to locate a bean with the scope and ID name you specified is made.

2. An object reference variable with the name you specified is defined.

3. If the bean is located, a reference to the variable is stored. The bean is then cast to the given `type`. If the cast fails, a `java.lang.ClassCastException` is thrown.

4. If the bean is not located, and:

   a. Neither `class` nor `beanName` is given, a `java.lang.InstantiatedException` is thrown.

   b. `class` is provided, but is either `abstract`, an `interface`, or has no `public` no-args constructor (meaning it cannot be instantiated), then a `java.lang.InstantiatedException` is thrown.

   c. `class` is provided and has a no-args constructor, then the `class` is instantiated.

   d. `beanName` is provided, then the `java.beans.Beans.instantiate()` is invoked and the reference is stored to the `id` name.

5. If the bean is instantiated, and it has body tags between the `jsp:useBean` tags, those elements are executed.

There are two major advantages of using JavaBeans within a JSP. The first is the ability to set attributes, and the second is the ability to define the scope of the bean. While we have discussed the latter, we now need to address the technique used to set properties within the bean.

jsp:setProperty

The most significant feature of a bean is its property values. The *setProperty action* is used to set the parameter values of the bean in use. The bean's "get" and "set" methods are designed to change these values through reflection. For the container to achieve this task, the methods must begin with a `get` or `set` followed by the property name using an initial capital letter. The power of this design is that it enables the container to transfer the request parameter values from a client request, which could come from a form, to a JSP, which uses a bean and sets the properties to that bean by using the information entered by the client.

Syntax

```
<jsp:setProperty name="beanInstanceName"
{
    property="*" |
    property="propertyName" [param="parameterName"] |
    property="propertyName" value="{string literal |
    <%= expression %>}"
}
/>
```

Examples

```
<jsp:setProperty name="bean" property="*" />
<jsp:setProperty name="bean" property="name" />
<jsp:setProperty name="bean" property="name"
                 param="user" />
<jsp:setProperty name="bean" property="name"
                 value="Ariela" />
```

The jsp:setProperty element enables the bean's properties to be set via the request parameters or directly. The first example uses a wildcard to indicate that all request parameters should be mapped to the instance bean and altered if there is a match. The second example defines the bean property name that needs to be assigned a value from the request. The third example is used when the request parameter name is not the same name as the bean property. By listing both, the container can map the two together. Finally, the fourth example directly assigns a value to the bean property regardless of the request. Figure 9.9 demonstrates how information from the client is transferred to the bean.

The image describes a scenario in which the user enters an ID and password into a form. The information is then bundled in a request object and sent to the JSP page. If necessary, a bean instance is created and the container will then use the "set" methods to mutate the bean properties to match those sent through the client request. If the names are different, the param attribute is used to map the property to the request parameter. Table 9.6 outlines the jsp:setProperty attributes.

FIGURE 9.9 The setProperty process

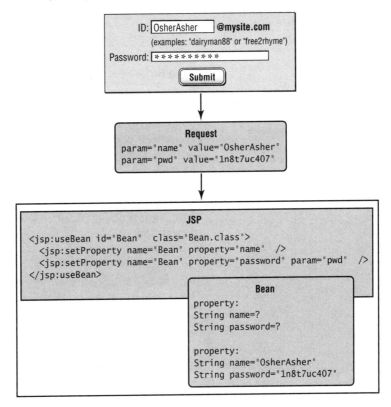

TABLE 9.6 jsp:setProperty Attribute List

Attribute	Description
name	The name of the bean instance. The name used must match the id attribute in the jsp:useBean element.
property	The name of the bean property. When a wildcard (*) is used to define the property, the container will search through all request parameters to find a match to the bean property. When a match is found, the request parameter value is assigned to the property. If the request parameter is an empty string (""), then the property is left unaltered.

TABLE 9.6   jsp:setProperty Attribute List *(continued)*

Attribute	Description
param	The name assigned to the request parameter. This attribute must be used in conjunction with property. Basically, it maps the request parameter name to the name of the property in the bean. If param is not used, it assumes the request parameter is the same as the property. If, however, there is no request parameter with the param name, or if its value is " ", then the container will leave the bean property unaltered.
value	The value assigned to the bean property. This can either be a request object parameter, a request time-evaluated expression, or a specific string.

There is one more important feature to know about the jsp:setProperty element. Not all bean properties are Strings; consequently, you need to know how the container manages bean properties of other data types. When the client sends a request, the parameter values are always of type String. These values are converted to their appropriate data types when stored in the bean's property. The JavaBeans specification states that the setAsText(*String name*) method should be used on a property if it has a PropertyEditor class. If a conversion failure occurs, an IllegalArgumentException is thrown. By default, PropertyEditors are provided for all primitive and respective wrapper classes. If the property is of a data type that is not available, the String will get converted to that of type Object.

After the property value is set, the JSP can retrieve this information by using the jsp:getProperty element.

jsp:getProperty

As easy as it is to set a bean's property from within a JSP page, you can get the values with similar ease by using the *getProperty action*, or jsp:getProperty action. When retrieving a bean's property, it is converted to a String by using either the toString() method or the wrapper class valueOf(String str) method if it is a primitive. Once converted, the results are passed to the output stream and finally to the client.

Syntax

```
<jsp:getProperty name="beanInstanceName"
    property="propertyName" />
```

Example

Let's start by using the following bean, which holds customer information:

```
public class CustomerBean {
    private String name;
    ...
    public void setName(String name) {
      this.name = name;
    }
    public String getName() {
      return this.name;
    }
    ...
}
```

The web page might allow the user to enter their name, and then that value could be set by using the jsp:setProperty action. Later, in another area, we could retrieve that value by using the jsp:getProperty tag. The following code snippet demonstrates the process:

```
<jsp:useBean id="custBean" scope="session"
    class="CustomerBean" >
    <jsp:setProperty name="custBean" property="*" />
</jsp:useBean>
<HTML>
    <BODY>
        <H1> Hello <jsp:getProperty name="custBean"
                        property="name" />!</H1>
</BODY>
</HTML>
```

Assuming the person entered their name as Yoav, the output generated would simply display the following message:

Hello Yoav!

The process of extracting data is similar to that of setting it. After the property value is set for the bean, a call to jsp:getProperty contacts the identified bean (in this case it's the CustomerBean) and invokes its getName() method. The return value is then sent to the JSP output stream and converted to a String for display purposes.

Here are some points to consider:

- You must first create an instance of the bean by using the jsp:useBean element before calling the jsp:getProperty tag.

- The jsp:getProperty tag works on JavaBeans, but not on enterprise beans. Enterprise beans are formatted to run within an application server and follow a template form very different from a basic Java-Bean. You could, however, have your JSP tag communicate with a JavaBean, which communicates with an enterprise bean. It's a fair workaround.

- If you use the jsp:getProperty tag on a property whose value is equal to null, a NullPointerException is thrown. If you are using a scriptlet or expression to retrieve this value, the null keyword is returned instead.

- You cannot use jsp:getProperty to retrieve values of an indexed property. An *indexed property* is an object that is either a collection or array.

Table 9.7 lists the available attributes for the jsp:getAttribute action.

TABLE 9.7 jsp:getProperty Attribute List

Attribute	Description
name	The name of the bean instance. The name used must match the id name in the jsp:useBean element.
property	The name of the bean property whose value you are looking to display.

The `jsp:getProperty` action is an easy way to retrieve a bean property value. It adds value to your code in that it makes it more readable and maintainable by someone who is more skilled in web design then in Java programming.

The exam expects you to know each action, its subactions, and associated attributes. Table 9.8 lists each action, its attributes, and possible subactions.

TABLE 9.8   Action Summary

Action	Attribute	Subtags
`<jsp:param>`	name and value	
`<jsp:include />`	page, flush	`<jsp:param>`
`<jsp:forward />`	Page	`<jsp:param>`
`<jsp:useBean />`	id, scope, class, beanName, type	`<jsp:getProperty />` `<jsp:setProperty />`
`<jsp:setProperty />`	name, property, param, value	
`<jsp:getProperty />`	name, property	
`<jsp:plugin />`	type, codebase, name, archive, align, height, width, hspace, vspace, jreversion, nspluginurl, iepluginurl	`<jsp:params />` `<jsp:fallback >`

Knowing the details associated with each action will help you pass the exam. Even more importantly, the meanings behind each attribute and how it is applied further solidify your success.

Real World Scenario

The Switch Over

International Phone Card, Inc. has recently decided to change their web application to allow for more flexibility and maintainability. As a startup company, they were limited to acquiring a development staff whose skills consist mostly of web design. As a result, they were paying huge funds to a consulting group to develop and maintain their servlet-driven web site. Recently, however, they decided on a new long-term approach. Instead of investing in training their staff in Java development, they will convert their application to utilize Java Server Pages, which talk to servlets on the front end. This approach limits their costs because their web designers can focus on designing the interface; the company needs to contract out only the servlet and bean pieces of the application. By separating the presentation layer from the business logic layer, they are able to utilize their staff more efficiently and cut down on long-term maintenance costs.

Summary

In this chapter, we covered the basic essentials of a JSP, starting with its life cycle and moving on to syntactical features. Two major coding options were discussed in this chapter: the utilization of a tag and the utilization of an action.

All four tag types were covered in great detail to ensure you understand the syntax and purpose behind a scriptlet, expression, declaration, and directive. Each directive type—include, page, and taglib—was described to further help define the particulars associated with a directive. Within these tags you were shown how to acquire access to common objects, known as implicit objects. They include request, response, out, session, config, application, page, pageContext, and exception.

The second half of the chapter focused on the available action types and their behaviors. The list of actions included jsp:param, jsp:include, jsp:forward, jsp:useBean, jsp:setProperty, jsp:getProperty, and jsp:plugin.

A solid understanding of the JSP (and XML) syntax, plus knowledge of how each of these features works will help increase your score substantially in the JSP section of the exam.

Exam Essentials

Be able to explain the JSP life cycle.   A JSP page goes through a morphing process before it can be accessed. Because certain actions take place before and after it translates, knowledge of the process helps you write a more efficient and accurate Java Server Page.

Be able to identify the JSP and XML syntax, purpose, and use of each tag type.   There are four tag types, known as directive, declaration, scriptlet, and expression. It is important to know how to write each correctly by using either JSP tags or XML tags. Although JSP scriptlet syntax was used originally, XML syntax is becoming the communication standard within the J2EE environment.

Be able to define and identify the purpose and functionality or use of implicit objects.   There are nine implicit objects available to a servlet page (JSP page translated) during the `service(...)` method. For convenience, they provide handles to critical information within the scripting section of your JSP page.

Be able to identify, use, and define JSP actions.   Again, you are expected to know the details associated with each action and its syntax. This information is necessary to build a suitable JSP page that can accomplish desired tasks. These actions also help separate the business logic from the presentation layer.

Key Terms

Before you take the exam, be certain you are familiar with the following terms:

actions	pageContext object
application	page directive
application object	page object
application scope	page scope
config object	param action
declaration	plugin action
directive	presentation layer
exception object	request
expression	request object
first-person penalty	request scope
forward action	response object
getProperty action	scriptlet
hidden comment	session object
implicit objects	session scope
include action	setProperty action
indexed property	static
JavaBean	taglib directive
JSP model	translation unit
out object	useBean action
page attributes	

Review Questions

1. Which of the following methods can be overridden by the author of a JSP page?

   A. `void_jspInit()`

   B. `void_jspService(HttpServletRequest request, HttpServletResponse response)`

   C. `void_jspDestroy()`

   D. None of the above

2. Which option best describes the life-cycle process of a JSP?

   A. JSP page is translated to a servlet, servlet is loaded into memory, code is compiled, instance is created.

   B. JSP page is translated to a servlet, code is compiled, servlet is loaded into memory, instance is created.

   C. JSP is compiled, JSP is translated to a servlet, code is loaded, instance is created.

   D. JSP is loaded into memory, code is compiled, instance is created.

3. Select the option that best describes the order in which JSP methods are invoked.

   A. `jspInit(), _jspService(...), jspDestroy()`

   B. `_jspService(...), jspInvoke(), jspDestroy()`

   C. `jspinit(), jspCreate(), _jspService(...)`

   D. `jspInit(), _jspService(...), jspDestroy()`

4. Which of the following classes must a JSP servlet extend?

   A. `javax.servlet.jsp.JspPage`

   B. `javax.jsp.JspPage`

   C. `javax.jsp.Jsppage`

   D. None of the above

5. The method _jspService(*HttpServletRequest request, HttpServletResponse response*) is declared in which of the following interfaces?

   A. javax.servlet.jsp.JspPage

   B. javax.servlet.jsp.HttpJspPage

   C. javax.servlet.jsp.tagext.Tag

   D. None of the above

6. Which of the following declaration types is not legal to use within a scriptlet tag?

   A. if block

   B. Method

   C. Variable

   D. Code block

7. Which of the following packages is not implicitly imported in a translation unit?

   A. java.lang.*

   B. javax.servlet.*

   C. javax.servlet.http.*

   D. None of the above

8. Which of the following page attributes has a default value of true?

   A. session

   B. buffer

   C. isThreadSafe

   D. isErrorPage

9. If a relative path begins with a forward slash (/), the path is relative to which of the following?

   A. Relative to the JSP application's document root directory

   B. Relative to the current JSP page

   C. Relative to the container's installation directory

   D. None of the above

10. Which of the following prefixes can be used for custom tag libraries?

   A. `jsp`

   B. `jspx`

   C. `servlet`

   D. `servletx`

11. When a JavaBean's scope is defined as `application`, it is stored as which of the following?

   A. A session attribute

   B. A request attribute

   C. A servlet context attribute

   D. An instance variable

12. Which of the following attribute types uses the `java.beans.Beans.instantiate()` method?

   A. `class`

   B. `beanName`

   C. `scope`

   D. `type`

13. If you are told a JSP page uses a plug-in bean whose source file is named `MyBean.java` and requires a Java Runtime Environment (JRE) of 1.2 and a compiled version is located within the classes directory of `/WEB-INF`, which of the following element tags would most likely execute successfully?

A. `<jsp:plugin type="bean" code="MyBean" jreversion="1.2" />`

B. `<jsp:plugin code="MyBean.class" />`

C. `<jsp:plugin type="Bean" code="/MyBean.class" jreversion="1.2" />`

D. `<jsp:plugin type="bean" code="MyBean.class" />`

14. Which of the following is not a directive?

A. `import`

B. `include`

C. `page`

D. `taglib`

E. None of the above

15. Which of the following is not an attribute of the **page** directive?

A. `session`

B. `autoFlush`

C. `isThreadSafe`

D. `uri`

Answers to Review Questions

1. D.   The method _jspService(*HttpServletRequest req,*
   HttpServletResponse res) should not be overridden by the JSP
   developer. The first and third options fail to define the correct method
   (These methods do not begin with an underscore.) If a developer defined
   either method, it would not be considered an override.

2. B.   When a client makes a request, and a JSP instance doesn't already
   exist, the appropriate JSP page (.jsp) is located and translated to servlet
   source code (.java). The JSP servlet is then compiled (.class), and
   the class file is loaded into memory. An instance of the servlet is then
   created.

3. D.   The jspInit() method is first called to initialize the JSP servlet
   when it is first loaded into memory. The _jspService(...) method is
   then called with each future request. Finally, when the JSP is about to
   be removed, the jspDestroy() method is called.

4. D.   javax.servlet.jsp.JspPage is an interface, not a class. Each
   JSP servlet must ultimately implement this interface.

5. B.   The _jspService(...) method is defined within the javax
   .servlet.jsp.HttpJspPage interface. The method should not be
   overridden as it is implemented by the container.

6. B.   A method must be defined within a declaration, not a scriptlet.
   All other code types are legal within a scriptlet.

7. D.   There are four packages that do not need to be imported in
   a JSP page, because they are implicitly imported. They include
   java.lang.*, javax.servlet.*, javax.servlet.jsp.*, and
   javax.servlet.http.*.

8. A.   A session attribute defaults to a true value, suggesting a client
   must join an HTTP session in order to use the JSP page. The buffer
   attribute defines the size of the out object, while isThreadSafe and
   isErrorPage default to false.

9. A.   A forward slash defines the file as relative to the JSP application's
   document root directory and is resolved by the web server. Without
   the slash, the file is considered relative to the current JSP page.

10. D. The first three tag prefixes are reserved by Sun Microsystems. However, `servletx` is available.

11. C. An `application` scope means the bean is available to the entire application. Because the servlet context applies to the entire application, the instance is stored as an attribute to this object.

12. B. The `beanName` attribute used within the `jsp:useBean` element instantiates a bean by using the passed-in bean name (assuming an instance does not already exist).

13. D. The type and code are both required attributes of the `jsp:plugin` element. The type must be marked as `bean` (remember, attributes are case sensitive) and the code must include the `.class` extension. Finally, if `jreversion` is not included, it defaults to the 1.2 version.

14. A. `import` is an attribute of the page directive, not a directive itself.

15. D. A `page` directive is used to define characteristics of the JSP page. This includes whether the page will participate in sessions, or whether the output buffer will automatically flush when it is full, or whether multiple clients can make simultaneous requests because the page is thread-safe. The majority of these options are defined with a `true` or `false` value. The `uri`, however, is the address or Uniform Resource Identifier for the tag library descriptor in a `taglib` descriptive.

Using Custom Tags

THE FOLLOWING SUN CERTIFIED WEB COMPONENT DEVELOPER FOR J2EE PLATFORM EXAM OBJECTIVES ARE COVERED IN THIS CHAPTER:

- ✓ **11.1 Identify properly formatted tag library declarations in the web application deployment descriptor.**

- ✓ **11.2 Identify properly formatted taglib directives in a JSP page.**

- ✓ **11.3 Given a custom tag library, identify properly formatted custom tag usage in a JSP page. Uses include:**
  - An empty custom tag
  - A custom tag with attributes
  - A custom tag that surrounds other JSP code
  - Nested custom tags

- ✓ **12.1 Identify the tag library descriptor element names that declare the following:**
  - The name of the tag
  - The class of the tag handler
  - The type of content that the tag accepts
  - Any attributes of the tag

- ✓ **12.2 Identify the tag library descriptor element names that declare the following:**
  - The name of a tag attribute
  - Whether a tag attribute is required
  - Whether or not the attribute's value can be dynamically specified

✓ **12.3 Given a custom tag, identify the necessary value for the body-content TLD element for any of the following tag types:**

- Empty tag
- Custom tag that surrounds other JSP code
- Custom tag that surrounds content that is used only by the tag handler

✓ **12.4 Given a tag event method (doStartTag, doAfterBody, and doEndTag), identify the correct description of the method's trigger.**

✓ **12.5 Identify valid return values for the following methods:**

- doStartTag
- doAfterBody
- doEndTag
- PageContext.getOut

✓ **12.6 Given a "BODY" or "PAGE" constant, identify a correct description of the constant's use in the following methods:**

- doStartTag
- doAfterBody
- doEndTag

✓ **12.7 Identify the method in the custom tag handler that accesses:**

- A given JSP page's implicit variable
- The JSP page's attributes

✓ **12.8 Identify methods that return an outer tag handler from within an inner tag handler.**

n the preceding chapter, we succeeded in separating the Presentation layer from the Business Logic layer through the use of JSPs. We showed how actions provide limited functionality to enable the JSP to perform certain tasks, while scriptlets handle everything else. A JSP page made up of these components is useful, but it does not provide a solution that enables you to completely exclude all Java code from the JSP page. For example, what if you wanted the JSP page to generate a table on-the-fly? This could be done with HTML, but the ability to highlight a row or change the content to another language is limited. Scriptlet or servlet code would be required.

Inevitably, the lack of functionality available in the standard JSP actions results in the developer having to write Java code in two ways: either embed a plethora of scriptlet code within the page or create a servlet to handle the functionality. The first option is not optimal because scriptlet code makes a page difficult to read, maintain, and expand. The second option is feasible, but requires the developer to provide an include or forward action every time a custom behavior is needed. Each attribute name must be known in order to set its value; in addition, each attribute must be listed in a separate jsp:param tag. Again, this approach works, but means that any complex graphical functionality must be handled within a servlet rather than a JSP. Ideally, all presentation-related logic should be handled by the JSP. This chapter discusses how to expand the current JSP library by enabling developers to create custom JSP actions.

The use of *custom tags* (also known as *custom actions* or *tag extensions*) helps provide a clear division of labor between the web page designer and the software developer. Similar to XML, a custom tag takes the place of scriptlets, and sometimes beans, to provide the web designer the functionality to accomplish a particular task. Instead of doing the following:

```
The random number assigned to you is:
    <%= (int)Math.random()*100 %>
```

The designer could use a tag to accomplish the task:

```
The random number assigned to you is:
    <custTag:randomValue/>
```

Designing the page becomes a matter of plugging in the appropriate tags to achieve the correct design. The developer, on the other hand, creates tag classes to accomplish generic tasks. In fact, custom tags can take the place of servlets to provide an all-JSP PRESENTATION tier. Each task can be customized via attributes passed from the calling page at runtime. The tag has access to all objects available to the JSP page, such as request, response, and out. In addition to being nested, custom tags can also communicate with one another. They allow for complex behavior while ultimately simplifying the readability and maintainability of the JSP page.

A Basic Custom Tag

Four components are required to ensure that a custom tag action performs correctly:

MyTagName.class is the custom action class you write to define the tag's functionality.

taglibName.tld is an XML file that defines a tag library and is also known as the tag library descriptor (TLD).

web.xml is an XML file that contains tag libraries available to the application.

MyJspPage.jsp is a JSP page that utilizes tags defined in the associated web.xml document.

A custom tag's body or functionality must exist in a special class that ultimately implements the Tag interface. This interface defines the life-cycle methods of the tag, enabling developers to include appropriate logic where necessary.

To simplify implementation, the API also provides a support class called BodyTagSupport. The BodyTagSupport class extends the TagSupport class, which in turn implements the Tag interface. BodyTagSupport also implements the BodyTag interface, which extends the Tag interface. This class reduces the number of methods the developer must define. We will talk about the interfaces and supporting classes in greater detail as the chapter progresses. Listing 10.1 is a code example of a basic tag, which generates a random value.

Listing 10.1: A Basic Custom JSP Tag

```
package tagext;

import java.io.*;
import javax.servlet.jsp.*;
import javax.servlet.jsp.tagext.*;

public class RandomValue extends BodyTagSupport {

    public int doStartTag() throws JspException {
        return SKIP_BODY;
    }
    public int doEndTag() throws JspException {
        int value = (int)(Math.random()* 100);
        try {
            pageContext.getOut().write("" + value);
        } catch (IOException e) {
            throw new JspException(e.getMessage());
        }
        return EVAL_PAGE;
    }

}
```

On a simple level, the two methods defined contain the behavior of the tag. The doStartTag() is called to process the start, or opening, of the tag instance. Depending on the constant returned, the body that lies between the opening and closing tags will be either executed or ignored. Although this method is not necessary in this example, because it performs default behavior, it is included to help you understand what is being called. Next, the doEndTag() method is invoked. In this example, a random value is generated and written to the tag's output stream. When compiled, the custom JSP class file should be placed within the application context's /WEB-INF/ classes directory.

The next step is to create a *tag library descriptor (TLD)* file. A TLD is an XML document that describes a tag library. It contains one or many related tag extensions. For this example, our TLD file `tagext.tld` might look like the following:

```
<?xml version="1.0" encoding="ISO-8859-1" ?>
<!DOCTYPE taglib PUBLIC
  "-//Sun Microsystems, Inc.//DTD JSP Tag Library 1.2//EN"
  "http://java.sun.com/dtd/web-jsptaglibrary_1_2.dtd">
<taglib>
  <tlib-version>1.0</tlib-version>
  <jsp-version>1.2</jsp-version>
  <short-name>demo</short-name>
  <description>Simple demo library.</description>

  <tag>
    <name>randomValue</name>
    <tag-class>tagext.RandomValue</tag-class>
    <body-content>empty</body-content>
    <description>First example</description>
  </tag>
  ...
</taglib>
```

Each custom tag is embedded within its own set of `<tag></tag>` elements. Name and content information is included to enable other JSPs to identify and use a particular tag. We will discuss each tag in detail later.

For now, we will map our `tagext.tld` file to the application via the `web.xml` document. The following elements must be included within the deployment descriptor to allow all JSPs to utilize the defined custom tags:

```
<?xml version="1.0" encoding="ISO-8859-1" ?>
<!DOCTYPE web-app PUBLIC
  "-//Sun Microsystems, Inc.//DTD Web Application 2.3//EN"
  "http://java.sun.com/dtd/web-app_2_3.dtd">

<web-app>
<!-- Tag Library Descriptor -->
```

```
<taglib>
   <taglib-uri>http://www.acme/tagext</taglib-uri>
   <taglib-location>
      /WEB-INF/tagext.tld
   </taglib-location>
</taglib>
...
</web-app>
```

The `taglib` element encapsulates information for the container to locate the library file. Once accessible, all JSPs within the application, including `MyJspPage.jsp`, can utilize each `taglib` or custom tag in the following fashion:

```
<%@ taglib uri="http://www.acme/tagext" prefix="custTag" %>
<HTML>
   <HEAD><TITLE>Your lucky number</TITLE></HEAD>
      <BODY>The random number assigned to you is:
      <custTag:randomValue />
      </BODY>
</HTML>
```

The JSP defines the `tag` element, which maps to the `web.xml` file, which maps to the `tagext.tld`, which maps to the specialized tag class. Figure 10.1 demonstrates the path taken.

FIGURE 10.1   Custom tag mapping

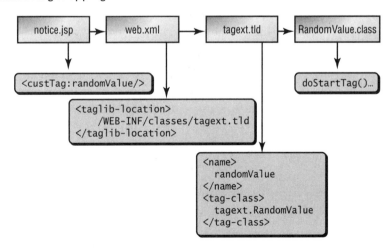

Each of these files would be located in the following directory structure:

```
MyJspPage.jsp
META-INF/
    MANIFEST.MF
WEB-INF/
    web.xml
    tagext.tld
    classes/
        tagext/
            RandomValue.class
```

Notice that the custom tag RandomValue is a `.class` file rather than a `.jsp` file. The remainder of this chapter will focus on the details associated with each of these components. In this section, we will address the nuances used to customize and add additional functionality to a custom tag:

- Defining a tag

- Using the `taglib` element

Defining a Tag

A custom tag, or tag extension, is similar in structure to a standard JSP action tag. It is made up of four parts: a name, attributes, nested tags, and a body:

Tag name   This is a name that uniquely identifies the element. It consists of two parts: a prefix and suffix. The *prefix* is a predefined name that links the action to a tag library. The *suffix* is the name of the element used to invoke the action. The prefix and suffix are separated by a colon.

Attributes   These help define the characteristics necessary for the element to perform its task. For example, `class` is an attribute for `jsp:useBean` that defines the class name used to instantiate the bean. An element can have as many or as few attributes as necessary. Attributes are optional.

Nested tags   A tag can contain subtags that provide further functionality, helping the outer tag complete its task. The subtags `jsp:setAttribute` or `jsp:getAttribute` enable the `jsp:useBean` action to change and access its attribute values. Nested tags are observed and executed at runtime.

Body   The content between the opening tag and closing tag, including subtags, is considered the *body content*. A tag extension can control the body content by extracting it from the element's class file and returning a changed value.

Syntactically, a tag extension can look like the following:

```
<prefix:suffix attribute1="value" attribute2="value" >
    <prefix:subSuffix attribute1="value" attribute2="value" />
    body
</prefix:suffix>
```

Each suffix represents a different JSP tag name associated with a tag class file. A JSP page can call any tag defined within the application's deployment descriptor, as long as the tag has been specified by the JSP `taglib` directive.

Using the *taglib* Element

Before a tag extension can be used within a JSP page, three things must happen:

1. The *JSP page* must include a `taglib` directive to identify which tag libraries to load into memory.

2. The *web.xml* document must use a `taglib` element in conjunction with the `taglib-uri` sub-element to declare, and identify the location of, the TLD file.

3. The *TLD* file must use the `taglib` element in conjunction with the `tag` sub-element to identify each custom tag and its attributes.

The JSP Page

You are required to use the `taglib` directive within the JSP page to identify the use of custom tags. Because the tag contains the necessary information to load the appropriate TLD, it must be defined before any custom tag is used. Once loaded, the TLD, or tag library, provides the current JSP with additional names and attributes of available custom actions.

Locating the correct tag library requires the inclusion of two mandatory attributes along with the `taglib` directive: `uri` and `prefix`. The syntax is as follows:

```
<%@ taglib uri="locationOfTLD" prefix="shortName" %>
```

You can use the `uri` attribute in two ways. First, you can map it directly to the URI used within the `web.xml`'s `taglib-uri` sub-element. When these two values match, the other sub-element within the `web.xml` file, called `taglib-location`, will define the absolute location of the file. The second option is for the `uri` attribute to provide the absolute path to the TLD. At that point, the `web.xml` file does not need to provide location information. The container will use the information from the JSP page to map to the TLD via the deployment descriptor. Both options are provided to enable the developer to conveniently define the location of the TLD file or to use more abstract measures that grant greater long-term flexibility.

The `prefix` attribute is also mandatory and defines the prefix name in the tag extension. For example, if `prefix="eei"`, then the tag for an element called `calculate` would look like `<eei:calculate />`. The actual value assigned to the prefix attribute is an arbitrary name defined by the HTML designer to enable the JSP container to map the tag to the real tag library. In addition to defining the first portion of a tag extension, the prefix also maps to the `shortname` element defined within the TLD. When the container encounters the `taglib` directive, it knows to download the library identified by the `uri`. When it encounters an element with a defined prefix, it then knows which library to search to efficiently locate the identified tag. This process is known as *prefix mapping*.

The Deployment Descriptor

The `web.xml` file is the mapping tool used between the JSP page and all other available container resources. The JSP uses the `web.xml` to locate the TLD. When a JSP attempts to invoke a custom tag, the tag must first be located, and then processed. By modifying the deployment descriptor to include mapping information to the tag library, the JSP can locate the necessary actions to invoke.

A tag library is defined within the `web.xml` by using the opening `<taglib>` and closing `</taglib>` tags. Embedded within, the URI and exact directory location are defined by using both the `taglib-uri` and `taglib-location` tags, respectively. The following code snippet demonstrates how to include two libraries within the application's `web.xml` file:

```
<?xml version="1.0" encoding="ISO-8859-1" ?>
<!DOCTYPE web-app PUBLIC
    "-//Sun Microsystems, Inc.//DTD Web Application 2.3//EN"
    "http://java.sun.com/dtd/web-app_2_3.dtd">
```

```
<web-app>
    ...
    <!-- Tag Library Descriptor -->
    <taglib>
        <taglib-uri>/taglib1</taglib-uri>
        <taglib-location>
            /WEB-INF/tlds/GeneralTagLib.tld
        </taglib-location>
    </taglib>

    <taglib>
        <taglib-uri>http://www.eei.com/taglib2</taglib-uri>
        <taglib-location>
            /WEB-INF/tlds/SpecificTagLib.tld
        </taglib-location>
    </taglib>
    ...
</web-app>
```

First, it is important to notice that the web.xml DOCTYPE is web-app. Later, when we provide a closer look at the TLD file, you will see that the DOCTYPE is defined as taglib. In addition, the actual DTD file (web-app_2.3.dtd) used to define the web.xml file is different from that used to define TLD files.

The taglib element has two sub-elements. The first sub-element is taglib-uri. It specifies the URI that all JSPs should use to access that tag library. Its path can contain either an absolute path, which includes host and port number, or a relative path using published directories. The mapping between the URI and the actual destination of the TLD is done by using the second sub-element, called taglib-location. This element is used to define the exact location of the TLD file. Unlike the URI, it can contain nonpublished directories such as /WEB-INF and its subdirectories.

When defining paths, it is important to know the difference between the three formats:

Context-relative path   If the path starts with a forward slash (/), then the path is relative to the application's context path.

Page-relative path   If the path does not start with a slash, then it is relative to the current JSP page or file. If the include directive is used, which incorporates the response of the identified file attribute, then the URI is relative to that defined file. If the `include` action is used, then the URI is relative to the `page` attribute's value.

Absolute path   This is the full path, starting with the protocol and host, necessary to locate the tag library file.

There should not be more than one `taglib-uri` entry with the same value in a single `web.xml` file.

Generally, the `taglib-location` element is mapped to a context-relative path, which begins with a forward slash (/), and does not include a protocol or host definition. Specifically, this path is referred to as the *TLD resource path*. The TLD resource path is relative to the root of the web application and should resolve to a TLD file directly, or to a JAR file that has a TLD file located in the `/WEB-INF` directory.

The following is an example of how the mapping applies.

web.xml file:

```
<taglib>
    <taglib-uri>/tagDir</taglib-uri>
    <taglib-location>
        /WEB-INF/tld/taglib.tld
    </taglib-location>
</taglib>
```

Maps to the JSP file taglib directive:

```
<%@ taglib uri="/tagDir" prefix="eei" %>
```

Both URIs map to each other, while the location identifies where the `taglib.tld` file resides. After the library is located, the container will load it into memory and examine its contents.

Tag Library Descriptor (TLD)

As you know, the tag library descriptor, or TLD, is an XML document used to identify and describe the list of tag extensions associated with a single tag library. The file contains general information about the library, and available extensions along with their attributes. Listing 10.2 displays a library containing two tags.

Listing 10.2: A Sample TLD

```xml
<?xml version="1.0" encoding="ISO-8859-1" ?>
<!DOCTYPE taglib PUBLIC
    "-//Sun Microsystems, Inc.//DTD JSP Tag Library 1.2//EN"
    "http://java.sun.com/dtd/web-jsptaglibrary_1_2.dtd">

<taglib>
   <tlib-version>1.0</tlib-version>
   <jsp-version>1.2</jsp-version>
   <short-name>examples</short-name>

   <description>Simple example library.</description>

   <tag>
       <name>hello</name>
       <tag-class>tagext.HelloTag</tag-class>
       <body-content>JSP</body-content>
       <description>First example</description>
   </tag>
   <tag>
       <name>goodbye</name>
       <tag-class>tagext.GoodByeTag</tag-class>
       <body-content>JSP</body-content>
       <description>Second example</description>
       <attribute>
           <name>age</name>
           <required>true</required>
           <rtexprvalue>true</rtexprvalue>
           <type>java.lang.Integer</type>
       </attribute>
   </tag>
</taglib>
```

The TLD begins with general information about the library. Table 10.1 lists the various tags that can be used to describe the library. The only two required are jsp-version and short-name.

TABLE 10.1 General TLD Tags

Tag	Explanation
tlib-version	The library's version number.
jsp-version	The JSP specification version required by the current tag library to function properly. This tag is mandatory.
short-name	The prefix value of the taglib directive. You should not use white space, or start the value off with a digit or underscore. This tag is mandatory.
description	A text string describing the library's purpose.

Optional tags for the library are available to provide additional flexibility and functionality. Table 10.2 displays these elements.

TABLE 10.2 Optional TLD Tags

Tag	Explanation
uri	An address that uniquely identifies this taglib.
display-name	The short name for the tag displayed by tools.
small-icon	An optional icon that can be used by tools to identify the tag library.
large-icon	An optional icon that can be used by tools to identify the tag library.
validator	An object used to ensure the conformance of the JSP page to the tag library. It can contain the following sub-elements:
	validator-class—The class that implements the javax.servlet.jsp.tagext.TagLibraryValidator interface.
	init-param—The optional initialization parameters.
	description—The explanation of the validator.

TABLE 10.2 Optional TLD Tags *(continued)*

Tag	Explanation
listener	A tag that defines an optional event listener object to instantiate and register automatically. It can contain the following sub-element: Listener-class—The class that must be registered as a web application listener bean.

After the broad library information is defined, custom tags can be declared by using the `<tag></tag>` elements. Configuration information for the specific action is embedded between these tags. Table 10.3 lists the basic tag options.

TABLE 10.3 Common Custom Tag Options

Tag	Explanation
name	The unique action name. The name defined after the prefix.
tag-class	The fully qualified class name for the custom action that implements the javax.servlet.jsp.tagext.Tag interface.
tei-class	This stands for the TagExtraInfo class. It provides information about the values exported to the corresponding tag class. This class must subclass the javax.servlet.jsp.tagext.TagExtraInfo class. This tag is optional.
body-content	Information used by a page composition tool to determine how to manage the tag's body content. The following options are available: JSP—A value that informs the container to evaluate the body of the action during runtime. This is the default. tagdependent—A value notifying the container that it should not evaluate the body of the action. Instead, its contents should be passed to the tag handler for interpretation. empty—A value stating that the body must be empty.

TABLE 10.3 Common Custom Tag Options *(continued)*

Tag	Explanation

attribute	The tag used to provide information about all available parameters and values exported by the tag. Its sub-elements are as follows:
	
	name—The name of the attribute. This is required.
	
	required—A value that indicates whether the attribute is mandatory or optional. This sub-element is optional.
	
	rtexprvalue—A value that indicates whether the attribute can be dynamically calculated by using an expression. This sub-element is optional. Options include:
	
	`    true | false | yes | no`
	The default is false. If true, then the tag might look something like the following:
	
	`    <prefix:action attrib="<%=obj.getValue() %>" />`
	
	type—The attribute's data type. For literals, the type is always java.lang.String.
	
	description—The explanation of the attribute.

In addition to the standard tags that define the element, supplementary elements can be included to enhance the use of the extension within a tool or to improve readability. Table 10.4 lists these additional tags.

TABLE 10.4 Additional Custom Tag Elements

Tag	Explanation
display-name	The short name displayed by tools.
small-icon	A file containing a small (16×16) icon image. Its path is relative to the TLD. The format must be either JPEG or GIF.
large-icon	A file containing a large (32×32) icon image. Its path is relative to the TLD. The format must be either JPEG or GIF.
description	An explanation of the tag.

TABLE 10.4 Additional Custom Tag Elements *(continued)*

Tag	Explanation
variable	An element that provides information about the scripting variables. Its sub-elements are as follows:
	name-given—The name as a constant.
	name-from-attribute—The name of the attribute whose value will be given the name of the variable at translation time.
	variable-class—The variable's class name. The default is java.lang.String.
	declare—A Boolean representing whether the variable is declared. The default is true. Available options are true | false | yes | no.
	scope—The scope of the scripting variable. NESTING is the default. The other legal values are AT BEGIN and AT END.
	description—An explanation of the variable.
example	A sample of how to use the tag.

A custom tag has a variety of elements to help define the tag's syntax and how it should be used. Some of the elements are basic requirements for the tag, whereas others are optional elements that make the tag more tool-friendly by adding robust features.

After a tag is defined, it can then be configured to perform its task by using the information and attributes provided. Let's begin by revisiting the second tag in code Listing 10.2:

```
<tag>
    <name>goodbye</name>
    <tag-class>tagext.GoodByeTag</tag-class>
    <body-content>JSP</body-content>
    <description>Second example</description>
    <attribute>
        <name>age</name>
        <required>true</required>
        <rtexprvalue>true</rtexprvalue>
        <type>java.lang.Integer</type>
    </attribute>
</tag>
```

We could invoke this tag within our JSP page in the following fashion:

```
<examples:goodbye age=
   "<%=
        new Integer(application.getInitParameter("age"))
    %>" >
</examples:goodbye>
```

This example provides one attribute called age. It is required and enables the value to be assigned at runtime by using an expression. Because its return type is of the java.lang.Integer class, the expression must convert the String value to an Integer object.

 Real World Scenario

Talking to the World

For several years, WorldTalk Inc. has provided the Internet community a service that translates websites to the clients' desired language. To ensure that their teams of designers are specialized experts in design and that their teams of developers are experts in programming, the company has begun to separate worker tasks.

Standard JSPs have greatly helped the company move toward this goal, because the JSPs enable designers to focus on HTML and use available tags to take care of basic functionality. The problem with this approach is that designers are forced to create complex HTML code that is not reusable because they are using JSP and have limited default programming functionality.

To solve this problem, management chose to migrate the application toward the use of custom tags. The development team began working on a library of tags that provide translation functionality. For example, designers can now use a tag called formatDate.jsp to present the date in the appropriate fashion. Optional attributes include the locale of the machine, the pattern describing the date style, the value being the actual date, and others. By creating a library of tags, the developers have enabled the designers to create pages by utilizing tags that handle all the functionality necessary to create the item or result desired. The developers handle Unicode translations, and the designers focus on layout.

The final piece needed to bring tag extensions together is the actual tag class. In the next section, we will discuss the various types of custom tags and their life cycles.

Tag Handler

As with all Java advanced technologies, creating a component that conforms to a particular API requires the implementation of an interface. Custom tags abide by this rule. When you are creating a custom tag, it is required that the class implement the interface `javax.servlet.jsp.tagext.Tag`. The interface provides several important methods that define the life cycle of the tag. By implementing the methods correctly, the container can manage the tag to deliver an expected and consistent behavior.

The `Tag` interface is the most basic protocol between the `Tag` handler and the implementing JSP page. It defines the methods that should be invoked at the starting and ending tag. The interface `javax.servlet.jsp.tagext.IterationTag` is a subinterface and provides additional functionality whereby the tag can loop through its body multiple times. Still one level lower is the `javax.servlet.jsp.tagext.BodyTag` interface, which allows the manipulation of the body content. By implementing any one of these interfaces and a little work, you can create a custom tag that suits your needs.

To minimize the work, the API provides support classes, which implement the interfaces for you. They define the most uncommonly changed methods and leave the most frequently modified methods abstract. Figure 10.2 demonstrates the hierarchy between the interfaces and support classes discussed. The solid lines represent "`extends`," and the dotted lines signify "`implements`."

A custom tag can implement any one of the interfaces or simply extend a support class. This section covers the functionality of each tag interface and abstract class:

- `Tag` interface
- `IterationTag` interface
- `BodyTag` interface
- Support classes

Deciding which class or interface to utilize is usually based on the life cycle desired and required methods the developer must define. We will discuss these features in detail.

FIGURE 10.2 The tag hierarchy to be fixed

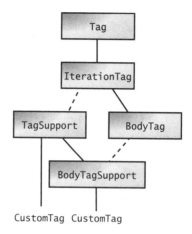

Tag Interface

As mentioned earlier, the `javax.servlet.jsp.tagext.Tag` interface defines the most basic protocol between the tag handler and the JSP page that invokes the instance. If you choose to implement this interface, you must define the following six methods:

- setPageContext(*PageContext pageContext*)
- setParent(*Tag tag*)
- getParent()
- doStartTag()
- doEndTag()
- release()

The first method that is invoked by the container sets the `pageContext` object, which provides a handle to all the implicit objects. Its signature is as follows:

```
public void setPageContext (PageContext pageContext)
```

The container passes the context to the tag to enable access to the application's implicit variables. Through the `PageContext` convenience methods, such as `getRequest()`, you can alter or provide more information to your tag handler. This method is usually defined by saving a local instance of the context object.

The second method that is invoked by the container is setParent(*Tag tag*). Its purpose is to provide a local handle to the closest enclosing tag handler. If a tag is nested within another tag, the handle to the outer tag is made available to the inner tag. Given the existence of the corresponding getParent() method, tags can communicate with one another by using the Tag handle instance. The signature to these methods is as follows:

```
public void setParent(Tag tag)
public Tag getParent()
```

After the setPageContext(...) and setParent(...) methods are called, the container can begin to process the beginning tag by first invoking any "set" property methods to set needed tag attributes. For example, if the tag has a string attribute called name, then a corresponding setName(...) method within the tag handler will automatically be invoked. The container will then continue to initialize the tag by calling doStartTag(). In addition to initializing the tag even further, this method is responsible for notifying the container about how to evaluate the body of the tag element. The body represents the logic between the opening and closing tags. The method signature is as follows:

```
public int doStartTag() throws JspException
```

Depending on how you would like the body to be handled, you can return one of the following constants:

int EVAL_BODY_INCLUDE   This constant indicates that the body should be evaluated. Results generated from executing the body are written to the current JspWriter out variable.

int SKIP_BODY   This constant indicates that the body should not be evaluated.

Depending on the return value, the body will be either evaluated or skipped. The doEndTag() method is then invoked. It processes the end tag for the element to determine how the remaining JSP page should be evaluated. The signature for the method is as follows:

```
public int doEndTag() throws JspException
```

As you can see, this method returns an int value as well. Again, the constant informs the container about how to proceed. The following return values are available:

int EVAL_PAGE   As the name suggests, this constant indicates that the container should evaluate the rest of the JSP page.

int SKIP_PAGE   This option indicates that the rest of the page should not be evaluated and that the request is in fact complete. If this request was created by a forward or include from another page, then only the current JSP page is complete.

 The specification states that if the TLD defines the action's body-content as empty, then the doStartTag() method must return SKIP_BODY.

 If SKIP_BODY is returned and a body is present, it is not evaluated.

Both the doStartTag() and doEndTag() methods throw a JspException in their signatures. If the method actually throws the exception, the container will generate an error page to notify the client of a JSP problem.

The final method that must be defined is used to clean up any loose ends. The signature is as follows:

```
public void release()
```

When the tag is done processing the beginning element, the body, and the ending element, the container invokes this method to release the tag handler's state. Figure 10.3 displays the life cycle for the Tag interface.

FIGURE 10.3 The Tag interface life cycle

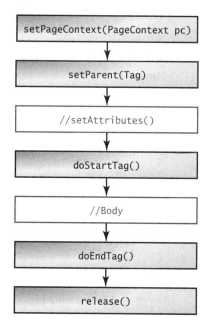

Let's revisit the custom tag example used to generate a random value. Previously, we showed you how we invoked such an action; now we will show you the actual code used to generate the action. Listing 10.3 displays the necessary code to implement the Tag interface.

Listing 10.3: Utilizing the Tag Interface

```
package tagext;

import java.io.*;
import javax.servlet.jsp.*;
import javax.servlet.jsp.tagext.*;

public class RandomValue implements Tag {
    private PageContext pageContext;
    private Tag parent;

    public int doStartTag() throws JspException {
        return SKIP_BODY;
    }

    public int doEndTag() throws JspException {
        int value = (int)(Math.random() * 100);

        try {
            pageContext.getOut().write("" + value);
        } catch (IOException ioe) {
            throw new JspException(ioe.getMessage());
        }
        return EVAL_PAGE;
    }

    public void release() {}

    public void setPageContext(PageContext pageContext) {
        this.pageContext = pageContext;
    }
    public void setParent(Tag parent) {
```

```
        this.parent = parent;
    }

    public Tag getParent() {
        return this.parent;
    }
}
```

In this example, the doStartTag() method notifies the container to skip the body and immediately invoke the doEndTag() method. This method generates a random value and writes it to the JspWriter out object. When the method completes, the rest of the JSP page will be evaluated. One thing you should notice is that within a custom action, you do not have direct access to implicit objects. Instead, handles to these variables are accessible from the pageContext object passed as an instance by the container. In the preceding example, the implicit out JspWriter is accessed by calling pageContext.getOut().

The PageContext class provides the following convenience methods for access to implicit objects: getOut(), getException(), getPage(), getRequest(), getResponse(), getSession(), getServletConfig(), and getServletContext().

IterationTag Interface

The javax.servlet.jsp.tagext.IterationTag interface extends the Tag interface and adds one additional method. As the name suggests, this interface enables the body of the element to be executed multiple times. The functionality is similar to a do/while loop.

In addition to the standard doStartTag() and doEndTag() methods, the IterationTag interface adds the doAfterBody() method. When this method is implemented, the developer can opt to have the body evaluated again. The signature is as follows:

```
public int doAfterBody() throws JspException
```

Depending on how you would like the body to be handled, you can return one of the following constants:

int EVAL_BODY_AGAIN This indicates that the body should be reevaluated. The doAfterBody() method will get called again after evaluating the body.

int SKIP_BODY This notifies the container that the body should not be evaluated. The value of out will be restored, and the doEndTag() method will be invoked.

If SKIP_BODY is returned, the body is not evaluated and the doEndTag() is then invoked.

As we said, this interface acts like a do/while loop. It enables the body to be evaluated (that's the do part), and calls doAfterBody() (that's the while part) to determine whether to reevaluate the body. Figure 10.4 displays the life cycle of an IterationTag.

FIGURE 10.4 The IterationTag life cycle

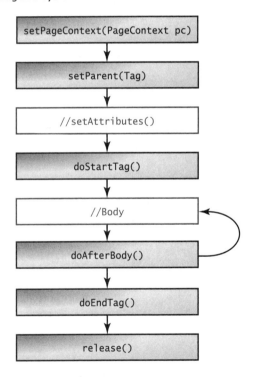

Although this interface is not often used directly, it can be utilized to cycle through an element's body to generate a response. Listing 10.4 takes our previous JSP, which generated a single random value, and now has it generate five random values.

Listing 10.4: Utilizing the IterationTag Interface

```
package tagext;

import java.io.*;
import javax.servlet.jsp.*;
import javax.servlet.jsp.tagext.*;

public class MoreRandomValues implements IterationTag {
    private PageContext pageContext;
    private Tag parent;
    private int counter;

    public void setPageContext(PageContext pageContext) {
        this.pageContext = pageContext;
    }
    public void setParent(Tag parent) {
        this.parent = parent;
    }

    public int doStartTag() throws JspException {
        return EVAL_BODY_INCLUDE;
    }

    public int doAfterBody() throws JspException {
        int value = (int)(Math.random() * 100);
        counter++;
        if (0 < counter && counter<5) {
            try {
                pageContext.getOut().write(" " + value);
            } catch (IOException ioe) {
                throw new JspException(ioe.getMessage());
            }
            return EVAL_BODY_AGAIN;
        } else {
            return SKIP_BODY;
        }
    }
```

```
public int doEndTag() throws JspException {
    return EVAL_PAGE;
}

public void release() {
    counter=0;
}

public Tag getParent() {
    return this.parent;
}
}
```

In this example, the doAfterBody() method generates a new random value if the body has been evaluated fewer than five times. It then takes that value and writes it to the JspWriter object. Because we are simply writing text to the response stream, we access the implicit out variable through the page-Context object and invoke the write(?) method, which takes a String value. The resulting output displays four consecutive random values.

You will not see the IterationTag interface implemented often because its subinterface, javax.servlet.jsp.tagext.BodyTag, offers the ability to iterate and manipulate the body content if necessary. If iterating through the body is not necessary, a support class implements all the necessary methods of this interface and makes coding a tag much easier. We will cover that topic later, in "Support Classes." For now, let's take a close look at the BodyTag interface.

BodyTag Interface

The javax.servlet.jsp.tagext.BodyTag interface extends the Iteration-Tag interface and adds the capability to evaluate and alter the body content multiple times. As you know, the body content is the logic between an extension's opening and closing tags. This functionality is made possible with the addition of the following methods:

- public void setBodyContent(*BodyContent bodyContent*)

- public void doInitBody() throws JspException

The setBodyContent(*BodyContent bodyContent*) method is called by the container to provide the tag a handle to the body content. It is invoked after the doStartTag() because the opening tag must first be evaluated to determine whether to execute or skip the body. The BodyContent object is a critical feature for BodyTag handlers. It is important to understand how this object works in order to get your output to display correctly.

With basic JSPs, output is written to the response stream by using the JspWriter out implicit variable. Until now, we too have written directly to the out variable by using the **pageContext** method getOut(). This approach works well when you need to write either a String, int, or char value to the stream. However, when the goal is to manipulate a tag's body content and then write its information to the response stream, the standard out object falls short. To accomplish this task, you must first write to the tag's BodyContent object. The class actually extends the JspWriter class, and is therefore a buffered writer. But what distinguishes it from its parent class is that it contains the tag's evaluated body content. From the Body-Content object, you can extract the body and manipulate its content. When you are ready to display your results, the BodyContent object must be written to the implicit out response stream. To understand how the container handles the body content, look at the following JSP code:

```
<syb:grandparent>
     This is the body
</syb:grandparent>
```

When the container reads the syb:grandparent tag, it executes the tag's doStartTag() method. This method creates a new BodyContent writer instance specifically for this tag. The implicit out variable is then redirected to the instance for future use. When the body is evaluated, the contents are transferred to the BodyContent object. After a BodyContent instance is initialized, you can invoke any one of the following methods on it:

- public void clearBody()

- public abstract String getString()

- public abstract Reader getReader()

- public JspWriter getEnclosingWriter()

- public abstract void writeOut(*Writer out*)

- public void flush()

The BodyContent has a buffer size that is unbound and cannot be flushed. In fact, the flush() method is overridden to prevent the parent class JspWriter from attempting to flush when this method is called.

As you can see, you can clear the body, read from it, or call getString() to convert the contents to a String and return its value. The last two methods are important, because they are used to alter the content.

When you specifically write to the BodyContent instance, you are not writing to the implicit out located on the bottom of the stack. Instead, you must access the outer-layer stream by calling getEnclosingWriter(). This method returns a JspWriter, which is the implicit out variable if your tag is an outer tag. The term *outer tag* means the custom action is not nested within another action. If it is nested, then you write your body content to the enclosing outer tag's body content. The task of sending the current body content to the enclosing writer is handled by the writeOut(?) method. This method writes the content of the calling BodyContent instance to the Writer object parameter. The parameter you pass is usually the result of a call to getEnclosingWriter().

The implicit out object can be accessed by most JSP actions by using the method pageContext.getOut(). The problem with accessing the out object directly is that custom tags need to access their body content and manipulate that data before sending it back to the response stream. A basic JspWriter does not offer such functionality. In addition, by writing directly to the pageContext .getOut(), anything that is currently in the buffer can be potentially overwritten.

The way data is written to the response stream is especially critical and essential for handling tags that are nested. *Nested tags* are tags within another tag. Consider the following JSP example, in which pc stands for the pageContext object:

```
<syb:grandparent>   <-- pc.pushBody() bodyContent 1 -->
    <syb:parent>    <-- pc.pushBody() bodyContent 2 -->
        <syb:child> <-- pc.pushBody() bodyContent 3 -->

        </syb:child>
    </syb:parent>
</syb:grandparent>
```

The code consists of three nested tags. The `child` tag is within the `parent` tag, and the `parent` tag is within the `grandparent` tag. The problem is that there is only one implicit `out` variable to which all tags must eventually forward their output. To prevent potential overwrites, each tag has its own `BodyContent` object. When the container accesses the opening tag, it calls the action's `doStartTag()` method, which causes the `pageContext` to call its `pushBody()` method. This method creates a new `BodyContent` object for that particular tag. With each tag owning its own `BodyContent` or `JspWriter`, your first instinct might be to have the tag write directly to its own `BodyContent` object. That, however, fails to work. The implicit `out` is located at the bottom of the stack, whereas each additional `BodyContent` writer is stacked one on top of the other. If you opt to `writeOut(...)` to the current `BodyContent`, then the output will not be sent to the implicit `out` stream. Instead, it will be sent to itself. The following code sample demonstrates this concept:

```
JspWriter jspOut = getBodyContent();
bodyContent.writeOut(jspOut);
```

The method `getBodyContent()` is available within the BodyTagSupport class. It returns the current body content instance. If you are implementing the BodyTag interface, a handle to the body content should be saved locally when the `setBodyContent(BodyContent bodyContent)` method is invoked by the container. We will discuss the support class in more detail later.

This example writes the contents of the current `BodyContent` into the current `BodyContent` writer `jspOut`. The implicit `out` variable is never accessed, and the stream is left empty. Basically, this example accomplishes nothing because it writes itself to itself.

When you call `getEnclosingWriter()`, you access the enclosing action's `BodyContent` object or `JspWriter`. If tags are nested, then each will call `getEnclosingWriter()` and access their outer tag writer, concatenating their information to the previous buffered data. Eventually, you'll reach the outermost layer and write the buffered stream to the response stream. The correct way to write output is as follows:

```
JspWriter bcOut = bodyContent.getEnclosingWriter();
bodyContent.write(" data ");
bodyContent.writeOut(bcOut);
```

If this code snippet is run as an outer tag, then bcOut is actually the implicit JspWriter out variable. If the tag is executed as a nested tag, then the bcOut variable is actually the outer tag's BodyContent.

Given the earlier nested example, the child tag must call getEnclosing-Writer() to access the content of the parent; the parent tag will then call getEnclosingWriter() to get the grandparent tag's content writer. Finally, the grandparent calls getEnclosingWriter() to gain access to the implicit out object writer, which transfers information to the response stream. Figure 10.5 shows how nested tags eventually access the response stream in comparison to a single tag.

When a stack of writers exists, the getEnclosingWriter() method ensures that you concatenate current data with the parent's data to eventually output all data to the response stream.

FIGURE 10.5 Accessing the enclosing writer

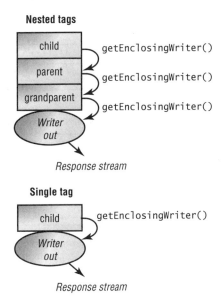

Now that you have a better understanding of BodyContent, let's get back to the life cycle of the BodyTag interface. As discussed earlier, the doStartTag() method is called to determine whether the body should be evaluated. If the answer is yes, then a BodyContent object is created and associated with the tag by an invocation of the setBodyContent(...) method. After the content is set, there is opportunity to initialize any variables prior to reading the body. This is done when the doInitTag() method is called. Its purpose is to process code that should be taken care of before the body of the BodyTag is evaluated for the first time. The doAfterBody() method is called next to determine whether the body should be reevaluated. After there is no longer a need to iterate through the body, the doEndTag() method is invoked. Finally, before the Tag handler is sent to the garbage collector, the release() method is called to release any unnecessary resources. Figure 10.6 demonstrates the life cycle for this interface.

FIGURE 10.6   The BodyTag life cycle

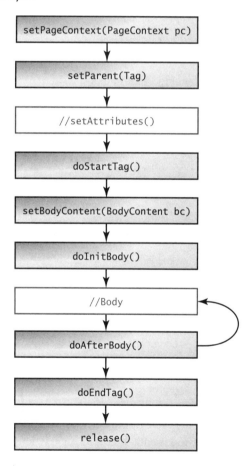

To demonstrate how this interface is used, we are going to create a LoopTag handler to print the body content to the client the number of times specified by an attribute.

First, we need to define the tag in the tag library descriptor:

```
<tag>
    <name>loop</name>
    <tag-class>tagext.LoopTag</tag-class>
    <body-content>JSP</body-content>
    <attribute>
        <name>iterations</name>
        <required>true</required>
        <rtexprvalue>true</rtexprvalue>
        <type>java.lang.Integer</type>
    </attribute>
</tag>
```

Notice that we define the body-content with the default value JSP. This tells the container to evaluate the body of the action at runtime. If you would rather have the *action* determine whether to evaluate the body, you can define the content type as tagdependent. Finally, to force the body to be empty, simply define the body-content as empty.

With this tag in place, we can now make the following call within our JSP page:

```
<examples:loop iterations="2">
    Test 1 <BR>
    <examples:loop iterations="2">
        Test 2 <BR>
    </examples:loop>
</examples:loop>
```

The code for the described tag is shown in Listing 10.5. You will notice that the doStartTag() method has an option to return the constant EVAL_BODY_BUFFERED. When the constant is returned, a bodyContent object is created to capture the evaluated body.

If EVAL_BODY_INCLUDE is returned, the setBodyContent(...) and doInitBody() methods are not invoked. Instead, the body is evaluated and "passed through" to the current out variable. The doAfterBody() method is then invoked the number of necessary iterations, until finally the doEndTag() is invoked.

Listing 10.5: Utilizing the BodyTag Interface

```java
package tagext;

import java.io.*;
import javax.servlet.jsp.*;
import javax.servlet.jsp.tagext.*;

public class LoopTag implements BodyTag {
    private PageContext pageContext;
    private BodyContent bodyContent;
    private Tag parent;
    private int iterations;

    public void setPageContext(PageContext pageContext) {
        this.pageContext = pageContext;
    }

    public void setParent(Tag parent) {
        this.parent = parent;
    }

    public void setIterations(int iterations) {
        this.iterations = iterations;
    }

    public int doStartTag() throws JspException {
        if(iterations>0) {
            return EVAL_BODY_BUFFERED;
        } else {
            return SKIP_BODY;
        }
    }

    public void setBodyContent(BodyContent bodyContent) {
        this.bodyContent = bodyContent;
    }
```

```java
public void doInitBody() throws JspException {}

public int doAfterBody() throws JspException {
    if(iterations > 0) {
        iterations--;
        return EVAL_BODY_AGAIN;
    } else {
        try {
            if(bodyContent != null) {
                JspWriter out=
                    bodyContent.getEnclosingWriter();
                bodyContent.writeOut(out);
            }
        } catch (IOException e) {
            throw new JspException();
        }
        return SKIP_BODY;
    }
}

public int doEndTag() throws JspException {
    return EVAL_PAGE;
}
public void release() {}

public Tag getParent() {
    return this.parent;
}
}
```

The point of this code is to determine whether the tag has a body. If it does, then the doAfterTag() method extracts the contents and writes it out to the bodyContent. The iteration counter is decremented and checked to determine whether to repeat the behavior in the doAfterBody() method.

By the time a tag's doEndTag() method is invoked, the container might have already reused the body content instance. Consequently, you should not use the BodyContent object in the doEndTag() method; instead, it should be handled within the doAfterBody() method.

The BodyContent object is flushed when the highest-level parent object (similar to the Object class) clears its buffer. The highest-level parent object would be a tag that is not nested within any other tag. When that object calls writeOut(...), the buffer is flushed.

Ultimately, the code example produces the following output:

```
Test 1
Test 2
Test 2
Test 1
Test 2
Test 2
```

A common use for the IterationTag or BodyTag is to extract data from a java.sql.ResultSet object returned from a database call. With each iteration, the current record is extracted in some standard format, which is defined within the body content.

Depending on the task at hand, you can implement any one of these three interfaces. To simplify matters, however, a few support classes are provided to limit the number of methods you have to define when creating a custom tag.

Support Classes

To reduce the amount of redundant work and provide additional functionality, *support classes* are made available. The API provides a variety of support classes; we will cover three that most closely pertain to the exam objectives.

Two of the three classes implement the Tag interface and define the methods for the developer. They include the following:

javax.servlet.jsp.tagext.TagSupport is used for basic tags that do not manipulate the tag's body. TagSupport implements IterationTag, which extends the Tag interface.

javax.servlet.jsp.tagext.BodyTagSupport is used for tags that intend to make changes to the tag's body content. Although these classes implement the methods of the interface, the most commonly used methods are written with limited functionality. This encourages the developer to override the intended method to define custom behavior. In addition to making tag extensions easier to write, the class also provide a few supplementary methods to expand the tag's capabilities. BodyTagSupport extends TagSupport. BodyTagSupport also implements the BodyTag interface, which in turn extends IterationTag.

The third support class is used to provide additional information to the tag:

javax.servlet.jsp.tagext.TagExtraInfo is provided by the tag library author to describe additional translation-time information not described in the TLD.

In this section, we will discuss these three classes as they are often used when creating custom tags.

The *TagSupport* Class

The javax.servlet.jsp.tagext.TagSupport class implements the IterationTag interface, granting it the standard Tag life cycle. The class is also able to iterate through the tag body multiple times, without making changes to the body. This utility class is considered the *base class*, which offers basic functionality for new tag handlers. Because all the life-cycle methods are implemented, they have default return values that you should know. Table 10.5 defines those defaults.

TABLE 10.5 Default Return Values for TagSupport Tags

Method	Default Return Value
doStartTag()	SKIP_BODY
doAfterBody()	SKIP_BODY
doEndTag()	EVAL_PAGE

In addition to defining the standard interface methods, the TagSupport class offers two instance variables and some convenience methods for greater functionality. The variables are as follows:

protected String id is a value that can be assigned to the tag for future reference.

protected PageContext pageContext provides the tag with access to the JSP page implicit objects, such as the JspWriter object out, or the HttpSession object, known as session.

Because the Tag interface method setPageContext(...) is now defined for you, the pageContext variable must be accessible to the class. The id variable is defined by using a method called setId(...) and indirectly accessible by using the getId() method.

Another feature of the TagSupport class is its capability to maintain a collection of values. A *tag value* is any java.lang.Object with an associated String key. This concept is similar to a java.util.Map. You can set and get the value of a tag by using the following TagSupport methods:

- public Object getValue(*String key*)

- public java.util.Enumeration getValues()

- public void removeValue(*String key*)

- public void setValue(*String key, Object o*)

As with a java.util.Map, you set the value of the tag by passing a unique key and the value itself. Internally, the TagSupport class maintains a Collection (it returns an Enumeration) of values that you can enumerate by using the getValues() method. Because you can add values, you can also remove them by identifying the object you intend to eliminate via its key.

In addition to the previous methods defined, one other convenience method is available to this class. It is static and used to help tags coordinate with one another. Its signature is as follows:

- public static final Tag findAncestorWithClass(*Tag from, java.lang.Class class*)

Sometimes you might need the help of an outer tag to resolve a problem with a current nested tag. You can get the handle to any parental tags from within a tag by using either the getParent() method or by calling findAncestorWithClass(...). The method getParent() returns only your immediate parent. In contrast, the findAncestorWithClass(...) method enables multiple-layer subtags to acquire a handle to any outer ancestral tag class. This method takes two arguments. The first parameter is the Tag handle from which you want the container to begin its search for the target class. The second parameter is the target java.lang.Class whose Tag handle you are requesting.

The findAncestorWithClass(...) method is used to return a handle to an ancestor tag class that is nested. For example:

```
<outer-outer>
    <outer>
        <inner (makes ancestor request)>
          Body
        </inner>
    </outer>
</outer-outer>
```

It is related to nesting tags within the JSP page, not a parental hierarchy. Consider the following code example:

```
public int doStartTag() throws JspException {
    Class className=com.company.TagName.class;
    Tag ancestor = TagSupport.findAncestorWithClass(this,
      className);
    TagSupport ts = (TagSupport)ancestor;
    ServletRequest req = pageContext.getRequest();
    ts.setValue("quantity", req.getParameter("qty"));
   return SKIP_BODY;
}
```

Imagine that the example's doStartTag() method exists within a tag that is nested within several other tags. The com.company.TagName.class is a great-great-great grandparent class. Given such a scenario, the findAncestor-WithClass(...) method will return a handle to that relative, allowing the current tag to modify a parameter value. In contrast, the method getParent() will return only the immediate enclosing tag class.

In order for the findAncestorWithClass(...) method to locate a parental relative, the child tag must be nested within the parent tag in the JSP page. In addition, the parent tag cannot evaluate its body.

The findAncestorWithClass(...) method can be called within any tag-handler method. Because the method is static, the handler class does not need to subclass TagSupport. A Tag instance is returned, so if the ancestral class is of a different data type, you must cast it in order to access the class's methods or instance variables.

When subsequent tags need to pass information or get information from a parental relative, they can use the Tag handle to access its attribute methods.

The *BodyTagSupport* Class

The javax.servlet.jsp.tagext.BodyTagSupport class extends the TagSupport class and implements the BodyTag interface. The design provides the BodyTagSupport class the added features of the TagSupport class and the capability to modify the body of the extension as defined by the BodyTag interface. This support class provides an iteration life cycle with the capability to alter the body content that exists between the opening and closing tags. It also can add and remove tag values.

In addition to the standard methods and variables defined by its inherited class and interfaces, the BodyTagSupport class offers a new instance variable and some convenience methods to access the BodyContent and the surrounding JspWriter. The new variable is as follows:

> **protected BodyContent bodyContent** provides a handle to the data that exists between the opening and closing tag elements.

In addition to the new variable, the class also adds the following two methods:

- public BodyContent getBodyContent()

- public JspWriter getPreviousOut()

Because the support class defines the **setBodyContent(...)** method, accessing the BodyContent object can be done either by accessing the instance variable bodyContent or by using the accessor method getBodyContent().

The other method, getPreviousOut(), saves you the hassle of first accessing the BodyContent object to then get the enclosing JspWriter. So instead of calling

```
JspWriter out= getBodyContent().getEnclosingWriter();
```

you can simply call

```
JspWriter out = getPreviousOut();
```

Again, this is simply a convenience method that provides access to the enclosing tag's writer. Given the potential for nested tags, this approach ensures that writing done in an inner tag will be concatenated to the outer tag's output.

Because the BodyTagSupport class extends the TagSupport class and provides implementation for the BodyTag interface, it offers the most default custom tag functionality. As a result, it is used most often when creating custom tags that utilize their body content. If we revisit the code for LoopTag, you can see how the code is greatly simplified; see Listing 10.6.

Listing 10.6: Utilizing the BodyTagSupport Class

```
package tagext;

import java.io.*;
import javax.servlet.jsp.*;
import javax.servlet.jsp.tagext.*;

public class LoopTag extends BodyTagSupport {
    private int iterations;

    public void setIterations(int value) {
        this.iterations = value;
    }

    public int doAfterBody() throws JspException {
        if(iterations>1){
            iterations--;
            return EVAL_BODY_BUFFERED;
        } else {
            try {
                if(bodyContent != null) {
                    bodyContent.writeOut(getPreviousOut());
                }
            } catch (IOException e) {
                throw new JspException();
            }
            return SKIP_BODY;
        }
    }
}
```

In this example, you should notice a few things. First, there is no need to define the standard set methods of the tag and its subclassing interfaces. Second, we use the `bodyContent` variable directly because it is available from the `BodyTagSupport` class. Finally, we call `getPreviousOut()` instead of using the `BodyContent` object to access the enclosing `out` variable.

The *TagExtraInfo* Class

Until now, we have shown you one way for a JSP page to access attribute values. When an action tag declares the value for an attribute, the JSP page can utilize the variable directly if a `setXXX(...)` attribute method is defined. Listings 10.5 and 10.6 use the `iterations` variable, which is passed from the JSP page. After the `setParent(...)` method is invoked, the container calls the `setIterations(...)` method, passing in the attribute value from the JSP page. Although this approach is effective, it requires the tag to individually define each and every attribute in the tag library descriptor. In addition, you are unable to specify the scope of the attribute. Instead, the attribute is available for the life of the action.

Another approach is available that provides more flexibility and manageable code (meaning you can create an action with 100 variables without having a huge TLD). By extending the abstract class `TagExtraInfo` and overriding one or two of its methods, you can provide a list of variables with differing scopes to the JSP page and scriptlets that the action might utilize. To create this list, you must override the first method in the list below. The second method is optional and simply adds greater functionality:

- `public VariableInfo[] getVariableInfo(`*TagData data*`)`

- `public boolean isValid(`*TagData data*`)`

The container invokes the `getVariableInfo()` method when attributes for the action are requested. A `TagData` instance is passed to the method containing translation time attribute/value pair information defined within the JSP page. Consider the following code:

```
<syb:profile name='Chris Cook'>
    Welcome to our site <%= name %><br>
</syb:profile>
```

In this example, the `TagData` object would contain a `String` key called `name` with an associated value `Chris Cook`. It acts like a `java.util.Map` by holding a collection of objects, which are accessible through their `String` key values. When overriding the `getVariableInfo()` method, you can use the TagData handle to call the getAttribute(*String name*) method and pass in the name of the attribute to acquire its value. The class ProfileTag-Info demonstrates how the method can be overridden.

```
public class ProfileTagInfo extends TagExtraInfo {
    public VariableInfo[] getVariableInfo(TagData data) {
        return new VariableInfo[] {
            new VariableInfo(
                data.getAttributeString("name"),"
                "java.lang.String",  // variable's data type
                true,                // True means variable
                                     // is new
                VariableInfo.NESTED  // scope
            )
        };
    }
}
```

Creating a VariableInfo object requires passing in four parameters to its constructor. The first is the name of the variable, which is passed as a String. To prevent runtime errors or unexpected results, the name of each variable should be unique, because it is the name of the actual attribute. The second argument is the fully qualifying class name of the variable's data type. The third is a boolean. When set to true, a new variable is created by the action and declared within the translated servlet. The variable overrides the value of an existing variable if necessary. A false declaration means the variable already exists. The last argument is an int value. It represents the scope of the variable. Table 10.6 describes your choices.

TABLE 10.6   VariableInfo Scope Options

Scope	Description
VariableInfo.AT_BEGIN	The variable is accessible from the start of the action tag until the end tag is reached.
VariableInfo.AT_END	The variable is not accessible until after the end tag is reached.
VariableInfo.NESTED	The variable is available only within the action's body.

Figure 10.7 shows the scope range for each constant graphically.

FIGURE 10.7 Scope range

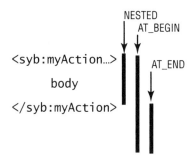

As you can tell, AT_BEGIN has the greatest possible scope, whereas NESTED covers the action's body, and AT_END covers everything thereafter. Some of these arguments can be defined dynamically with the use of the TagData object passed by the container.

The second method that is commonly overridden, but optional, provides elegance to the action's attribute. The isValid() method is used to validate the attributes passed to a tag at translation time. It receives a TagData instance, which can be used to filter out unacceptable values. For example, you might accept only certain object types or numbers within a particular range. The default implementation returns a true for all attributes. If configured to return false, it is still the developer's responsibility to utilize the attribute correctly.

Now that we've shown you how to create the list of variables, we will show you how to link the variables to the JSP page. The process begins with the container. When it comes across a variable within a scriptlet, it attempts to locate the value by looking to the tag library descriptor. An instance of the implementing class of TagExtraInfo is available by using the tei-class element to define it. Let's take a look at an example:

```
<taglib>
    <tag>
        <name>profile </name>
        <tag-class>ProfileTag</tag-class>
        <tei-class>ProfileTagInfo</tei-class>
        <body-content>JSP</body-content>
        <attribute>
            <name>name</name>
```

```
            <required>true</required>
            <rtexprvalue>true</rtexprvalue>
        </attribute>
    <tag>
</taglib>
```

The container locates the class and loads it into memory. At that point, all the variables are available by mapping the JSP variable name to the variable's key name.

In our example, we defined the scope of the variable name as NESTED. That works fine when we want to use the variable within scriptlets located inside nested actions. If, however, the scope is defined as AT_END, the variable must be saved to the JSP's PageContext. Remember, the PageContext object is one of the first objects set within the page. It lasts for the life of the page and can hold attributes. Consider the following code:

```
public int doEndTag() throws JspException {
    pageContext.setAttribute("name", "Sasha");
    return EVAL_PAGE;
}
```

In this example, the attribute name is accessible from within a JSP page after the closing tag for this action is read. If the scope for the variable were AT_BEGIN, you would need to associate it to the pageContext before the doStartTag() method. Fundamentally, it is important to know that attribute variables defined within the PageContext are accessible from within the JSP page and embedded scriptlets.

The PageContext object is a major resource for storing and accessing variables. It contains handles to implicit objects and page attributes.

Utilizing the TagExtraInfo class provides a clean way to incorporate a significant number of attributes into an action. The attributes can be used from within the custom tag class, the action itself, and scriptlets.

Summary

In this chapter, we covered the topics needed to understand custom tags. We began by discussing custom tag fundamentals, including the ways to call a custom tag and the elements that are necessary within the JSP and web.xml file in order to locate the tag library. We discussed how to create a tag library descriptor file, which maintains all the tags and their attributes. Finally, this left us with the core behind custom tags—the actual action or tag class.

The unique features of each interface and class that utilize the parent Tag interface were addressed. Although most people will always use support classes to create their tags, the exam tests your knowledge of the behaviors and semantics of each method, which depend somewhat on the ancestral class or interface being utilized. For example, the return type of the doStartTag() method is different if your class extends BodyTagSupport versus any other class or interface. We emphasized the details associated with each Tag interface to ensure a thorough understanding of the Tag, IterationTag, and BodyTag life cycles. Each interface serves a slightly different purpose and should be utilized accordingly.

We also covered the importance and role that the pageContext plays in a custom tag by providing access to the application's implicit variables and TagExtraInfo attributes. Finally, we covered the impact of the BodyContent object and how to effectively write information out to the client.

Exam Essentials

Be able to format tag library declarations in the web application deployment descriptor. The deployment descriptor uses the taglib element to identify the URI name, or taglib-uri, used by the JSP page to then locate the actual tag library by using the taglib-location element.

```
<taglib>
    <taglib-uri>/taglib.tld</taglib-uri>
    <taglib-location>
        /WEB-INF/taglib.tld
    </taglib-location>
</taglib>
```

Be able to identify taglib directives in a JSP page. You can use the taglib directive within a JSP page to notify the container of the tag library you are interested in utilizing. The uri attribute maps to the taglib-uri identified in the web.xml document. The prefix attribute is used to call the tag from within the page.

```
<%@ taglib uri="/taglib.tld" prefix="test" %>
```

Be able to identify properly formatted custom tag usage in a JSP page. A custom tag is defined by a prefix value, a colon, and the name of the action. Attributes are optional and can be listed within the opening tag. Nesting tags within the body of another tag is also acceptable.

Be able to identify the general tag library descriptor elements. A custom tag must be embedded within its own set of `<tag></tag>` elements. Nested within are the `name`, `tag-class`, and `body-content` elements used to define the tag's calling name, fully qualifying class name, and identifier to notify the server about how to handle the tag's body.

```
<tag>
  <name>theDate</name>
  <tag-class>DateTag</tag-class>
  <body-content>JSP</body-content>

</tag>
```

Be able to identify attribute tag library descriptor elements. Each tag can have multiple attributes to help provide greater flexibility to the `tag` extension. Nested within the `tag` element, you will usually find attribute information, such as its name, an indication of whether it is required, an indication of whether the value can be dynamically determined within an expression, and the data type.

```
<attribute>
  <name>age</name>
  <required>false</required>
  <rtexprvalue>true</rtexprvalue>
  <type>java.lang.Integer</type>
</attribute>
```

Be able to identify valid values for the body content TLD element. The `body-content` element has three valid types: `JSP`, `tagdependent`, and `empty`. `JSP` notifies the container that it should evaluate the tag's body, whereas `tagdependent` tells the container to pass the body through to the action class so that the class can determine what to do with the body. Finally, `empty` means the tag cannot have a body.

Be able to describe the life cycles for tag event methods. It is important to know the three major interfaces that provide unique functionality for a custom tag. They consist of `Tag`, `IterationTag`, and `BodyTag`. The two supporting classes, TagSupport and BodyTagSupport, share similar life cycles. Know which methods are called under certain circumstances.

Be able to identify valid return values for tag event methods. The interface or class your custom tag utilizes has a significant effect on which return types your doStartTag(), doAfterBody(), and doEndTag() methods deliver. Know the distinction between the SKIP_BODY and SKIP_PAGE, and when to use EVAL_BODY_BUFFERED versus EVAL_BODY_INCLUDE.

Know how to utilize the PageContext variable to access page attributes and implicit variables. Keep in mind that implicit objects are not directly accessible. You must use the PageContext convenience methods in order to utilize those variables. Using the PageContext object also enables you to set attributes for the JSP page to access.

Know which methods are used to write information to the implicit out variable. There are three general ways to access the implicit out variable. Depending on the class your tag extends or implements, you can use one of the following options:

```
JspWriter out = getBodyContent().getEnclosingWriter();
JspWriter out = getPreviousOut();
JspWriter out = pageContext.getOut();
```

Key Terms

Before you take the exam, be certain you are familiar with the following terms:

absolute path	prefix
base class	prefix mapping
body content	suffix
context-relative path	support classes
custom actions	tag extensions
custom tags	tag library descriptor (TLD)
nested tags	tag value
outer tag	TLD resource path
page-relative path	

Review Questions

1. Which of the following is an invalid declaration for a `tag-uri` element? (Choose all that apply.)

    A. `<taglib-uri>/taglib</taglib-uri>`

    B. `<taglib-uri>`
    `        http://www.eei.com/taglib</taglib-uri>`

    C. `<taglib-uri>taglib</taglib-uri>`

    D. `<taglib-uri address="taglib" />`

2. A `taglib` directive must define which of the following attributes?

    A. `value`

    B. `prefix`

    C. `uri`

    D. `uri` and `location`

    E. `uri` and `prefix`

3. Given a custom tag library with a `short-name` of `math`, and a tag with the `name` of `calculate`, identify which of the following options best displays an empty custom tag.

    A. `<math:calculate />`

    B. `<calculate:math>`
    `        4 + 4`
    `    </calculate:math>`

    C. `<math:calculate />`
    `        </math:calculate>`

    D. `<math:calculate %>`

4. What interface defines the following method invocation life cycle?

    `setPageContext → setParent → (setAttributes) →`
    `    doStartTag → doInitBody → doAfterBody →`
    `    doEndTag → release`

    A. `IterationTag`

    B. `Tag`

    C. `BodyTag`

    D. None of the above

5. Which of the following methods is always invoked exactly one time? (Choose all that apply.)

    A. `doEndTag()`

    B. `doStartTag()`

    C. `doInitBody()`

    D. `doAfterBody()`

6. Which constant is used to notify the container to reevaluate the custom tag's body?

    A. `EVAL_BODY_TAG`

    B. `EVAL_BODY`

    C. `EVAL_BODY_AGAIN`

    D. `EVAL_BODY_INCLUDE`

7. Which of the following tags identifies the `TagExtraInfo` class used to pass attributes to a custom tag?

    A. `class`

    B. `tinfoclass`

    C. `texiclass`

    D. `tei-class`

8. Which of the following statements is true?

    A. The `doInitBody()` is called before the body content has been evaluated for the first time.

    B. The `doInitBody()` method is always called with tags that implement the `BodyTag` interface.

    C. The `doAfterBody()` method is always called at least once.

    D. All of the above.

9. If the doStartTag() method returns the constant Tag.SKIP_BODY, which of the following methods will be invoked?

    A. doInitTag()

    B. doAfterBody()

    C. doEndTag()

    D. It depends on which tag interface is implemented.

10. Which of the following is the default return type for the doStartTag() method if the tag handler subclasses TagSupport?

    A. EVAL_BODY_BUFFERED

    B. SKIP_PAGE

    C. SKIP_BODY

    D. EVAL_BODY_INCLUDE

11. Which statement is illegal?

    A. pageContext.getOut().write(
          bodyContent.getEnclosingWriter());

    B. bodyContent.getEnclosingWriter(
          getPreviousOut());

    C. bodyContent.writeOut(
          bodyContent.getEnclosingWriter().write("data"));

    D. All of the above

12. Select all legal ways to obtain a JspWriter object if the tag handler class extends the BodyTagSupport class. (Choose all that apply.)

    A. getBodyContent().getEnclosingWriter();

    B. getPreviousOut();

    C. bodyContent.getOut();

    D. None of the above

13. Identify the tag library descriptor element used to define the class of a custom tag.

   A. class

   B. tag-class

   C. tclass

   D. taglib-class

14. Which of the following code samples best shows how to get the requested locale?

   A.
   ```
   public class MyTag extends BodyTagSupport {
     public int doStartTag() throws JspException {
       Locale locale = request.getLocale();
       return SKIP_BODY;
     }
   }
   ```

   B.
   ```
   public class MyTag extends BodyTagSupport {
     public int doStartTag() throws JspException {
       ServletRequest request=
         pageContext.getRequest();
       Locale locale = request.getLocale();
       return SKIP_BODY;
     }
   }
   ```

   C.
   ```
   public class MyTag extends BodyTagSupport {
     public int doStartTag() throws JspException {
       ServletRequest request=
         pageContext.getRequest();
       Locale locale = request.getLocale();
       return SKIP_PAGE;
     }
   }
   ```

   D.
   ```
   public class MyTag extends BodyTagSupport {
     public int doStartTag() throws JspException {
       Locale locale = getLocale();
       return SKIP_PAGE;
     }
   }
   ```

15. Which of the following is not a valid type for the tag library descriptor
element body-content?

    A. JSP

    B. servlet

    C. tagdependent

    D. empty

Answers to Review Questions

1. D.   The first option is valid because a forward slash simply means the URI is relative to the context path. The second option utilizes an absolute path, which is acceptable as well. The third option defines a page-relative path, meaning the taglib file is relative to the current JSP page or file. Finally, the last option fails because there is no address attribute, and a tag-uri path cannot be defined in that fashion.

2. E.   The uri attribute defines the path within the web.xml file to locate the TLD file. The prefix is also mandatory and denotes the short-name used to identify which library the custom tag is associated with.

3. A.   An empty tag has no body. The easiest way to write the tag is to provide only an opening tag.

4. D.   The life cycle is very close to that of the BodyTag; however, one step is missing. After a call to the doStartTag() method, the setBodyContent(*bodyContent*) method is invoked. After that completes, the doInitBody() is called.

5. A, B.   The doStartTag() is invoked early in the life of a JSP. If it returns an EVAL_BODY_BUFFERED or EVAL_BODY_INCLUDE, then the doInitBody() method will run one time. If, however, it returns a SKIP_BODY variable, the doInitBody() method is not executed. The doEndTag() is also executed once. When it is determined that the body will no longer be evaluated, the doEndTag() method is invoked.

6. C.   When the doStartTag() method is called, it will evaluate the body if EVAL_BODY_INCLUDE is returned. When the doAfterBody() method is called, a return value of EVAL_BODY_AGAIN must be returned.

7. D.   The tei-class is used to help the container load an array of attributes for the action to utilize.

8. A.   The second option is false because it assumes that the body is always evaluated. If the doStartTag() returns a SKIP_BODY value, the doInitBody() method is not invoked. The third option fails as well. It too assumes the doAfterBody() method is always called. Again, if the body is not evaluated, neither is the doAfterBody() method.

9. C.   Regardless of the tag interface, a return value of SKIP_BODY will cause the doEndTag() to be invoked next. The first two options are invoked only if a body is evaluated for certain custom tags.

10. C.   The first and last options are valid return values only if the tag handler subclasses BodyTagSupport. For a TagSupport implementation, the default value for the doStartTag() method is SKIP_BODY.

11. D.   The first option fails because the JspWriter class does not have a write method that accepts a JspWriter as a parameter. The second option fails for similar reasons. The method getEnclosingWriter() does not take any parameters. Finally, the last option fails because the write method returns a void instead of a JspWriter object, which is what writeOut(?) expects.

12. A, B.   The first option is legal because it uses the bodyContent object to get the enclosing action's output stream. The second option is merely an abbreviation of the first. It is a helper method that takes one step rather than two. The third option fails because the bodyContent object is an OutputStream and does not provide a getOut() method to access embedded streams.

13. B.   The element tag-class is used to define the fully qualifying tag class name.

14. B.   Implicit objects are not directly accessible. You must use the PageContent variable to acquire these objects. This leaves both B and C as options. C fails because SKIP_PAGE is not a valid return for the doStartTag() method.

15. B.   The term servlet is not legal. JSP signifies that the container should evaluate the action's body, whereas tagdependent suggests it should not. If empty is defined, then a body cannot be used.

Chapter

11

Web Tier Design Patterns

THE FOLLOWING SUN CERTIFIED WEB COMPONENT DEVELOPER FOR J2EE PLATFORM EXAM OBJECTIVES ARE COVERED IN THIS CHAPTER:

✓ **13.1 Given a scenario description with a list of issues, select the design pattern (Value Object, MVC, Data Access Object, or Business Delegate) that would best solve those issues.**

✓ **13.2 Match design patterns with statements describing potential benefits that accrue from the use of the pattern, for any of the following patterns:**

- Value Object
- MVC
- Data Access Object
- Business Delegate

he development of an application is often sparked by the need to resolve a particular problem. The decisions behind resolving that problem are usually influenced by cost, time, and functionality; the order of priority usually depends on the project. The difficulty, however, is that for every problem, there are multiple solutions. Depending on existing variables and long-term desires, a solution can vary from situation to situation.

Design patterns offer a proven "cookbook" answer to resolve the problem while managing various extraneous issues. There are many books on this topic alone, defining more than 30 patterns, but we will cover only four as they pertain to the J2EE model and the Sun Certified Web Component Developer for J2EE Platform exam:

- Value Object pattern

- Data Access Object pattern

- Business Delegate pattern

- Model View Controller pattern

We will define the behaviors of each pattern and identify ways to distinguish one from another. We will also cover the advantages and disadvantages of each pattern. Our goal is to ensure that you have a thorough understanding of each pattern and the knowledge necessary to answer scenario- and benefit-based questions.

Before we jump into discussing each pattern, you need to have an understanding of the major components utilized within the J2EE architecture. Figure 11.1 displays each tier and its purpose.

Until now, we have discussed only the Presentation tier and the Web tier; however, we've neglected the Server tier, which manages all Enterprise Java Beans, or EJBs. Although the exam does not test your knowledge of these components, a general discussion of the Server tier will help clarify each design pattern.

FIGURE 11.1   The J2EE tier design for the Web

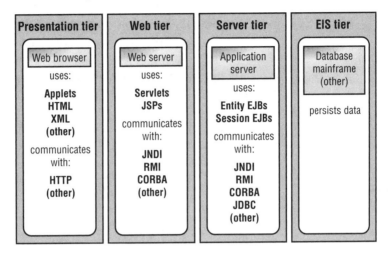

Server Tier Components

The web browser (Presentation tier) and web server (Web tier) communicate by way of servlets and JSPs, and the web server (Web tier) and application server (Server tier) communicate by way of *Enterprise Java Beans (EJBs)*. Contained within an application server, EJBs are Java classes that implement business services and rely on the server to manage their life cycle and their architectural services such as security, transaction management, and persistent data storage, to name a few. A Java *application server* is a vendor product that, at a minimum, adheres to the EJB specification to provide support for the various forms of EJBs. To understand the benefits of certain design patterns, you must first have a general understanding of EJBs.

In this section, we will explain the purpose and functionality of the two main types: entity beans and session beans. After you understand how each component behaves, we will begin our discussion on J2EE design patterns.

Entity Beans

An *entity bean* is a transactional object that represents persistent data. In layman's terms, this means it is a special Java class that manages the inserts, updates, deletes, and selects from a database for a particular record. Usually, each entity bean represents a record in a single table or multiple tables. Each entity class contains data representing the attributes from the database tables. Using an entity's getXXX() or accessor methods, a servlet (or client, or session bean) can request information from the entity. When an entity bean is invoked, it usually results in a query or change to the associated database. Because entity beans are pooled to improve efficiency, they have a many-to-many relationship with the client. This means that multiple clients can access more than one entity bean of the same kind. Figure 11.2 shows where entities fit into the J2EE architecture.

FIGURE 11.2 Entity beans

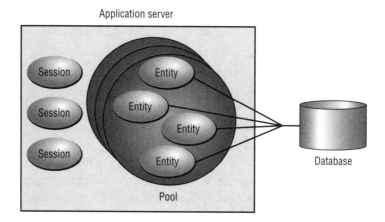

In the image, you see each entity bean communicating with the database. Usually, application servers provide a connection-pooling mechanism to reduce the number of unnecessary connections; pooling enables a system to service a larger population with few instances (or connections). The result is an increase in performance.

Performance is also influenced by the design of the entity bean itself. Because each database call is potentially remote, reducing the number of unnecessary calls will improve the application's performance. Consider the scenario of an entity providing a "get" method to return each data field associated to a record. The client would need to make multiple requests to retrieve a single record. Assuming each call is remote, this approach utilizes excessive bandwidth, resulting in inefficiency.

The proper use of an appropriate design pattern could improve the efficiency of an entity. Before we discuss pattern options, we will first address session beans.

Session Beans

Unlike entity beans, *session beans* generally do not modify the database. Instead, they provide business services to the client. These services are usually task oriented. For example, you might have a `TravelAgent` session bean that provides a method to locate available flights or book a flight.

To accomplish a particular task, a session bean usually employs the help of entity beans. Figure 11.3 shows how a session uses entities to communicate with the database.

FIGURE 11.3   Session bean

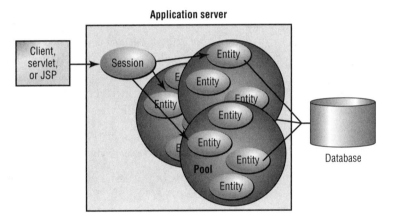

A service or task is usually made up of several database calls. Going back to our `TravelAgent` example, the act of booking a flight entails the following process:

1. Acquire available flights.

2. Reserve flight with client's information.

3. Charge client's credit card.

At least two entity beans could be used to handle the airline and client information. After the transaction is complete, the client receives the necessary confirmation data, which might include the flight number, the time of departure, the cost, and so on.

There are several approaches a developer could take to provide the client with all their flight information. The first requires the application to make multiple requests to obtain each individual field item associated with the trip; the second simply has the application request a single object containing all the necessary flight information. Because the second approach utilizes less bandwidth, resulting in one network call instead of many, the application's performance increases. This particular technique utilizes the common design pattern called the Value Object pattern.

Now that you have a basic understanding of the role that both session and entity beans play in the J2EE architecture, we can discuss the Value Object and other patterns used to improve an enterprise application's performance, maintainability, and expandability.

Value Object Pattern

The *Value Object pattern* is designed to reduce the number of method calls a client must make to obtain information. It is made up of a single class called a *value object*. This lightweight class is created by an entity or session bean, populated with bean attribute values, and passed to the client for easy access. Its structure is as follows:

- It usually provides a variety of constructors that accept attribute values designed to create the value object.

- The members of the value object are defined as `public` to eliminate the need for "get" or "set" methods.

- If there is a need for `private` or `protected` data, "get" methods can be provided; however "set" methods should still be avoided unless absolutely necessary.

In general, it is considered bad coding practice to make variables `public`. This, however, is not a huge concern with value objects. Because the value object is created via a remote entity bean and passed *by value* back to the client, the client operates on a local copy of the value object and is not modifying the data of the remote copy.

There are design strategies you should consider when creating value objects. You can make the member variables `public`, with no "get" or "set" methods. Or you can make the member variables `private` or `protected`, and include "get" methods and "set" methods if necessary. Figure 11.4 shows the general life cycle of this pattern.

FIGURE 11.4 The Value Object life cycle

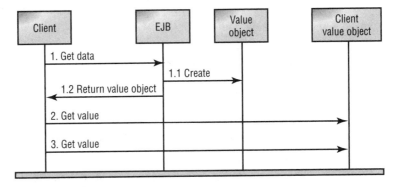

A client makes a request to an EJB, which in turn creates a value object containing all the necessary data to fulfill the client's demand. A copy is then sent to the client, which can use its copy of the value object to extract data from the instance.

Whether you allow the user to set values in a value object is influenced by the pattern strategy you choose to implement. The exam requires that you know how to identify a value object. Consequently, you should be familiar with how the pattern is used. There are four defined strategies for this pattern. The first creates a value object whose attributes can be changed. The second enables a bean to create and utilize more than one value object. The third has the entity bean extend the value object. Finally, the fourth is the most complex; it allows the entity bean to inherit from more than one value object. In the remainder of this section, we'll describe each strategy and then discuss the pros and cons of the Value Object pattern as a whole.

Updateable (or Mutable) Value Object

A value object that has "set" or mutator methods or `public` members is considered *updateable*, or *mutable*. The *Updateable (or Mutable) Value Object strategy* is utilized when you want the client to be able to change its value object instance. There are three ways to create mutable value objects; their class can supply any one or a combination of the following features:

- `public` variables

- constructors

- "set" methods

Generally, there are two common approaches. The first uses both public variables and constructors to create the value object. For example:

```
public class Ticket {
  public double cost;
  public Date purchaseDate;

  public Ticket() {}
  public Ticket(double cost, Date purchaseDate) {
    this.cost = cost;
    this.purchaseDate = purchaseDate;
  }
}
```

The second approach enables the user to change its private data through the use of constructor or "set" methods:

```
public class Ticket {
  private double cost;
  private Date purchaseDate;

  public Ticket() {}

  public Ticket(double cost, Date purchaseDate) {
    this.cost = cost;
    this.purchaseDate = purchaseDate;
  }
  public void setCost(double cost) {
    this.cost = cost;
  }
```

```
public void setDate(Date purchaseDate) {
  this.purchaseDate = purchaseDate;
}
public double getCost() {
  return this.cost;
}
public Date getDate() {
  return this.purchaseDate;
}
}
```

Either approach is acceptable and used depending on security and memory requirements.

There is one other consideration. Sometimes value objects are amazingly complex and have a large number of "set" methods. In such cases, it might be beneficial to include a setData(...) method to set all values at once.

```
...
public void setData(double cost, Date purchaseDate) {
  this.cost = cost;
  this.purchaseDate = purchaseDate;
}
...
```

Some books suggest passing in an instance of your value object to the setData(*ValueObject obj*). We choose not to recommend this approach because it merely causes the user to go through an extra step. Creating a new instance ultimately provides no additional benefits.

A call to the setData(...) method simply causes all attributes to change in one step. By providing a setData(...) method within the value object, you reduce the number of calls a client needs to make if they intend to make multiple changes to the object's data. After the value object is configured to an acceptable state, it can be passed to an entity or session bean to update some other source.

On a basic level, this is quite a simple design and strategy. It gets more complex when a single EJB utilizes more than one value object.

Multiple Value Objects

It is quite feasible that either an entity or session bean will utilize more than one value object. Imagine a Bank bean that provides information to all your accounts. The bean provides client information; checking, savings, and money market history; and more. Each category could warrant a separate value object. The *Multiple Value Objects strategy* enables the EJB to create associated value objects with "get" methods to each referenced object. Figure 11.5 shows how a single EJB object can utilize multiple objects.

FIGURE 11.5 Multiple value objects associated with a single EJB

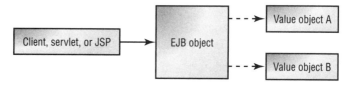

This strategy is quite common in complex application systems. In general, session beans are more likely to use multiple value objects as they attempt to accomplish multiple tasks to complete a process. In such cases, each task can reference a separate value object.

Simple entity beans are less likely to use this strategy because they map to a single record. If, however, a record contains fields that represent entire records from other tables, then the entity will likely use multiple value objects. If a Ticket value object references another value object, which represents the *type* of ticket, then creating the object becomes a bit more complex. Consider the following:

```
public class Ticket {
    private double cost;
    private Date purchaseDate;
    private Type ticketType;

    public Ticket() {}

    public Ticket(double cost, Date purchaseDate,
                  Type ticketType) {
        this.cost = cost;
```

```
        this.purchaseDate = purchaseDate;
        this.ticketType = ticketType;
    }
    public Type getType(){
        return this.ticketType;
    }
    ...
}
```

For a client to create or modify the Ticket object, they must first create or access the Type object.

When using this approach, it is critical that value objects are designed to be granular but not too granular. If a value object is too large, and only a small portion of its content is modified regularly, then you are unnecessarily transferring a larger-than-needed object between client and server, causing traffic and inefficiency.

Entity Inherits Value Object

As its name indicates, the *Entity Inherits Value Object strategy* applies only to entity beans. Its purpose is to eliminate code duplication by having an entity bean extend the value object class. This means a value object is created when an entity is instantiated. As soon as a client utilizes the entity, the container will populate the entity with the necessary data values that represent the desired record. Instead of storing the data directly in the entity class, the data is actually inherited from the value object. Let's revisit the basic Ticket example:

```
public class Ticket {
    protected double cost;
    protected Date purchaseDate;

    public Ticket() {}

    public Ticket(double cost, Date purchaseDate) {
        this.cost = cost;
        this.purchaseDate = purchaseDate;
    }
```

```
   public void setCost(double cost) {
     this.cost = cost;
   }
   public void setDate(Date purchaseDate) {
     this.purchaseDate = purchaseDate;
   }
   public double getCost() {
     return this.cost;
   }
   public Date getDate() {
     return this.purchaseDate
   }
 }
```

If an entity bean extends this class, then it does not need to provide value object logic:

```
public class TicketEJB extends Ticket
    implements EntityBean {

    //mandatory entity methods

    public Ticket getData() {
      return new Ticket(cost, purchaseDate);
    }
 }
```

The design calls for the following method to be included in the entity bean:

```
public ValueObject getData() {...}
```

To obtain the value object reference, the client calls **getData()** on the entity bean. The bean, in turn, returns an instance of its superclass.

The benefits of this strategy are as follows:

- It eliminates code duplication within the entity and the value object because data is stored in one location—the value object.

- It helps manage changes to the entity and value object because the data exists in only one class rather than two.

The less appealing aspect of this strategy is the following:

- A change to a value object can affect all its subclasses.

Significant changes to an application's hierarchy can be cumbersome. A solution to this problem is to layer the Value Object Factory strategy on top of this one.

Value Object Factory

The Entity Inherits Value Object strategy allows the entity bean to extend only one value object. Yet the Multiple Value Objects strategy shows that an entity bean can often utilize more than one value object. The *Value Object Factory strategy* solves this problem. Through the use of interfaces, the Value Object Factory strategy enables an entity to inherit from more than one value object.

The process consists of the following steps:

1. Create an interface for each value object.

2. Create a value object class to implement its respective interface.

3. Create a factory class with a constructor that takes the following arguments:

- The entity bean instance intending to create the value object

- The interface that identifies which value object to create

4. Instantiate the factory from within the entity to create the needed value objects.

The following example breaks down each step by providing pseudo-code samples of each piece required to create a value object factory.

Step 1. Create the interfaces:

```
public interface Ticket {
    public void setCost(double cost);
    public void setPurchaseDate(Date purchaseDate);
    public double getCost();
    public Date getDate();
}
public interface Airline {
    public void setFlightNo(int no);
```

```
    public int getFlightNo();
}
```

Step 2. Implement the interfaces:

```
public class TicketVO implements Ticket {
  private double cost;
  private Date purchaseDate;

  // implement all the get and set methods
}

public class AirlineVO implements Airline {
  private int flightNo;

  // implement all the get and set methods

}
```

Step 3. Create the factory:

```
public class VoFactory {
  public static final int TRIP =0;
  public static final int CUSTOMER =1;
...

  public VoFactory (EntityBean bean, int type) {
    switch(type){
      case TRIP:
        Field[] field =
          bean.getClass().getDeclaredFields();
        for (int i=0; i< field.length; i++) {
          ...
          // use reflection to associate
          // bean instance to appropriate value objects
        }
        break;
      case CUSTOMER:
        ...
```

```
                break;
              }
            }
          }
```

Step 4. Create the client:

```
public class TripEJB implements EntityBean {
  private Ticket ticket;
  private Airline airline;

  public TripEJB() {
    VoFactory fact = new VoFactory(this,
      VoFactory.TRIP);
  }

      ... // All mandatory entity bean methods
  }
```

With a handle to the entity bean, the factory class can instantiate all the required value objects for the specific entity and assign it the bean's attribute values through reflection.

Although this approach offers expandability, flexibility, and maintainability benefits, it sacrifices performance due to the overhead involved in using reflection to set the variables.

Advantages and Disadvantages

Depending on the project constraints and design goals, there are certain advantages and disadvantages you should consider when creating value objects.

Advantages

There are three main benefits associated with using value objects. They reduce network traffic and code duplication, while protecting transactional data blocks:

Reduces network traffic   The Value Object pattern acts like a data carrier and enables data to be passed between client and server by using one remote method call. This improves network performance.

Reduces code duplication   When an entity inherits from a value object, there is no need to include attribute data within the entity. Instead, the members are inherited. This results in reduced code duplication. If the Value Object Factory strategy is utilized, then the same benefit occurs; however, you face an increase in application complexity.

Enables concurrent access and transactions   The EJB container offers transaction isolation levels to help manage multiple access to the same data. An *isolation level* defines the degree of strictness an application will maintain for data access. By defining the correct isolation level, the integrity of a value object can be protected.

Disadvantages

Unfortunately, poor use of design patterns can actually harm an application. There are three potential problems that should be considered when utilizing value objects. The first relates to maintaining stale data; the second is about threading issues; and the third pertains to the effects of transferring large objects over the network:

Updates propagation and stale value objects   When a value object is mutable, the client could be holding onto an instance that no longer represents the current record state. Imagine multiple clients making requests to the same record. If each client captures the same data and one makes a change, all other clients will hold stale data. This could have negative effects, as further changes might not be warranted based on the new values.

Creates synchronization and version control issues   After an entity bean modifies a record in the database, it must then save the new values to its own set of attribute values. If more than one client simultaneously makes an update to the same record, the bean could end up with incorrect data. To solve this problem, the entity can synchronize the bean or value object to prevent more than one thread from accessing the same record at a time. The other solution is to have the value object have a time stamp and version number attribute. Thus the bean can determine whether it has the latest update.

Decreases network performance   Performance can decline if the data shipped is very large. A value object provides the application with the capability to transfer information by using one remote call instead of multiple calls. The downside to this technique is that it causes larger amounts of data to be shipped in one call. Depending on the object size, this can sometimes be more of a problem than a benefit.

Data Access Object Pattern

Behind every large and successful application is a strong information storage system. Most web applications deal with stored data in one way or another. Whether the data consists of inventory for purchasing, session activity for client history, or static information to display, an application eventually needs to write to or read information from some repository. The problem is that the repository or data-storage mechanisms can vary greatly. Many systems maintain data on mainframes, relational database management systems (RDBMS), object-oriented database management systems (OODBMS), Lightweight Directory Access Protocol (LDAP) repositories, flat files, and more.

One benefit the Java language offers is the ability to "write once, implement anywhere." Well, that phrase is only as effective as the developer writing the code. Java Database Connectivity, or JDBC, is a common way Java communicates with RDBMS databases. Making database calls is a prime example of where the "implement anywhere" can fail.

Using the JDBC API, you can easily write code that will execute on any JDBC-supported database. That is because the vendor implements the defined interfaces, and you, the developer, use the standardized method names and interfaces that compliant vendors define. The shortcoming, however, occurs when you send a custom String value that represents a database command (Structured Query Language, or SQL, statement) to the driver. Some drivers will accept more complex statements, and others accept only the basic. The end result is that you can write vendor-specific code while using Java.

Unfortunately, eliminating vendor dependence altogether usually comes with a cost. Often that sacrifice is efficiency or flexibility. Because both are important, a design pattern has emerged to provide both vendor flexibility and the ability to seize the benefits a particular vendor can offer. The pattern is called the *Data Access Object (DAO) pattern*. Adhering to the object-oriented principle of isolating object tasks, the pattern separates the logic needed to communicate with the Enterprise Information Systems (EIS) into its own class. This means a business object such as an entity or session bean, or a servlet or JSP component, utilizes a *data access object (DAO)* to handle all EIS-related transactions.

 A *business object* is a client object that requires access to the data source in order to obtain and store data.

Figure 11.6 diagrams the process.

FIGURE 11.6 The Data Access Object diagram

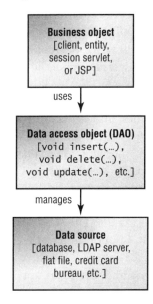

If your application utilizes a relational database, you might have separate DAO objects to handle inserts, updates, deletes, and queries for each table, value object, or entity bean. If a new data source is required, the DAO objects are modified, leaving the business objects untouched. At a minimum, this pattern requires the following three elements:

- A business object, utilizing each DAO interface and its methods to communicate with the EIS tier

- A DAO class, providing the specific vendor implementation for communication

- A data source, representing the data storage device

It is considered good coding practice to create an interface for each DAO object. Business objects should utilize the interface name to minimize the number of modifications necessary when a new DAO implementation is provided.

You can utilize three implementation strategies to maximize the benefits of this design pattern. The first is to simply hard-code the communication logic for each method accessing the data source, the second is to use a mechanism to automatically generate the data source communication code, and the third is to create a factory class that handles the construction of each DAO object. We will discuss each in detail.

Basic Database Access Object

When writing an entity bean, which normally maps to a database record, you can handle the persistence data two ways: either the bean can provide the SQL (this is known as Bean Managed Persistence, or BMP) or the EJB container can generate the SQL (this is known as Container Managed Persistence, or CMP).

With CMP beans, the container automatically services all persistent storage access, so there is no need to use the Data Access Object design pattern.

If you write the SQL yourself, you are encouraged to create a separate class that handles all this logic; this is known as the *Basic DAO strategy*. The SQL class you create is actually your DAO object. Your bean can then call the DAO object to use its methods and communicate to the database. Let's consider a DAO object representing an airline object. Its pseudo-code might look similar to the following interface and class:

```
public interface AirlineDAO {
    public void insert(String query);
    public void delete(String query);
    public void update(String query);
}
```

```
class AirlineDAOImpl implements AirlineDAO {
    ...
    private AirlineDAOImpl(String source) {
        // make connection
    }
    public static AirlineDAO getDAO(String source) {
        return new AirlineDAOImpl (source);
    }
    public void insert(String sql) {
        ...
    }
    public void delete(String sql) {
        ...
    }
    public void update(String sql) {
        ...
    }
    ...
}
```

In this example, we force the user to acquire an instance to the class by using the static getDAO(*String source*) method. By passing a qualifier, such as a driver for a database or filename for a flat file, we generate the necessary connection in the constructor and pass a new handle to the client. If the data source is changed, the DAO object will need to be modified, along with one line of code used to obtain the DAO object in the business object.

 By passing a unique instance to each caller, we are avoiding threading issues that could occur if multiple callers had access to one single instance.

Automatic Code Generated Data Access Object

While the Basic DAO strategy improves code management with respect to the business object, the *Automatic Code Generated Data Access Object strategy* eliminates the need to modify the DAO object in addition to the business object.

The Automatic Code Generated Data Access Object strategy assumes the use of a tool or technology to eliminate the need to manually write the code of each DAO object. This technique can be used to investigate the underlying system and create mappings between the information and the DAO object to then generate the appropriate code. One example is the Java reflection API, which uses introspection to dynamically determine table names and fields that can be mapped to each access object. Another example might be a tool that maps objects to relational databases. If you are familiar with Container Managed Persistence for an entity bean, the container provides such a device.

The benefit of this strategy is that it reduces the amount of code the developer needs to generate. If changes to the DAO object are updated dynamically, the client will probably experience a runtime delay the first time the instance is created. The reason for the delay is that techniques such as introspection and reflection take time up front.

Factory for Data Access Object

The third strategy can utilize either the basic or the automatic code generation approach to generating the DAO. Its main focus, however, is to create a pool of DAO objects that can easily be accessed from any data source without requiring code modifications.

In Java terms, a *factory* is a class that creates instance variables for a specific class type. The *Factory for Data Access Object strategy* is designed to have a class provide DAO objects for a specific data source. An application calls on the factory to acquire a particular data source DAO instance. When a new data source is introduced, it is added to the factory and made available to the user through a static method call. Old code is not broken, and new code has greater flexibility. For a single data source, the design requires the following code pieces:

- A DAO factory interface, which defines the "create" methods for each accessible data access method

- A DAO factory class, which implements each factory interface method to return an actual DAO object

- A DAO object, which is created by the factory and passed to the client to handle data source management

To demonstrate the parts necessary to make this pattern come alive, we are going to revisit the `AirlineDAO` data access object example. This time, however, we are going to assume that the DAO object might reside in different data sources.

Step 1. Create the factory interface:

```
public interface DAOFactory {
    public AirlineDAO createAirlineDAO();
    public HotelDAO createHotelDAO();
}
```

Step 2. Provide a data source implementation of the factory interface:

```
public class RdbDAOFactory implements DAOFactory {
    private Connection con;

    public RdbDAOFactory(String url) {
      // make connection
      conn = ...;
    }

    public AirlineDAO createAirlineDAO() {
        return new AirlineDAOImpl_RDB(conn);
    }
    public HotelDAO createHotelDAO() {
        return new HotelDAOImpl_RDB(conn);
    }
}
```

Using an interface to define each "create" method enables a new data source to provide its own implementation without modifying existing code. For example, if you wanted to create another factory implementation for an object-oriented database, you would write yet another class that implements the `DAOFactory` and defines all its methods in a custom fashion.

Step 3. Create the DAO objects:

```
public interface AirlineDAO {
    public void insert(String query);
```

```
    public void delete(String query);
    public void update(String query);
}

class AirlineDAOImpl_RDB implements AirlineDAO {
    ...
    public AirlineDAOImpl_RDB(Connection conn) {
    ...
    }
    public void insert(String sql) {
    ...
    }
    public void delete(String sql) {
    ...
    }
    public void update(String sql) {
    ...
    }
    ...
}
```

Each data access object must be implemented for this type of data source.

Step 4. Create the class that provides access to the desired factory:

```
public class EISFactory {
  public static DAOFactory getRdbDAOFactory(String
    driver) {
    return new RdbDAOFactory(driver);
  }
  public static DAOFactory getOdbDAOFactory(String
    driver) {
    return new OdbDAOFactory(driver);
  }
}
```

A factory class must be provided to enable the client to obtain a handle to the desired data source. Usually the factory class will pool instances; for our example, it will simply return a new instance to the caller.

In the end, the client will make the following calls to gain access to the data access objects for a specific relational database:

```
public class Client {
  public static void main(String[] args) {
    DAOFactory dao =
        EISFactory.getRdbDAOFactory("com.sybex.driver");
    AirlineDAO airline = dao.createAirlineDAO();
    airline.insert(...);
    ...
  }
}
```

What you gain from this approach is the ability to add a new data source type to the `EISFactory` class, which produces an independent implementation of each data access object. Previous code that relies on existing resources will not require change. If code must be moved to the new system, one change in the business object is required to call the correct `getXXXFactory(...)` method. All other code is unaffected if the database query code is acquired from an external source (such as a file). Ultimately, the client is left untouched.

The other reason for using this design is to manage pooled connections to a particular resource. While we didn't show that technique, it is a common reason for using any kind of factory.

This approach takes a little more work up front, but limits the amount of work required when a new data source is introduced into an application. What you gain is an application that is easy to manage and *extensible*—it can grow without affecting previously written code.

Advantages and Disadvantages

As with all advances or approaches, there are advantages and disadvantages. Depending on the size of the application and potential for change, this pattern can offer benefits or cause unnecessary work.

Advantages

In general, there are many benefits to the Data Access Object design pattern. They include:

Hides data access implementation code When the business object invokes a DAO method, the actual implementation is hidden and transparent to the client.

Eliminates code dependencies   Separating the DAO object from the business object makes migrating to a new data source seamless. When using factories, a change in data source affects only the Data Access Object layer, leaving the client ignorant of the modification.

Improves code readability and development productivity   This happens for two reasons. The first is a result of separating the business object logic from the data access logic. Complex data manipulation code is maintained within its own DAO object. This form of organization can vastly improve the productivity to generate and maintain a complex application. The second reason the code is more readable and faster to develop is because this pattern centralizes all data access into a separate layer. Isolating sections of code from others can vastly improve code maintenance.

Disadvantages

As with all technologies, the Data Access Object pattern can be used incorrectly or create additional overhead. Disadvantages include the following:

Provides more classes to manage   By separating access code into different classes, you have more classes to handle.

Causes excessive code maintenance   Sometimes developers get overzealous about using patterns and utilize them when they aren't needed. For example, if it is highly unlikely for the application to change data source types, the factory approach might be overkill.

Business Delegate Pattern

Now that you have an understanding of how and why to use data access objects to help communicate with the information storage system, we will cover a design pattern that helps the presentation components communicate with business services.

The *Business Delegate pattern* is used to prevent the exposure of all business services to the client. A *business service* is a specific behavior or method(s) performed by a servlet, JSP, or EJB. There are several reasons why client code should not access server-side services directly:

- It makes the client vulnerable to change. As the business evolves, there is a good chance the business service API will change as well; with the client communicating directly with services, the client code will also need to be changed.

- There is an impact on network performance. To look up and access data, the client might need to make more method calls than truly necessary.

- The client must deal with network issues associated with EJB technology. For the servlet to communicate with an EJB, it must deal with the lookup and access details of the EJB architecture.

By placing a layer between the client and server, changes made to one side do not affect the other. This layer is called the *Business Delegate layer*. The delegate hides the details of the underlying system. For example, it can handle:

- The naming and lookup services for EJBs

- Business service exceptions such as `EJBException`

- Server result cacheing

The naming and lookup services should be transparent to the client. This is a task that can be handled by the delegate. Generally it takes two steps to access a single EJB object handle. The first step is a lookup technique that provides access to the bean's Home object. The second step is to use the Home object to either find or create the desired bean. When a delegate is used, the client is shielded from this process.

Another task handled by the delegate is the interception of server-side exceptions. When an EJB exception is thrown because some error occurred with a bean, the client should not be responsible for considering EJB architectural issues to develop an alternative plan. Instead, the delegate can capture these exceptions and, in turn, generate an application-level exception to send to the client. This keeps the client focused on client-related issues and problems.

The final task a delegate can handle is caching client results. Instead of requiring the client to cache all potentially needed information, making the servlet or JSP object very large when transferred over the network, the delegate can store the information and provide it to the client upon request. This greatly improves performance and limits the number of network calls.

Figure 11.7 shows how the delegate fits into the application design.

FIGURE 11.7 The Business Delegate pattern

This figure shows the client communicating to the delegate, which then communicates with the business services. Some common business services are enterprise beans or Java Messaging Service (JMS) components. Two strategies can be applied to this pattern. The first is the Delegate Proxy and the second is the Delegate Adapter. Both are discussed next.

Delegate Proxy

The *Delegate Proxy strategy* places a layer between the client and server, exposing all business methods to the client. The proxy handles the underlying tasks needed to invoke each business method without the client needing to worry about lookup, location, or exception information. From the client's perspective, it simply calls the business methods and they "magically" work.

Delegate Adapter

The *Delegate Adapter strategy* is used when two systems do not use the same integration language. Let's say the client is written in XML and the server components are EJBs; an adapter would be required to join the two distinct systems. The XML client would invoke the adapter, which would parse the XML request to then create a delegate and invoke its methods. The delegate would perform its normal communication with the business service (or bean) and ultimately return results back to the adapter. The adapter could then prepare the appropriate XML and return it to the client.

Advantages and Disadvantages

Adding yet another layer to an application can provide benefits if used under the right circumstances. It can also add unnecessary complexity if the design does not require a translation layer.

Advantages

On the whole, this pattern requires more work up front, but provides several long-term benefits. They include:

Improves code manageability   Code is more manageable because client components are not directly linked to server-side components.

Provides easier exception handling   Because the delegate can translate business service exceptions, the client needs to deal only with application-level issues. The delegate can capture network-related exceptions and send more client-oriented exceptions. This simplifies client code management, because the client does not need to decipher details that are not related to the Presentation tier.

Offers a simpler business service API   While a server application might have many session beans available, the delegate provides a clean list of available methods to the client without worrying about which session to invoke to access a particular behavior. All session management and transactions are handled either at the delegate level or on the Server tier—away from the client.

Improves performance   Because the delegate can cache services, the Presentation tier does not need to make as many network calls to access commonly requested data.

Disadvantages

There are a few minor disadvantages to this pattern. They include:

Adds complexity   By adding an extra layer, you increase the intricacy of the application.

Decreases flexibility   The client is restricted to the options provided by the delegate.

Model View Controller Pattern

Until now, we have discussed the Value Object and Database Access Object patterns, which separate server-side tasks into individual components. We also covered the Business Delegate, which is used to separate the clients from the business services. The *Model View Controller (MVC) pattern* affects the Presentation layer to improve the application's extensibility, flexibility, and managcability. MVC divides the display logic from the code that causes change.

A project's success is often measured by its immediate return value, and its future ability to expand, change, be maintained, and adapt. Most applications should be written with extensibility in mind; this means that changes or additions do not break existing components. The Model View Controller design pattern is geared toward creating an application that can increase client-side functionality without warranting changes to the server-side code.

The pattern was originally developed by using the language SmallTalk and later gained popularity in the Java market through its extensive use within the Swing component library. The pattern takes a single graphical object and breaks down its tasks into three pieces:

- The *controller*, which triggers a change to the component

- The *model*, which manages the data by providing methods to alter or access the information

- The *view*, which provides a visual display of the current data

A scrollbar component is a perfect example of MVC in action. It has a few controllers,—up and down buttons, and the slider. When any of these elements is used, the controller invokes the model. The data associated with a scrollbar is usually an `int` value that represents the location of the slider. The up-arrow controller tells the model to increase the `int` value, and the down-arrow controller calls the model's method to decrease the value. It is then the model's responsibility to update the data and notify listeners or views interested in the recently changed data. Figure 11.8 provides a visual representation of each MVC component within a scrollbar.

FIGURE 11.8   MVC within a scrollbar

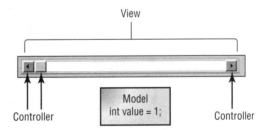

The class that handles the visual presentation is notified of a change and is able to repaint the image to correctly represent the current data. In this case, the slider would be repositioned to represent the increase or decrease in value.

The benefits you gain from creating three classes, rather than two or one, are as follows:

- Changes to the controller do not affect any view classes.

- Changes to the view do not affect any controller classes.

- You can add additional view or controller classes without affecting existing code.

By removing the data from the graphical components and by separating these components into two categories, one that controls and one that displays, you create an application environment that is easily extensible.

The order of operations is as follows:

1. When the controller is triggered, it communicates a change to the model.

2. The model makes a change to the data and pushes the new data to the appropriate views.

3. The view receives the new data and displays the new image or form.

In a J2EE environment, JSPs or servlets are often used to communicate server content graphically to the client. There are two defined model types used to determine which class is the controller:

Model 1 The Model 1 design places client control in the hands of JSPs. Basically, the controller is a JSP, usually managed by using custom tags, and the view is also a JSP.

Model 2 The Model 2 design is currently the favored approach because it assigns roles based on the purpose of the component. Because servlets are better suited for handling Java coding logic, they fit nicely into the role of controller. JSPs, on the other hand, are designed to focus on presentation. Consequently, they represent the view.

In both strategies, the model is not specified, because it can be any number of components, such as a component on the Web tier side, or EJBs. Given the design patterns we have presented in this chapter, the business delegate object is often an ideal candidate for the model role.

Imagine a basic web application that requires the client to log in prior to accessing their account information. An MVC implementation of that design might look similar to the general layout of Figure 11.9.

FIGURE 11.9 J2EE MVC

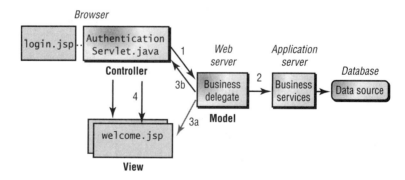

In Figure 11.9, the login.jsp page is a view that communicates with an AuthenticationServlet to determine whether the user is valid. The servlet corresponds with the model (step 1), which might invoke a session or entity bean to check the information against the database (step 2). If the user is valid, two things can happen: either the model pushes the response to the view (step 3a), ending one cycle, or the model returns the response to the original controller (step 3b). Most commonly, the model returns the response to the controller, and the controller then forwards it to the view (step 4). The welcome.jsp view is then displayed with the user's name and necessary information. If authentication failed, a loginAgain.jsp view would appear. The process cycles until the user successfully logs in or ends the session.

You might want the underlying controller to be a servlet so that you can:

- Control authentication

- Handle application-specific logging

- Access a database

- Process requests

- Utilize the Java debugger

When a process requires a lot of Java code, embedding it within a JSP object can make the resulting application difficult to read, making it hard to develop, debug, and maintain. Often your choice is to either use a servlet or, if you feel the need to utilize only JSPs (Model 1), create custom tags. Either approach is functionally acceptable.

Separating controller and view often requires JSPs to communicate with servlets and servlets to communicate with JSPs. Next, we will cover how these two entities exchange information.

JSP to Servlet

For a JSP component to communicate with a servlet is a simple task. It requires the use of a bean, which stores the information that is transferred from one to the other. Consider the following components:

- A JSP page: login.jsp

- A bean: UserInfoBean.java

- A servlet: AuthenticationServlet.java

Let's first look at how the JSP page (`login.jsp`) sets up the data to transfer to the servlet:

```
<jsp:useBean id="userInfo" scope="request"
     class="com.syb.jsp.beans.userinfo.UserInfoBean">
     <jsp:setProperty name="userInfo" property="*" />
</jsp:useBean>

<jsp:forward page="/AuthenticationServlet" />
```

When this section of code is read by the interpreter, a bean instance called `userInfo` is either retrieved or created. As you might remember from Chapter 9, "Java Server Pages (JSPs)," the `jsp:setProperty` action uses reflection to link and change all bean attributes to match the values generated from the request. After the JSP creates the bean with all the necessary information, it forwards it to the servlet.

It is now up to the `AuthenticationServlet` to use this bean and extract its information obtained from the request. Consider the following pseudo-code:

```
public class AuthenticationServlet extends HttpServlet {
...
    public void doGet(HttpServletRequest request,
                        HttpServletResponse response)
     throws ServletException, IOException {

     UserInfoBean userInfo =
       (UserInfoBean)request.getAttribute("userInfo");

     // Access the bean's get methods to extract its data
     String name = userInfo.getLoginName();
     String pwd = userInfo.getPassword();

     // Use the model handle (made available from another
     // method) to access and authenticate the bean.

       boolean status = model.validateUser(loginName, pwd);

     if (status == true) {
      // forward to the next JSP page in the application
     } else {
```

```
        // forward to a "login failed, try again" JSP.
      }
    }
  }
```

After the information from the bean is extracted, the servlet acts like a controller and requests that the model perform a validation. The model then determines whether the user is valid. Depending on the design, the model can either return a boolean to the AuthenticationServlet to determine where to forward the request/response, or the model itself can handle this task. In our example, the model passes forwarding responsibility back to the servlet. Now let's look at how the servlet communicates with JSPs.

Servlet to JSP

In order for a controller to push data forward to a view, the servlet must communicate with a JSP. As covered in Chapter 2, "The Servlet Model," the RequestDispatcher can be used to forward the response generation to another servlet or JSP. To demonstrate this concept, we will build on the AuthenticationServlet. In this interpretation, we explicitly show you how the servlet accesses the model or delegate called Delegate.java.

```java
import java.io.*;
import javax.servlet.*;
import javax.servlet.http.*;

public class AuthenticateServlet extends HttpServlet {

    public void init() throws ServletException{
        Delegate model = new Delegate();
        ServletContext context=
          getServletConfig().getServletContext();
        context.setAttribute("delegate", model);
    }

    public void doGet(HttpServletRequest req,
                      HttpServletResponse res)
      throws ServletException, IOException {

        UserInfoBean userInfo =
          (UserInfoBean)req.getAttribute("userInfo");
```

```
String name = userInfo.getLoginName();
String pwd = userInfo.getPassword();

ServletContext context=
  getServletConfig().getServletContext();
Delegate model=
 (Delegate)context.getAttribute("delegate");
boolean status = model.validateUser(name, pwd);

if(status==true) {
  RequestDispatcher disp=
   req.getRequestDispatcher("/app/Welcome.jsp");
  disp.forward(req, res);
} else {
  RequestDispatcher disp=
   req.getRequestDispatcher("/app/loginAgain.jsp");
  disp.forward(req, res);
}
    }
  }
```

The `AuthenticateServlet.java` (controller) file creates a `Delegate` object when the class is first initialized by the web container. When a login request is made, the controller accesses the delegate and asks it to validate the user. Depending on the response, the request is forwarded to the appropriate JSP (or view).

Advantages and Disadvantages

MVC is one of the most popular design patterns and is being utilized whenever possible. From a managerial perspective, the benefits are great and the problems minor, if any.

Advantages

Like the Business Delegate pattern, MVC requires more work up front, but provides several long-term benefits. They include:

Provides job separation   Web designers can focus on creating graphic presentations through JSPs, while code developers can generate code to perform tasks using servlets.

Improves code manageability   Because each task is contained within its own object, it is easy to locate and determine where a problem exists. This decreases the time needed to fix errors or expand the code.

Disadvantages

Any pattern that is not used correctly can actually cause the problems you are attempting to correct. Here is one disadvantage to this pattern:

Adds complexity   Once again, the addition of objects means there are more classes to handle. However, if the application is carefully designed, this problem is negligible.

The pattern does require more work and careful planning, but that is usually the sign of a good application.

 Real World Scenario

Justifying the Need for a Robust System

Skeptical investors for a new startup company, ePayroll Inc., recently requested that the company provide an application design that models the web application they wish to develop. The application is intended to enable businesses to enter their payroll over the Internet. The developers justified the need to develop the following components:

EJBs   Given the need for strict security, data integrity, and use of external resources, enterprise beans offer a way to manage these issues through the application server without requiring developers to write code to handle these issues.

Value objects   To reduce the number of network calls, value objects should be used to contain groups of related data.

Data access objects   As the business expands and technology improves, there is a strong chance that there will be a need to upgrade the back-end data storage system. These objects will ensure a smooth transition.

A delegate   Because their groups of developers are specialized in specific areas, the Delegate model enables one person to manage the link between web and server components.

> **Views** Web application designers can focus on developing an aesthetically pleasing interface, without having to be trained in Java programming.
>
> **Controllers** Their strong team of Java programmers can help develop front-end components.

Summary

In this chapter, we covered the four main design patterns:

The Value Object pattern is a data object used to reduce code duplication and traffic. By creating an object containing all the necessary data, a single call for the object can be made rather than multiple calls for the same data.

Benefits:

- Reduces network traffic

- Reduces code duplication

- Enables concurrent access and transactions

Drawbacks:

- Update propagation and stale value objects

- Creates synchronization and version control issues

- Decreases network performance

The Data Access Object pattern is used to decouple a business object's code and that used to access a storage system. By separating the two, it is easier to maintain the code if storage system changes are required.

Benefits:

- Hides data access implementation code

- Eliminates code dependencies

- Improves code readability and development productivity

Drawbacks:

- More classes to manage
- Causes excessive code maintenance

The Business Delegate pattern places a layer between the Web and Server tiers to limit the number of dependencies between the two.

Benefits:

- Improves code manageability
- Provides easier exception handling
- Offers a more simple business service API
- Improves performance

Drawbacks:

- Adds complexity
- Decreases flexibility

The MVC pattern separates web components used to control the application versus those components designed to display information. The application is more flexible and expandable as a result.

Benefits:

- Provides job separation
- Improves code manageability

Drawbacks:

- Adds complexity

Exam Essentials

Given a list of architectural issues, be able to select the appropriate design pattern to solve the problems.   The Value Object and Data Access Object design patterns help modularize server-side code to improve manageability and expandability, whereas the Model View Controller pattern is used to produce the same result for client-side code. Architecturally, the Business Delegate places a layer between the Web and Server tiers to eliminate any dependencies.

Be able to identify the benefits associated with any one of the following design patterns: Value Object, MVC, Data Access Object, or Business Delegate. Knowing the benefits associated with each pattern will help you determine which pattern is appropriate for a given scenario.

Key Terms

Before you take the exam, be certain you are familiar with the following terms:

application server	extensible
Automatic Code Generated Data Access Object strategy	factory
Business Delegate layer	Factory for Data Access Object strategy
Business Delegate pattern	isolation level
business object	Model View Controller (MVC) pattern
business service	Multiple Value Objects strategy
data access object (DAO)	mutable
Data Access Object (DAO) pattern	session beans
Delegate Adapter strategy	updateable
Delegate Proxy strategy	Updateable (or Mutable) Value Object strategy
design patterns	Value Object Factory strategy
Enterprise Java Beans	Value Object pattern
entity bean	value object
Entity Inherits Value Object strategy	

Review Questions

1. Which of the following design patterns is used to limit the amount of network traffic necessary to transfer data?

    A. Business Delegate

    B. Data Access Object

    C. Value Object

    D. Model View Controller

2. If your company is likely to change their EIS tier within the next year, what pattern would you recommend utilizing to minimize the amount of change the application will need to endure?

    A. Business Delegate

    B. Data Access Object

    C. Value Object

    D. Model View Controller

3. Which pattern(s) are used to isolate tasks? (Choose all that apply.)

    A. Business Delegate

    B. Data Access Object

    C. Value Object

    D. Model View Controller

4. Which pattern helps eliminate code duplication?

    A. Business Delegate

    B. Data Access Object

    C. Value Object

    D. Model View Controller

5. Which pattern is known for encouraging job separation for web designers and Java programmers?

   A. Business Delegate

   B. Data Access Object

   C. Value Object

   D. Model View Controller

6. If your current application exposes business services to the client, what pattern could you recommend to alleviate this problem?

   A. Business Delegate

   B. Data Access Object

   C. Value Object

   D. Model View Controller

7. Which strategy enables an application to switch between EIS systems with the fewest modifications to existing code?

   A. Basic Data Access Object

   B. Automatic Code Generated Data Access Object

   C. Factory for Data Access Object

   D. None of the above

8. Some web developers have been expressing concern over having to handle `EJBExceptions`. Because they lack an understanding of EJB architecture, they are unable to determine the appropriate action. What pattern can be used to help resolve this problem?

   A. Business Delegate

   B. Data Access Object

   C. Value Object

   D. Model View Controller

9. Which pattern(s) help improve code manageability? (Choose all that apply.)

   A. Business Delegate

   B. Data Access Object

   C. Value Object

   D. Model View Controller

10. Which pattern reduces the size of objects by providing `public` data members?

   A. Business Delegate

   B. Data Access Object

   C. Value Object

   D. Model View Controller

11. Which pattern can use a tool to help generate the embedded code?

   A. Business Delegate

   B. Data Access Object

   C. Value Object

   D. Model View Controller

12. A company is told that they have access to five web designers and two Java programmers. What design pattern should they consider when developing their graphics-intensive web application?

   A. Business Delegate

   B. Data Access Object

   C. Value Object

   D. Model View Controller

13. You are told that your company's current two systems do not use the same integration language but they need to communicate. Which pattern could solve this problem?

    A. Business Delegate

    B. Data Access Object

    C. Value Object

    D. Model View Controller

14. Which pattern can be used to hide SQL database commands?

    A. Business Delegate

    B. Data Access Object

    C. Value Object

    D. Model View Controller

15. Which of the following patterns uses accessor and mutator methods to reduce the number of network calls needed to alter or access data?

    A. Business Delegate

    B. Data Access Object

    C. Value Object

    D. Model View Controller

Answers to Review Questions

1. C.   A value object contains data that can be transferred in one call.

2. B.   Using data access objects enables J2EE applications to swap out the EIS tier without requiring much change to code. If done correctly, the only change is made to the data access objects themselves.

3. A, B, D.   All three patterns isolate tasks. The Business Delegate isolates the Web tier from the Server tier; Data Access Object isolates database communication from business objects; MVC isolates the controller code from presentation code.

4. C.   When using the Entity Inherits Value Object strategy, there is no need to define the value data in the value object and entity bean.

5. D.   MVC separates the controller code, which is developed by using servlets, from the presentation code, which is developed by using JSPs. The skill set used to create the two is different. A web designer can create JSPs with ease, whereas programmers are better suited to focus on functionality, such as that handled by a servlet.

6. A.   The Business Delegate places a layer between the client and the business services. This prevents the client from dealing with access and lookup issues to utilize the server.

7. C.   The factory strategy simply requires access classes to be added to the current list of DAO objects. Existing code is left untouched.

8. A.   Including a Business Delegate enables exceptions to be intercepted before reaching web components. The delegate can then send a user-friendly application an exception to help web developers better understand the problem.

9. A, B, C, D.   All four patterns separate tasks into individual classes. This is the key to code manageability. Problems can be located easily, and changes have minimal, if any, effect on other classes.

10. C.   One strategy of the Value Object class is to provide `public` members, thus removing the need to have get or set methods.

11. B.   Third-party or Java's reflection tools can be used to introspect a database or data source to generate code for data access objects.

12. D. Although this situation isn't ideal, the web designers can be thoroughly utilized to generate appealing view components. The developers, on the other hand, can deal with controller and back-end components.

13. A. The Adapter Delegate strategy can be used to translate between two systems. One system can write to the delegate, which can interpret the request and then communicate it to the appropriate source.

14. B. Data access objects hide all SQL implementation. Instead of including database-specific code within a business object, it is placed within a DAO.

15. C. The Value Object can contain "get" and "set" methods to access or change its member variables. These methods are used locally rather than over the network.

Glossary

A

absolute path   The full path, starting with the protocol and host, necessary to locate the tag library file.

access list   Sometimes it's a simple file containing each user's login name, password, and role. Other times it's stored as a database with encrypted employee information.

actions   Java tags that affect the runtime behavior of the JSP.

application   See "`application` object."

application object   An implicit object that represents the `ServletContext` object. It provides a set of methods to communicate with the container.

application scope   Indicates that objects are available for the life of the application.

application server   A vendor product that, at a minimum, adheres to the EJB specification to provide support for the various forms of EJBs.

attackers   See "hackers."

attribute   A name/value pair associated with a request.

authentication   The process whereby the client supplies credentials to prove their identity. Most often proof is provided via a password. Other examples include the swipe of a card, retinal scans, fingerprints, or digital certificates located on the user's system.

authorization   A process whereby a client makes a claim to be a particular user.

Automatic Code Generated Data Access Object strategy   A strategy in which a tool or resource generates the code needed for a DAO object to communicate with a data source.

B

base class   A support class that offers basic functionality for new tag handlers.

body content The content between the opening tag and closing tag, including subtags.

Business Delegate layer A layer of code placed between the client and server to protect the client from experiencing change when alterations are made to the server code.

Business Delegate pattern A pattern that prevents the exposure of all business services to the client.

business object A client object that requires access to the data source in order to obtain and store data.

business service A specific behavior or method(s) performed by a servlet, JSP, or EJB.

C

certificate authority (CA) A company that sells certificates to individuals to enable them to sign their public key.

CHECKED An attribute used for radio or check-box controls. It's a boolean value that identifies whether the control should be selected.

class variables Variables that are shared among all instances of a servlet.

client certificate An encrypted object, known as a signature, personalized with data for a particular person. It provides a secure way to authenticate users communicating over a network. Instead of simply logging into a system and providing a password, which can be decrypted, the user provides a certificate that can be read only by using a special key.

clustering See "distributable."

conditional GET An entity that can be returned only under specified circumstances. The request message header contains at least one of the following fields: `If-Modified-Since`, `If-Unmodified-Since`, `If-Match`, `If-None-Match`, or `If-Range`.

config object An implicit object that is of the `ServletConfig` data type. It enables the container to pass information to the JSP page before it is initialized.

container   A software application that exists within an application server to manage the services associated with a component—including security, transactions, life-cycle management, pooling, and so on.

content type   Defines the type of content being delivered with the response object.

context   The root directory containing all files associated with one application.

context attributes   Global data associated with the `ServletContext` object that is accessible by the entire application.

context object   An object that acts as a reference to the web application. When a servlet is initialized, the container provides it a handle to the context object for the servlet to communicate with the container. All servlets within the application use the single context object to access information about the container and server in which they reside.

context path   The first section of the path. It defines the *context* for which the servlet resides. Within a single Java Virtual Machine, several web applications might be running. For each web application, there is one context.

context-relative path   A path that starts with a forward slash (/) is relative to the application's context path.

controls   GUI components that enable the user to interact with the interface.

cookie   An object containing small amounts of information sent by a servlet to a web browser, then saved by the browser, and later sent back to the server.

custom actions   See "custom tags."

custom tags   Similar to XML, a custom tag takes the place of scriptlets, and sometimes beans, to provide the web designer the functionality to accomplish a particular task.

D

data access object (DAO)   An object containing code used to access and manipulate a data resource.

Data Access Object (DAO) pattern   A design pattern separating the logic to access a resource into its own separate class. It provides both vendor flexibility and the ability to seize the benefits that a particular vendor can offer.

declaration   Declares Java variables or methods that future Java code can access within the JSP page.

declarative security   Uses the deployment descriptor to specify which resource a role can access.

default mapping   A process in which the container provides server content appropriate for the resource request, such as a default servlet. The string begins with a forward slash (/), and the servlet path is the requested URI minus the context path. The path info is null.

Delegate Adapter strategy   A strategy used when two systems do not use the same integration language. The adapter knows both languages and acts as a translator.

Delegate Proxy strategy   A strategy that places a layer between the client and server, exposing all business methods to the client.

DELETE method   A method enabling you to remove a file from a particular URL.

design pattern   A proven approach to resolving specific programming issues.

digest   A one-directional, encrypted value that represents data.

digital certificate   Attaches identity to a public key. It acts like a driver's license or passport in that it proves you are who you claim to be. A certificate contains your public key and some additional information signed by a third party's private key.

digital signature   An object that associates an individual with a particular piece of data. It adds one more level of security to a digest. Not only does it provide authentication, but it also links the user to the data. This means that the request cannot be intercepted, re-signed, and sent by an imposter without the server realizing the error.

directive   Enables a JSP page to control the overall structure for the translation phase of the servlet. Directives provide global information independent of a specific request.

distributable   Describes a system that utilizes multiple back-end servers to distribute processing responsibilities. This technique promotes efficiency and dependability. By using multiple servers to handle requests, the application can manage a large number of simultaneous requests on different systems. When one machines crashes, requests can be redirected to another server to keep the application alive.

document type definition (DTD)   A file used to specify the structure of an XML document and to validate the document.

dynamic error page   An error page that is generated when a problem occurs and contains information specific to the current problem. Dynamic pages enable the message, the page, or the data to change depending on the set error code. Instead of using HTML pages, a servlet could be written to handle errors.

E

Enterprise Information Systems (EIS)   A generic name for all storage mechanisms.

Enterprise Java Beans (EJB)   Java classes that implement business services and rely on the server to manage their life cycle and architectural services such as security, transaction management, and persistent data storage, to name a few.

entity bean   A transactional object that represents persistent data.

Entity Inherits Value Object strategy   A strategy that eliminates code duplication by having an entity bean extend the class, acting as the value object class.

event   An object that holds data about an activity that took place.

exact mapping   When searching for the URL associated with the requested file or directory, all strings match exactly.

exception object   An implicit object that is an instance of the java.lang .Throwable class. It represents the uncaught Throwable object that results in the error page being invoked.

exceptions   Objects used to describe the reasons behind a particular problem. When caught, an exception can be used to resolve, log, and communicate the problem.

expression   A valid statement of logic used within a JSP page. It indicates a variable or method invocation whose resulting value is written to the response output stream.

extensible   Describes a class that can grow without affecting previously written code.

extension mapping   When searching for the URL associated with the requested file, an asterisk is used to define the string name, leaving only the extension as the mapping field.

F

factory   A class that creates instance variables for a specific class type.

Factory for Data Access Object strategy   A strategy designed to have a class provide DAO objects for a specific data source. An application calls on the factory to acquire a particular data source DAO instance.

filter   An object that can transform a request or modify a response.

firewall   A security system that blocks network traffic by limiting access to most ports and unauthorized users. The firewall requires the client to authenticate in order to enter the system. Unfortunately, firewalls are not foolproof: there are ways to bypass security by impersonating another.

first-person penalty   The delay experienced by the first person accessing a JSP page. The delay is caused by the container needing to translate the JSP page to a servlet class.

form   A section of an HTML page that contains various controls.

forward action   An action that transfers control of the current request handler to a specified resource. The target source is then responsible for generating the response.

G

GET method   A request designed to retrieve static resources such as an HTML document or an image from a specific location on the server.

getProperty action   An action used to get the parameter values of the bean in use within a JSP.

H

hackers   Individuals who invade systems and either corrupt or capture vital data.

HEAD method   A method resulting in a request that does not return the entity body. It returns the response line and headers only.

hidden comment   Identifies text that should be ignored by the JSP container.

hidden HTML values   Values that are not visible to the client and that enable you to store client data between servlets to use at a later date.

HttpSession   An object created by the servlet to maintain data for the entire duration of a transaction. Assuming the client's browser supports session management, an HttpSession object is created when the client first accesses a web application. Data can then be written to or retrieved from this object.

Hypertext Markup Language (HTML)   The intermediary language between the browser/client and all other technologies, such as Java or networking protocols.

Hypertext Transfer Protocol (HTTP)   The network layer built on top of Transmission Control Protocol (TCP). HTTP is a stateless protocol—meaning its data is not retained from one request to the next. After a request is made, the connection is closed. Because clients are not holding open connections to a server, the server can have more clients connect over a long period of time.

I

idempotent   Describes a request that can be safely repeated without necessarily consulting the user.

immutable   Describes a variable that is final and cannot change.

implicit objects   A standard set of objects implicitly available to a JSP. These objects are available to a servlet through methods not available to the JSP.

include action   An action used to temporarily transfer control and allow another resource access to the current request and response objects.

indexed property   An object that is either a collection or an array.

instance variables   Variables defined within the class body and separately assigned to each instantiated object.

isolation level   Defines the degree of strictness an application will maintain for data access.

J

Java archive (JAR) file   A compressed file containing any combination of Java classes, such as servlet, JSP, bean and utility classes, used within the application. JAR files should be stored in the /WEB-INF/lib directory.

Java Server Pages (JSPs)   Java objects that communicate between the client and server, and can also execute business logic. JSPs are optimized for the layout.

JavaBean   A class that contains private data with accessor and mutator methods.

JSP model   The model that utilizes JSP for the graphic presentation of a web application, leaving servlets to handle or communicate the needs for business logic.

K

keys   Two identifiers generated by a client prior to any login attempts. The first is a private key that holds the individual's authentication code and is stored in a secure location, on a SmartCard or in a file. It should be known and accessed only by its owner. The second is a public key given to all receivers to validate the authenticity of the user attempting to log in.

L

listener   Interfaces that once implemented get notified when specific events are triggered.

local variables   Variables defined within the body of a method.

M

malicious code   Synonymous with "virus."

MAXLENGTH   An attribute of the `INPUT` tag used for the types `text` and `password` to specify the maximum number of characters the user is allowed to enter.

/META-INF   The *meta information* directory, which contains, at a minimum, one file named `MANIFEST.MF` (the manifest file).

Model View Controller (MVC) pattern   A pattern that divides the display logic from the code that causes change.

Multiple Value Objects strategy   A strategy that enables the EJB to create associated value objects with "get" methods to each referenced object.

Multipurpose Internet Mail Extension (MIME)   An extension of the e-mail protocol used to allow the exchange of different kinds of data files over the Internet.

multithreaded   Indicates that a single instance can be accessed by more than one thread.

mutable   Describes a value object that has "set" or mutator methods or `public` members.

N

NAME   An attribute of the `INPUT` tag that represents the human-language name assigned to the control. It is also used to identify the element in the servlet.

nested tags   Tags within another tag.

nonce   A random value that is unique. An example of a nonce could be the client's IP address followed by a time stamp and some random data.

non-error   A flag that indicates a noncritical problem.

O

OPTIONS method   Used to return all supported HTTP methods on the server. It returns an `Allow` header and acceptable HTTP methods as values.

out object   The implicit object used to write response information to the client. It is of the class `javax.servlet.jsp.JspWriter`, which is a buffered version of the `java.io.PrintWriter` class.

outer tag   A custom tag that is not nested within another tag.

P

packet sniffer   Software that enables you to view all the traffic on your network.

page attributes   Information about the current request stored within a pageContext object.

page directive   Defines attributes that apply to an entire JSP page.

page object   An implicit object that is similar to the this keyword in Java. It represents an instance of the servlet generated by the JSP page for the current request.

page scope   Indicates that an object is available only within the current page.

pageContext object   An implicit object that provides the JSP with information about the current request.

page-relative path   A path that does not start with a slash and is relative to the current JSP page or file.

param action   An action used to provide a name/value pair to a servlet. It is used in conjunction with the jsp:include, jsp:forward, and jsp:param actions.

partial GET   A type of GET method requesting that only part of the entity be transferred.

path info   The extra path information between the servlet path and the query string.

path mapping   A process used to locate a specified path. When the container attempts to locate the most appropriate file associated with the request, the stored string begins with a forward slash (/) and ends with a forward slash and asterisk (/*). The longest match determines the servlet requested.

permanently unavailable   Describes a servlet throwing an exception that cannot recover from the error until some action is taken. Usually, the servlet is corrupt in some way or not configured properly.

plugin action   An action defined as jsp:plugin and displaying or playing an applet or bean in the browser. The plug-in is either built into the browser or downloaded from a specific URL.

POST method   A request designed for posting information to the server.

prefix   A predefined name that links the action to a tag library.

prefix mapping   The process used to locate the tag library by using the tag name and the associated library.

Presentation layer   The layer of code developed for the front-end user.

principal   The identifier used to map the person logging into the system. A principal is usually recognized by their user ID.

private key   A key that holds the individual's authentication code and is stored in a secure location, on a SmartCard or in a file.

programmatic security   A type of security using code to determine whether to grant access to a particular group or user.

public key   An encryption scheme, either generated by software or issued by a third party, used to encode or decode information. It is given to all receivers to validate the authenticity of the user attempting to log in.

PUT method   A method type that requests to store static information. A PUT method asks the server to store the content body to the URI identified in the request line.

Q

query string   A URL-encoded string that contains data stored in name/value pairs.

R

redirect URL   A converted URL in which all non-ASCII values must be converted to their hexadecimal values; this includes ampersands and equal signs.

request   An object containing client intent and data.

request attributes   Objects associated with the request.

request dispatching   The forwarding of a request from one servlet to another servlet for processing.

request object   An implicit object that represents the HttpServletRequest object. The request object initiates the _jspService(...) method upon a client's call. When created, the request object generates header information, such as cookies, the intent or type of request, such as a GET or POST, and possible parameters passed by the client.

request scope   Indicates that an object is accessible from all pages processing the same request.

RequestDispatcher   A wrapper class that can be used to forward a request to an error page.

response   An object containing the information requested by the client.

response object   An instance of the implementation-specific subclass of the javax.servlet.ServletResponse interface, often known as HttpServletResponse. Unlike servlets, it enables HTTP status codes and headers in the JSP to be changed after output has been sent to the client.

role-based   Describes a system in which users are assigned to roles, such as Manager, Employee, or Guest. Each role is assigned certain privileges, and access is granted to roles rather than users.

S

scope   The life span of a data element.

scriptlet   A code fragment used within a JSP page.

sendError(...)   A method that gives the developer an opportunity to set an error status code for the response header and enables the servlet to replace the response body with a server-specific page explaining the error.

servlet   A platform-independent web component. Servlets are loaded dynamically into a web server, from where they can process business logic and generate a layout for the client on an as-needed basis.

servlet life cycle   The various stages a servlet encounters during different points of an application's life. The cycle consists of a servlet being loaded and instantiated. It then waits for requests for service. When the server deems it appropriate, the servlet can be taken out of service.

Servlet model   A model that provides small reusable server programs the ability to process a variety of requests from a client and then return a response efficiently.

servlet path   The mapped directory name associated with the actual servlet. Usually this consists of either the mapped servlet name or a mapped path to the servlet, but nothing more.

ServletConfig   The object created after a servlet is instantiated and its default constructor is read. It is created to pass initialization information to the servlet.

ServletException   A `javax.servlet.ServletException` is thrown by a servlet to indicate a general servlet problem has occurred.

session   An object that provides servlets access to the multiple actions of each user utilizing the site.

session attributes   Temporary client information stored within an `HttpSession` object.

session beans   Provide business services to the client.

session object   An implicit object created when a client makes its first request to an application. It is unique to a client and can exist longer than a single request or even longer than the life of a client. It is an object used to track client-specific data for the duration of the conversation or a specified period of time.

session scope   Indicates that objects are available for the life of the session. Until the session is closed manually or automatically due to a method call or a timeout, components can exist and share data.

setProperty action   An action used to set the parameter values of the bean in use.

SingleThreadModel   An interface used as a flag to notify the container how to handle the servlet life cycle. As per the API specifications, a servlet that implements the SingleThreadModel is "guaranteed" to allow only one thread access to the service() method at a time.

SIZE   An attribute of the INPUT tag used to identify the initial width of the control.

SRC   An attribute of the INPUT tag used to specify the location of an image control type.

stack trace   The computer path taken to arrive at the current problem.

static error page   Usually an HTML-formatted page that contains a response to the occurring problem. Its information explains the problem, but does not change it.

static include   The process of including a file in your current JSP page. The text of the included file is added to the JSP page.

suffix   The name of the element used to invoke the action.

support classes   Several API-provided classes that reduce the number of methods a developer must implement to create a custom class.

synchronization   A locking mechanism used to ensure that data cannot be accessed by multiple requests.

synchronized   Describes a method or code block that forces the requesting thread to acquire the instance lock in order to gain access to the code block.

T

tag extensions   See "custom tags."

tag library descriptor (TLD)   An XML document that describes a tag library. It contains one or many related custom tag extensions.

tag value   Any java.lang.Object with an associated String key.

taglib directive   Defines a tag library and prefix for the custom tags used in the JSP page.

temporarily unavailable   Indicates that a servlet cannot handle the request for a period of time due to some system-wide problem. For example, there might not be sufficient memory or disk storage to handle requests, or a third-tier server might not be accessible. Some of these problems are self-correcting, and others might require a system administrator to take corrective action.

TLD resource path   The context-relative path to the tag library descriptor file, which begins with a forward slash (/) and does not include a protocol or host definition.

TRACE method   Returns the entire network route that the request took, from the client to the server and back.

traceroute   A Unix command that identifies all the locations or IP addresses that a request has utilized to get to its target address.

translation unit   The combination of an attribute that applies to an entire JSP page and any static `include` files.

TYPE   An attribute for the `INPUT` tag used to specify the type of control to create. Your choices are the following:

```
text|password|hidden|submit|reset|button|checkbox
radio|file|image
```

U

UnavailableException   An exception thrown to indicate a servlet is either temporarily or permanently unavailable.

Uniform Resource Identifier (URI)   The part of the URL excluding the domain name and the query string.

Uniform Resource Locator (URL)   Defines the information the client needs to make a connection to the server.

updateable   Describes a value object that has "set" or mutator methods or `public` members.

Updateable (or Mutable) Value Object strategy   A strategy you utilize when you want the client to be able to change its value object instance.

URL rewriting   A methodology that associates a session ID to all URL addresses used throughout the session. Using the ID, a developer can map client-related data to the session object for that client.

useBean action   An action that incorporates a JavaBean within a JSP.

V

VALUE   An attribute of the INPUT tag that specifies the initial value of the control. It is not a required attribute for any control.

value object   A single class with functionality to create, access, and possibly set field values.

Value Object Factory strategy   A strategy that enables an entity to inherit from more than one value object.

Value Object pattern   A pattern designed to reduce the number of method calls a client must make to obtain information.

W

web application   A single application that can consist of any or all of the following elements: servlets, JSP pages, utility classes, static documents, client-side Java applets, beans, and classes, and a standard configuration file.

web archive (WAR) file   A compressed file containing all the necessary classes and resources for a single web application.

/WEB-INF/classes   The directory containing all the server-side Java classes, such as servlet and utility classes.

/WEB-INF/lib   The directory containing all necessary compressed Java files that are used for the web application. These files are referred to as Java archive files or JAR files. They can consist of servlets, JSPs, beans, and utility classes.

/WEB-INF/web.xml   The file that contains the deployment descriptor.

web server   An application that directs and manages web requests.

Index

Note to the reader: Page numbers in **bold** indicate primary discussions of a topic or the definition of a term. Page numbers in *italics* indicate illustrations.

I

T

X

SYBEX & Oracle9i™ Certification

Sybex Study Guides Provide the Most Comprehensive Preparation for Oracle Certification Exams

Special Features in the Books

- **Assessment Test** allows readers to check their level of knowledge before they study.

- **Key Terms** sections at the end of each chapter highlight crucial vocabulary.

- **Review Questions** for each chapter allow readers to check their grasp of the material.

- **Practice Exams** give readers a chance to test themselves on material covering the entire book.

- **New Real World Scenario Sidebars** take readers well beyond the basics.

Cutting-Edge Test Prep Software on the CDs

- **All the Questions from the Book**—Chapter-by-chapter testing of all the Review Questions, as well as the Assessment Test and the Practice Exams.

- **Electronic Flashcards** for PCs and Palm devices—Hundreds of flashcard-style questions for both PCs and Palm devices that reinforce reader understanding of key concepts.

- **Bonus Exams**—Sample tests available exclusively on the CDs.

- **Searchable e-Book** allows readers to study anytime, anywhere.

Highlights

- With over 100% growth in the past year, the Oracle Certified Professional program recently surpassed 80,000 certifications in 65 countries.

- Authors are all experienced Oracle DBAs and developers, with years of consulting and training experience.

- Each Study Guide corresponds to one Oracle9i exam and includes exam objectives aligned with instructor-led training.

SYBEX®

www.sybex.co

Java™ 2 Web Developer Certification Study Guide

Sun Certified Web Component Developer for J2EE™ Platform (310-080)

SYBEX